Roman Family Empires

Dedicated to John L. White, Mentor and Friend

In thanks for pointing me toward this investigation long ago
and for providing an example of gracious presence
as a scholar, an example that I too seldom emulate.

Family Empires, Roman and Christian

VOLUME I
Roman Family Empires
Household, Empire, Resistance

Susan M. (Elli) Elliott

POLEBRIDGE PRESS
Salem, Oregon

Polebridge Press is the publishing arm of the Westar Institute, a non-profit, public-benefit research and educational organization. To learn more, visit westarinstitute.org.

Cover and interior design by Robaire Ream

Cover: Funerary relief from the monument of Onessimos and his family, 150–180 CE. Photo by Tilemahos Efthimiadis. Wikimedia Commons.

Gemma Augustea reproduced by permission of the Kunsthistorisches Museum, Wien.

Phrygian votive steles (Inv. 68.21.64 and Inv. 15.99.64) reproduced by permission of the Museum of Anatolian Civilizations (Anadolu Medeniyetleri Müzesi), Ankara, Turkey.

Cutaway view of a Roman domus reproduced by permission from Jonathan Rutland, *See Inside a Roman Town* (London: Macmillan Publishers International Ltd.) © 1986 by Macmillan Children's Books.

Library of Congress Cataloging-in-Publication Data
Names: Elliott, Susan (Susan Margaret), author.
Title: Family empires, Roman and Christian / Susan M. (Elli) Elliott.
Description: Salem, OR : Polebridge Press, 2018- | Includes bibliographical
    references and index. Contents: Volume 1. Roman family empires: household,
    empire, resistance.
Identifiers: LCCN 2017057844 | ISBN 9781598152074 (volume 1 : alk. paper)
Subjects: LCSH: Families--Religious aspects--Christianity--History. |
    Families--Religious life--History. | Church history--Primitive and early
    church, ca. 30-600. | Families--Rome--History.
Classification: LCC BR195.F35 E45 2018 | DDC 306.850937--dc23
LC record available at https://lccn.loc.gov/2017057844
10   9   8   7   6   5   4   3   2   1

Contents

Abbreviations

CIL	*Corpus Inscriptionum Latinarum*. 17 vols. Berlin: Berlin-Brandenburg Academy of Sciences and Humanities 1862–2012. Online: http://cil.bbaw.de/cil_en/dateien/datenbank_eng.php
ILLRP	Degrassi, Attilio. *Inscriptiones Latinae Liberae Rei Publicae*. 2 vols. Florence: La Nuova Italia, 1963, 1965.
ILS	Dessau, Hermann. *Inscriptiones Latinae Selectae*. 3 vols. Berlin: Weidmann, 1892–1916.
LSJ	Liddell, Henry G., Robert Scott, Henry Stuart Jones, and Roderick McKenzie. *Greek-English Lexicon*. 9th ed. Oxford: Clarendon Press, 1996.
OCD	Hammond, N. G. L., and H. H. Scullard. *The Oxford Classical Dictionary*. 2d ed. Oxford, UK: Oxford University Press, 1970 (1976).
POxy	Oxyrhynchus Papyrus

Preface

Take a look at this image.[1] This image was made in the time of Jesus. Take a long look at it. Try to resist the temptation to turn the page and read ahead. First look at the image and note what you see. Even if you recognize this image and have examined it before, take a good long look. What do you see?

Figure 1: *Gemma Augustea*, Roman cameo, onyx, 9–12 CE. Gold frame, seventeenth century. Vienna*

This image is known as the *Gemma Augustea*, the Gem of Augustus, a low-relief cameo carved approximately 10–20 CE from a double-layered piece of onyx about 7.5 inches high and 9 inches wide, about the size of an iPad. Originally the cameo was probably part of the personal property of the imperial household.

You may have recognized Caesar Augustus seated prominently in the upper portion of the image. Scholars disagree about the

---

*Kunsthistorisches Museum, Wien, collection of Greek and Roman Antiquities, Inventory no. IXa 79.

interpretation of many elements of the image. Even the consensus
that the central figure is Augustus is broad but not unanimous. You
may have seen the central figure as the god Jupiter in the heavenly
court. The figure is both the emperor and the god. Augustus is represented enthroned as Jupiter, but in place of the god's thunderbolts
he holds a staff in his left hand and in his right an augur's *lituus*,
the crooked rod of a priest who interprets signs from the deities.
The eagle of Jupiter is at his feet. To his right, the goddess Roma
sits gazing with favor upon him, portrayed perhaps with the face of
Augustus' wife Livia. From behind, Oikoumene, the personification
of the inhabited world (or the global empire after Alexander the
Great) reaches to crown Augustus with the *corona civica*, the sign
of having saved Roman citizens. Beside her is the god of the seas,
Oceanus. Italia sits beneath them surrounded by children. Augustus
receives the victorious figures in the upper left portion of the image, Tiberius descending from the chariot driven by Victoria and
the young Germanicus standing beside Roma. The cameo celebrates
their victory but the eyes of all the figures in the upper register turn
toward Augustus. His stepson and adoptive grandson bring their
victory to him. A disk above bears the ibex, the symbol of Capricorn,
Augustus' birth star. The heavens shine favorably upon him as well.
For the people who commissioned and prized this carved gem,
the image portrayed a "divinely ordained world order" upheld by
Roman military might.[2]

The ruler and deity sits in his rightful place. The other deities and
the heavens are in concord to affirm his role. Beneath them, below
the line through the middle of the image, the barbarians are under
control. Victory over them has been achieved, and world order is
secure from the threat of chaos.

For the subdued peoples, the image would read differently. They
might have identified, as you may have, with the bound man or the
despairing woman hunched next to him on the left, or the woman
being dragged by her hair or the pleading man beneath her on the
right.

When I show this to groups of church people and ask them what
they see, someone usually wonders whether that pleading man on
the right is Jesus or whether the beam being raised above the bound

man on the left is the cross. The artist who created the image was not portraying Jesus, just a generic barbarian, perhaps a specific Celtic or German tribal leader, forced to his knees. The beam is not the cross of Jesus but a *tropaion*, a trophy being prepared for the victory parade. The bound barbarian will be tied to it and lifted up to display the victory of Rome.

Is Jesus in the picture? That is a topic for ongoing discussion. Inasmuch as the *Gemma Augustea* presents an encapsulated view of the world into which Jesus was born, we can look for responses to that world in his and his followers' teachings.[a] We can also consider where his followers saw him in that world, both raised on the *tropaion* and seated on the victor's throne. Consider this picture and the place of Jesus' early followers in it as you read. We can picture them in the lower register, and it will be important to understand elements of resistance to see where they fit and how they resisted. In the first volume of this work, we will mostly see the context in which early Christianity grew, the Roman family empire and those who resisted it. As we turn to early Christian responses and modes of resisting in the second volume, we will see their repositioning of Jesus onto the throne as a pivotal move not only for early Christianity but also for Western culture, a move that happened quite early. Many of the images of the alternative family empire of Jesus Christ that they created rhetorically in the early years later became a new form of Christian family empire. Such images of Christ's empire bear striking similarity to the images in the *Gemma Augustea* and the family model that will be the subject of this volume.

But why, you might ask, does an introduction to a book about the family and the early Christians[b] begin with this image of the world of the Roman Empire? This little image encapsulates the vision of

---

a. On balance the evidence suggests that it is more probable than not that an historical Jesus existed who raised some form of movement among people in Galilee in the early first century. This issue will be discussed in Volume 2 in the discussion of teachings attributed to Jesus.

b. The terms "Christians" and "early Christianity" refer to the Jesus-following movements and groups from the time of Jesus on. While they were not referred to as "Christians" until much later, it remains the least cumbersome way to refer to the progenitors of what became "Christianity." In later chapters and Volume 2, more precise distinctions will be made.

the family that was the Empire, the vision promoted by those who
dominated the world of Jesus' time, a vision of a divinely crowned
emperor surrounded by his family as their enemies are destroyed.
Alternative visions of the family and the world emerged among those
who desired a world different from the one depicted. This book ex-
plores how the vision revealed in the *Gemma Augustea* came to rule
by creating a family empire and how people, including some early
Christians, resisted and struggled to create alternatives in it.

Introduction

Family, Religion, and Politics

Then and Now

Before we enter the ancient world, however, let's begin where we are. Many of us live in the United States of America, a nation with, shall we say, a "global reach"? The United States is still the only superpower on earth. Even if you do not live in the United States, your world is undoubtedly affected by what happens here, and what we do most likely has a disproportionate influence on your nation. Within this powerful nation, we are finding ourselves increasingly polarized politically. Frequently two perspectives talk past one another, each mystified by the other's apparent lack of logical consistency.[a]

When I served as a pastor in churches in the United States rural heartland, I came to understand that almost everyone there was a Southern Baptist. There were Baptist Southern Baptists and Lutheran Southern Baptists and Presbyterian and even Catholic Southern Baptists. One example, though, is telling. In a conversation with a very intelligent and creative teacher, a member of a mainline church, it became clear to me that she took it for granted that I did not believe in evolution because I was a Christian minister. She assumed this as a Christian tenet. I let her know my own perspective, that the theory of evolution is clearly the most plausible reading of the evidence, and explained to her how I read the Bible from an historical understanding. A few months later it was clear that she had changed her mind. Yet here was a well-educated person, a public-school teacher, who assumed that Christianity and

---

a. As this volume is being completed, change is happening rapidly, however. The status of the USA and its economic power among the world's nations is changing, and while political polarization is intensifying, it is also multiplying so that more than two perspectives are talking past one another.

1

acceptance of the validity of evolution are mutually exclusive. We must wonder about the colossal silence of any other perspective—a colossal silence now bearing fruit in widespread antagonism in the name of "faith" toward scientific understanding, and in a politi... transformation that is terrifying to many. Many of us now share the baffling and bewildering realization I used to express to colleagues: "These folks are living in a different symbolic universe. I don't live there. I understand that it's different and I accept them and I love them anyway. Yet it's a different symbolic universe. I can catch pieces of it, but I cannot fully comprehend it." Later, at the recommendation of my dissertation director, John L. White, I read George Lakoff's *Moral Politics* for a better understanding of such "symbolic universes,"[1] the repercussions of which will become apparent as the book progresses.

This book began as a lecture series in 2004 for an audience in a wealthy theologically liberal congregation, under the title, "Whose Family Values?" At the time, that audience made little or no connection between the Roman Empire and the American Empire and were generally averse to perceiving an American Empire. It has since evolved in dialogue with different audiences, especially a group from the Billings Unitarian Universalist Fellowship, and in my own transition out of the Christian narrative. Since 2004, political discourse in the United States has only become increasingly polarized, and, on the liberal side of the divide, the notion of the American Empire is not as opaque as it was then. Indeed, the gulf may have become unbridgeable.

Before describing the content of this book, one more observation needs to be made. All interpretation is done from a social location, a basic recognition to be discussed in chapter 2. Authors write books out of particular concerns connected to particular communities. Readers read out of particular concerns connected to particular communities. What are mine? What are yours? Economically, I am among the United States working poor, an income level that is, nevertheless, in the upper 1 percent worldwide. I have assets that put me in a different position than most of my low wage co-workers, especially the log cabin inherited from my parents in a Montana mountain town that is quickly gentrifying. Socially, I come from educated working class roots that gave me the encouragement and resources to obtain a high level of education and a professional identity. This allows me to be accepted among environmentalists, progressives, and feminists in our town and also among my co-workers who are from the Montana small-town culture that is being overtaken.

Family location is also a social location. My sister and brother and I were raised in as close to a model "Nurturant Parent" family as existed in our generation, and we thus understand our family to extend into a community of human beings and the web of life on planet earth. As a result, I have spent much of my life participating in groups struggling in one way or another in opposition to the impact of the American economic and military empire in our own time, from the rights of undocumented workers to the strip-mining of coal and many other issues. Experiences of living in poor urban neighborhoods, in a village in Mexico, and in ministry with farming families on the high plains also offer me insight into early Christian texts and contexts and hold me accountable to a community of struggle that currently includes the Northern Plains Resource Council; a community of progressives in Carbon and Stillwater counties; a fledgling grassroots think tank provisionally called the Shining Mountain Institute; the Billings Unitarian Universalist Fellowship; and increasingly the majestic land on which I dwell with all our human and nonhuman relations.

My education and scholarly work also allow me access to the academy and the discussion among scholars in the study of early Christianity. This connection offers not only insight into early Christianity and methods of investigating Christian origins but also a community of accountability. I am a member of the Society of Biblical Literature and the Catholic Biblical Association and its Feminist Hermeneutic Group, but I participate most actively as a Fellow of the Westar Institute. This investigation is intended as a contribution to the current work of Westar's Christianity Seminar.

This work is also intended as a contribution for the grassroots think tank that is being shaped, however unhurriedly, as a project to learn to think "in place," as an effort, ironically, that is ultimately about NOT thinking about Christianity and the Roman Empire. Nevertheless, because this book attempts to probe the foundations of the Christian imperial mission, I hope it will help readers to consider how the Christian imperial mission has been imposed upon the North American continent. By more deeply understanding the root family metaphors and the larger narrative that we have unconsciously assumed, I hope we will be empowered to learn instead how to perceive and share a root family metaphor and narrative being generated by the place in which we dwell, whether that is the Big Sky region of Montana and northern Wyoming, in my case, or wherever it is readers call home.[2]

Structure of this Book

This book draws from the fruits of historical criticism and the data of traditional history, now amplified with archaeological data and interpretive methods that emphasize the lives and history-making of non-elites. It consists of five parts.

Part 1 will describe the interpretive approach for this project. Chapter 1 will summarize the work on which this project is based, linguist George Lakoff's work on the family models he has discerned as root metaphors in contemporary political discourse, designated as "Strict Father" and "Nurturant Parent" family models. Chapter 2 will outline related interpretive approaches to be used in this work and will place this project at the confluence of several streams of current interpretation of early Christian texts.

Part 2 will present a thick description of the Roman Strict Father family model that was the root metaphor for the Roman Empire as a social reality, "up close and personal" in the microcosm of the Roman household. We will see the household and the family model as a dramatic performance to enhance the image of its *paterfamilias*, the father-owner at its center. Chapter 3 will describe the architecture of the house as the stage for a daily performance of his power. Chapter 4 will introduce the cast of characters assigned the leading parts and will survey the roles and responsibilities of the individuals at the center of the household. Chapter 5 will offer a view of the slaves in the household, both as the human stage set in the script of the master's drama and as characters in their own right. Then chapter 6 will outline some elements of interaction that provide the plot of the drama in the relationships of the characters.

The macrocosmic version of this Roman Strict Father family will take center stage in Part 3 as we see how the Roman Strict Father Family model became the basis of one-man rule of the Roman Empire in the ascendancy of Caesar Augustus. In chapter 7, we will see the movement of Augustus into the center of the imperial stage as the empire's *paterfamilias*. Then chapter 8 will explore his disciplinary role as the imperial *paterfamilias* in his efforts and strategies to impose more rigid stratification in his family empire. The role of the imperial cults in unifying the family empire under one-man rule will be the topic of chapter 9.

Part 4 will move the focus to the wings and offstage to consider the many strategies people used to resist and survive with dignity in the Roman family empire. We will see a few samples of armed and national resistance in chapter 10. Then chapter 11 will discuss intellectual resistance in philosophical movements, including imagining alternatives in utopian community visions and the radical witness to an alternative worldview found especially among the Cynics. Chapter 12 will consider the strategies of ritual and spiritual resistance found in popular religious efforts, especially in cults designated as "mystery cults." This will include an examination of the example of the cults of Cybele and Attis. Chapter 13 will investigate the social structures of the Greco-Roman meal and the voluntary associations as potential locations for strategies of survival and resistance.

In Part 5, a first look at a Christian community will offer a case study to bring together many of the elements discussed in previous chapters. Part 5 will begin a change of gears that will continue in the second volume with a focus in more detail on early Christian texts. The letter of an organizer of early Christian communities, Paul, to the slaveholder Philemon and the community meeting in his house will be introduced in chapter 14. Chapter 15 will move through the letter in a verse-by-verse analysis to consider the multi-layered dynamics of this early community.

Readers will note that in parts 2, 3, and 4, mention of the scholars on whose work I rely is kept to a minimum in the text and attributed in the endnotes. This will, I hope, allow non-specialist readers to engage this material more easily. The endnotes also provide sources for many topics so that scholars and non-specialists alike can follow and verify threads of interest, although the endnotes are not exhaustive in citing every single mention of a topic or issue in every work listed in the bibliography.

Readers will also note that in parts 1 and 5 more mention is made of scholars in the text. As a discussion of scholarship and methods, Part 1 mentions individual scholars as the matter at hand. The discussion of Paul's letter to Philemon in Part 5 intentionally foregrounds the ground-breaking work of a group of African-American scholars on this text by mentioning them in the main text rather than citing them in the endnotes.

A brief epilogue will mention the relevance of this discussion of family empires for contemporary culture wars.

Part I

Family Metaphor and Related Interpretive Approaches

What images do the words "family empire" evoke? We might think of the royal dynasties of Europe, the Habsburgs of Austria or the House of Windsor. Television dramas may come to mind, the drama of the sibling rivalry of *Empire* or the earlier family intrigue of the Ewings on *Dallas*. Family corporate empires could cross our minds: Rockefeller, Vanderbilt, Morgan, or a name emblazoned on hotels and golf courses now moving into governmental control as well.

The transition of the Roman Empire to one-man rule under Caesar Augustus had some traits in common with such "family empires." Yet when we focus on the machinations of family members jockeying for personal power in the ruling family of such empires, we miss the deeper connections. Family relationships and expectations in the grassroots, the image of a nation or an empire as a family, the family in control at the center of an empire, and the relationships of a nation or empire with its deities are all in a dynamic relationship in the "family empires" to be explored here.

Before we turn to examine the family form that dominated the Roman Empire and to the empire itself as a family, and to a consideration of the opposition to both during the Greco-Roman era, an explanation of the methods that ground this study will be helpful.

1

Family and Nation

Models and Metaphors in Contemporary Political Discourse

George Lakoff's insights into the roots of today's political divide are becoming increasingly useful. His analysis of the language used in political discourse indicates that while everyone speaks of the nation as a family, two different family models are being assumed. His work will provide a tool to use in examining the family systems of the world in which Christianity originated.[a] This chapter will summarize Lakoff's work to provide an understanding of the elements of the family models as he discerns them. The elements he uses to contrast two contemporary models will prove useful as a tool to explore multiple family models operating in the Greco-Roman era, none of which are identical to either of Lakoff's.

Different Assumptions
Root Metaphor

Lakoff begins with the notion of root metaphor. If you were not paying attention in your middle school English class and have had

---

a. This project does not involve the form of linguistic analysis that Lakoff used to discern the root metaphors in contemporary political discourse, nor does it address issues in the field of cognitive science or metaphor analysis or other multiple criticisms of Lakoff's work. Here I will use his results to look more generally at the Roman Empire and movements within it.

no occasion to remember the word since, metaphor is about "understanding and experiencing one kind of thing in terms of another."[1]
We think of metaphor as something used in poetry to picture one
thing as another. If you were paying attention in middle school, you
may remember a line from "The Highwayman": "The moon was a
ghostly galleon tossed upon cloudy seas."[2] Metaphorically, the moon
is understood in terms of a ship sailing in a night sky understood as
a turbulent sea. Another familiar example is from Shakespeare, "All
the world's a stage | And all the men and women merely players."[3]
The monologue for the part of Jaques continues to develop the metaphor describing the ages in the life of a human being as parts in a
dramatic performance. Many familiar expressions are metaphors. We
speak, for example, of "screaming headlines" and to "nip the problem in the bud" without suggesting that the newspaper makes any
actual sound or that any actual pruning shears are involved.

Metaphor is sometimes viewed as merely decorative or illustra-
tive, non-essential but useful for aiding understanding and catching
interest. Its purpose is only to make writing more interesting and
vivid—frosting on the cake, to use a metaphor about metaphor.

The notion of *root* metaphor points instead to how metaphor
forms our thinking and how we perceive reality. What Lakoff and
other linguists are discovering is that our language and thought is
structured by metaphor.[4] Rather than being the frosting, metaphor
is the pan in which the cake is baked, what gives the cake its very
shape.

Root metaphors are metaphors we assume that ground our language. We seldom think about these metaphors. We use them without much conscious awareness. Basic spatial and physical metaphors
enter our language all the time. For example, in the introduction,
I used a common metaphor of light and dark to describe a mental
insight: the lightbulb flashing on as a metaphorical description of a
mental insight. Other expressions of that root metaphor of light and
darkness for how we think about thought itself can be readily generated: "illumination" as a word for understanding, "shed a little light
on the subject" as a metaphor for adding relevant information for
understanding an issue; "unenlightened" to describe those who lack
information and thus hold misguided opinions, and being "kept in

the dark" to refer to the experience of being prevented from knowing information.

In using such terms, we rarely consider that we are speaking metaphorically. The physical experience of light and darkness grounds our language about thought. Similarly, we describe our lives assuming a metaphor of walking, with the past behind us and the future in front of us. A physical experience in space grounds how we speak about time. Even to speak of "root" metaphors "grounding" our language implies a spatial framework and our experience of gravity from below and the growth process of trees and vegetation.

The study of root metaphors is part of a larger investigation of how we think. While we are not always aware of the basic metaphors that structure our thought, these metaphors shape our thinking and logic. The field of investigation for this metaphorical structuring of reason is called "cognitive science." A description in the preface of one of Lakoff's theoretical works indicates how the aims of cognitive science differ from a traditional view of reason. Cognitive science seeks to understand what reason is and how it operates:

> On the traditional view, reason is abstract and disembodied. On the new view, reason has a bodily basis. The traditional view sees reason as literal, as primarily about propositions that can be objectively either true or false. The new view takes imaginative aspects of reason—metaphor, metonymy, and mental imagery—as central to reason, rather than as a peripheral and inconsequential adjunct to the literal.[5]

This is a different view of reason, the reason that begins with our bodily and social experience and makes coherent sense even though it may not follow the logical propositions of a legal argument. We cannot reduce reason to a sequence of logical propositions in an orderly progression.

"Everybody's Doing It"
Family as Metaphor for the Nation

Lakoff applies his work on root metaphor to a study of contemporary United States political discussion in his book *Moral Politics*. From a study of political discourse, he discerns a widespread tendency to assume a family metaphor when we are speaking of the nation. We are all doing this, liberals and conservatives alike. The use of family language has been more self-evident and more self-conscious in conservative political discourse, but liberals also assume a family metaphor. The difference is not pro-family or anti-family. The root metaphor—"The nation is a family in which the government is the parent"—applies across the political spectrum. The difference is in the *model* we are assuming when we speak of family. In Lakoff's analysis, the essential polarized political alignments in the United States are rooted in two contrasting models of family.[b]

We must keep in mind that these two models usually operate as unstated assumptions to organize moral reasoning. They function as organizing metaphors that are not always clear but tend to define what is common sense, what is obviously moral and immoral, and what we assume the family is. The difficulty is that what is common sense and obvious if we are assuming one model can be downright nonsensical and opaque if we are assuming the other. In many ways, it comes down to what we "just know." While the values of each model are not mutually exclusive, how the priorities of those values are ordered is different. In those emphases, we may come at some times to experience that never-the-twain-shall-meet. From one perspective, what I "just know" is right may be "just plain nonsense" from your perspective.

The "Strict Father" Family Model

Lakoff labels the model of the family that grounds *conservative* political and moral thinking the "Strict Father" model. He outlines the moral and political reasoning that operates as common sense when this model is assumed. Here is Lakoff's description:

> This model posits a traditional nuclear family, with the father having primary responsibility for supporting and protecting the

---

b. In current political shifts in the USA, as a wider range of perspectives is co-alescing and these perspectives are talking past one another, additional family forms could be discerned as well. For example, analysis of libertarian perspectives could, perhaps, yield a parentless family model for the nation. Such analysis is beyond the reach of this study, however.

family as well as the authority to set overall policy, to set strict rules for the behavior of children and to enforce the rules. The mother has the day-to-day responsibility for the care of the house, raising the children, and upholding the father's authority. Children must respect and obey their parents; by doing so they build character, that is, self-discipline and self-reliance. Love and nurturance are, of course, a vital part of family life but can never outweigh parental authority, which is itself an expression of love and nurturance—tough love. Self-discipline, self-reliance, and respect for legitimate authority are the crucial things children must learn.

Once children are mature, they are on their own and must depend on their acquired self-discipline to survive. Their self-reliance gives them authority over their own destinies, and parents are not to meddle in their lives.[6]

The highest moral priorities in the Strict Father model are

- *moral strength*, meaning "the self-control and self-discipline to stand up to external and internal evils"
- *respect for and obedience to authority*
- the setting and following of *strict norms of behavior* that conform to a moral order conceived of as naturally defined[7]

Competition is a crucial ingredient in this moral system and is viewed as good because it develops self-discipline and self-reliance. A moral world metes out rewards and punishments justly, and some people are thus better off than others. That is only reasonable. It would be wrong to deprive those who have justly earned them of their rewards. In this framework, if that tenet were not true, the world would be unjust.

The Strict Father family model is organized around the need to prepare children for survival in a competitive and fundamentally dangerous world. The father protects young children from danger and prepares them to meet the challenge of that world. He is especially concerned to make sure that his sons are tough enough to take whatever the world dishes out.

Table 1
Family Models in George Lakoff, *Moral Politics**

STRICT FATHER	NURTURANT PARENT
▓ Form	
Traditional Nuclear Family— Father, Mother, Children	Co-resident households with extended relationships
▓ Roles & Responsibilities	
Father: support & protect family, set & enforce rules & guidelines, administer rewards & punishment Mother: day-to-day responsibility in the home, care of children, upholding father's authority. Children: respect & obey parents, gain character; learn self-reliance & respect for legitimate authority	Adults: support & protect children & family (which requires strength and courage); foster communication & climate of respect in the family; make clear decisions & explain them; foster capacity for responsibility Children: be cooperative family members; learn & grow; increase capacity for responsibility; question to learn to think for themselves
▓ Priority Childrearing Mission	
Prepare children for survival in a competitive and fundamentally dangerous world	Prepare children to be fulfilled and happy in their lives as responsible community members
▓ Moral Priorities	
Moral Strength (self-control, self-discipline, strength to resist external and internal evils) Authority (respect and obedience) Strict Norms (setting & following norms that conform to a moral order)	Love & Empathy (compassion, awareness of others' needs, helping others) Taking Care of Oneself (in order to be able to help others & not be a burden) Nurturance of Social Ties (cooperation, connection, community)
▓ Conception of Moral Order	
A natural and timeless order of role division and a just system of reward & punishment	An interdependent world in which everyone must cooperate to survive and no one is left out

*Root Metaphor: The Nation is a Family
(Government = Parent; Citizens = Children)

14

STRICT FATHER	NURTURANT PARENT
▦ Conception of Character	
An individual moral essence that is established by adulthood and must be kept pure from corrupting influences	A moral essence that resides in society; corrupting influences must be healed & transformed, not purged
▦ Internal Role of Government	
Formation of character, promoting self-discipline, responsibility, self-reliance; helping the truly needy; ensuring punishment for lack of self-discipline; uphold moral order in the nation-family	Promote fairness & equity in distribution of society's goods; help & protect those who cannot help & protect themselves; foster a climate of respect among all members of society
▦ External Role of Government	
Protect citizen-family from external evils	Cooperate with other nation-"families" to make the world safer for all

To prepare children for survival, this family model focuses on the cultivation of character, and character is understood as "a kind of essence that is developed in childhood and then lasts a lifetime."[8] An important metaphor for character is uprightness, not falling into corruption and impurity, and hence also a spatial metaphor with protected boundaries. Those of upright character must protect themselves and the world from impure and immoral influences. This protection is achieved by isolating those whose essence is corrupt and fallen so that they do not infect the morally pure. In this conception, it is the Strict Father moral system itself which must be defended from corrupting influences. The influences currently seen as most threatening to the system are homosexuality and feminism as well as excessive sexual content in the mass media.

As a metaphor for the nation, government is the parent in the Strict Father family system. The aim of the government-parent is the formation of the character of its citizens, promoting "self-discipline, responsibility and self-reliance."[9] It is *immoral* for the

parent-government to foster dependency and *unjust* to reward irresponsibility. Only the "truly needy" whose need does not result
from their own or their parents' irresponsibility are to be assisted.
The government-parent's proper role is to maintain the morality of
reward and punishment, rewarding people for their self-reliance and
responsibility and insuring punishment for lack of self-discipline.
Like a good strong father, the government is responsible to protect
the citizen children from external evils and to uphold the moral
order internally, the moral order defined in the natural order of the
Strict Father family.[10]

The seeming illogic that liberals perceive in the conservative
stance that attacks "big government" while simultaneously tolerat-
ing enormous expenditures for wars and governmental intrusions
into privacy is not at all illogical in this framework. It is not about
"big government" or "small government." Big is fine if it serves
the obvious purposes of government as seen from this metaphorical
framework.

There are many other implications, but these are some basic elements of the Strict Father model to get us started.

The "Nurturant Parent" Family Model

The Nurturant Parent family model, on the other hand, grounds
liberal moral and political thinking. Here is how Lakoff describes it:

> Love, empathy, and nurturance are primary, and children be-
> come responsible, self-disciplined and self-reliant through being
> cared for, respected, and caring for others, both in their family
> and in their community. Support and protection are part of nur-
> turance, and they require strength and courage on the part of
> parents. The obedience of children comes out of their love and
> respect for their parents and their community, not out of the fear
> of punishment. Good communication is crucial. If their authority
> is to be legitimate, parents must explain why their decisions serve
> the cause of protection and nurturance. Questioning by children
> is seen as positive, since children need to learn why their parents
> do what they do and since children often have good ideas that

should be taken seriously. Ultimately, of course, responsible parents have to make the decisions, and that must be clear.

The principal goal of nurturance is for children to be fulfilled and happy in their lives. A fulfilling life is assumed to be, in significant part, a nurturant life—one committed to family and community responsibility. What children need to learn most is empathy for others, the capacity for nurturance and the maintenance of social ties, which cannot be done without the strength, respect, self-discipline, and self-reliance that comes through being cared for. Raising a child to be fulfilled also requires helping the child develop his or her potential for achievement and enjoyment. That requires respecting the child's own values and allowing the child to explore the range of ideas and options that the world offers.

When children are respected, nurtured, and communicated with from birth, they gradually enter into a lifetime relationship of mutual respect, communication, and caring with their parents.[11]

In Nurturant Parent morality, the highest priorities are

- *love and empathy*, compassion, awareness of others' needs, helping those who need help
- *taking care of oneself* in order to be able to help others and contribute and not be a burden to others
- the *nurturance of social ties*, that connect people in a larger community

Moral strength functions in the service of nurturance, not as a central priority. Cooperation is a crucial ingredient for this moral system, and a moral world is one in which everyone cooperates and no one is left out.

The Nurturant Parent family prepares children to be responsible citizens in an interdependent world in which survival depends on broad cooperation and responsibility, mutual nurturance, and recognition of common dependence on the earth.

Let me note that some of Lakoff's language about the world that the Nurturant Parent model assumes indicates that it is a world under construction, a world that the family prepares matured children to help create. Yet it is not an idealistic assumption but views survival not as individual survival but the survival of humanity, civilization, and life on the planet. In this model, the world is a dangerous place precisely as a result of the unbridled operation of the competitive values of the Strict Father model. On the other hand, those who assume the Strict Father model perceive danger in the immorality they expect from too much permissiveness.

The children's preparation in the Nurturant Parent family is focused less on the development of character as a moral essence than it is on the continuing capacity for growth and the cultivation of skills to make the world a better place. Better is defined in terms of inclusion and love and cooperation. Moral essence is not understood to reside in the individual but in society. If society is corrupted, healing is conceived as a holistic transformation rather than a purge of the corrupting influences.

For the nation understood as a Nurturant Parent family, the role of the government-parent is to promote fairness and equity in distribution of society's goods and to help and protect those who cannot help and protect themselves. Externally the parent-government is a member of the society of nations who must cooperate to solve the world community's problems. Internally, it promotes the health of the nation-family by ensuring fairness and inclusion among the citizens. From the perspective of the conservative Strict Father morality this looks unfair and feels dangerous.

This, then, is a brief sketch of Lakoff's two family models. Table 1 will be helpful as a summary.

Some Clarifications

What Lakoff is offering is a typology of models that frame ethical and political discussion. They are metaphorical models that frame our thought. The model does not necessarily equate to all actual families. Most families will be some hybrid and the values of the models may be in constant negotiation. Many people reflect on their families and must acknowledge, "My family doesn't look like either of these models." Many examples can be cited of political conservatives whose families look more like a Nurturant Parent model or liberals whose families reflect a Strict Father tendency.

The values in each model are also not exclusive. The values are a matter of priorities, and priorities can shift. In the conservative Strict Father model, empathy is a value. It is not considered evil to be empathetic. It is good, in fact, so long as strength of character prevents empathy from leading to corruption. In the liberal Nurturant Parent model, likewise, appropriate reward and punishment is not wrong or evil if it does not harm the long-term development of the one being rewarded or punished.

Lakoff also presents just two models in binary opposition. What his analysis offers is the presence of an alternative to the Strict Father family model that has presumed to define itself as "the family" as if it were a natural form. Defenders of the Strict Father model assume that they are defending THE family, and not just one family form. Lakoff's articulation of the Nurturant Parent family model clarifies that another family model legitimately contends for the defense of "family values." His discernment of the Nurturant Parent model also indicates that there may be more than two possibilities. Lakoff's work is helpful for de-naturalizing the Strict Father family model. As we turn to the Greco-Roman era, we will see a distinctly different form of Strict Father family and an array of other possible models. Seeing two forms instead of just one, however, will allow us to examine multiple forms.

Using this brief summary of the family models Lakoff outlines, subsequent chapters will show how the Roman Strict Father family model is similar to the contemporary one but hardly identical, and that alternatives in the Roman era may resemble aspects of the Nurturant Parent model but are also distinct and varied. The project here is not a search for the Nurturant Parent model in the Greco-Roman era. Neither is it an effort to congratulate the early Christians for introducing the Nurturant Parent model to a world languishing under the rule of the Strict Father. That would be both misguided and entirely inaccurate. The project here is to discern how the distinctly Roman version of the Strict Father family became the foundation of a long-lasting empire under one-man rule and how people living under that empire, including early Christians, both resisted and accommodated to the empire and the family model on which it was founded. The elements of Lakoff's models will be helpful for examining the form of Strict Father family as both a social reality and as a metaphor that shaped the Roman Empire as the household of the emperor.

2

Family as Root Metaphor and Other Interpretive Approaches

Lakoff's analysis of the family metaphors used in contemporary political discourse will be a framework here, but other approaches will also come into play. It will be useful to locate this project at the confluence of other interpretive streams that feed it as well and to indicate how this investigation using Lakoff's insights relates to other approaches. I will not attempt to address all the various methods of interpretation that have emerged in studies of early Christianity in recent decades or even to provide much detail about the interpretative approaches mentioned here, each of which is a broad field of investigation in its own right.

Family Studies

Family studies have emerged in the past few decades, including an expansion of studies of the family in the ancient world and early Christianity. Somewhere along the way, however, it surely dawns on anyone who has taken the study of the family seriously that this topic is so pervasive that we may as well take up the topic of "life in all its fullness" or, "Life, the Universe, and Everything."[1] This is especially true when we understand an empire as a metaphorical family.

Broad social changes in the last decades of the twentieth century have led to an interest in family studies in a variety of fields. As a major factor, the most recent feminist movement has stimulated attention to this basic reality of human life as women's lives have become a matter of interest. In archaeology, social history, sociology, political science, anthropology, psychology, religious studies, and more, the family is becoming a topic of great interest. Study of the family has brought an increased focus on family systems rather than individuals and on everyday private life rather than major public events.

Study of the Greco-Roman world has also seen an explosion of research and publication on family, domestic architecture, and related topics. Studies on specific topics in Greek and Roman family life by such scholars as Keith R. Bradley, Suzanne Dixon, Beryl Rawson, Richard Saller, Andrew Wallace-Hadrill and others began to proliferate in the 1980s. Topics from wet-nurses to corporal punishment, from Roman mothers and sons to architectural changes in houses began to be studied in detail. Such studies continue with the purpose that Bradley stated in the introduction to his 1990 volume of essays, "to gain some appreciation of the dynamics of Roman family life, at more than one social level, indeed, and to understand the family as a social organism."[2] The many detailed studies in recent decades are making it more possible to see an organism rather than a static entity. More recently, Beth Severy has examined the importance of family for the establishment of one-man rule of the Roman Empire, both as a metaphorical model and as a literal extension of Augustus' own family. Her study will be invaluable in the survey presented here.[3]

Scholars of early Christianity are also turning increasing attention to the family, often in conversation with the classicists mentioned and others. Studies focused on early Christian families and the family context of early Christianity began to appear in greater numbers in the 1990s. This project will draw heavily from the work of scholars who have participated in collaborations in North America and in Europe, especially the Early Christian Families Group in the Society of Biblical Literature, led by Carolyn Osiek and David Balch,[4] and an overlapping group of European scholars assembled by Halvor Moxnes.[5]

Most of these scholars recognize "family" as a social construction and as a term that eludes a firmly fixed definition. Metaphorical uses of family terminology in New Testament and early Christian texts have long been the subject of many scholarly studies, but many studies assume "family" is some form of natural and static entity and show little awareness that these terms for family were used differently in Greco-Roman antiquity. More recent studies incorporate more developed understandings of the social reality of the family in the Greco-Roman world to understand the use of family terms like "brothers" and "sisters" for other community members as metaphors and as fictive kinship terms in early Christian texts.[a] Bringing the notion of family as root metaphor for the nation and the empire to these metaphorical uses in early Christian texts will help place them in a larger context.

In introducing a volume of contributions to a conference that helped define the scope of study in this field as both the study of "family as metaphor" and "family as social reality," Halvor Moxnes delineates several approaches.[6] To understand the "family" as a social reality, Moxnes indicates that it is important to study the "family" not in itself but as part of a wider social, economic, political, religious context.[7] Then he explains several overlapping areas of inquiry for understanding the "family" as a social reality in antiquity. These approaches loosely correspond to terms for "family" in Greek and Latin, keeping in mind that no term existed to denote what we now refer to as the "nuclear family."[8]

Families as domestic groups can be seen in terms of households, as "task-oriented residence units."[9] This is an important aspect of understanding the Roman *domus* and Greek *oikos*, although it is not precisely equivalent. For example, the *domus* could include the family lineage. Studies that approach "family" as "household" will be important in what follows as part of understanding the Roman Strict Father family model as a social reality.

Families can also be understood in terms of kinship. Some studies define families and family metaphor in the world of early Christianity using anthropological methods and kinship definitions. Some of these studies will also prove useful in what follows.[10] The Latin *familia* must be distinguished from an understanding just in terms of kinship, however, because it usually included the property and slaves, not just blood relations, as did the Greek *oikos*.

---

a. "Fictive kinship" means referring to members of a group using family terminology even though the individuals have no blood tie.

Focusing specifically on marriage as an institution provides another approach to understand the core group in ancient households that most closely resembles the modern "nuclear family," a domestic group that existed but for which there was no specific term. In the Greco-Roman era, however, marriage, at least among the upper echelons, was less a romantic bonding between husband and wife than a union with larger purposes: linking kinship groups, forming a new economic unit, and continuing a lineage.[11] At other levels of society, the evidence is more complex.

Marriage relationships are seen within another wider view of the family as a system of relations. This approach investigates the relationships between and among the various social locations in the family: mother-son, husband-wife, master-slave, brother-sister, son-pedagogue, male siblings and more.[12]

To understand the Roman Strict Father family model, it will be important to view it as a system of relations. Its various roles and relationships will be explained in Part 2. Here, it is worth emphasizing, however, that slaves were an essential part of the Roman Strict Father family. Slaves were present in households as well as toiling their brief lives away in the mines and in the fields of vast plantations, and they were part of the property of the household. The Roman Empire was a slave economy and a slave society, a civilization unsustainable without slaves. Yet the holding of slaves was part of family life and slaves were part of the metaphorical family empire. We cannot discuss the family without discussing slavery. Slavery was part of the family system. Slavery and the family were one system of relationship.

I will not attempt to mention or survey the vast literature on slavery in the Roman Empire in this introduction, with one exception. To make the simple statement that slavery and the family are one system of relationship, it would be hard to underestimate the importance of Orlando Patterson's *Slavery and Social Death*, a first comprehensive analysis of slavery as a relationship in a way that incorporates the slaves' point of view, defining it in terms of the slaves' experience of "social death."[13] Patterson's work will be explained in more detail in chapter 5.

In what follows, the notion of intersectionality will also be informative. "Intersectionality" emerged in Black Women's Studies in the 1990s to examine how gender, race, class, and nation "mutually construct one another," rather than functioning "as separate systems of oppression."[14] Intersectional analyses demonstrate the importance of the family in contemporary political and social rhetoric. Patricia Hill Collins, a social theorist whose work has defined intersectionality, considers the family a "privileged exemplar" in this form of analysis. The imagined "traditional family ideal" in the family rhetoric of contemporary United States political and social discourse around "family values" that she describes closely resembles Lakoff's description of the Strict Father family mode. While she does not use a linguistic analysis of root metaphor, her rhetorical analysis has much in common with Lakoff's linguistic one: "The power of this traditional family ideal lies in its dual function as an ideological construction and as a fundamental principle of social organization."[15]

Collins' analysis reveals key aspects missing in Lakoff's work in *Moral Politics*, however, by examining "how family links social hierarchies of gender, race, and nation."[16] For contemporary United States society, her insight that the traditional family is projected as a naturalized hierarchy and that "family writ large is race," is crucial. In the traditional image, each race is considered as a family unit with its own internal family hierarchy. In the nation as a family, racial groups form another racial hierarchy with whites seen as the adults in the national family and all the other races seen as children. Women are to subordinate themselves to men, children to adults, within each racial group, and the non-white racial groups are to subordinate themselves to whites. She also points to the reliance on violence to maintain the familial social hierarchy at all levels.[17]

Collins also shows that the defense of boundaries that Lakoff mentions as important in the Strict Father family model also relates to both the feminization of domestic space and to racial segregation. She discusses key points that will be relevant in what follows: the role of control of women's sexuality in maintaining family lineage and the blood ties that define family inheritance and racial boundaries; the rights and responsibilities of membership in a family-race-nation;

the importance of moving to family and wealth as the basic unit of social analysis rather than the individual and income; and racial and class differentials in family planning policies.[18]

In what follows, the notion of intersectionality and Collins' analysis of family will be applicable in understanding the Roman Strict Father family model. We will see that it differs from the contemporary Strict Father family in several key aspects that Collins' discussion points out. While Collins does not present an alternative family model as Lakoff does, she points to the need to articulate alternatives:

> Given the power of family as ideological construction and principle of social organization, Black nationalist, feminist, and other political movements in the United States dedicated to challenging social inequality might consider recasting intersectional understandings of family in ways that do not reproduce inequality. Instead of engaging in endless criticism, *reclaiming the language of family for democratic ends and transforming the very conception of family itself might provide a more useful approach.* [emphasis added][19]

The chapters that follow will not offer a complete intersectional analysis that relates family to race or to the many subordinated ethnic groups in the Greco-Roman era, but notions of intersectionality will inform the relation of slavery and the family and of the gendering of subjugated peoples in the Roman Empire. We will also see that the project of "reclaiming the language of family" that Collins recommends is not new.

Empire Criticism and People's History

Scholars in recent decades are recognizing the Roman Empire as the main context for understanding the development of early Christianity. Previous scholarship had envisioned a Jewish context as the major power influencing the world of early Christianity. A shift has taken place quite rapidly, in fact. I remember some of us meeting in the early 1990s in pre-meetings at the Society of Biblical Literature (SBL) to share our work on the specific contexts of Paul's letters in the context of the Roman Empire and to frame what is meant by "people's history." One time we literally met in a hallway because our room request had been lost.[20] Only a decade later, MOST of the New Testament sessions in the SBL meetings had many papers addressing topics related to the empire and several ongoing sections are devoted to empire criticism. A major shift has taken place from viewing early Christianity in a Jewish context to viewing early Christian and Jewish groups in the context of the Roman Empire. Here I will draw upon work of empire-critical scholars in those gatherings and others.

Two basic concepts will be helpful to explain in this introduction. One is the notion of religion as a "public cognitive system." Chapter 9 will include more explanation of the imperial cults, but some initial clarification will be helpful for understanding the importance of the family as a root metaphor for empire in the Roman era. It is important to recognize that the separation between church and state guaranteed in the United States constitution simply does not apply to the Greco-Roman world. This legal separation applies, in fact, in few other locations. Scholars have also assumed that religion and politics are discrete categories.[21] Religious observance and organization need to be understood instead as a real societal binding force, not separate from politics but part and parcel with it. Richard A. Horsley has coined a descriptive mouthful as a term for this: "Roman imperial religio-politics."[22] The Roman Empire was not just a political or military dominion. It was a religious and, as we shall see, familial one as well. The notion of "cult" as it is used here may also be unfamiliar to some readers. See Box 1 p. XXX.[23]

The assumption of a division between religion and politics has concealed the central importance of the imperial cult, "emperor worship." A conventional approach to Roman history relegated the imperial cults to the sidelines as "mere propaganda" while focusing on the diplomatic and administrative functions of the state.[24] Politics, conventionally defined, was the main issue while religion was considered ritual frippery of no real consequence.

The imperial cult, in fact, functioned as a fundamental means of binding the empire together. By allowing wide participation and ritual connection to the emperor and by connecting the emperor and the Roman pantheon to the deities of conquered peoples, the

"Cult" and "Cults"

The term "cult" is used here to describe religious practices in the Greco-Roman world and does not have the modern connotation of a small group with dangerous nonconformist beliefs. "Cult" simply indicates a form of organized religious practices. The term is used rather than the term "religion" because that term denotes a modern concept of mutual exclusivity and definition of one religion as distinct from others that does not apply to religious activities in the Greco-Roman era, at least until the rise of Christianity.

The term will most often be used in the plural, "cults," to indicate the lack of a monolithic organization. To speak of "the imperial cult," for example, or "the cult of Dionysius" can imply unity and central organization that did not characterize these religious expressions.

imperial cults fostered loyalty and inclusion to unite the empire as a family. The imperial cults made the empire a family and integrated elements of what today we experience as separate spheres of "religion" and "politics."

The imperial cults also used to be seen as a top-down propaganda mechanism, mere propaganda dressed as religion without any real adherents. This assumes an understanding of religion in Christianized terms as a belief system focused on individual internal experience. Instead, religion in the Roman era meant an active practice including rituals and other expressions of devotion. These could include ritual processions, the construction of temples, votes to change the calendar to reckon time from the birth date of the emperor, sponsorship of gladiatorial games, daily devotions at the household shrine, and more.

Instead of seeing religion as an internalized belief system, with classicist Simon Price we need to treat religious ritual as "a public cognitive system."[25] Rather than considering religion and ritual as a primarily internal experience, religious ritual outwardly and publicly displays how members of a human group think of themselves together, and ritual is the collective thought process and "a way of conceptualizing the world."[26] While it certainly affects and shapes members' internal self-concepts, ritual constructs a system to display relationships. It shows who fits where in society and reveals and reinforces a worldview, an understanding of the cosmos that contains society. To revise ritual is to reconstruct, or attempt to reconstruct, the societal relationships and the worldview expressed.

Such a public cognitive system conveys the root metaphor of the empire as family. Ritual is the enactment, the embodiment, of the family empire. "Religion" is thus both the public ritual which is real and significant for organizing the population and how they think of themselves as a sacral unit,[b] and the individual internal experience that is being shaped by and shaping the language of the public cognitive system.[27] The development of ritual can also be a means for groups to rethink themselves and reconstruct their relationships, and some of this rethinking can form what will be proposed in chapter 12 as a "hidden cognitive system" using a second important concept.

That second concept comes from the work of political scientist James C. Scott. He has coined some useful terms for understanding the early Christians in the Roman Empire: the "public transcript" and the "hidden transcript." His work is based on his studies of contemporary strategies of resistance exercised among Malaysian peasants. Their modes of resistance stay off the radar screen of the power elites who dominate their lives, and their strategies leave precious little trace in any written or public record, yet such peasants effectively undermine the elites' many efforts to dominate them.[28]

These modes of resistance form what Scott labels the "hidden transcript" as opposed to the "public transcript" that forms the public and historical record. The term "public transcript" describes "the open interaction between subordinates and those who dominate."[29] This is how people who dominate wish to have things appear, what they wish to believe.[30] The "hidden transcript" is the stream running beneath the surface, what subordinates say and do and their strategies of self-preservation formed out of view of those in power.

---

b. A sacral unit is a group defined by common ritual or a common relationship to a deity or deities.

Rituals as Public Cognitive Systems

Religion has often been understood as an internalized belief system with an implied emphasis on individual choice and intellectual assent. Simon Price has instead used the term "public cognitive system" in his discussion of the Roman imperial cult. His notion is based on early work in cognitive science that identified "symbolic knowledge" as well as on anthropological studies of ritual.

Understanding religious ritual as a "public cognitive system" emphasizes the role of religious ritual as a series of collective physical actions rather than religion as an individual mental activity. In ritual, collective actions display how members of a human group think of themselves and their relationships. Ritual can be understood as a collective thought process that displays a group's conceptualization of themselves and their world, their social relations and the role of their deities.

As a "public cognitive system," ritual projects a system of power relationships to which individuals may or may not assent intellectually as they participate. The ritual may, in fact, provide a display that provokes thought about the system of power relations. The very display may move participants to struggle to revise or resist the public ritual or to create counter-rituals in hidden transcripts. (See the box on "Hidden and Public Transcripts.") To revise ritual is to reconstruct, or attempt to reconstruct, the societal relationships and the worldview expressed in public cognitive systems.

Several forms of public rituals formed the "public cognitive system" of the Roman empire. The imperial cults included various rituals, such as processions and sacrifices, and with the ritual display of the violent spectacles in the Roman arena, conveyed a public cognitive system of the root metaphor of the empire as family. Rituals of other deities also framed public cognitive systems. Such rituals enacted and embodied the family empire.

"Religion" is thus both the public ritual which is real and significant for organizing the population and how they think of themselves as a sacral unit and the individual internal experience which is being shaped by and shaping the language of the public cognitive system. The development of ritual can also be a means for groups to rethink themselves and reconstruct their relationships.

For example, if you have ever worked in a factory or some other job where there are a lot of subordinates and a boss, you are aware that there is one set of behavior and opinion expressed in the workplace, keeping up appearances and acting like the boss is a good guy or gal, and another in the coffee shop or the corner tavern where workers gather after work and their real opinions and frustrations can be shared. If you are that boss and are not completely clueless, perhaps you label it as pathology and accuse them of passive-aggressive behavior. In a relatively open society you may even be able to foster honest communication. Where power is more disproportionate this becomes less possible. As Scott puts it, "the more menacing the power, the thicker the mask."[31]

A whole world of discourse and opinion lies hidden from the elites of any given generation and is absent from the historical record for subsequent generations. Wherever we see extreme disproportions of power, however, we can assume that hidden transcripts are present in a variety of forms. Scott outlines strategies that subordinated peoples use. People may speak in coded metaphors. They may gossip. They may proclaim allegiance to a supposed "real" good and just king or czar to undermine the authority of the repressive local representative of the actual czar. The list of subterranean strategies is long. On occasion the discourse happening among subordinated people out of earshot of the elites emerges to be assertively heard, "speaking truth to power," and there may be a trace of this open resistance in the historical record, or not. Every time we see the pressure of the

Hidden and Public Transcripts

Political scientist James C. Scott has coined the terms "hidden transcript" and "public transcript" to describe the dynamics of resistance in situations where elites hold disproportionate power.

The "public transcript" describes what the elites want to believe about themselves and their relationships to their subordinates. The "public transcript" is the discourse that occurs openly when the elites are present, the public image. The "public transcript" upholds the elites view of themselves.

The "hidden transcript" describes what subordinates say and do out of earshot and out of view of those in power. Subordinates use a variety of strategies to create and maintain their own discourse about themselves and those in power. They may find and create physical spaces for discussion out of earshot of those who dominate them. They may also create code language and metaphors that they use within earshot. In the "hidden transcript," they develop alternative narratives and worldviews counter to the worldview projected in in the "public transcript."

stream popping through to form a little geyser, a much larger body of discontent is bubbling under the surface.

This notion and the descriptions of a variety of modes of resistance in the "hidden transcript" are proving quite fruitful for our approach to early Christian texts. In some cases, we can see something quite close to an historical record of the "hidden transcript." A few sayings attributed to Jesus might fit that description, as well as some elements embedded in Paul's letters. Most often we are looking for the hidden transcript just below the surface of the text. In that we can begin to recognize the resistance of the women and the slaves and the peasants and the vast impoverished majority. We listen for the voices of the conquered people represented in the lower register of the *Gemma Augustea*.

We can see them and begin to hear their voices, however, not in searching for responses to the public transcript of our world but of theirs. It is vital that we understand that the "hidden transcript" is not an ideologically unified perspective. In spaces out of earshot of the upholders of the public transcript, people fashion diverse responses to it. They respond in their own ways to their own context. They shape modes of resistance in language that responds to the public transcript of their own context. To understand their language and modes of resistance in the hidden transcript, we need to understand the public transcript of their time, the Roman Empire and the family metaphor that undergirded it and the imperial cults as a ritual expression of that family as a "public cognitive system."

One point is crucial for our understanding here. In later chapters, we will see Roman imperial propaganda. This propaganda is the public transcript, and only that. The Roman Empire projected its power as absolute, but it did not possess actual absolute power. We must be careful not to believe imperial propaganda as fact. We look for the hidden transcript to see who was unconvinced and how they responded to assert their own power.

Early Christian texts preserve some glimpses into the hidden transcript, and we have them because they were preserved by the later Christian empire. We cannot assume that early Christians were unique or special in producing a hidden transcript, only that we have more evidence preserved from them. Yet it bears repeating that it is important not to believe Roman imperial propaganda, not to believe that Roman emperors or the empire had actual absolute power. This is important in order to understand the reality and power of the resistance in the "hidden transcript" both then and now.

People's History and Historical Criticism
Reading History against the Grain

Not believing the imperial propaganda as fact, many scholars involved in empire criticism are also engaged in people's history, investigating history as made by ordinary people, history from below. People's history focuses not on the great men, the elites and kings and their wars, but on ordinary people and all aspects of their lives.[32] For studies of Christian origins, traditionally focused on the interpretation of texts, this means refocusing on the communities revealed through the texts and considering all aspects of their lives, not just the religious meaning of the texts, and not just focusing on Jesus and Paul as the great men.

This shift of the focus away from the individual great men and toward the ordinary people and communities will be relevant for the framing of this project, especially in volume 2. Approaching Christian origins as people's history, this project will work to de-center Jesus and Paul as the great men who created Christianity and to focus instead on the early communities. Paul will be considered as one leader in those communities. His letters are a major body of evidence about those early communities, and his thought has formed a major influence on later developments of Christianity and on Western culture. Greater attention may appear to be given to him than the effort to de-center might suggest. Yet the approach here will not assume that his efforts are to be either uncritically applauded or dismissed. Jesus will also be considered using his teachings in the early communities. The efforts of the Jesus Seminar to discern a body of material most likely to originate with the historical Jesus will be taken into consideration, but his words and the words attributed to him will be viewed more broadly as teachings of the early communities. Jesus and Paul will be considered as major influences, but the focus will be the early communities and the variety of their social experimentation.

As people's history, the nitty-gritty questions of people's circumstances and lives will take center stage rather than theological issues created as their writings were used in later centuries. Consideration of the family as root metaphor will raise the theological issues, but in ways that reveal the impact of these issues on peoples' lives.

We will also understand these texts primarily as the products of oral presentations in communities rather than as texts written by solitary authors, as part of popular traditions rather than as elite cultural productions.[33] Sources and methods that move us beyond written texts and archives will be important, including archaeological research that investigates the lives of common people and sociological research.

Texts will be revisited with the basic notion current in a wide spectrum of liberation-oriented study of early Christianity: "reading against the grain." This phrase comes from Walter Benjamin's brief but penetrating *Theses on the Philosophy of History*.[34] Benjamin contrasts "historicism" as the history that serves the elites with "historical materialism," something closer to people's history. For both, history is a "process of empathy," but the traditional historian empathizes with the victor.

"Historicism" describes the Enlightenment project of history, and its corollary, historical criticism of biblical texts. Enlightenment thinkers and historical critics were attempting to free the texts and themselves from authoritarian Christian dogmatic interpretation by establishing the authority of "objective" methods of interpretation.[35] More recently, as many scholars who are not males of European extraction have entered the field, the supposed objectivity both of the tools of these Enlightenment-based historians and of their results has come under scrutiny. In the words of one analyst of the issue, "much of the so-called 'objectivity' for which historians aimed appears to be a universalization of their own particularity."[36]

A first step in perceiving the limitations of and the damage done by "historicism" is to see those who do not benefit from the rewards enjoyed by the elite. This means seeing the experience and empathizing with the anguish of the people in the lower panel of the *Gemma Augustea*. In the words that precede Benjamin's statement about reading against the grain, he describes the recovery of history as a "process of empathy" in which the "adherents of historicism," in contrast to the "historical materialists," empathize with the victor. He uses the metaphor of a continuing Roman victory parade like the one we have seen depicted being readied in the lower panel of the *Gemma Augustea:*

And all rulers are the heirs of those who conquered before them. Hence, empathy with the victor invariably benefits the rulers. Historical materialists know what that means. Whoever has emerged victorious participates to this day in the triumphal procession in which the present rulers step over those who are

lying prostrate. According to traditional practice, the spoils
are carried along in the procession. They are called cultural
treasures, and a historical materialist views them with cautious
detachment. For without exception the cultural treasures he
surveys have an origin which he cannot contemplate without
horror. They owe their existence not only to the efforts of the
great minds and talents who have created them, but also to the
anonymous toil of their contemporaries. There is no document
of civilization which is not at the same time a document of barbarism. And just as such a document is not free of barbarism,
barbarism taints also the manner in which it was transmitted
from one owner to another. A historical materialist therefore dis-
sociates himself from it as far as possible. He regards it as his task
to *brush history against the grain.* [emphasis added][37]

When we bring this recognition of horror to texts and artifacts,
the "cultural treasures" from the past, then, we develop a different
perception of history. These are the data we have, but we do not
read them at face value. We detach ourselves not from the informative value of the data but from any empathy with the victors who
have produced and preserved (and sometimes looted) much of the
data we have. Rather than believe that the "objectivity" that historicism pretends is even possible, we choose our empathy in order to
read the data "against the grain" to find what we can of those who
have been left out of the victors' history. While imagination may
be needed to fill in blanks, the primary task is re-reading the data
"against the grain." To do this, we start with the basic assumptions
of people's history already mentioned.

In this process, it is important to take care not to universalize
the experiences of the under-classes. Power elites tend to universalize their own experience as "human experience" and thus make the
experiences of those outside the elites invisible. In apologizing for
the limitations of their experience, privileged interpreters sometimes
attempt to universalize the viewpoint of "oppression," still perceiving the underclasses as a single unit.

To "brush against the grain" means to find the many and varied
voices. Audre Lorde's basic notion of the power of *difference,* the

power of recognizing and unifying different experiences rather than imposing an elite perspective as universal, reveals the presumption of universalizing.[38] She articulated this perspective in response not to traditional historians, however, but in response to feminist theorists who wanted to universalize women's experiences of oppression.

Feminist Approaches and a "Hermeneutics of Hunger"

Whether identified as "people's historians" or not, many feminist scholars of early Christianity are re-centering attention on the community rather than the great men. Many also understand Lorde's critique and investigate particular communities. Without necessarily using the term, feminist scholars have been active in discerning and reimagining the "hidden transcript" and the approach of "reading against the grain" has gained a wide currency among feminist interpreters.

Feminists tend to engage texts as artifacts preserved by history's (male) victors. During the past few decades, feminist interpreters have struggled with texts of the Jewish and Christian canon and, in the words of Sandra Schneiders, "the awareness that, in Western society at least, the Bible is a major source and legitimator of women's oppression in family, society, and Church."[39] Feminist scholars and interpreters have brought a "hermeneutics[c] of suspicion" to the Bible and have labored diligently to expose male-centered ideological biases integral to many of its texts and to reveal the omission of women from much of the Bible.[40]

The importance of exposing the role of the Bible in legitimating women's oppression extends not only to the communities that recognize these texts as scripture but also to the broader society influenced by Christianity. We should not underestimate the importance of this "hermeneutics of suspicion" and ideological criticism, notions we have already seen as undergirding empire criticism and people's history. Schneiders succinctly summarizes the notion more broadly in two assumptions: first, the text is not neutral, and second, the interpreter is not "objective."[41]

---

c. "Hermeneutics" is an academic term for "interpretation."

Many feminist scholars do not limit their interpretation to ideological critique or "suspicion," however. These interpreters all illustrate a move beyond suspicion. Rather than just analyzing and critiquing the oppressiveness of the Bible, they look for constructive alternatives in various forms.

Some offer empowerment in the form of a "hermeneutics of retrieval" for feminists who choose to remain within the Judeo-Christian tradition and interpret texts as scripture, but from a critical position.[42] Here I do not approach the texts as scripture nor do I personally approach them as a Christian seeking validation in Christian scripture. Some of what will be explored could nevertheless be useful for a "hermeneutics of retrieval" for Christians so inclined.

Other feminists have explored forms of reconstructive interpretation that, as has been mentioned, de-center Jesus and Paul as the great men and focuses instead on the early communities. Antoinette Clark Wire, for example, uses Paul's Corinthian correspondence to reconstruct the presence of women in the Corinthian community.[43] This type of approach has inspired creative methods to brush the grain of the text to reveal the faint presence of women and to reveal the central role of women in some early Christian communities.

Another ground-breaking feminist scholar, Elisabeth Schüssler Fiorenza, also advocates an interpretive focus on the early communities rather than the great men and seeks methods that do not limit feminist interpretation to suspicion. A hermeneutics of suspicion is just one in an array she lists of seven hermeneutical strategies in a "dance of interpretation" that also includes "a hermeneutics of experience, of domination, of suspicion, of critical evaluation, of memory and re-membering, of imagination, and of transformation."[44] Schüssler Fiorenza envisions a dance that moves into construction of an alternative vision of present-day community in relationship to the liberating communities she visualizes in her reconstruction of early Christianity.

This study shares some assumptions with Schüssler Fiorenza's feminist approach. Here we will investigate the Strict Father model, but this model shares much with the androcentric (male-centered) community model or, as she terms it, "kyriocentric" (master/ruler-centered) language and rhetoric. Examining this "kyriocentric" Strict Father family model as root metaphor will allow us to look at additional dimensions of its language and rhetoric.

This effort also shares the quest Schüssler Fiorenza advocates "to both identify and establish connection to certain potential roots of historical struggles for emancipation."[45] To consider these struggles for emancipation, family models offer something more than the dead-end question, is it egalitarian? This study will neither focus upon nor assume that there was an original egalitarian Jesus movement or "community of equals."[46] Instead, I will focus on the experimentation in these early communities as their world became increasingly dominated by the Strict Father family of their time, the Roman Empire, and as that empire increasingly developed and promoted its Roman version of the Strict Father family. The reality is not static family models in opposition to one another but a dynamic interaction of a variety of impulses toward liberation responding to a more hegemonic model that itself was in flux. In other words, it's a dance of moving targets—creative resistance efforts and imperial responses.

By investigating alternative family models, we can consider the varieties of experimentation in the early Christian era in what Schüssler Fiorenza calls "the critical alternative spaces of emancipation."[47] Those alternative spaces include experiments in lived relationships "up close and personal" in households and groupings that describe their relationships using family language, in the microcosm, as well as experiments in language and rhetoric that envision relationships of a changed world, in the macrocosm.

The approach used here to connect to those "alternative spaces of emancipation," the social locations where hidden transcripts emerge, is informed as well by a new turn among some feminist interpreters to a "hermeneutics of hunger" a term introduced by German theologian and activist Dorothee Sölle in her book *The Silent Cry: Mysticism and Resistance*.[48] Sölle takes up an interpretive stance in a "zone of freedom" offered by mysticism in a variety of religious traditions, a position in the margins of religious traditions where women have often found direct access to the divine, especially when they have been excluded from the symbolic centers of divine power in religious institutions. By "mysticism" she means "the knowledge of God through and from experience," as defined by medieval scholastics.[49] She takes a stance in mysticism because its religiosity, "its 'substance,' seeks to overcome the basic presuppositions of patriarchal thinking: power and dominance over 'the other,' be it the other sex, other nature, or other races and civilizations."[50]

In her effort to move beyond the necessary but limited project of a hermeneutics of suspicion that continues to focus on the centers of power by critiquing them, Sölle moves to a hermeneutics of hunger. She asks "what it is that women and men are looking for in their cry for a different spirituality."[51] The hermeneutical lens is the people's hunger. Her work links the physical hunger and oppression of the Third World addressed in liberation theology to spiritual hunger in the First World where there are people "yearning to live a different kind of life."[52] Sölle's book traces elements of mysticism connected to various religious traditions and places them in their respective social-historical contexts. She offers a "democratization" of mysticism in its link to resistance to dominating structures, mysticism as an experience of God open to everyone.

Sölle's hermeneutic interprets a history of religious traditions rather than specific texts from any tradition's scriptures. Applying this "hermeneutic of hunger" to scriptural texts should allow us to perceive this hunger in the text. This hermeneutic acknowledges a present-day stance in a mysticism of "yearning to live a different kind of life" as a hunger for a world of justice and sustainability for the planet, a hunger that unites mysticism and resistance.

Especially in Part 4, this book will consider various forms of resistance to Roman imperialism primarily using James C. Scott's language of the public and hidden transcripts already mentioned. In chapter 12, the notion of popular religiosity will supplement it as well. Yet the notion of a "hermeneutic of hunger" and the zones of freedom created in the mystical margins of established religious forms will also inform the view of the social locations in which hidden transcripts can develop even without direct references to Sölle's terminology. We will see hunger and hope among the vast impoverished majority of the Roman era as the "yearning to live a different kind of life" and to create spaces for it and to envision a different world. We will not look at this vast impoverished majority as a single mass, however, but with the assumption of a wide variety of difference.

While Sölle describes the spaces in which a democratized mysticism breeds resistance, the notion of a hermeneutics of hunger will not here be taken to require belief in God. Here those spaces will be understood as human creations and the mystical will be assumed as part of human experience. Connection across time to those spaces of resistance does point toward a subjective and emotive experience, empathy to use Benjamin's word, in the process of investigation.

I should clarify, however. In this project, I will of necessity bring subjective experience and yes, empathy, to interpretation of the texts and archaeological evidence and images, all the data that have been preserved. All interpreters do this whether they acknowledge it or not. This does not mean imagining data, however. To brush against the grain means that we have something in hand that we are brushing. This project is not intended to create a usable past or to envision a time when there was some form of pure egalitarian reality in the early Christian movement, a "myth of origin."[53] Even when a movement is young and relatively authentic and idealistic, the reality is messy and complicated with personal power struggles and limitations in members' abilities to become what they envisioned and to envision beyond the constrictions of their contexts. That will be the assumption here, at least. The purpose is to explore their efforts with empathy, neither to imagine them in the perfection of a golden age nor to judge them for their lack of perfection.

The variety of their efforts is also important as part of a broader shift that is part of a feminist approach, a shift away from binary vision that considers a question like, is it egalitarian or not? One aspect of the Strict Father family model, even in the variant forms to be examined in this study, is the tendency to define the world in dualities: the civilization inside its boundaries and the barbarians outside. George Lakoff also describes two family models in a way that gives the impression of a binary opposition, either a Strict Father model or a Nurturant Parent model. His study, however, reflects the polarization that has developed in contemporary political discourse. A broader array of family models is possible.

As we consider the models in the Greco-Roman era, we will see not only that the Strict Father model of the Roman Empire differs significantly from the model Lakoff describes for contemporary culture in the United States but also that those who resisted the Roman Strict Father family empire experimented with a variety of models and alternatives that cannot be neatly described as the Nurturant Parent model Lakoff discerns. Experiments could include elements of the Strict Father model and still be efforts to resist the empire. Considering family models can help us move beyond binary thinking to be able to assess experimental counter-imperial and counter-kyrio-centric efforts on their own merits without having to judge them by a contemporary yardstick.[d]

---

d. The term "counter kyrio-centric" is based on Elizabeth Schüssler Fiorenza's coinage of the term "kyrio-centric" for what is often termed "patriarchy." The term, based on the Greek work often translated "lord," points to a system of domination and hierarchical relationships rather than the focus on male power associated with the term "patriarchy."

Conclusion to Part I

If we look again at the *Gemma Augustea*, then, and contemplate today's victors as the heirs of the emperor-god seated on the throne and see the conquered peoples in the lower register, we need to see more than their subjugated state and their suffering. The peoples portrayed came from worlds not contained in or shaped by this image, not necessarily idyllic but also not necessarily in the same shape. People like them envisioned worlds not shaped in this image. Ultimately it is the shapes of those worlds that we seek to understand.

Part II

The Roman Empire as a Strict Father Family in the Microcosm

The Roman Strict Father family model undergirding the Roman Empire was a social reality as well as a metaphor. Part 2 will focus on this form of family as a lived social reality, primarily as a system of relations in a household or "task-oriented residence unit."[1] Kinship and marriage are important as part of the system of relations. While not everyone in the Roman era lived in a Roman Strict Father family "up close and personal," this was the form that came to dominate the lives of the population of the empire. To understand the context in which early Christianity grew, we need to understand this family form as a distinctively Roman Strict Father family. This was the family of the public transcript, the one that was being defined as natural. In the hidden transcript, a different story was being told, and a few initial notes to acknowledge another perspective will be helpful.

Family in Hidden Transcripts

Cameras are widely available today, and families from a wide social spectrum are portrayed in images available in many print and on-line forms. People in the Greco-Roman world also had family portraits made in paintings and stone reliefs, but the images give us a disproportionate view of those who could afford such media.[2] The discussion of the Roman Strict Father family model in the public transcript will be informed by many such images. Yet we have a few glimpses of people of meager means as well.

Portrayals of families in social locations where hidden transcripts could develop are rare, due less to their need to be "hidden" from the powerful than to their simple lack of resources. Votive monuments from rural Phrygia (the interior of what is now Turkey) provide an unusual archaeological record from this era. Carved for local shepherds from scraps from a marble quarry, these small monuments, most less than a foot high, indicate a variety of family forms.[3] In addition to individuals,[4] many of these steles portray a family grouping.

The family configurations vary widely.[5] Some portray two men in shepherd's capes.[6] Many are male and female pairs, most probably married couples.[7] Several may portray a nuclear family with a man, a woman and one or more children.[8] Yet others are varied: a woman with two men[9] or a man with two women,[10] and various other configurations with adults and children.

Figure 2 : Marble relief. Ankara. Inscription reads: "… on behalf of his own association … from … (dedicated this) vow to Zeus …"*

---

*20.1 x 10.3 x 4.2 cm. LH 1 cm. Museum of Anatolian Civilizations, (*Anadolu Medeniyetleri Müzesi'nin*), Ankara. Inv. 68.21.64." Drew-Bear, Thomas, Yildizturan, *Phrygian Votive Steles*, 137, no. 167.

Some of the steles portray larger groupings. One notable example portrays seven figures. Three men in shepherd's capes stand together on the left, and two women over two children on the right. The inscription reads, "... on behalf of his own *doumos.*" The authors translate "*doumos*" as "association," but it could also be the Latin word for "household."[11]

In another example, the left side portrays a man in a shepherd's cape and two women as slightly larger figures, with a boy and a girl on the upper right over a donkey on the lower right. Amia, a woman, dedicates this stele to Zeus Alsenos, the god to whom many others are also dedicated.[12]

We cannot be certain about how the people portrayed in these images were related to one another or to the dedicators, but we can see a wide variety of family configurations. Most likely these were combinations created not by choice but by default, families made up of the members who have survived the many threats to the lives

Figure 3: Marble stele. Ankara. Inscription reads: "Amia (dedicated this) vow to Zeus Alsenos"*

*32.2 x 27.8 x 5.0 cm. LH 1.6 cm. Museum of Anatolian Civilizations, (*Anadolu Medeniyetleri Müzesi'nin*), Ankara. Inv. 15.99.64. Drew-Bear, Thomas, Yildizturan, *Phrygian Votive Steles,* 127, no. 150.

of people of sparse means and those who have stayed on the home place when others went to seek a living in the urban areas. We can see how important the family groupings were to these lowly shepherd families, however, in the fact that they used some of their meager resources to have them carved and placed in the temple as a public display not only of their devotion to the deity but also of their own images and family identity. Given a rare opportunity to project their relationships in enduring stone, peasants in the countryside showed that they valued family connections in many forms.

Hidden Transcripts in the Family

Within the Roman Strict Father family form, a hidden transcript was also taking place among people in the margins right within the family. One example can provide an initial reminder that they also had their own points of view and their own emotional lives. In one epitaph, a freedwoman of enough means to erect a stone monument mourns her daughter, Posilla:

> Posilla Senenia, daughter of Quartus and Quarta Senenia, freedwoman of Gaius.
>
> Stranger, stop and, while you are here, read what is written: that a mother was not permitted to enjoy her only daughter, whose life, I believe, was envied by some god.
>
> Since her mother was not permitted to enjoy her while she was alive, she does so just the same after death; at the end of her time, [her mother] with this monument honours her whom she loved.[13]

We do not learn much about the details of their lives, but the epitaph recalls the real affection of a mother for her daughter and gives some intimation of a rich emotional life among mothers and daughters as well as among the many others who were subordinated in the family structure.

Not only in the countryside and among the urban poor but also within the Roman Strict Father household, people claimed their own family relationships despite a lack of resources to portray them in lasting media and despite structures that did not recognize them.

These connections in the hidden transcript form a web of relationship that resisted the dominant culture in a variety of ways.

High status women form another part of the picture of the hidden transcript of the household. In the public transcript, they appeared in several roles, as benefactors and as priestesses as well as in their dignified but defined role in the family.[14] Such women nevertheless engaged in activities not necessarily associated with their role in the household model, as philosophers, writers, gladiators, and in one protest movement, even enrolling themselves as prostitutes.[15]

As just one example of a writer from the first century CE, we have this account:

> Pamphile was an Epidaurian, a learned woman, the daughter
> of Soterides, who is also said to have been an author of books,
> according to Dionysius in the thirteenth book of his *History of
> Learning*; or, as others have written, it was Socratides her husband. She wrote historical memoirs in 33 books, an epitome of
> Ctesias' history is three books, many epitomes of histories and
> other books, about controversies, sex and many other things.[16]

This is just one example to keep in mind because it indicates that women did not necessarily fit themselves into the role we might assume was prescribed for them in the Roman Strict Father family model, a complex role to be discussed below. We should suspect that many of them, too, were writing a hidden transcript within their households.

Much of the discussion that follows will describe the Roman family model on which the Roman Empire was based. The image of these other relationships provides a tantalizing counterpoint, a different story of how family was lived among the vast impoverished majority and at the margins within the dominating form of family.

3

The Stage and the Daily Performance

Roman *Domus* as Edifice and Social Structure

We turn, then, to the family model that dominated the Roman Empire. Visualize this family in a constant performance, a daily and annual and life-cycle routine that enhances the honor of its leading man, the father at the center of the family model, its *paterfamilias*. After clarifying discussion of some difficulties of terminology around "family" and "household," this chapter will describe the house that provided the stage for this performance.

Familia, Domus, Oikos
Terms and Forms of "Family" in the Greco-Roman Era

When we speak of "family" in the first century, we must identify some difficulties with the terms we use. Not only is translation of terms from one social system to another difficult, but determination of precisely what the Greek and Latin terms meant in the Greco-Roman era is also a challenge.

The Latin term *familia* apparently included the kinship grouping descended through the male bloodline as well as the slaves and animals. *Domus* was a broader term that also encompassed the house and property and the male line of ancestors and descendants. The Greek term *oikos* referred to both.[1] No term for what we now know as the nuclear family existed,[2] although visual representations of families portray a core unit of father, mother, and child that was a pervasive aspect of the kinship grouping. We should not be surprised at such complexity if we consider the variety of meanings for the term "family" today. Why would we think it was any simpler or clearer in the Roman era? What we think of as "family" is only tenuously a meaningful term when applied to the Greco-Roman world. "Proximate social relations" could be a more accurate term, but it is cumbersome and too general.

We must, however, imagine a different world. We cannot, for example, translate the Latin term *familia* as "family" and imagine life in a single nuclear family home of the 1950s where dad goes to work in the morning and comes home at night, mom stays home and does volunteer work, and children go to school, and mom and dad and the three children sit down around the dinner table at night and talk about Dick's problem with his teacher and Jane's tiff with her friend while Sally mashes her peas. This is not the "family" of the Greco-Roman era. Adding extended family relationships of grandparents and aunts and uncles and cousins would not be inaccurate but would not be the necessary mental shift to envision family life in the Greco-Roman world.

We make some unstated assumptions when we speak of "family" and "home." In the world of the early Roman Empire, we cannot assume that these terms apply in the same way. The nuclear family was recognized as an emotional unit but was in many ways more complex than the dynamics of our nuclear family. It was kinship and more. Private and public interacted differently, and the presence of slaves created a significantly different relational dynamic.[3]

So, if the family in the Greco-Roman era was not the emotional unit we currently assume, what was it? Halvor Moxnes' definition is a start: "a co-resident group that performs various tasks: production, distribution, transmission, reproduction, and that serves as the primary group of identification."[4] To this list we should add ritual and worship. In other words, we need to imagine family as a group that shares space that is both a living space, where people eat and sleep and raise children, and a working space, where things are made for use and for sale to others, business is conducted, guests are entertained, and deities are offered worship. When individuals in that group leave this living-working space, they are known as members of the group who occupy that space and are associated with the family's head. With this picture, we are closer to an image of family life in the Greco-Roman world.

A summarized list from a second-century legal digest indicates that defining *familia* was a complex task back then, too, but it can help reorient our vision. In proposing a definition, the *Digest* explains that the term applies "both to property and to persons." The term is used when the question is about ownership of the *familia* as well as about membership in it. "*Familia*" also specifies "a certain body of persons" defined either in a strict legal sense or more loosely by kinship. Legally, the term indicates "a number of people who are by birth or by law subjected to the *potestas* (power) of one man," the *paterfamilias*. Upon the death of the *paterfamilias,* or when his sons are emancipated, they also each form a new *familia*, yet the term continues to apply to all those descended from the deceased *paterfamilias*. A male blood lineage is maintained as *familia*, while, as the *Digest* states, "A woman ... is both the beginning and end of her own *familia*." As property, slaves are generally part of the *familia* as well.[5]

A nuclear family appears to be at the core of this household with sons moving to new residences with their wives when they married and daughters moving to live with their husbands upon marriage. Yet there were also some multi-family households with adult sons and daughters and their spouses and children. Some of this depended, then as now, on household financial fortunes.[6]

As we begin to understand the house and who would populate it, we must realize that especially in the early first century CE, the "family" and the design of the houses in which families lived was a shifting target and was under discussion.

Setting the Stage
Picturing the *Domus* as the Roman Strict Father Family

The Roman *domus* was both an edifice and a social organism. An examination of the edifice will show how it functioned as a stage for the social life of its inhabitants. The architecture of the *domus* also indicates some of the social changes around family structures that were taking place in the transition from the Roman republic to the empire. Changes in architecture and the extension of a Romanized style into the provinces of the empire indicate that a Romanized conception of family structure was part of the change.[7] In Part 3, we will see that this was consistent with Caesar Augustus' program to promote his version of Roman family values based on a Roman Strict Father family presented as the timeless natural order.

The *domus* included the house, everyone in it, everything in it, the other properties of the *familia*, the ancestors and their tombs, and the descendants to come. *Domus* is also a term used for the physical houses of wealthy and prominent Roman citizens, houses with a characteristic architecture that projected *Romanitas*, "Romanness."

Domus as Edifice and Social Stage

The Roman *domus* was a status symbol that expressed the standing and social identity of its owner, the *paterfamilias* (father/owner) of the family who lived there. The house was not only a dwelling; it was a projection of the owner himself.[8] Such houses could be quite opulent, with luxurious decoration and plenty of unused space, so opulent that moralizing philosophers criticized owners of such houses for the vices of *luxuria* (squandering of an inheritance) and *aedificatio* (excessive building).[9] Yet such *luxuria* was necessary for the *paterfamilias* to maintain and advance his social status and enhance his honor and prestige, not so much by the show of wealth in the houses themselves as by providing a space for voluminous social activity within them.[10] The greater the hubbub of people coming and going for both business and entertainment, the greater the owner's social standing. The owner needed the opulent edifice as a social stage.

For members of the Roman aristocracy and others with social pretensions, the house began to function as the location for their social and political power. In the early decades of his reign, Augustus began to eliminate the rituals by which the aristocracy had previously displayed their status in triumph parades, sponsorship of public buildings, and on coinage.[11] Augustus was also displacing their political power in the Roman Senate. They began to exercise their influence more informally through social activity in their own houses as well as in secluded areas in the imperial palace. Power moved from the public sphere to informal conversations and dinner parties in the houses of the elites.[12]

The Roman *domus* was thus a location for *public* life in a distinctively Roman way, and the public nature of the house was a conscious architectural choice under discussion.[13] The house was part of the owner's public presentation rather than a refuge for privacy.[14] This meant that members of the household were also part of his public life, or perhaps more accurately, that much of what we now consider public life was taking place in the *domus*.[15]

The pattern of the Roman house indicates a social change that was occurring as Roman domination increased in the Eastern Mediterranean, a change that made the elite household an even more public space.[16] The elite Roman house, at least the house in town, was envisioned as itself a public space. Villas in the countryside functioned in some periods as a form of private sphere. Yet there was always a large staff, and the villas often hosted many travelers. The house in town, however, was not only the *paterfamilias*'s office and business headquarters but also a projection of his person into public view. Far from viewing their homes in the city as a retreat from the rough and tumble of the outside world, the Roman elites saw their houses as a way to make themselves visible and known in public. Being known meant being known to be Roman, following the traditions and mores that expressed their Romanness, their *Romanitas*, and *Romanitas* became the standard imitated in architecture, décor, and mores by aspiring elites across the empire.[17]

The concepts of "public" and "private" applied differently than they do today, however,[18] and recent work using archaeological evidence is suggesting even less distinction than previously thought between public and private space.[19] In his first-century CE work, *De Architectura*, the architect Vitruvius categorized houses as "private architecture," but the Latin word *privatus* designates property not owned by the state, not a "private" space in the modern sense of a place of retreat.[20]

A more important distinction for our purposes is his use of the terms *communia* and *propia* for spaces within the Roman *domus*.[21] Houses were designed with *communia*, rooms and areas where people could enter uninvited and where clients could gather, and *propia*, rooms where an invitation was required.[22] Rooms that Vitruvius mentions as *propia* include bedrooms, dining rooms, baths, and others where an invitation is required. Rooms and features he names as *communia* include entry ways, peristyle courtyards with covered walkways, central "office" rooms, and main halls. He also points out that householders who do not receive large numbers of visitors, whose social obligations mostly take them instead to others' houses, would not require the features named as *communia*.[23]

The architecture of houses was understood more in terms of relationship and social structure than in terms of luxury, even when extravagance was on display. The vocabulary of *communia* and *propia* defined parts of the *domus* in relational and dynamic terms. The levels of access could change throughout the day as well. Within the elite house, the defining difference between *communia* and *propia* was the degree of invitation from the *paterfamilias* of the household. The differences among houses were defined by how much space was needed for the reception of guests, if any at all.

Houses excavated at Herculaneum and Pompeii offer a model of the *domus* and indicate features that emerge in houses across the empire during the late republic and early principate. Figure 4 offers a basic schema of a Roman *domus,* although the houses were not in Rome itself, and a variety of architectural forms are found across the empire.[24] The layout of these houses was a miniaturized version of enormous elite dwellings that started to appear on the Palatine Hill at Rome in the late sixth century BCE, excavated relatively recently by Andrea Carandini. At the beginning of the imperial era, the houses were even larger, one with an atrium that could accommodate two thousand people.[25] Architectural features associated with civic buildings and temples, such as columns and curved walls and ceilings, were included to associate these houses with such public buildings and to indicate the purpose of the house as a public display.[26] Wall decoration and murals, sometimes alluding to stage scenery, also evoked public buildings.[27]

The rooms and features of the house formed a stage for activities throughout the course of the day, and we can best picture the Roman *domus* by describing the features of the house as its inhabitants moved through it during the day.

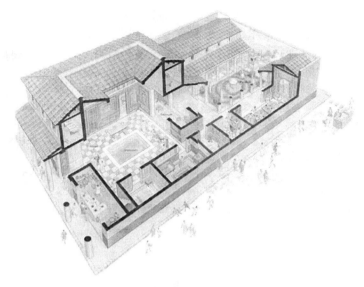

Figure 4: Cutaway view of "A House in Town"*

In the wee hours of the morning, some of the inhabitants would be asleep in rooms in the upper stories of the house. Slaves would rise from having slept wherever they could, or in rooms that doubled as storerooms, rather than in any designated slave quarters.[28] They were busy in the early hours with the many tasks of preparation for the day. Members of the family ate a light breakfast.

One of the first activities in the morning was probably a gathering at the household shrine. In the house reconstructed in the illustration (Fig. 4), the shrine is shown as a base with four posts and a stone canopy at the very rear of the house against the back wall in the peristyle garden. Shrines could also be in niches and in other locations in the *domus*.[29] This shrine was called a *lararium* for the *lares*, Roman household deities. The *paterfamilias* would function as a priest to conduct a religious ceremony, reciting prayers and burning incense to request protection of the deities held in honor by the household.[30] Other family members could offer personal devotions at the shrine as well.

---

*Jonathan Rutland, *See Inside a Roman Town*, 10–11.

In the house illustrated here, as in many of the houses at Pompeii
and Herculaneum, the shrine at the very rear would be visible from
the street when the front door was opened in the morning. The
house was designed with a straight-line view through the entryway
and atrium, past the *tablinum* and through the peristyle, so that
there was a view to the very back of the first floor of the house.
This arrangement would display the family's devotion to the deities,
although the household shrine might be in a less visible location
in many homes. Elite Greek houses, by contrast, were not on such
display from the street, and the entrance could be off a separate cor-
ridor from the street.[31]

The areas considered *communia* for much of the day were part
of the straight-line view. In the morning, after the door was opened
by the slave assigned to guard the door, clients and others seeking
favors from the *paterfamilias* or with other business matters that
needed his attention would gather in the first large room, the atrium.
Owners of the shops at either side of the door could also be opening their establishments, but these shops were usually constructed
without access to the interior of the house.

Clients and others seeking access to the *paterfamilias* at his morning *salutatio* waited in the vestibule between the front door and the
street until the door was opened. The first floor of the house was
then visible from the street through the entrance, the vestibule in
front of the door and the entryway (*fauces*) between the door and
the atrium. When the door was opened, the atrium became a public
space, *communia*, as the waiting clients passed into the atrium. In
the schema in the illustration, an opening in the roof of the atrium
supplied rainwater to a pool there, the *impluvium* at the center of
the atrium that would help to maintain a moderate temperature in
the house. Houses were also designed with other forms of atrium as
well.

At the morning *salutatio*, clients offered the obligatory morning greeting (*ave*) to the *paterfamilias* of the *domus*, their patron.
He would be prominently visible from the street, conducting his
business from the *tablinum*, the area between the atrium and the
peristyle garden at the rear in the illustration. At other times, this
tablinum area could be made more secluded by drawing curtains or

screens on either side to create space that was *propia*. It was open
for the morning *salutatio*, where the number of clients assembled
would enhance (or diminish) his social standing. A slave *nomenclator*
announced each of the callers, sorting them by their rank and relationship to the *paterfamilias*/patron. Clients would receive a dole
(*sportula*) and might then proceed to another *domus* to offer a greeting for similar remuneration there.[32]

The atrium where the morning audience occurred was hardly
empty even without the crowd of clients. In addition to the murals
and painted wall decoration, ancestral masks of the male line of the
paterfamilias would be hanging on the walls of the atrium and the
adjacent *tablinum*. These relief images of their faces would display
his proud lineage and represent the deceased members of the *domus*.[33] The masks of the ancestors overlooking the scene also served
to morally inspire the *paterfamilias* and members of the household.[34] This memorial display enhanced the prestige of the household and provided a setting for the household's life-transitions. The
atrium was also the location for a special altar when a child was born
to the *paterfamilias* and for laying out the body when he or his wife
or child died.[35]

The atrium often contained emblems of the wife's (*materfamilias*)
womanly virtues. A loom would represent "wool-working" (*lanificium*) extolled as one of the virtues for a woman of her position. The
materfamilias might be working at the loom as well, accomplishing
the task of producing useful textiles in full view, thus enhancing the
moral reputation of the household. A symbolic marriage bed might
also be present as an emblem of her chastity and modesty (*pudicitia*).[36] The display, especially the display of the wife's virtues, was
distinctively Roman, at least in distinction from the Greek household where women were more restricted in their designated domestic space.[37] In the early imperial era, display of the wife's virtue was
becoming more prominent on the stage of the household.

During the middle of the day and early afternoon, the *paterfamilias* would go out to participate in civic business. Accompanying him
was an entourage composed of clients from the morning *salutatio*
who were invited to accompany him and members of the household
whose presence would enhance his status, such as a long-bearded

philosopher. His young sons would attend a school, accompanied by a slave pedagogue, and other members of the household would be busy with various tasks and errands and producing goods for use and sale. Slaves oversaw access to the various areas of the house, including the side entrance (*posticum*) that slaves and others used for all the comings and goings that were not part of the display. All in all, the house was an open and busy place, not a secluded or quiet retreat.

Some rooms and areas were designated as *propia*. These might be used for a variety of purposes during the day. Large houses could include dining rooms off the atrium and peristyle. These dining rooms were of a distinctive form known as a *triclinium*. The Latin word means "three couches" and indicates the custom of reclining at these social meals. The couches could be portable furniture or built into the room, but a *triclinium* generally accommodated about nine guests to recline in socially ranked order by proximity to the host. If the household was hosting a meal with guests, the feast would begin in the mid-afternoon and extend into the evening hours. The resident philosopher who had been a status symbol in the entourage that accompanied the *paterfamilias* during the day would be expected to give a flattering speech at such a meal. Picture dining rooms that might be in the view of those who had access to the areas designated as *communia* but where access to participation in the meal itself would be by invitation. Murals on the walls of the *triclinium* could be visible from the more accessible areas as well and would frame the social activities of those of higher rank from the viewpoint of those "at the bottom end of the room" and those looking in.[38]

Bedrooms were also designated as *propia*, areas of the house entered by invitation only. Bedrooms could be located on the first floor as well as in the upper stories. In addition to being a location for sleeping and sexual activity, as well as childbirth and care of the sick and dying, the bedroom could also be a location for the conduct of confidential business and the reception of close friends.[39] The bath and kitchen were often off the peristyle and were also considered *propia*.

As members of the household retired for the night, slaves would complete the tasks of the evening, closing the door, cleaning up, and tending to various responsibilities. Some slaves would place themselves to be available to serve the needs of their owners. Others would find places to sleep wherever they could.

Domus as Social Structure

From the description of the domus and the activity within it, we can already perceive a social structuring of its inhabitants and guests. We have glimpsed how, within the house, social ranking can be seen in the degree of access to the *paterfamilias* on the part of his kin and his socially ranked friends and guests. Slaves were everywhere but were not viewed by their owners as of any social importance. Some functioned to control access to the *paterfamilias* and various areas of the house. To understand the *domus* as a social structure, some distinctions about the internal ordering of its space and inhabitants will be helpful.

The description of the house as a social stage throughout the day emphasized the central factor of social ranking defined by degrees of access to the *paterfamilias*. Areas in the house were distinguished as *communia* and *propia*, more applicable terms for what is often described as "public" and "private." Two common assumptions about the usual distinction of "public" and "private" and the definition of household space do not apply to the Roman *domus*.

First, a prevalent notion of domestic space as primarily the domain of women does not apply very cleanly to the Roman *domus*. Envisioning *communia* or "public" spaces as the male sphere and *propia* or "private" spaces as the female domain would be inaccurate. Emblems of the Roman matron's virtue, and the matron herself, could be found on display in the public space, and the *paterfamilias* might well conduct the most important and confidential of his dealings in his bedroom. While such division of the household into male public spheres and female private domains on the upper floors may have been applicable to Greek and other elite houses, the Roman pattern was distinct. In elite Greek houses, the women were not generally present in the front areas, while in Roman houses, women moved more extensively within the house.

Second, if we are prone to apply the image we may have of large households from historical dramas on British television, a division of spaces in the house by age might also inaccurately inform our concepts. Children were depicted as playing in the atrium, for example, not segregated into specific nursery spaces or play rooms in the upper stories. They were part of the hubbub and part of the display. Household slaves did not have their own quarters, either. The divide was not "upstairs-downstairs." Space was differentiated by degrees of access to the *paterfamilias*, as we have seen.[40] Social ranking was part of the performance on the stage of the household.

For the Roman elites in the early empire, the activity in the household became the intersection of public and private life which generated the power of its *paterfamilias*, in the words of Andrew Wallace-Hadrill as:

> a constant focus of public life … where a public figure not only received his dependants and *amici* ["friends," often as a euphemism for clients] … but conducted business of all sorts. His house was a power-house: it was where the network of social contacts was generated and activated which provided the underpinning for his public activities outside the house."[41]

The Roman house was becoming much more than the location of daily life where people lived and worked. It was becoming the center of political and public life as well, in a way it had not been in the republican era and in a way distinct from the households of other ethnic groups subsumed by the empire, particularly the Greeks.

Family and household life took diverse forms across the empire, of course, and most people did not live in such houses. Most people at the time, the vast impoverished majority, did not live at the heart of this family structure. Many may have lived elsewhere, in crowded apartment buildings or neighborhoods in the cities, or in a wide variety of family forms and houses in the rural areas of the provinces. Yet, while the elite Roman *domus* may not reflect the family relationships of this vast impoverished and multi-cultural majority, the conceptual model of family based in the elite Roman *domus* was the metaphorical reference point for the Roman way of life coming to dominate the Mediterranean world. Many urban residents also fell under the sphere of influence of a *paterfamilias* and his *domus*. Recent evaluations of archaeological research on urban areas point toward the centrality of the *domus* in cellular neighborhood units where social relationships placed the *paterfamilias* and his *domus* as the nucleus.[42] Many people oriented their lives around such "families" whether they lived inside the *domus* or not. This Roman Strict Father Family model was the ideologically dominant family model.

Conclusion

As a house, then, the *domus* provided the physical stage for the household's performance for an audience that included the neighbors and the city and the peers of the *paterfamilias* as well as the performers themselves. The *domus* also shaped the performance as a social structure by controlling who could see what and when and who could speak to whom and who could listen. With the stage in place, then, we can introduce the cast of characters, the roles in the Roman household.

4

The Leading Parts

Roles and Responsibilities of Free Members of the Core Family in the *Domus*

We have already seen some of the household personnel of the Roman Strict Father Family model in action on the stage of the *domus*. This chapter will offer a more complete introduction to the central *dramatis personae*. In the Roman Strict Father Family, each of the household members had a role specified by gender, status, age, and relationship to the central figure, the *paterfamilias*. Each role also had its own specified moral priorities, the virtues expected for the role. Within the parameters of their specified role, household members were expected to improvise their scripts throughout the course of a life cycle defined for their role and to exhibit virtues appropriate to their stations.

This chapter and the next will introduce each of the roles in order of rank, starting with the deities. The household venerated its deities and looked to them for protection, and the deities were regarded as the top of the household hierarchy. Next, the *paterfamilias,* the head of the household, was at its center, and the other roles were defined in relation to him. He was *pater* to the sons and daughters, master (*dominus/kyrios*) to the slaves and other dependents, and patron to the clients who relied on him. His title in Greek, *kyrios,* is the word usually translated "Lord" in New Testament texts. After the *paterfamilias*, the role of his legitimate wife will be discussed. The *paterfamilias* had one wife at a time, and she was *mater* (mother) mother to the sons and daughters and *domina/kyria* (female master) to the slaves. The household also included their sons and daughters, as well as the children of the *paterfamilias* by previous marriages. Chapter 5 will offer more detail about the variety of slaves present, from the most menial to the managerial slaves, men and women from children to elderly. There could also be slaves who had been manu-mitted, now *liberti* (freed persons) still attached to the household as clients who might dwell in the house or have their own dwellings. We should note that prominent heads of household also had clients whose role will not receive further discussion. Clients did not reside in the house but appeared for a variety of favors in the atrium in the morning hours and were obligated to be present when "invited."

Each of the positions and relationships in the family had its own virtues or, to used Lakoff's term, "moral priorities." These are not all enumerated in one place, and there tend to be variations, but different moral expectations clearly applied to different members of the household. Although no handbook exists with a summary of four characteristic virtues for each position in the household, the descriptions of each position in what follows will enumerate four characteristic virtues to characterize the moral framework of this family model.

The differentiation of the virtues is an element of a Strict Father Family model. The lack of differentiation will be an element to note in alternative models as we look at forms of resistance to the Roman Empire and its Roman Strict Father family model.

Deities and Ancestors in the *Domus*

In the Roman Strict Father family, household deities and ancestors were a presence in the *domus*, watching over the household and providing moral exemplars to its members. The household shrine tied members of the household to their past and future, beyond the lifetimes of the current occupants of the *domus*. All the members of the household could approach the deities there, and all owed them dutiful devotion and loyalty (*pietas*), including the *paterfamilias*.[1]

The ancestors were present in the masks that adorned the walls of the atrium and *tablinum*, providing a constant presence of their

moral example. The household would also display its status and virtue at the family tomb where they honored the dead members of the
domus, in one of many cemeteries or "cities of the dead" (*necropo-
leis*) that lined the streets coming into and leaving Roman towns
and cities.[2] The visibility of these tombs and the Romans' annual
observance of Parentalia, a nine-day festival in February to honor the
dead, shows the central presence of the dead in the living *domus.*[3]

In the fire at the hearth, they recognized the presence of the goddess Vesta. Daughters of the *paterfamilias* probably tended her fire,
and his wife decorated the hearth with floral garlands during religious festivals.[4] In the *fauces,* the entry way to the house from the
street, Janus, the spirit of boundaries and entryways, was present.[5]

The *Penates,* always plural deities, guarded the food supply for
the household and inhabited the area behind the hearth. Members
of the household venerated them in regular rituals, along with the
Lares, more general guardian deities present in images and statues,
commonly portrayed in a dancing pose. The *Lares* in their *lararium,*
the shrine discussed in the description of daily life in the *domus* in
chapter 3,[6] received frequent offerings of grain, grapes, honey, wine
as well as blood offerings. Household members might also crown
their heads with flowers.[7]

The household also observed regular devotion to the *genius* or
"guiding spirit" of the *paterfamilias.* This image in the shrine portrayed the *paterfamilias* wearing a toga with a portion pulled up
to cover his head, or "veiled," and in the posture of offering sacrifice to the deities. A serpent was often included in the depiction to
show the life force of the *genius* and as an additional guardian force.[8]
Members of the household saw in the *genius* the procreative force
of the *domus* and the guardian of the household's name and genera-
tional continuity.[9] The image itself could be used from generation
to generation. The chief festival of the *genius* was on the birthday of
the current *paterfamilias.*[10] Some evidence suggests a female counterpart to the *genius* of the *paterfamilias.* His wife may have had a
guiding spirit with an image, known as a *iuno,* which was part of the
household cult and received special devotions on her birthday.[11]

We can imagine the household gathered for devotions at the
shrine, then, where the *paterfamilias* functioned as the priest. We

Table 2
Roman Strict Father Family Model

ROMAN STRICT FATHER FAMILY

▦ Form

Roman Household—*Paterfamilias,* son(s), legitimate wife, daughters, slaves, freed persons, clients, others

▦ Roles & Responsibilities

Paterfamilias: Monarchical authority over all aspects of household; support & protect household, set & enforce rules & guidelines, administer rewards & punishment, ensure continuation of household through generations; exercise *auctoritas*

Sons: Loyalty to father and to mother, and mutual defense of siblings; prepare to inherit role of *paterfamilias* in household; respect & obey parents, gain character; learn self-reliance & respect for legitimate authority

Mother: Day-to-day managerial responsibility in the household; bearing of legitimate heirs; overseeing nurturance of children; upholding father's authority.

Daughters: Loyalty to father, mother, and brothers;

Slaves: Obedience to *paterfamilias;* anticipation and fulfillment of his will and desires; display of honor to *paterfamilias* by self-abasement; extensions of *paterfamilias's* body (tools of master)

Freed persons: Continued acknowledgement of *paterfamilias* and demonstrations of support for his honor and status

Clients: Same as freed persons and specific roles (house philosopher)

▦ Priority Childrearing Mission

Prepare male heirs for survival in competitive and fundamentally dangerous world;

Prepare female heirs for supportive roles and cooperative alliances;

Prepare all others for assigned social station

▦ Moral Priorities

(Virtues determined by status)

Paterfamilias: Virtus: courage, virtue, virility, moral strength, manliness, moral perfection; *Clementia:* clemency and mercy; *Iustitia:* justice and legal fairness (reward and punishment); *Pietas:* devotion, loyalty, duty, religious observance, behavior appropriate to one's social position

Legitimate Wife/Daughters as Future Legitimate Wives: *Pudicitia* (chastity); *Modestia* (modesty); *Obsequium* (obedience to husband);

ROMAN STRICT FATHER FAMILY

Lanificium (wool-working);
Slaves: *Fides* (loyalty, faithfulness = Greek *pistis*, "faith"); *Obsequium* (obedience to master); *Benevolencia* (good will); *Pietas* (behavior appropriate to one's social position)

▤ Conception of Moral Order

A natural and timeless order of role division within the household, the natural and entitled rule of Rome over the known world, and a just (Roman) system of reward & punishment in both

▤ Conception of Character

Roman *virtus/pudicitia* as an individual moral essence that is established by adulthood and must be kept pure from corrupting influences; other virtues and character determined by status

▤ Internal Role of Government

Ensuring punishment for lack of self-discipline; upholding moral order in the nation-family; providing for citizens (bread & circuses)

▤ External Role of Government

Protecting Rome from barbarians and citizen-family from external evils

---

might see him contemplating the image of the *genius*, perhaps a painting of himself, in the same dress and pose that he would assume at the shrine, the same pose and dress as his father and grandfather before—in a toga with his head covered, arm outstretched to offer a sacrifice. His *genius* was flanked by dancing images of two of the *Lares* of the household. We can imagine him looking at this image of his best self and offering signs of subordination to the deities, including his own *genius*.

We can hold this moment as the center of the Roman Strict Father family, the *paterfamilias* seeking the aid of his *genius* to display the virtues required of him. Such a ritual would have provided a "public cognitive system" for the household as well, and enforced the concept of a divinely ordained order in the *domus,* an order centered in the *paterfamilias.*

The *Paterfamilias* (and Roman Citizen Males)

The Roman family was centered on the *paterfamilias.*[12] While he could be described as a "strict father," his power and societally sanctioned role was qualitatively different from the version we know in the conservative family model of the present-day United States. The responsibilities and powers of the Roman *paterfamilias* far exceed those of a contemporary "strict father."

Responsibilities of the *Paterfamilias*

The *paterfamilias*-patron surely felt himself to be a man burdened with responsibilities. He had to provide for the members of his household and for a variety of needs of the various clients to whom he also owed assistance.[13] His daughters would need to be matched with suitable husbands and have a dowry to take with them, and his sons would need his assistance in advancing in their political careers. Everyone needed basic food and clothing, and his nuclear family needed luxuries to promote his prestige. Managerial oversight for his estates and activities was required.

At the same time, he bore the responsibility for the discipline of the household. He had to maintain the moral order of the house by his example and exhibit the effective exercise of his authority. This was part of the display required of him to maintain his reputation and status.[14]

His religious functions as the chief priest of the household were part of the display. The *paterfamilias* was the family's priest for festivals of the household's deities. Part of his responsibility was setting an example in the demonstration of appropriate devotion to these gods and to the deities of the larger pantheon, including the divine emperor. This may seem to be an afterthought, but it is an essential element of the family and the role of the *paterfamilias.* The family was a *sacral* unit as much as it was an economic and kinship unit.

The responsibilities of the *paterfamilias* extended to his role as patron as well. The Romans ruled the world with a vertically integrated social system of patronage, a system that extended the family unit beyond the walls of the physical *domus*. The *paterfamilias* of a large household was a patron with responsibilities not only for the members of the household but also for an entourage of clients as a kind of outer ring of the family.

When the *paterfamilias* manumitted a slave, the slave became one of his clients, now as a freedman or freedwoman. A freed slave did not go off to some other place for a new life but was expected to stay on in a new subordinate relationship with the old master, now as a client. Other dependent people for whom the *paterfamilias* provided a wide variety of favors would be his clients as well. The more fortunate members of the impoverished majority who sought assistance of various types and received the patron's favor could also become clients. In the mornings, there would be a line-up of clients at the patron's door seeking assistance as we have seen. Clients owed their patron honor and devotion (*pietas*), both by social convention and by law. The honor of the *paterfamilias* and his household was enhanced or diminished by the size of the entourage accompanying him when he went out. The longer the entourage, the greater the honor. The disproportionate power relationship of patron and client was masked by the language of "friendship," so that favors were given and received with the mask of a mutuality that did not, in fact, exist. This euphemistic language is something to keep in mind when we read about "friendship" in early Christian texts.

All this is not to mention his civic responsibilities as a member of the ruling elite of the city and empire, responsibilities that included participation in civic life and organizational structures and civic financial obligations as well as complex political maneuvering behind the scenes in the private recesses of his and his associates' houses.

Powers and Limitations of the *Paterfamilias*

Yet the responsibilities of the *paterfamilias* were not without real societally sanctioned powers. A defining aspect of the Roman family system can be seen in the pervasive notion expressed in the Latin term *patria potestas*, the power or authority or perhaps most accurately, the *sovereignty* of the father, his rule of the household in an "assimilation of paternity to ownership."[15]

The powers of the paterfamilias included physical discipline not only of his slaves but of his children, but the father-child relationship also included affection and an expectation of mutual obligation that was an aspect of the Roman virtue of *pietas*.[16] Certainly there is evidence of considerable affection, and significant mitigating aspects, not the least of which was a generally short life expectancy.[17] One does not preclude the other, however, and we can assume that the degree of affection and violence experienced in particular family units varied as widely as it does today. Yet the relationship was still based in an assumption of nearly absolute authority in a pervasively violent context of slavery that we do not assume today.

Several aspects of the Roman father's powers were notable at the time by contrast to other cultures. Writing in the second century, for example, the Roman jurist Gaius noted that the power that a Roman man had over his legitimate children was unique among nations, except that Galatian fathers had similar powers.[18]

The Roman *paterfamilias* owned the family property as long as he lived and ruled most aspects of his children's lives. He controlled their marriages. His approval was required for a legitimate marriage, and he could compel a divorce. He could disinherit his children at any time and transfer the property to unrelated heirs. As long as the *paterfamilias* was alive, his sons did not control their own property or their lives.[19] He could offer his adult children as well as trusted slaves a *peculium*, an allotment of money that he owned but his child or slave was free to manage with a fair amount of freedom. With the *peculium*, his children and slaves could establish themselves with some independence, but this was always at his discretion.[20]

One of the most discussed aspects of the sovereignty of the Roman *paterfamilias* is his power of life and death over all those in his family domain, the *vitae necisque potestas*. Legally this power included even the right to order the execution of his adult sons in the case of serious offences. Instances of the actual implementation of this power in the case of adult sons are extremely rare, however, and they all predate the imperial period.[21]

The employment of this power was not so rare, however, for adult daughters. The recorded cases in which adult daughters were executed by order of their fathers imply many other unrecorded cases.

The noteworthy aspect that caused cases to be recorded was that the daughter was innocent or her father was morally disqualified from making the judgment.[22] A daughter's sexual transgression was most often the cause. Families were responsible for carrying out the death penalty even when the state was involved in the judicial decision. During the republican era, for example, in the suppression of the cult of Bacchus by the Roman Senate by large numbers of executions, women convicted of participation in the cult were turned over to their families to be executed in private.[23] Most wives remained under the authority of their fathers and thus under his *patria potestas* in such matters.

The most common use of this power of life and death was not in the case of adult children, however, but of infants.[24] When a baby was born to his legitimate wife, the *paterfamilias* decided whether to accept the child as a member of the household or to reject the child, in which case the baby would be exposed, left in the street.[25] The decision could be made from a distance, as a letter from a husband with instructions to his pregnant wife indicates: "If—good luck to you!—you bear offspring, if it is a male, let it live; if it is a female, expose it."[26] The exposed babies died either literally by exposure or metaphorically by being retrieved to be raised as a slave in another household.[27] This was a power exercised not only by Roman fathers but also by the Greeks, both of whom thought the Egyptians, Germans, and Jews a bit peculiar because they raised all their children themselves.[28]

Biological birth also did not determine who was a child, specifically a son and heir, in the case of a lack of biological children. A *paterfamilias* without an heir would often adopt a son, related or not, but generally a citizen. The status of the adopted son was equal in every way to that of a biologically fathered son. Recognition by the *paterfamilias* was more important for the determination of who was a son and heir than biological relationship, and to be a son and heir meant to be in line to be a real person at the center of the family, a *paterfamilias*.

The powers of the *paterfamilias*, while seemingly absolute, were mitigated to some extent by his limited life expectancy. A *paterfamilias* frequently did not see his children grow to adulthood.[29]

Adolescent sons could inherit, but the estate would be managed by a financial guardian until they reached the age of twenty-five.[30]

The seemingly unlimited powers of the *paterfamilias* were also significantly curbed by the Roman system of honor and the design of the *domus* to put the household on display. The success of the *paterfamilias* depended on his ability not only to control those under his power in the *domus* but also to gain their respect, their "visibly willing recognition of his authority."[31] Even though the relationship was hierarchical and the *paterfamilias* had more power than his subordinates, an ideal of reciprocity also held so that mutual recognition was expected. The *paterfamilias* needed his inferiors' recognition to appear to be reciprocal.[32]

The power to withhold that visible recognition of his authority could be a potent "weapon of the weak" that subordinates could use to tarnish his public image. He needed their willing obedience to be visible and his image depended on projecting a harmonious household to all the world around him. His subordinate could lower his superior's social standing by showing dissent.[33] Yet the forces of self-interest wove a web of protection to shield the whole household from shame, and conflict was generally solved internally.[34] This tended to protect the *paterfamilias* and his power.

Virtues Expected of the *Paterfamilias* and Sons

The family's honor required its members to display the virtues appropriate to their roles. For Roman male citizens, the *paterfamilias* and his sons in preparation for that role, two virtues were central:

- *virtus* (manliness, courage, virtue, virility, moral strength, moral perfection)
- *pietas* (devotion, loyalty, duty, religious observance, behavior appropriate to one's social position)[35]

Two additional virtues are added on a golden shield presented to Augustus by the Senate in 27 or 26 BCE, canonized as these four more by modern scholarship than by ancient writers, but they generally express the moral character expected:[36]

- *clementia* (clemency, mercy)
- *iustitia* (justice, legal fairness, fair administration of reward and punishment)

Greek philosophers had enumerated another canon, usually: bravery (*andreia*); temperance (*sophrosyne*); justice (*dikaiosyne*); and wisdom (*phronesis/sophia*).[37]

The especially "manly" virtue of *virtus* (*andreia*) was a competitive virtue and relied not only on upright moral conduct but also on victory and recognition.[38] Virtues, and especially *virtus*, were closely related to honor. The Greco-Roman world placed a high value on honor. Honor was more important than material goods, although the display of wealth enhanced a household's honor. Honor was a limited good, and men competed to win honor in all kinds of venues. Every exchange between men was a contest for honor. There was an order of honor in the arrangement of guests on the couches in the *triclinium*. Speech-making was a contest. A man's honor was displayed in his name and reputation, his status, his clothing, and his profession.[39] As manliness, *virtus* implied a victory at the expense of someone else's "unmanliness" or inferior manliness.

Pietas, as a "quintessentially Roman virtue," expressed the social responsibility that was a complement to competitive *virtus*.[40] *Pietas* was expressed by acknowledgement of social bonds, and a household's honor was enhanced in its members' visible expression of *pietas*, displaying deference according to their social positions. The *paterfamilias* displayed deference to the deities just as all of his subordinates displayed deference to him. He also expressed *pietas* by fulfilling his fatherly and patronal responsibilities to his subordinates.[41] The loyalty of the male members of the household in defending the family honor was also a vital expression of *pietas*, and the disloyalty of one brother would bring shame on the household. As a virtue, *pietas* involved not only duty but affection, sincere devotion, and required "unselfish effort of all for the common good."[42]

Clementia and *iustitia* as well as the virtues of temperance, justice, and wisdom enumerated by the Greek philosophers express the role of the *paterfamilias* as the disciplinary and legal authority in the household, and authority based on his moral example. These are virtues consistent with a Strict Father family model that values just rewards and punishment.

If we return to imagine the morning ritual then, we can see the *paterfamilias* with his many responsibilities and the sovereignty he has assumed as his role, displaying *pietas*, devotion, to his own *ge-nius*. We can see the members of the household surrounding him. They are his responsibility not only as mouths to feed but also as expressions of the virtue and honor of the household, his honor. He must keep them not only fed and clothed but in line, functioning properly in their places. We can see them gaze together upon his *genius* in the moments before their performance of the household's virtue begins again for the day.[43] We can only imagine their thoughts about the *paterfamilias* and the expectations the *genius* placed upon them.

All in all, the *paterfamilias* was a formidable figure in their lives and in the household.

The *Materfamilias*
Wife, Mother, Matron, and Female Master (*Domina*)

In the modern Strict Father family, the mother may be expected to provide the affection and emotional support as a complement to the father's disciplinary role. Although a similar assumption about the role of mother and father is not unknown in ancient writers, the mother of the Roman Strict Father family model was not as specifically associated with the affective aspects of parenting as is currently assumed.[44] Like her husband, the *materfamilias* was a formidable figure.[45] While the image of Mother Earth on the Ara Pacis[a] may portray a bucolic image of a mother holding sweet chubby infants, elite Roman matrons mostly did not provide much direct physical care for their children.[46] Even the mother portrayed there betrays something of a stiff distance from the toddlers she holds. Her reserve can help us perceive the position of the elite Roman mother.

The Roman *materfamilias* was a wife to the *paterfamilias* but was most often still a member of her own father's family and under his authority. When her father died, she had more independence. In the most common form of marriage, *sine manu* or "free marriage," she did not come under the authority of her husband.[47] She brought a dowry to the marriage which he managed, but it would

---

a. To view this image, use an online image search of "Ara Pacis."

be returned to her if the marriage were dissolved.[48] Elite wives, and especially widows, had a measure of financial independence and personal power.

We should not imagine Roman elite women as powerless figures in the shadows of the house. This image may fit women in other parts of the empire. For example, when women of Tarsus went into the street, it would appear, they were entirely covered and only able to see the ground.[49] Women's activities were also set apart in more sequestered areas in elite Greek homes. We should recognize that the position of women varied across the empire. An overview of the position of the Roman *materfamilias*, however, will help us to understand the family model on which the empire was based.

Responsibilities of the *Materfamilias*

Motherhood was central to the role of the *materfamilias*. Her purpose was to bear legitimate children, sons to carry on the lineage of the *domus* and daughters to marry for the alliances the *domus* needed. Wet-nurses and child-minding slaves did most of the direct care of her infants and young children, the ones acknowledged by her husband and allowed to live. Mothers of all classes used wet-nurses.[50] Roman mothers were more involved in the lives of their children in their adolescence and adulthood. As their children grew to adulthood, Roman mothers were responsible for their discipline and considered "custodians of Roman culture and traditional morality."[51] Tacitus, for example, emphasizes the mother's disciplinary role and the importance of the ethical and linguistic standards she provides.[52]

The *materfamilias* was also a master of slaves under her charge, *domina* in Latin, *kyria*, in Greek. She supervised daughters and slaves in the textile production of the household and oversaw much of the day-to-day running of the household.

Powers and Limitations of the *Materfamilias*

Elite wives and mothers wielded considerable power. Most held property and had the power to transmit it. This gave them some economic independence from their husbands as wives and even

more once they were widows. Due to the age difference at marriage, many a wife became a widow, an honored position in Roman
culture.[53] Elite widows who held the inheritance of their husbands'
estates had power in their relationship with their children.[54] Many
were in the position of administering the business affairs of their
minor children.[55]

The *materfamilias* did not have the same legal rights over her
children as the *paterfamilias*, however. She might sit on the family
council, but she did not have the right as a mother to decide whether
her child would be exposed or not, nor the right to abort a legitimate
child.[56] How women influenced such decisions or acted outside of
their legal rights is not precisely known. Accusations by philosophers
and satirists indicate their suspicion that elite women used abortion
and contraception to avoid the inconvenience of pregnancy.[57] From
this we can assume only that women used abortion and contraception and not what their actual motivations were.

Mothers also played a major role in arranging marriages for their
children, as both a power and a responsibility, although the approval
of the *paterfamilias* legally validated the marriages of children under
his power.[58] Mothers took a greater role in arranging their daughters' marriage than their sons'.[59]

Most elite mothers appear to have had a close relationship with
their daughters. Daughters, more than sons, were expected to defer to their mothers. When they lived in separate households after
the daughter's marriage or the mother's divorce, daughters were
expected to visit their mothers. They commemorated one another's
deaths in tender epitaphs.[60] Mothers and daughters were closely
identified, sharing a common interest in supporting and protecting one another. The daughter's honor or shame reflected on the
mother.[61]

The mother-son relationship, while not without conflict, was
"depicted as a happy one founded on mutual esteem."[62] Mothers
were expected to advise their adolescent and young adult sons and
to "worry over" them and encourage them in their aristocratic careers.[63] Mothers exercised political influence through their sons
rather than directly.

While women of the Roman elites were not as restricted within the household as women in the Greek East and other parts of the empire, they were not allowed to participate in many areas of public life. Women were excluded from the Roman Senate, for example.

The story of Papirius Praetextatus illustrates this. His father took him along to the Senate one day when he was still an adolescent, and afterwards he refused to tell his mother what had happened there. When she pressed him, he invented a story and, swearing her to secrecy, told her that they had discussed whether men should be allowed to have more than one wife. A crowd of women surrounded the Senate the next day demanding that they not pass this law. The Senators congratulated the son for humiliating his mother in this way.[64] Defending the Senate and its affairs as the exclusive province of aristocratic males clearly took precedence over a son's defense of his mother's honor. Yet even though the assembly of the women was based on a false rumor, we can see that elite women were quite capable of public action.

Women were hardly absent from public prominence. At Pompeii, for example, a wealthy woman, Eumachia, built the headquarters of a worker's association, and was identified as a public priestess (*sacerdos publica*). She was hardly unique.[65] Slaves and freed women, workers in bakeries and eateries, put up notices of support for political candidates as well. Women from the top to the bottom of society were not hidden from public involvement.[66]

We have also seen that the *domus* increased in importance as a location for the conduct of public affairs as the Senate and other public political institutions lost influence in the transition from the republic to the empire. This would put the elite women of the *domus* in closer proximity to the discussion of public matters, in a position to exercise influence.

Virtues Expected of the *Materfamilias* and Daughters

Honor was a wife's purpose, so said the emperor Marcus Aurelius according to one ancient biographer. He was said to have retorted to his jealous wife that "she must let him have his pleasures with others:

a wife is for honour, not for pleasure."[67] The implication, of course, is that the wife's virtues serve her husband's honor.

The first emperor apparently struck a similar chord. Cassius Dio, writing in the early third century, attributes words on the joys of marriage and family life to Augustus extolling the virtues of the wife:

> Is there anything better than a wife who is discreet (*sophron*, "of sound mind"), domestic (*oikouros*, "watching"), a good manager (*oikonomos*, "one who manages a household") and childbearer (*paidotrophos*, "child-rearer"); a woman to rejoice you in times of health and look after you in illness, to join you in prosperity and console you in misfortune; to restrain the very impetuosity of youth and to temper the untimely harshness of age?[68]

For Roman matrons and their daughters as future matrons, a set of virtues different from those expected of men was held in esteem. Traditional virtues for wives and mothers include those listed in a eulogy by a husband for his wife, Turia, usually referred to as the *Laudatio Turiae*.[69] He lists her traditional domestic virtues as those that should go without saying, among them several virtues that appear frequently on other epitaphs:

- *pudicitia* (chastity, sexual virtue, shame-facedness, sense of decency, self-respect)
- *modestia* (modesty)
- *obsequium* (obedience to her husband)
- *lanificium* (wool-working)

Pudicitia, as the maintenance of bodily integrity and an unblemished reputation, was especially important in the sexual mores of the Roman family, and we will return to discuss this virtue more extensively in the discussion of sexual mores in chapter 6. *Modestia* was expressed as "sobriety of attire" and "modesty of appearance."[70] The expectation of a wife's deference to her husband, her *obsequium* and the companion virtue of loyalty (*fides*), were also virtues expected of slaves, and were the subject of "Tales of Loyalty" in Roman *exemplum* literature that held up examples of wives' and slaves' courageous loyalty to their husbands and masters in times of crisis.[71]

Wool-working (*lanificium*) may seem surprisingly specific and material as a virtue. Note that all the virtues are for display, however. Objects on display in the atrium of the house publicly display the wife's virtues: the loom for wool-working and the model of the marriage bed for her sexual decorum and *pudicitia*. Her deference to her husband in public and her modest style of dress were also part of the display. The display of the wife's virtues brought honor not only to her but to her husband. Her purpose, after all, was to enhance the honor of her husband, as Marcus Aurelius reportedly emphasized.

The virtues of the *materfamilias* introduce another aspect of the honor of the household and its *paterfamilias*, honor related to women's sexuality.[72] Bodily protection of the women of the nuclear family in the household was part of the household's honor, and the ability to protect them from violation, whether with their consent or not, reflected on the *paterfamilias*. Women preserved the family honor by preserving their own sexual purity in exclusive sexual relations only with their husbands. In widowhood, a Roman wife received praise if she did not remarry, upholding the tradition of devotion to one man (a *univira*) although the Augustan family legislation to be discussed in chapter 8 attempted to change this. A period of ten months of mourning before remarriage was mandated in any case to make sure that the paternity of any child she might bear was clear.[73]

Women's virtue, including her sexual purity, thus displayed the honor or dishonor of the whole *domus*, not just the woman herself. Rumors about her behavior could damage the honor of the *domus* whether they were true or not.[74] The behavior itself was not the issue so much as the public knowledge of it.[75] A daughter provided honor to the family by observing female virtues and by bearing children when she married. Like her mother, she exhibited her virtue in her skills, some of which reflected a formal education.[76] Her display of virtue as a wife and mother brought honor to her father's *domus* as well as her husband's.

Women of the elites were not praised exclusively for domestic virtues. Wealthy women received acknowledgement for public virtues in their role as benefactors of various civic projects, virtues such as:

generosity (*munificentia, liberalitas*), kindness (*beneficia*), and worthiness (*merita*).[77]

The *materfamilias*, matron, wife and mother, held a central role in the Roman *domus*, deferring to the *paterfamilias* but still an imposing figure in her own right. A mural in the House of Lucretius Fronto at Pompeii portrays the centrality and continuity of the idealized role of wife and mother in the household. The painting depicts the story of Pero and Mycon, her father. When Mycon was condemned unjustly to starve in prison, his daughter Pero saved him by visiting him and giving him milk from her breast, and the painting shows Pero nursing her father in prison. She is thus mother and daughter in the same image, and the accompanying poem on the wall includes praise of female virtues of *pietas* and *pudicitia* (*pudor*).[78] While most elite mothers did not nurse their own infants, this idealized image is one to hold in mind as emblematic of the Romans' expectation of the *materfamilias* to nurture the *paterfamilias* as father and son at the center of the household. If we see the *paterfamilias* at the shrine gazing on his *genius*, an image of his better self that also evokes his ancestors, we can also imagine the *materfamilias* present to nurture him as well as uphold his honor, perhaps gazing on her own *iuno* image, and taking her place in a line of nurturing mothers and dutiful daughters. We might see her at the shrine, then, as a Roman maternal disciplinarian also watching over the behavior of the children who were visibly present in the daily life of the Roman *domus*.

Children of the *Paterfamilias*

The presence of children of the *paterfamilias* enhanced the image of the *domus*. Children provided visible evidence, as did the symbolic marriage bed in the *atrium*, of socially appropriate sexual relations between the *paterfamilias* and *materfamilias* and of his generative power. They also represented the continued existence of the *domus*.

Bearing and Rearing

A Roman child became a person upon birth. In the early imperial era, abortion was a widespread practice invoking no legal or religious sanctions, but inheritance rights of an unborn child were recognized in the restrictions on recently divorced or widowed pregnant women.[79] The issue in abortion was not about any inherent right of the fetus or the mother but on the husband's right to decide.[80]

A wife usually gave birth at her husband's home, attended by a midwife, and probably surrounded by female relatives. Those assembled called upon divine assistance, most prominently from the goddess Juno Lucina. The midwife inspected the newborn and advised the parents whether the child was fit to rear.[81] As has been mentioned, the child's father decided whether the child would be raised in the household as his. The adults, mostly women, surrounding the child in its early hours and days, carefully observed rituals and taboos, and continued their petitions to the deities. The household prepared for the child's *lustratio*, a ritual meal and celebration in the *atrium* of the house.[82] At the *lustratio*, the child received a name, and thus an identity, and a *bulla*, a pendant with an amulet for protection until adulthood.[83] In spite of the *bulla*, and their parents' many appeals to deities and doctors, many children died in their early years.[84]

Wet-nurses minded and cared for children during their early years.[85] Children played. Dolls and toys and games were popular, and a toy-making industry thrived.[86] In addition to the devotions to the deities that took place within the household, public religious festivals helped socialize Roman children for their role in the family during their formative years. The frequent festivals promoted the ideals of "marriage, childbearing, and respect for ancestors."[87] Children were participants as well as observers in such festivals.[88]

Educating

Children received education in the home, and Romans considered parents and nurses as key influences. In his first-century CE handbook on the training of orators, Quintilian recognized the importance of nurses and pedagogues in the shaping of speech and recommended that children not learn patterns in infancy that they would have to unlearn.[89] He acknowledged the importance of both mothers and fathers in the development of elite orators and suggested the cultivation of the mother's style of speech.[90] He indicated that young boys usually began to learn to read at age seven but recommended that they start earlier.[91] His discussion of the issue of whether to send the boys out to school as he recommended or to educate them at home indicates that Roman families did both.[92] Girls were also educated, some by tutors at home and some, at least, went out to school.[93] Slave children could also be educated to prepare them for various roles in the household.[94]

The schools were rudimentary classrooms, often in the open air, run by teachers paid a meager fee by the parents.[95] The Roman state did not involve itself with schooling except to sanction teachers who innovated outside of the traditional curriculum. The traditional curriculum has been aptly described as determined by "the collective wish of upper-class fathers that their children should not be confronted with new ideas—or indeed with ideas at all."[96] They dictated, memorized, and recited a standard set of Greek and Latin texts.[97] Teachers were the ones with the active role, dispensing the knowledge and forming the children, and physically beating them into shape as necessary.[98] Physical training was also a major part of the instruction of children.[99]

Becoming Adults

In elite families, children moved toward adulthood during early adolescence. For girls, adulthood began at marriage, when they put on the *stola* worn by elite adult women and began their lives as wives in a separate household. At around the age of fourteen, boys would begin their political apprenticeship with their fathers. The *paterfamilias* would take his son to accompany him in his civic involvements. In his mid-teens, when the father deemed him ready, the son put on the toga of manhood at the festival of *Liberalia*.[100] He also enrolled as a voter when his father decided it was time.[101] In late adolescence, at seventeen or eighteen, he began his military service.[102] Adulthood did not mean independence from parental authority, as has already been mentioned in the discussion of *patria potestas* above.

Children of the lower classes began their work lives much younger.[103] Free non-elite children of peasants, skilled workers and small traders often worked outside the home. Some were apprentices to skilled workers. Others engaged in unskilled labor. Their work was part of the family's economic strategy.[104] Slave children took part in work as soon as they were able, and as slaves were never viewed as full adults.

Children and Slaves

Children of the elites were viewed in many ways as slaves until they became adults. The elite male citizen writers of antiquity articulated a view of children that lumped them together with slaves due to their lack of the capacity for rational thought, the *logos* elite adult males saw as their own preserve. In women of their class, they perceived a deficiency of *logos*, but not a total lack.[105] Plato characterized children, women, and slaves as susceptible "to desire, pleasure, and pain," and these categories were in a similar status for giving evidence in court.[106] Children were also compared with animals. Plato described children, slaves, and animals as similar because they all need supervision, but children are "of all wild creatures ... the most intractable," and require the most supervision because they have uncontrolled reason and are thus treacherous.[107] Philosophers also saw children as weak and helpless.[108]

In both Greek and Latin, a common word was used for both slave and boy, *pais* in Greek and *puer* in Latin. The terms indicated a common characteristic, that both are "small" and viewed has having a "lesser intellectual capacity," but the comparable status relationship was the key element in the identification.[109] Elite male writers tended to lump together all the people subordinated and see them as similar,[110] but slaves and children had this identification in a common term.

They had an additional commonality. Slaves and sons who had not reached adulthood could both be beaten, but the beatings inflicted on boys of the elite were apparently not as severe as those that slaves suffered.[111] Sons could reach adulthood and no longer be subject to beatings. Slaves could not.

Virtues and Vices Expected of Children

As they were being raised and educated and cultivated in the virtues to be expected of them in their respective future adult roles, the sons and daughters of the *paterfamilias* shared some aspects of the moral status of slaves to be discussed in the next chapter. As *logos*-deficient beings, children were lacking in the self-control they would need in order to exhibit the adult virtues to which slaves were not supposed to aspire, especially the *virtus* and *auctoritas* of free males and the *pudicitia* of free women.

As children were trained to assume the virtues enumerated for their adult roles, they shared in the virtue common to all the roles in the *domus*: *pietas*.[112] As one of the virtues of the *paterfamilias* already mentioned, *pietas* was characterized as dutiful devotion, especially to the deities. As a virtue expressed in the relationship of the *paterfamilias* and his children, *pietas* also expressed affection and mutual obligation, as a relational virtue. *Pietas* denotes the deference children were expected to display from an early age as well as the warm regard expected in the relationship.[113] Displays of deference that appeared as affectionate and voluntary would, of course, enhance the honor of the *paterfamilias* more than forced submission.

Conclusion

The *dramatis personae* on center stage in the *domus* are thus in place. In the spotlight, quite literally standing in the morning light cast from the opening of the ceiling in the atrium of the houses we saw in chapter 3, is the *paterfamilias*. Yet before turning to assume that position, he and many of the bustling performers around him may well have assembled at a more sequestered stage within the household, at the shrine (*lararium*) where he faced his *genius* as it stood flanked by dancing *lares* with the other household deities arranged in a frozen and silent display of protection and moral example.

With the *paterfamilias* in the spotlight, we can also see the *materfamilias* in view, perhaps at her loom, vigilant in overseeing the many activities that keep the household running smoothly. She, too, may have turned from the moment of devotion at the *lararium*, perhaps facing her own *iuno*, or perhaps she turns as well from devotion to Vesta in the fire at the hearth, to take her place in public view.

Children of the family come and go, depending on their ages, and are part of the general hubbub of the busy *domus*. Yet other people fill the stage as well, the slaves assigned to function as both players and stage set.

5

The Human Stage Set

Slaves in the *Domus*

Slaves provided the stage set for the Roman Empire and the Roman Strict Father Family. The Roman Empire was a slave system, one of a very few civilizations that can be defined as a full-blown slave economy. The antebellum United States South was, by the way, one of the few others. The Roman slave system encompassed multiple thousands of slaves mostly out of view. Slaves worked as field laborers on the vast *latifundia* (plantations) producing the grain that was the foundation of Roman prosperity. Many also toiled their lives away quickly in the mines or the galleys of ships. These are the slaves who were chained into their barracks in rows by night and used as little more than laboring beasts by day.[1] In a traditional view of a slave economy, slaves are the nameless backdrop, among the resources on which the economy is built.

The slaves in view in our sources, however, are the ones who were part of Roman households, slaves visible to us as part of the web of relationship in the *domus*. These slaves, too, have often been viewed as a human stage set for the drama enacted by the central players in the family. We can picture their lack of personal identity in the image of the annual Compitalia festival when the family sought the Lares' protection for members of the household symbolized in male and female woolen dolls for the free members and a genderless and faceless ball of wool for each of the slaves.[2]

Slaves come into view as players, however, in a pivotal shift in view inaugurated by Orlando Patterson, mentioned already in chapter 2, that sees slavery in terms of relationship rather than a form of utilization of human beings as economic resources. Slaves were assigned roles as part of the stage set, yet they also were part of the web of relationship as players on the stage of the *domus*.

Slavery as Relationship
(Work of Orlando Patterson)

In the Roman era, we cannot discuss the family without discussing slavery. Slavery and the family are one system of relationship as Orlando Patterson explains in *Slavery and Social Death*, a first comprehensive analysis of slavery as a relationship in a way that incorporates the slaves' point of view. Patterson's definition of slavery is important to contemplate as we form a picture of the Roman family system, especially as we understand early Christian language within that system, language about redemption and salvation, life and death. Patterson defines slavery as "the permanent, violent domination of natally alienated and generally dishonored persons," or more tersely as "social death."[3]

The phrase "permanent, violent domination" indicates, first, that slave status generally originated at some level as a substitute for death, such as death in war, death by exposure as an infant, or death by starvation.[4] The Romans relied on military campaigns for slave procurement more than most other slave societies, and they enslaved massive numbers of people. Major campaigns resulted in tens of thousands, often over one hundred thousand captives for sale in the slave markets.[5] Infants rejected by their biological fathers and consigned to exposure were another source. Roman law recognized the right of fathers to sell their children into slavery, a choice usually made to avoid starvation.[6] Social death in slavery replaces physical death.

"Natal alienation" is another key element in that social death. "Natal alienation" means that slaves are denied the social recognition of their intergenerational relationships and have legally and socially recognized relationships only through their owners. In the Roman family, a slave's parent was the *paterfamilias*. Slaves could have only a *praenomen*, what we would call a "first name." Even that name was usually more like a pet's name than the name of a free citizen. "Felix," meaning "Lucky," for example, was a slave name.

The name was assigned by the master. The name could itself indicate slave status, such as "Marcipor," meaning "Marcus's slave-boy."
Slaves were not allowed to have names that connected them to any
lineage except that of their masters.

Enslaved men had no recognized children or descendants as freeborn men did. The children of a slave mother inherited her slave status and become the property of her owner. For enslaved women, this
also meant that they had little choice in the matter of child-bearing
and child-rearing.[7] Their infants would often be nursed by a wet-
nurse and minded by another slave so that they could work.[8] Their
children could also be sold. Slaves continued to assert parent-child
and marital relationships as a means of resistance, but their natal
alienation was the public transcript.

Slaves are also defined as "generally dishonored." Mention has
already been made of the importance of honor in the Greco-Roman
era. Honor was the central concern for male citizens. Family honor
was enhanced for the *paterfamilias* when his subordinates showed
him proper deference and exhibited the virtues appropriate to their
roles. Slaves had no honor. They were considered physical extensions of their masters. For both men and women slaves, this also
meant they had no societally sanctioned bodily integrity. They were
sexually available to their male owners and whomever their owners
allowed to use them.[9] Their virtue was to obey, and their obedience
enhanced the master's honor.

Three facets of the power relations of slavery reveal how the domination operates: social, psychological, and cultural. The social facet
uses or threatens violence. For the Roman system, we need to recognize violence as a constant. Slave gladiators fought one another, often to the death, for the entertainment of the elites and masses alike.
Slaves could be and were beaten and sexually used at the master's
will. We must imagine the "family" suffused with this atmosphere of
violence and abuse.

Yet it is not all about constant physical violence. People tend to
adapt psychologically and culturally. These are the other two facets
Patterson outlines. The psychological facet involves influence and
persuasion so that the way the slave perceives his or her interests and
circumstances is changed. The slave psychologically "tunes in" to

the needs and wishes of the master, even unstated needs, and lives constantly accommodating to the master in psychological subordination. The cultural facet, thirdly, is that of authority. Expectations of the slaves imposed ultimately by violence become transformed into duty so that the official moral code imposes willing compliance and obedience as a virtue.[10] As has been noted, virtues expected of masters differed from those expected of slaves.

In the system of social relations as defined by the masters, the slave is not alive as a distinct person, but only as an extension of the master. Slaves resisted this "social death" in a variety of ways not always visible in the historical record, and hints of that resistance can be glimpsed in the early Christian movement, as will be suggested in volume 2. For now, we need to understand that this relationship of slaves and masters is essential for understanding the Roman *family* system. We must understand the slave system as part of the context of regular life. Slavery was integral to the family model at the metaphorical foundation of the Roman Empire.

Roman Slavery Compared to Slavery in the United States South

Even as we recognize that the Roman family was part of a slave system, we must also understand that it differed in several important ways from the slave system we know from the antebellum United States South.

Slavery was not a racial matter. Individuals of all races and ethnicities could be found as slaves. It was an equal opportunity employer. Some ethnicities, notably the Phrygians, were especially associated with slavery, but nothing exempted any ethnicity.

Nor was slavery occupation-specific. A few occupations were associated with slavery, particularly mining and some of the household positions, but these were the exception. At a construction site, for example, slave carpenters could be working next to free wage-earning carpenters. Physicians might be slaves. Trusted slaves could be the managers of large portions of a family business or entrusted with a portion of capital of their own to multiply, a *peculium*, as in the parable of the talents. If they were successful, they might purchase themselves and become freedmen or freedwomen. The term "freed person" indicates another distinction. In the Roman system, slavery was not perceived as a necessarily permanent condition. The United States system defined a racial sector as slaves without any significant possibility of manumission, and slavery was a permanent state. In the Roman system, while most slaves were never manumitted, the possibility was always present, and there were significant numbers of freed persons.[11] Slaves who were freed continued to be subordinate members of the household whether they lived in the house or not. Once freed they took on their former master's family name (*nomen*) as a sign of freedom and Roman citizenship. For example, when Marcus Tullius Cicero freed his slave, Tiro, he became Marcus Tullius Tiro.[12] The freed slave's biological parents were not acknowledged in the name, and legal lineage would begin only upon manumission. Then the legal lineage would extend the family name of the *paterfamilias* of the household, not the freedman's.[13] Freed slaves were still a part of the family, not outside it. Manumission did not mean independence.

There was also a developmental dimension in the language about slavery. As has been mentioned, Greek and Latin terms for child and slave were the same and their status was similar. A son, however, eventually outgrew this status while a slave never did, remaining permanently in the status of child, a "Boy," as in the language that persists from the slave system in the United States South.

Slaves were part of the emotional dynamics of family life in both systems. Just as grown children of slave owners in the United States South spoke affectionately of the childhood "mamie," Roman era adult masters often spoke affectionately about the slaves charged with raising them as children.

Many similarities and differences in the array of roles played in the Roman household could be pointed out to compare it to slave households in the United States South, but our purpose here is to get a picture of the Roman one.

Slaves' Roles in the Roman Household

The elite household required many slaves. Slaves of all ages were everywhere in the *domus,* from the most menial to slave managers of the house and of the vast offsite holdings of the *domus.* Slaves cooked, cleaned, sewed, kept notes and filed papers, tended gardens, produced thread and fabrics, bathed and dressed their owners, kept watch at outer entrances and at bedroom doors, laundered clothes, emptied chamber pots, dismissed unwanted visitors, washed the feet of guests, served and entertained at meals, chopped vegetables and stoked ovens and much more.

Some slaves were *vernae*, slaves born in the household. These "house-born slaves" usually received better treatment than other slaves in the household.[14]

Of special interest are the nurses and childminders who raised the young children and were part of their emotional support. Some of the nurses were free and worked for wages on contract, and others were slaves in the household. They provided physical care, nursing and changing the babies and minding the young children of the household. They nursed slave children as well.[15]

A slave pedagogue took charge of a boy who could be a future *paterfamilias* from about the age of six until he reached the age of majority. The figure of the pedagogue was frequently regarded with affectionate ridicule and often visually portrayed as "an old, grumpy-looking Socrates."[16] The ugliness of some of the portrayals of pedagogues is said to indicate the "proverbial dread that children had" of them, and the role of pedagogue was considered appropriate for slaves unfit or unsuitable for other tasks due to age, injury, or alcoholism.[17] The pedagogue was responsible for discipline and protection of the future master from unsavory influences while he was young. Pedagogues had a reputation for vigorous administration of corporal punishment with their professional accoutrements, the cane, whip, rod, and crooked staff.[18]

During the son's childhood, the pedagogue inflicted upon the future *paterfamilias* a version of the violence that slaves were exposed to for a lifetime.

Violence and Sexual Use in Roman Slavery

Slavery requires violence. A lengthy inscription from Puteoli illustrates how much violence was taken for granted in the Roman slave system. The inscription details regulations for the profession of the undertakers, who were also the professional torturers and executioners of slaves. Torture and execution of slaves was so common that a specific profession devoted to this task was required. The regulations in the inscription specify conditions when an owner "wishes to have a slave—male or female—punished privately," and "wants to put the slave on the cross or fork." The contractor must supply everything needed: the cross for crucifying or the fork for impaling, and the chains and ropes that the floggers will use, as well as the floggers themselves. For a punishment ordered by a magistrate, the contractor has similar responsibilities to provide the crosses as well as the "nails, pitch, wax, tapers and anything else that is necessary." The regulations specify that the work-gang that hauls away the corpse or corpses must be "dressed in red and ring a bell."[19]

Not every offense provoked measures that were quite as draconian as the cross or fork. Less injurious beatings than the punishments described in the Puteoli inscription could be inflicted, and slaves prone to run away might instead be fitted with collars. One well-preserved example from the late empire is an iron collar that would have been put around the slave's neck, with a bronze tag inscribed, "I have run away; hold me. When you shall have returned me to my master, Zoninus, you will receive a gold coin."[20] Slaves were also tattooed, some with "Stop me, I'm a runaway" on their eyebrows and others with a "tax paid" stamp.[21]

Sexual use of slaves was widespread. One use was in slave breeding. A child born of a slave mother was the property of her owner. Women slaves were encouraged to produce children, but there is no evidence of "systematic, coerced human reproduction comparable to the breeding of livestock."[22] The practice of designating some slave women as wet-nurses for others' infants, however, was intended both to free the mothers for other work and to allow them to become pregnant again more quickly.[23] Fertility was clearly an important selling-point for female slaves. Roman jurists discussed whether a buyer of a slave who turned out to be sterile could expect the seller to return the price.[24] Slave women were given incentives to reproduce. For example, Columella's agricultural handbook from the first century CE recommends giving an exemption from work to slave women who produce three sons and even granting freedom to those who produce many children.[25]

Slaves, male or female, adult or child, were also sexually available to the *paterfamilias* and to whomever he offered them for sexual use—within some complex legal and social limitations. Such use could lead to complex emotional relationships as owners sought emotional as well as physical domination, and as slaves competed for the master's affections as well.[26] Whether masters intentionally bred slaves by selecting male partners to "breed" with slave women is unclear. That slaves were used sexually is not.

Sexual use was beyond what we might wrongly imagine as benign licentiousness. A part of the violence of slavery was the sexual use of children. Slave children could also be designated for their various forms of entertainment value as *delicia*. Wealthy Romans selected these "pet children" for their deformities as well as their beauty and appealing ways of speaking. The *delicia* could serve as playmates for the younger children of the *paterfamilias*, and some were also used sexually by their adult owners.[27] Some comely little boys were also castrated to prolong their sexual appeal.[28] This type of sexual use was taken for granted as part of the family system.[29]

No right to bodily integrity was acknowledged for slaves.

Roman Slaves Claiming Themselves

As we saw above, slaves nevertheless found ways to own their own lives despite being defined in the public transcript as socially dead and extensions of the masters. They formed and honored relationships in a hidden transcript. Some slaves also formed lasting marriages acknowledged in the public transcript and in extant evidence in epitaphs and gravestones after they were freed.[30]

Other freed slaves leave a record of their relationships as well. For example, a funerary inscription that reveals the mutual commitment of two slaves:

> For Aulus Memmius Clarus, Dedicated by Aulus Memmius
> Urbanus to his fellow freedman and dearest companion. I can-
> not remember, my most respected co-freedman, that you and I
> ever quarrelled. By this epitaph, I invoke the gods of heaven and
> of the underworld as witnesses that we first met on the slave-

dealer's platform, that we were granted our freedom together in the same household, and that nothing ever parted us from one another until the day of your death.[31]

We do not know whether these two freedmen were friends or lovers, but they nevertheless forged a loyalty to one another without legal or societal sanction. As slaves, they could have been parted at any time if one were sold. Yet they maintained a close bond until Urbanus provided a decent burial for Clarus.

These small examples indicate that slaves did not conform to being merely bodies for the use of their masters. In the hidden transcript, they formed lasting relationships that upheld their reality as human beings.

Slaves who were manumitted became *liberti*, freed persons, but they would still be subordinates of the *paterfamilias*. They would still owe *pietas* to the paterfamilias as his subordinates, and many would join his clients at the morning *salutatio* described above.

Vices and Virtues Expected of Slaves and *Liberti*

The slaveholders' ethical view of the household held that slaves were, by nature, to be ruled by those who, by nature, were their masters. Slaveholders saw slaves as extensions of themselves, part of the property, akin to things or lifestock.[32] Masters would value their slaves' marketable or functional traits as "virtues": their physical beauty, useful skills, or compliant sexual availability.

To recognize ethical action, virtues and vices, on the part of slaves requires acknowledgement of their humanity. Slaveholders defined slaves ethically as much by the inconvenience of their chronic vices as by positive expectations, using "the longstanding literary convention of the criminous slave."[33] Masters assumed that troublesome behaviors were normal for slaves, expecting them to steal, to be careless with the household's resources, to run away when they could, and to betray the household's secrets to neighbors.[34] Such "vices" were viewed as part of the nature of the slaves and the moral degeneracy attributed to them was an element of their masters' argument that they were, by nature, in need of masters.[35] Household management included strategies to ameliorate slaves' expected vices as well as to inculcate virtues appropriate for slaves. A major ethical discussion among slaveholders centered on the appropriate ways to contain such behavior, whether by corporal punishment or by positive incentives.[36]

A primary vice of slaves was behaving as if they were free. A slave who behaved as a free man and head of household was a threat. Slaves were not expected to exhibit the traits of Roman "manliness" but expected to be cowardly and to display servile deference.[37] In the economy of honor, a slave's display of manly *virtus* would deprive the master of honor and shame him since the master's manliness was based on others' "unmanliness." Courageous slaves could also pose a physical threat to slaveholders as the "domestic enemy" capable of murdering their owners.[38]

The ethical virtues that the Roman Strict Father family system expected of the slaves, expectations that continued even if they were manumitted, were the opposite of such vices.[39] A slave who displayed servile deference, did not steal, exercised care for the resources of the household, and kept her or his mouth shut outside the household would be considered a virtuous slave. Such virtuous loyal slaves were presented in Roman "Tales of Loyalty" (*exemplum*) that narrated examples of slaves' loyalty, just as they offered moral examples of dutiful wives, as mentioned in the previous chapter. Exemplary slaves demonstrated their loyalty by following their masters into exile, undergoing torture or dying on their master's behalf, and committing suicide at the death of the master, often in a household suicide in which they assisted. Such tales were a reassurance to masters confronting the threat of slaves as the "enemy within," and an attempt to educate slaves in their role, to show that in honoring their masters with their loyalty they could acquire a share of honor for themselves.[40]

The Roman Strict Father family model accentuated two virtues as most desirable in slaves, although these were expressed as an ideal rather than a realistic expectation:

- *fides* (Latin) or *pistis* (Greek) (loyalty, faithfulness, dependability)
- *obsequium* (obedience and deference to the master)[41]

Other virtues are also named in the *exemplum* literature. One oft-
told tale, for example, relates that a slave who had previously been
brutally treated and branded nevertheless saved his master by killing
an old man and burning his corpse on a funeral pyre and telling the
would-be assassins that the burning corpse was his master.[42] Valerius
Maximus describes the slave's action as a display of *fides* and two additional slave virtues:

- *beneuolencia* (good will, implying happy acceptance of one's
  status)
- *pietas* (behavior appropriate to one's social position)[43]

In the Roman Strict Father family, then, virtuous slaves not only
displayed their loyalty and deference to their masters but also acted
happy and grateful as they bowed properly to their social superiors.
Their role in the social drama of the *domus* required a very thick
mask, indeed.

Yet the virtues that masters expected of their slaves can hardly
be expected to match the slaves' own moral expectations. The vices
their masters expected as the bothersome costs for the benefits of
slave-owning can be seen as virtuous acts of resistance, virtuous from
the slaves' perspective. They would see successful thievery to feed
oneself and other slaves, for example, as resistance rather than as
an immoral action.[44] The contrast of moralities is illustrated in the
words of a slave character named Epicrates in a comic play quoted by
Athenaeus's second-century work on banqueting:

> What is more hateful than to be summoned with Slave, Slave!
> [or Boy! Boy!] to where they are drinking; to serve, moreover,
> some beardless stripling or fetch him the chamber-pot, and to
> see things lying spilt before us—half-eaten milk-cakes and bits
> of chicken which, though left over, no slave may touch, as the
> women tell us. But what makes us rage is to have them call any-
> one of us who eats any of these things an impudent glutton![45]

Here we have a glimpse of the slave's point of view. Slaveholders'
ethics viewed a slave who ate leftover scraps from a meal as a thief
and a glutton, but the slaves' ethics saw the waste and the arrogant
behavior of the young guests as the moral issue, and pointed out the
ironic implicit question of who the real gluttons were.[46]

In the ethical view that would develop in slaves' daily acts of resistance, the slaves would develop their own view of virtues and vices
that surely included a valuing of the talents for successful pilfering
and effective dissembling, as well as other virtues that their masters
would view as vices.

Conclusion

Slaves filled the stage of the *domus*. They were busy with every imaginable household task, coming and going on errands, and managing
access to various parts of the house. They were present and available
at all hours in all parts of the house. Slave children were part of the
scene as well, some filling entertainment roles from amusing speech
to the sexual use to which all slaves could be subjected. When slaves
filled their assigned roles on the stage of the *domus* with every indication of willing obedience, exhibiting their assigned servile virtues,
they enhanced the image of the *paterfamilias* as a respected and
honored head of his household. To do so required them to make
their faces and postures a mask, a thick mask. Their assigned roles
made them a human stage set for the performance of the central
roles in the family. We should remember, however, that the assigned
"script" was only the public transcript. The slaves could and did continue to assert their own humanity in hidden transcripts "offstage"
among themselves. Keep this in mind as we turn to focus on plot
lines that still center on those assigned the lead roles on the stage of
the *domus*, even as we consider some of the offstage aspects of the
central roles as well.

6

Plot Themes

Relationships and Emotional Dynamics

We have seen that the Roman Strict Father family household included quite an array of personnel, an array of roles assigned by gender, age, and status. Each role had its own moral expectations, its own script. On the social stage of the *domus*, members of the household improvised within the parameters of their assigned roles. Yet when actors in a play perform their parts onstage, their offstage lives are also present. An actor may subordinate her offstage hopes and allegiances to the onstage role, yet her whole person is nevertheless present. For a lifetime on the stage of the *domus*, this interplay between onstage role expectations and the players' personal identities generated a bewildering complexity in relationships and emotional dynamics.

Improvising a script from birth to death within a prescribed role was already complex. All the relationships in the family were affected by deaths of members of the household, often at a young age.[1] The violence in the system of slavery and slaves' sexual availability to the *paterfamilias* also affected all the relationships in the family, as did differentiation by gender.

As just one example, we might imagine the resentment for harsh discipline and gratitude mixed with a close emotional bond that the son of the *paterfamilias* would have for his slave pedagogue as he grew up. As a caretaking slave, the pedagogue would also have mixed feelings about his master's son, emotions that would be every bit as complex as that of the slaves of the antebellum South and of servants who mind the children of the elites in our own day. We have seen that those same slaves also maintained relationships that were not part of their assigned roles, unacknowledged in the public transcript.

Complex emotional dynamics pervaded the Roman household both on and off its social stage. Consideration of a few of the key relationships in the family system, even within the confines of the assigned roles, can give us an idea of the complexity. Here we will look at sibling relationships, relationships between husband and wife, and sexual mores.

Sibling Relationships

The sibling relationship was the longest lasting relationship in the lives of most members of the Roman elite due to the demographic factors of age and death rates.[2] The rivalries and loyalties among these siblings were as complex as you might imagine, or more so, yet sibling solidarity was a large factor in how the whole system worked.

Several demographic factors affected sibling relationships. Children belonged to their fathers, not their mothers, and stayed with the father in cases of divorce. This meant that children of more than one marriage could be part of the household. While the father was alive, his sons competed for his favor and the financial benefits that depended on his favor.[3] Children also lost their fathers early in life, often before they were twenty.[4] Not only could this create tensions over inheritance, it could also pull the siblings together to face a variety of common threats. High child mortality meant that the siblings who survived into their teens had usually experienced the loss of brothers and sisters. High child mortality also meant that adoption was a factor in the relationship as well. Elites often used adoption of a son as a strategy to ensure succession and to preserve the family name.[5] At the center of the household, we can picture a combination of siblings, half-siblings, perhaps an adopted brother with a sister, and most often as a small group of two or three.[6]

Siblings were expected to provide support for one another in various circumstances, and the expectations depended on birth order and gender.[7] The sibling relationship was also idealized as a bond of harmony and mutual love.[8] Sibling relationships appear to express something more "egalitarian" than other relationships in the Roman Strict Father family, but in discussion of sibling relationships in antiquity, the focus was more on harmony, unity, and conformity to one's role in the family than on egalitarian notions.[9] Hierarchies among siblings were relatively fluid, however, and not always detectable, and the sibling relationship was where some equality and mutual relationship existed.[10] In spite of a high ideal of sibling love, conflicts between and among siblings were common, often over inheritance.[11]

Marriage, Divorce, Adultery

The relationship of husband and wife provided additional plot lines in the drama of the *domus*, and the relationship was no more dependably one of "happily ever after" than it is today. It could include not only marriage but divorce and adultery, but these were understood differently than they are now.

Marriage

Marriages formed families as they do today, but marriage was understood differently. Weddings in the Greco-Roman era usually took place in the household, and the ceremony involved the bride moving from her father's household to the groom's household, often with a noisy nocturnal procession of rowdy revelers accompanying the bride on her journey. No ceremony was legally required, perhaps other than the "leading" of the bride to the groom's house.[12] Custom called for feasting and celebration, including offerings to the deities.

The current image of marriage includes the expectation of love, intimacy, romance, mutuality between partners, and companionship, even if the partners are expected to fulfill differentiated gender roles in a modern Strict Father family model. Does this image also apply in the Roman Strict Father family? No, and yes.[13]

In Roman marriage, a distinct emphasis on the virtue of *concordia*, a state of harmony between husband and wife, applied. Some scholars view this virtue as an indication of marital chilliness. Because many couples married by arrangement, not by choice, successful accommodation was the goal. Since the virtue of *concordia* was most extolled in the public sphere precisely at crisis moments, the times of greatest discord, similar praise of this virtue for the marriage relationship is taken as an indication of its frequent absence. If anything, it may indicate something a little chillier than romance.[14] This is not to say that actual affection did not develop, but the sexual availability of slaves and the role of slaves in childcare introduced more distance into the relationship than is expected in modern marriage.

Nevertheless, ample evidence exists of a romantic ideal of marriage in which actual affection and companionship were expected.[15] An ideal of marital companionship was emerging in the early empire. For example, Tacitus recounts a debate in the Roman Senate about whether wives should be allowed to accompany their husbands to their service as provincial governors.[16] The debate indicates that the senators valued their wives' companionship.[17] In the discussion of the virtues of the *materfamilias* in chapter 4, we saw ideal wifely virtues articulated by Cassius Dio.[18] She is discreet and domestic, and a good manager and child-bearer, and looks after her husband physically and emotionally and manages his excesses of impetuosity in youth and severity in old age. A wife's companion role was vital to the success of her husband, but clearly subordinate. Romance was part of marriage to some degree as well. Wedding hymns extolled expectations of romantic love, affection, and sexual attraction in marriage.[19] Men also wrote affectionately to their wives.[20] Philosophers could also wax eloquent about emotional equality and companionship in marriage while also presenting a hierarchical view of the relationship.[21] Romantic idealism about marriage was as realistic and unrealistic as such notions are today.[22]

Notably, however, "a husband's display of restraint (*moderatio*) toward his wife can be taken as a sign of his affection (*caritas*) toward her."[23] We can assume what the converse lack of restraint would be, but we should note that verbal and physical abuse of wives was a matter for the courts, and not assumed under the powers of the *paterfamilias*. The wife's continuing membership in the family of her father would also help to mitigate this, especially if she had brothers to assist her. In addition to protection provided by her siblings, a wife's position in her husband's family could be secured by having a living son.

The elite wife was not a slave to her husband, but the relationship was expected to be asymmetrical, not mutual. The relationship of husband and wife was understood as analogous to that of father and child or tutor and ward.[24] Frequently the age differential corresponded to the analogy. Brides were generally a decade younger than the grooms at first marriage. Brides were as young as the age of menarche, twelve to fourteen, although some argue that most girls married in their later teens.[25] Grooms were older, in their late twenties.[26] Marriages were usually arranged by the couple's parents, although the children had some rights to refuse. Sons, being older at the time of marriage, had more leverage than daughters, and girls were in no position to refuse the choice of husband without serious grounds.[27]

The asymmetry in the expected relationship is revealed in one of Plutarch's essays. The influential late first-century CE moral philosopher offered advice for the bride and groom about how to have a successful marriage.[28] Plutarch recognizes that the wife is a human being expected to develop intellectually with her husband's influence and to improve her husband morally.[29] He admonishes the husband against asserting supremacy over her by force. For example, he uses the analogy of men who are too weak to mount a standing horse and instead train the horse to kneel in order to caution husbands who marry women who are their "betters" to rise to the quality of their wives rather than using humiliation to reduce their wives to their own level. In his continuation of the analogy, however, the husband is still the rider and the wife is the horse.[30]

Plutarch consistently advises the wife to subordinate herself to her husband, using various analogies. The couple are to sing in harmony, but the tune is carried by the bass, just as the husband's leadership is disclosed in all that the household does.[31] She is to be the moon to his sun, so she should appear with him when he is present to outshine her and stay in secluded shadows when he is away.[32] Most telling, perhaps, is her status as a mirror to reflect his emotions and to have no feelings of her own.[33] She is to have no friends of her own and no deities of her own, and she is to defer to her husband's parents before her own and be especially cognizant of placating her mother-in-law.[34] He recommends that the husband not allow his

wife to wear shoes so that she will stay indoors.[35] The wife should
avoid speaking so that outsiders can hear and instead let her husband
speak for her.[36] The couple's financial resources are to be held "in
common," which means in the control of the husband.[37] Plutarch's
advice indicates some common expectations in the marriage relationship, and his counsel to wives to subordinate themselves also
suggests that not all of them did so.

Marriage is a much more complex topic than this, but we can see
that it differed from contemporary expectations.

Divorce and Remarriage

Roman divorce was an informal procedure and could be initiated
by either partner unilaterally. The wife's family could also initiate a
divorce. Divorce occurred for a variety of reasons and was not uncommon. Blame was unnecessary, although a frequent cause was the
failure to have children, a failure attributed to the wife's inadequacy.
Most motivations for divorce were considered private family matters
that did not need to be stated publicly.[38] Divorce did not involve
legal procedures.[39]

When an elite woman was divorced, her dowry was restored to
her. Any children from the marriage belonged to the father and
stayed in his house and received a portion of their mother's dowry.[40]

Divorce and remarriage, a pattern of serial marriage, created an
additional web of relationship among the Roman elites. Children of
more than one marriage were often present in the *domus* and each
maintained ties to the families of their respective mothers. While the
tensions among half-siblings would be expected, the alliances that
resulted also extended their connections.[41]

Adultery

When a married woman had an affair, it was considered adultery. In
the republican era, a husband could legally kill his wife and her lover
if they were caught in the act, but adultery was otherwise considered
an internal family matter. This changed under the Augustan family
legislation starting in 18 BCE. The husband's right to kill in these
circumstances was restricted and adultery became an issue for public
courts. Husbands were required to divorce wives who were caught

and have them tried. There were no criminal charges for a husband's extramarital activities, but wives could divorce their husbands for this as well as other reasons.[42] The husband could take a concubine instead of a wife, but not both at the same time, and this occurred mostly in cases where status differences or other factors made a legal marriage problematic.[43] Slavery, and the husband's sexual use of slaves as an assumed social convention, also complicated the emotional dynamics of sexual relationships in the family.

Sexual Mores

Adultery brings us to the matter of sexual mores. To understand the Roman family model and its ethical implications, we need to revise some assumptions about sexual morality. In contemporary society, we tend to assume a set of sexual mores based on the question of fidelity to a partner and the general question, with whom? where the issue is the gender and age of the sex partner.

For the Romans, the question of fidelity applied disproportionately to married women and to daughters—especially in the elite classes. For the married woman, the gender and age were hardly relevant in answer to the question, with whom? For wives, the answer was "with no one but her husband," and for the unmarried daughters, of course, "with no one at all." There is evidence that some married women at Rome did, in fact, register themselves as prostitutes for a little side entertainment,[44] but such behavior was morally frowned upon, and the stakes were high for illicit relationships. This was truer for daughters who could pay with their lives, as we have seen. A radical double standard applied. While the *paterfamilias'* sexual access to slaves was taken for granted, a wife or daughter of the *paterfamilias* or any other free woman who had sexual relations with a slave was committing adultery. The double standard also applied to the character of sexual activity as well. Sex in the marriage bed was to be "modest" and wives were expected to accept their husbands' more "debauched" sexual activities with other partners as a way of preserving their honor as wives.[45]

Considering the breadth of options available for elite men, the question, with whom? might at first seem to have more relevance for them. To understand traditional sexual *mores* for men, however, we need to comprehend that the issue was not so much with whom? but how? The strictures of chastity and fidelity applied to freeborn women were not such important moral values for citizen men. Nor was the gender or age of the partner. What mattered more was who penetrated whom, who acted upon whom, and whether the form of the sexual act was appropriate to the respective power positions of the partners. This penetration pecking order has been discussed as a "priapic" model in which "sexual intercourse is seen as penetration, which confers (social) power on the penetrator and detracts power from the one who is penetrated—the active-passive mode."[46] Thus sexual relations with slaves of either gender and any age, children included, were not considered immoral unless the master dishonored himself by allowing himself to be the passive partner. His role and his *virtus* was defined by being the "impenetrable penetrator."[47] In the interests of good taste, the graphic details of the hierarchy of orifices and what in which need not be described in detail.[48] Your imagination is probably correct.

For slaves and, to some extent, freed persons, sexual morality was a different question. From the perspective of the *mores* that defined the Roman Strict Father family, slaves were objects to be used. Their morality was demonstrated in their obedience. The moral viewpoint of the slaves themselves is another question. Many slaves came from peoples the Romans had captured in their many conquests, and it would be simplistic to assume that upon capture all cultural memory and moral values from their original traditions were erased.

Funerary portraits of family units of wealthy freed couples reveal a desire to project an image of the wife as a Roman *matrona,* resisting the sexual availability she was subjected to in her former slave identity.[49] This exemplifies a sexual ethic that differs from the "priapic" model focused on penetration, sexual morality based instead on the sexual virtue of *pudicitia*: modesty, chastity, shamefacedness.[50] The freed woman displayed her *pudicitia* as a quality very much associated with free status in Roman thought.[51]

Pudicitia was a distinctively Roman virtue, with some similarities to Greek concepts of self-control (*sophrosyne*) and shame (*aidos*).[52] It had specific connotations related to sexual purity but the sexual integrity of *pudicitia* was also associated with a sense of decency and self-respect.[53] Around this term, Romans discussed gender differences, the relation of body and mind, and power dynamics.[54] Upholding *pudicitia* was, for freeborn members of the family other than the *paterfamilias*, a way of life similar to his efforts to maintain his *auctoritas* and was a way to maintain a sense of personal power and honor.

Pudicitia was also similar to *auctoritas* because the "moralising gaze of the community" played an important role in motivating conformity to the requirements of its display.[55] Virtues were not just for their own sake, but for the sake of the family honor in the eyes of the community. *Pudicitia* required attention not only to maintaining bodily integrity but also to the scrupulous avoidance of anything that the community's gaze could perceive as an opportunity for impropriety and thus the equivalent of impropriety itself.[56] The quality of *pudicitia* internalized this community gaze in a cultivated sense of shame that was part of the system of maintaining the household's honor.[57]

This brief reorientation of our concepts of sexual mores can give us some insight into the array of virtues expected of the different roles in the Roman *domus*. From the perspective of bodily integrity, the virtues of the elite members were also an aspect of the privileges of their positions. The *materfamilias* and the daughters of the *paterfamilias* were not only expected to maintain their bodily integrity; they were *allowed* to do so as an essential aspect of their privilege. When we consider the slaves whose bodies could be penetrated in any orifice and even be mutilated for the pleasure or profit of their masters, we can see that *pudicitia* as the bodily integrity expected of elite wives and daughters was not only an expectation but also a privilege, the privilege of self-respect.

Viewed from the perspective of penetration as the central aspect of Roman sexual *mores*, then, the virtue of the *paterfamilias* and his sons was enhanced by sexual penetration in dominant positions. Such domination enhanced their power and their moral superiority. For subordinates, especially the slaves, penetration was an embodiment of their subordination and their social death and dishonor.

Viewed from the perspective of *pudicitia* of the mother or daughter, exemption from this penetration or its limitation to the marriage bed provides another understanding of the virtue and power she is allowed in her ability to maintain her personal bodily integrity rather than in the ability to dominate.

Conclusion

A variety of relationships were played out on the stage of the *domus*. Siblings were jockeying for power and offering one another support. Husbands and wives, often matched by their parents, were negotiating their marriage for public view to meet societal expectations as well as navigating whatever personal bond they might form. Sexual relationships were also taking place, some according to the mores based on male domination and some not according to social conventions of the day. This discussion has hardly scratched the surface of relational dynamics in the household, however, and relationships that have been left unconsidered also include fathers and sons, fathers and daughters, mothers and sons, mothers and daughters, slaves and slaves, slaves and freed persons, sons and pedagogues, daughters and wet-nurses. The list is long. This discussion does indicate that the family of the *domus* was not the family of our day.

Conclusion to Part II

As a prelude to the discussion in Part 5 of an early Christian letter being read in such a household, Paul's letter to Philemon, let us pause for a moment to consider what Christian baptism might mean in this context.

Picture yourself as a member of one of those households, then. Odds are you are a slave. Odds are you have experienced some form of abuse. You have been beaten or threatened with beatings. You have witnessed a great deal of violence. You may have been used sexually from childhood on. It was simply part of how things were.

Today we know what this does to people in a society that does not condone it. Imagine yourself in this world that does.

Now imagine yourself coming through the waters of baptism in the Christian ritual. You come up from the water, and as someone wraps you in a fresh white robe, the assembly greets you speaking the words from God to Jesus,

"You are my beloved child! With you I am well-pleased!"

Can you understand what this would do, to have a divine *paterfamilias* who loves you and claims you? Can you imagine what this could make community members capable of? Can you imagine what changes in relationships the baptized might aspire to?

While the early Christian movement was hardly the only form of resistance in which those subordinated in the Roman Strict Father family engaged, this can give us a glimpse of what resistance could mean. Without understanding how the metaphor of the family was embedded in the understanding of the Empire, we might think it was just about the personal experience, however. When we understand this movement in the context of the empire as a Roman Strict Father family and the missionary movement of its imperial cult, we will see that it has not only personal but world-changing implications as well, at least at its inception. Volume 2 will consider how that loving divine *paterfamilias* who met the early Christians coming through the waters of baptism also became the *paterfamilias* of a new form of Strict Father family empire. First we need to examine how the Roman Empire was constructed as such a family.

Part III

The Roman Empire as a Family in the Macrocosm

Aelius Aristides, a second-century orator from Mysia in Asia Minor, delivered a speech to the imperial court at Rome in 155 CE, the *Encomium of Rome*. He praised Rome for being cohesive and noted that Rome was no longer a specific city but "everywhere in the empire is equally Rome." He congratulated the empire for being a household, according to one paraphrase, "Whereas the city-state was once compared with a private household, now the whole empire is one house."[1] Rome had become an idea more than a geographical location, expressed in the Romanized architecture of the cities and the elite houses and the Romanized self-identification of their owners.[2] The root metaphor of that idea was the Roman Strict Father family, the *domus*. Just as the *domus* was a stage for the presentation of a performance of the honor of the household and its *paterfamilias*, the empire became a stage for the performance of Roman honor now in the person of their *paterfamilias* and emperor.

Making the Roman Empire one household under one *paterfamilias* was the strategy of Caesar Augustus (ruled 27 BCE to 14 CE), an effective strategy that endured for centuries. The Romans already saw themselves as a family, with cults that were writ large in the city and small in each household. Vesta's hearth fire, for example, burned in her temple at the heart of Rome and in the hearth at the heart of each household as well.[3] Under Augustus, the empire became a household not only metaphorically but, in many ways, literally. The Roman Strict Father family outlined in Part 2 became the basis for centuries of one-man rule by a series of emperors. In establishing one-man rule using this Roman household form, Augustus worked to enforce his vision of that family form as the superior Roman way. Here in Part 3, we will see how the Roman Strict Father family we have looked at as a social reality in the microcosm worked at the level of the empire in the macrocosm. We have already mentioned a few of the social changes that were part of the shift from republic to empire, such as the shift of the conduct of political affairs from public institutions like the Senate into the *domus*.

The change from the Roman republic to an empire under one-man rule was a change in the family model assumed as its root metaphor. We will not attempt to retrieve the family model of the republic here, other than to note that it appears to have focused on the male siblings as the center of power. We will see the family model of the republic only in its breakdown in the metaphorical battle of brothers that resulted in the sole rule of Augustus. We should note, however, that the family model outlined in Part 2 became the metaphorical basis of the empire even as this supposedly "traditional" Roman family was being "revived" along with other "time-honored" Roman values. Family and family values were a central topic of discussion in the early imperial era. One-man rule of the Roman Empire that had already conquered a vast territory was reshaping every aspect of life for those under its dominion, a dominion that grew much larger under Augustus.

The shift to one-man rule predictably directs our gaze to center stage, to the one man ruling, Augustus. Yet the changes during the Augustan era, the changes Augustus envisioned, were more comprehensive than a simple desire for individual power. The strategy Augustus used to establish his rule, based on the transformation of the empire into his family, was also the goal. Augustus had a vision for the empire, and he created his own image to be the leader (father) he thought Rome required and to legitimate a new political order around himself. His empire was to be a Roman Strict Father family, as he defined and redefined it, and his family was to be an empire. That empire was to rule the world, as he indicates in the title and first line of his account of his achievements, the *Res Gestae*: "The achievements of the Divine Augustus, by which he brought the world under the empire of the Roman people."[4]

7

A Father's Rule in the Roman Family Empire

A Monarchy without a King

Like the word "family," the word "empire" conjures images in our heads. The "Evil Empire" of the Star Wars series may come to mind for some. Military conquest is likely to be part of the picture. The Roman Empire was certainly founded on military domination, and its military strategies and innovations in the conduct of warfare allowed it to conquer many peoples and territories.

The empire relied on a huge military force to occupy a vast territory. Yet the size of the Roman military was in fact small to rule such a large area.[1] Military might alone does not explain the success of the Roman Empire. Other dynamics were at work in the success of the Augustan project, a project presented as "cultural renewal." Much of this program revolved around a new attention to the Roman family in the basic understanding of the empire. To rule this vast empire, Caesar Augustus, and his successors following his lead, deftly used and transformed themes and myths and an ideal of the Roman family that were already elements of the Romans' self-definition.

Augustus' Titles and Powers

In the name of the restoration of the republic, Augustus managed to become the first Roman emperor without becoming a king and thus avoided appearing to be the threat to the traditions of Rome that his adopted father's murderers had perceived in Julius Caesar's bid for power. This was no small feat. While he increasingly became the sole

proprietor of state and sacral power, Augustus refused the monarchical titles and powers associated with the tyrannical kings much-de-
spised by the Romans from their early history. Instead he identified
his position as *princeps civitatis*, "First Citizen." He accepted powers
that he used to consolidate his control while refusing public offices.
For much of his reign, he ruled as a private citizen (*privatus*).

Augustus was granted increased military, financial, and foreign
affairs powers, and he legitimated his supremacy using permanent
powers of a tribune (*tribunicia potestas*) granted to him in 23 BCE.
In his record of his accomplishments, known as the *Res Gestae*, he
dates the beginning of his own reign to the granting of this power.[2]
Traditionally a body of tribunes were chosen from the among the
common people (*plebs*) to represent their interests, and the tribunes
had powers to restrict actions of the aristocratic Senate (patricians).[3]
As a body, the *plebs* guaranteed the physical safety of the tribunes.
During the last century of the republic, the authority of the tribunes
was diminished under the dictator Sulla and then Julius Caesar. The
powers Augustus assumed included the right to introduce legislation
to the popular assembly and to the Senate, veto power, the right to
coerce citizens to obey his orders, and the right to investigate cases
against magistrates' decisions and overrule them.[4] While Augustus
proudly recounts the benefits he bestowed on the common people,
his assumption of these powers as a patrician, permanently by grant
of the Senate and not as a term-limited elected *pleb*, functioned over
time to remove the *plebs'* formal channels for influence, pushing
them to informal protest methods, such as organized chants from
the stands in public events.[5] While Augustus assumed responsibilities
for the fatherly care and feeding of the *plebs*, they were losing their
voice in the family council of the empire, even though their council
continued to meet to ratify Augustus' policies.

Augustus described another measure of fatherly supervision as
requested by these same people and the Senate. He recorded that
on three occasions in 19, 18, and 11 BCE, he refused to accept their
appointment as supervisor of laws and morals (*curator legum et morum*) "without a colleague and with supreme power."[6] Historians
of the next generations recorded that he did accept this role, a role
consistent with his image as the *paterfamilias* of the Roman people.[7]

After 27 BCE, Augustus used the name *Imperator Caesar divi filius Augustus* in the pattern of the names of other prominent Romans.[8] For example, Cicero was *Marcus Tullius Marci filius Cicero*. Marcus was his individual given personal name (*praenomen*), Tullius the name of his clan (*nomen*). *Marci filius* indicates that he was the son of Marcus, and Cicero was his *cognomen*, a name with several purposes and origins that usually identifies him. The *cognomen* could be a further specification of the branch of the clan designated in the *nomen*, an honorific, an additional personal name, or, for an adoptee, an indication of his original *nomen*.[9]

Imperator (Commander) thus took the place of Augustus' given name, Gaius, with Caesar as the name of his adoptive father, Gaius Julius Caesar. This formulation omitted the name of the Julian clan, and the name Caesar became synonymous with "emperor" later in the first century CE. The title "*Imperator*" signified his consolidation of military power. Augustus reported that he was saluted twenty-one times as *imperator*,[10] a title traditionally awarded for outstanding military victories along with a triumph parade. Augustus had added more territory to the empire than any other *imperator* and was proud to mention that, "In my triumphs nine kings or children of kings were led before my chariot."[11] Julius Caesar had already used *Imperator* as part of his name, to indicate his role as a military dictator with absolute power. Even during the civil wars and before the victory at Actium, as the adopted son of Julius Caesar, Octavian began to use *Imperator* as part of his name along with the cognomen "Caesar" inherited from his adopted father. The Roman Senate conferred the title officially in 29 BCE.[12] The Prima Porta statue of him as Commander in Chief provides an imposing image of him as Imperator.[a]

Augustus also derived "*Divi Filius* (Son of a God)" from his adopted father, Julius Caesar. After the assassination of Julius Caesar on the Ides of March in 44 BCE, during the games Octavian (to become Augustus) defiantly held in July in honor of his adoptive father's victories, a comet appeared and was interpreted as Julius

---

a. Use an online image search of "Augustus Prima Porta" for pictures of the statue.

Caesar becoming a deity, his apotheosis.[13] The Roman Senate who
had murdered him in their meeting hall two years earlier now voted
to declare him a god as part of the state cult with temples and altars
to him.[14] As his adopted son, Octavian was thus *Divi Iuli Filius*, Son
of the God Julius, but he dropped the specification "*Iuli*" to use the
more generally divine designation, *Divi Filius*, "Son of a God" or
"Son of God." Thus, where other Roman men's names identified
them as their earthly father's son, Augustus was identified as a son
of a deity.

Augustus (Revered, Consecrated, Sacred) became his cognomen,
the name by which he was known, replacing Octavian as the name
of his earlier career. The omission is consistent with what appears to
be an intentional removal of reference to his "Octavian phase" elsewhere.[15] As Augustus, he could project himself as a more merciful
ruler than his previous identity as the crueler Octavian who joined
in ordering the proscriptions during the Second Triumvirate (43–33
BCE) that killed off hundreds of Roman aristocratic leaders, including Cicero.[16] A new image of Augustus, sculpted using the harmony
of classical proportions, also replaced statues of Octavian.[17]

The name "Romulus" had been considered to evoke the image
of a second founder, but it came with too much problematic symbolism. "Augustus" had been an epithet usually applied to a place,
meaning that it had been consecrated by auspicious signs that revealed divine favor.[18] As a name, it was new and evoked divine favor,
an auspicious new founding, and a savior of the state.[19]

The Roman Senate awarded Octavian the title of Augustus in
January of 27 BCE along with his status as *Princeps*, the first citizen,
when he restored the republic after the civil wars. As he tells it:

> In my sixth and seventh consulships, after I had extinguished
> civil wars, and at a time when with universal consent I was in
> complete control of affairs, I transferred the republic to the
> dominion of the senate and people of Rome. For this service
> of mine I was named Augustus by decree of the senate, and the
> door-posts of my house were publicly wreathed with bay leaves
> and a civic crown was fixed over my door and a golden shield
> was set in the Curia Julia, which, as attested by the inscription

thereon, was given me by the senate and people of Rome on account of my courage (*virtus*), clemency (*clementia*), justice (*justitia*), and piety (*pietas*). After this time I excelled all in influence (*auctoritas*), although I possessed no more official power than others who were my colleagues in the several magistracies.[20]

As Augustus, and later as *Pater Patriae* (Father of the Fatherland), he projected himself as ruling by virtue, not by might. He emphasized that he ruled specifically by the virtue of *auctoritas* expected of the Roman *paterfamilias*, and that it was his victory in the contest of this virtue that gave him his ability to rule. We can see in his description of the centrality of virtues, and the virtue of *auctoritas* specifically, that the rule he envisioned relied on moral leadership and the virtues specific to the *paterfamilias*.[21]

The word *auctoritas* has a range of associations helpful for understanding Augustus' vision. It is a quality that inheres in an individual, based originally in the special insight attributed to an *auctor*, a guarantor who gives a stamp of approval to an action.[22] *Auctoritas* connotes mutuality as well and is based on voluntary allegiance rather than a mandate, relying on "consensus, goodwill, and compromise in getting things done rather than on a rigid system of parliamentary rules and cross-checks."[23] *Auctoritas*, therefore, must be constantly confirmed. As such, *auctoritas* indicates what has been termed "actual" power for "transformational leadership" involving morality and values, in contrast to "transactional power" based in the machinery of government and "transactional leadership" that relies on exchanges to create and maintain political support.[24]

Augustus also indicated that he "excelled all in *auctoritas*," declaring himself the winner in a competition for virtue.[25] The competition was not, however, the conventional zero-sum competition for honor in which honor is gained by the shame of the opponent. Augustus constructed his *auctoritas* and the virtues associated with it to increase the *auctoritas* of other Romans as well. He thus superseded the *auctoritas* of the Senate without usurping it.[26] *Auctoritas* was a power created with the participation of the Roman people, meant to increase their honor and to justify their moral right to rule the world.

The focus on *auctoritas* indicates a type of leadership that intends to multiply the virtues associated with it.[27] The virtues expected of the *paterfamilias* listed in chapter 4 would be included: courage (*virtus*), clemency (*clementia*), justice (*justitia*), and piety (*pietas*). These were the virtues as inscribed on the golden shield that the Roman Senate presented to Augustus.

Virtus exemplifies the courage and manliness required to establish *auctoritas*, and the restoration of this quality in Roman citizen males was part of Augustus' overall program for his version of the Roman republic. Augustus displayed his own *pietas* as an encouragement to all the members of the population to be respectful to their "betters" as he was to the deities. He displayed his *clementia* by enslaving the peoples he conquered rather than slaughtering them wholesale and his *justitia* in his unflinching severity in his handling of internal affairs.

To his name as *Imperator Caesar divi filius Augustus*, two more titles were added to complete his identity as the leader of the new political order he envisioned.

When Julius Caesar was assassinated in 44 BCE, his office as the *pontifex maximus* (chief priest) was granted to Lepidus, the sidelined third man in the "three-man rule" (triumvirate) along with Antony and Octavian. As long as Lepidus lived, Augustus refused the office, but after Lepidus died in 13 BCE, Augustus became *pontifex maximus* in 12 BCE.[28] As the chief priest of the Roman state, he now had official authority to interpret divine law and was the head of the college of pontifices who presided over the affairs of the state cult.[29] Just as the *paterfamilias* was the chief priest of the household, Augustus now became the chief priest of the Roman family empire, and the image of his *genius* became a binding force as we will see below in a discussion of the imperial cult.

In 2 BCE Augustus officially received the title of *Pater Patriae* (Father of the Fatherland). He had refused the official title for some twenty-five years although he had been addressed by the title without the formality of a decree.[30] Augustus concluded the *Res Gestae* with this title as the culmination of his catalogue of achievements:

> In my thirteenth consulship the senate, the equestrian order
> and the whole people of Rome gave me the title of Father of

my Country (*pater patriae*), and resolved that this should be inscribed in the porch of my house and in the Curia Julia and in the Forum Augustum below the chariot which had been set there in my honour by decree of the senate.[31]

Inscribed in the Curia Julia where the Senate met, the title would remind the senators of his role. In the Augustan Forum, the title visually connected him to the mythic and legendary founders of Rome, Aeneas and Romulus. The chariot where the title was inscribed stood at the center of the plaza in the forum, in front of the temple to Mars Ultor. To either side of the temple, areas constructed with semi-circular walls were dedicated to these legendary founders, Aeneas to the viewer's left, Romulus to the right. The inscription on Augustus' chariot indicates his identification with them as founders as the new Father of the Fatherland in their line.[32]

The inscription on the porch of his residence indicates that Augustus' *domus* shared the blurring of the distinction between public and private that characterized the Roman *domus* of this time.[33] His home was also a place for the conduct of the public affairs of the Roman people. With the placement of the inscription "*pater patriae*" on his porch, his role as *paterfamilias* of his own *domus* and *paterfamilias* of the Roman people merged. His household became the Roman family empire and the empire became his household.

Augustus was not the first Roman *pater patriae*. Romulus as Rome's legendary founder was considered a *parens* or *pater patriae*, as was Marcus Furius Camillus, acclaimed in the title as the second founder of Rome after the Gallic invasion (387/6 BCE). Before Augustus, the Senate awarded the title twice. The first award was to Cicero in 63 BCE after he exposed the Cataline conspiracy. As Octavian, Augustus had this honored *pater patriae* killed during the proscriptions under the Second Triumvirate. The second award was to his adoptive father, Julius Caesar, awarded the title *Parens Patriae* shortly before his assassination. Coins honoring Julius Caesar with this title were issued after his death.[34] Perhaps Augustus refused the title for twenty-five years out of some superstition about its association with violent death?

For Augustus, however, his title as Father united the content of his other powers and titles into one identity. As the *princeps civitatis,* First Citizen, he ascended to the metaphorical position of the eldest brother, first in line for the inheritance of the role of the *paterfamilias.* He assumed paternal care-taking functions with his assumption of powers as a tribune (*tribunicia potestas*), and fatherly responsibility for the moral behavior of family members with his role as supervisor of laws and morals (*curator legume et morum*). As *Imperator,* he had the responsibility to defend the Roman *domus* from external and internal enemies and to expand it. As *pontifex maximus,* he assumed the priestly responsibilities of the *paterfamilias.* His designation as Augustus denoted his choice to rule by the virtues of the *paterfamilias,* especially by *auctoritas.*[35] As *divi filius,* Son of (a) God, his position as father is part of the lineage of the *domus,* where every *paterfamilias* was also a son in a proud line. As son of (a) god, he placed himself and the Roman *domus* in a divine lineage and aligned the Roman family with a celestial family as well.

The identification of the family or household of which he was the Father as the *patria* was equally significant. He was not a king of a kingdom. He was the Father (*pater*) of a *patria,* a homeland with a proud ancestry, a beloved territory, the familial "home place." While his role as *paterfamilias* functioned to give him monarchical powers over the Roman Empire without the identity as king that the Romans loathed, his identity as *pater patriae* also offered a relational identity. The Romans would not have accepted a king, but they could be persuaded to accept themselves as a Roman household in macrocosm, a family with a *paterfamilias* with monarchical powers. This divinely connected household became the ideological foundation that allowed the ostensible republic to function as an actual empire under one-man rule, an empire entitled to rule the world under its divine emperor.[36]

Take another look at the image of the *Gemma Augustea* at the beginning of this book. In the upper register, all eyes, including those of the deities, turn their gaze toward the seated Augustus, portrayed as the divine *paterfamilias* Jupiter, ruling with the divine *auctoritas* they acknowledge. They also concur in their joint mandate to rule the world, to triumph over the barbarians depicted in the lower register. We will return to them later, but for now we can see the compelling image of the divine Augustus.

Battle of Brothers
Apollo versus Dionysius

Augustus did not ascend instantly to the role of Jupiter/Zeus, the *paterfamilias* in the household of the Empire, however. He began as one of the brothers in a painful contest for ascendancy. In fact, his ascension to the role of father and the formation of what we call the empire were part of the same transformation. It began in the battle of brothers, a battle that concluded the turmoil of a century of bloody civil war at Rome.

Augustus came to power out of a series of contests that shaped his imperial strategy. We can see this played out especially in the last contest decided at the Battle of Actium in 31 BCE. There the forces of Octavian, who had not yet become Caesar Augustus, defeated the forces of Mark Antony and Cleopatra. At the level of the propaganda war both before and after, this last contest was played out as a battle between the god Apollo, represented by Octavian/Augustus, and the god Dionysus, represented by Mark Antony.

Dionysus, was the "party-god," the god of wine and even drunkenness, the god of actors and the theater, the god of enjoyment in living, and the god of disorder and things outside the lines, Zeus's love-child by a mortal, not quite accepted among the Olympians, and a god of the foreigners. Mark Antony himself took up this image with enthusiasm, but his Dionysian image was not as popular as he expected and made him an easy target for his enemies' negative propaganda.[37]

Apollo was the responsible god, the god of reason and order, justice and music, the god who colors inside the lines, one of the inner circle of the Olympians and a son of Zeus-Jupiter. Augustus cultivated an association with Apollo. A story circulated as early as the 30's BCE that he had, like Alexander the Great, been conceived by Apollo, coming to his mother in the form of a snake.[38]

Augustus and Antony both staged costume parties where they dressed as gods. Augustus himself was rumored to have appeared as Apollo at a "a notorious 'feast of the twelve gods.'"[39] The Roman

plebs were not particularly happy about it, suffering as they were
from a grain shortage at the time. At roughly the same time, Antony
appeared at a costume party at Alexandria "dressed as the sea god
Glaucus, his nude body painted blue, and, with a fish-tail swaying
behind him, danced on all fours."[40] Most often, however, Antony
cast himself as Dionysus on the public propaganda stage.

When Octavian-Augustus defeated Mark Antony at the Battle
of Actium, the victory was thus cast as the victory of Apollo over
Dionysus. Andrew Wallace-Hadrill summarizes the mythic dimension of the victory:

> For the myth-making required that Actium should be seen as far
> more than a battle between individuals for supremacy. It was a
> battle for Roman values, to save the Roman world from a frontal
> assault on its gods, its ideals and its moral fabric. The threat was
> not a tipsy Antony but the evil incarnate in Cleopatra; the victory
> was one of Roman decency over barbarism and corruption.[41]

In the role of Apollo, Augustus (Octavian) was thus defending
Roman civilization from the corrupting influences that Dionysus-
Antony threatened to allow in. At Actium, then, Augustus/Octavian
fought not as a rival for power but as a savior of the Roman civilization against the corrupt Eastern menace that included Cleopatra. He
defended what he would come to enforce as Roman "traditional"
family values, specifically the values of the Roman male head of the
household: moral strength, authority (*auctoritas*), and strict norms.
His program of cultural "renewal" was intended to strengthen the
boundaries against corrupting influences and to strengthen the
moral fiber of good Romans to withstand them. This played very
well with the values of the sectors of society from which the Roman
armies were drawn and with military values in general, values to
which Antony was seriously oblivious, perhaps due to a haze of alco-
hol and Cleopatra's legendary charms. Augustus portrayed himself
as restoring solid Roman values in the face of this, values that evoked
the Romans' simple peasant origins. The image we have seen on the
Gemma Augustaea is the image he takes up, then, in his identification as Jupiter-Zeus, the "alpha-male god" crowned as savior of
Roman civilization. This fits his title as "father of the fatherland."

Administration of the Roman Empire
as a Household and the *Familia Caesaris*[42]

The Augustan transformation at the level of image-making included a corresponding transformation at the level of organizational management. Before looking further at the construction of the empire as a familial identity, a word about changes in organization is needed. Augustus was not only the *pater patriae* as a figurehead but also as a manager. He began to manage the empire as his household.

Augustus began to provide public services using his own financial resources, funding the fire brigades at Rome and the imperial guard, as well as a substantial portion of the soldiers' retirement fund.[43] Both Augustus and his wife Livia donated to maintain members of the elite whose resources were depleted.[44] Augustus' personal financial resources also increased with inheritance of individuals condemned and executed for treason as well.[45] He controlled Rome's public treasury as well, as the *Pater Patriae*.[46]

The mechanism for the control of those state accounts shifted into a bureaucracy under Augustus' direct control, by a staff of his slaves and ex-slaves, part of the *familia caesaris*.[47] Members of the *familia caesaris* also administered substantial imperial holdings, vast estates and mines and much of the civic administration of the provinces that were under direct imperial control.[48] Under later emperors, this bureaucracy increased and administered many civic institutions, from aqueducts to libraries.[49] There were benefits to being part of this retinue of slaves and freedmen, and antiquarians and academics became incorporated as well, including one of the librarians on the Palatine, Gaius Melissus, who rejected his free birth status to be part of the *familia caesaris*.[50]

In her traditional role as *materfamilias*, now with the empire as her household, Augustus' wife Livia also oversaw a large personal staff and managed extensive business interests that gave her influence, in addition to her role as her husband's advisor.[51] She also managed the familial international relations in her role.[52] Augustus' male relatives increasingly controlled the military.[53]

Augustus made the empire not just a metaphorical Roman Strict Father family but a quite literal one. With his wife and close family at

his side and his retinue of slaves and freedmen as his staff, he administered the empire as his own *domus.* Just as a *domus* passed from one
generation to the next, succession for control of the empire began to
pass by inheritance as well. Augustus' family and his "restoration" of
the family was placed on center stage as the inauguration of the new
"Golden Age" that began with his rule.

Pax Romana and the Golden Age

In the image promulgated by the poets and writers and artists who
championed the cause of Augustus, a Golden Age dawned with
Augustus in a Pax Romana after a century of civil strife. The Golden
Age represented a new configuration of the Roman republic, the
one-man rule we view in retrospect as the empire. Family images
are essential in the image of the Pax Romana and the campaign to
promote the Golden Age. Augustus replaced images that glorified
his military victories with images of religious renewal, as part of his
effort to remove images of Octavian.[54] Images evoking peace and
stability, family harmony (*concordia*), and devotion to deities and
parents (*pietas*), portrayed the Augustan victory.

The Ara Pacis Augustae, the Augustan Altar of Peace, commissioned by the Roman Senate after Augustus returned from pacifying
Spain and Gaul was constructed starting in 13 and dedicated in 9
BCE.[55] The Ara Pacis provided an emblem for the Golden Age that
displays family imagery.

A prominent panel on the screen that surrounds the altar displays
the so-called Tellus relief mentioned above in the discussion of the
materfamilias in chapter 4. A deity with several possible identifications in addition to Tellus as the earth, she is seated with her chubby
infants on her lap surrounded by symbols of abundance, cultivated
plants and domesticated animals and flanked by figures representing
the winds.[56] Whether or not she should be identified as another deity, the image conveys the Pax to which the altar is dedicated and the
importance of the mother in that Pax.[57]

Many of the other images depict members of Augustus' own family, human and divine.[58] His ancestors are portrayed, Aeneas in the
posture of sacrifice with his son assisting, in one panel, and Aeneas'
descendants Romulus and Remus, the founders of Rome, as infants

suckled by the she-wolf.[59] On either side, the screen depicts processions that display priests and the members of Augustus' family portrayed in idealized forms, along with representatives of Rome's dependent allies as part of the family. They move together toward the sacrifice at the altar that Augustus will offer in imitation of his ancestor Aeneas.[60] The Ara Pacis, then, celebrates the abundant life of peace of the Golden Age won by military victories and places family life and Augustus' own family at the heart of that peace.

The victory presented as achieving this Golden Age involved more than the military victory at Actium and the restoration of peace after the civil wars, however. The moral victory, a victory over "sin," was central. Vergil and Horace, for example, portrayed the image of Augustus ushering in the Golden Age and the need for Augustus to expiate and abolish "sin" (*scelus*).[61] For Romans, *scelus* was an offense that would bring down the wrath of the gods if not expiated in the proper ceremony and if the offense were not eliminated. Before the victory at Actium, attention focused on civil strife as the central "sin." As Augustus began to consolidate the peace, adultery moved into view as the central "sin" at the root of Rome's problems, especially in Horace's propaganda poetry.[62] The propagandists cited neglect of the traditional Roman morals and religious customs as the cause of Rome's troubles.[63] Augustus addressed the rampant societal "sin" (*scelus*) of adultery as one element of a more general program of family legislation that was supposed to restore Roman family values, in his fatherly disciplinary role, as we will see in the next chapter.[64]

Conclusion

Augustus became the sole ruler of the Roman Empire without becoming a king, a role odious to the Romans, by instead ascending to rule as Rome's *paterfamilias*. We have seen how he assumed titles to shape this role, after having won both a military conflict and a propaganda battle that concluded a century of civil war. His position as the *Pater Patriae* was more than an honorific title, however, and indicates not only his self-identification but also his project to reshape the empire as his family.

8

Discipline in the Family Empire

"Back" in your places, everyone!

Augustus provided the Romans with a vision for the restoration of the republic. When his victory at Actium concluded the civil war, he relinquished his dictatorial powers and restored the republican institutions to a semblance of functionality. His vision, however, was for moral restoration, a return to the traditional Roman values of the sectors of society that provided Rome's soldiers. The Golden Age was to be one of traditional discipline, discipline and tradition as he defined it. This moral campaign included his family legislation and efforts to make the stratification of society more visible, as an expression of the value of *pietas*.

Augustan Family Legislation

Augustus mentioned the family legislation among his accomplishments in the *Res Gestae*, briefly praising the laws as a "restoration" of the ways of the ancestors:

> By new laws passed on my proposal I brought back into use many exemplary practices of our ancestors which were disappearing in our time, and in many ways I myself transmitted exemplary practices to posterity for their imitation.[1]

Poetic propagandists of the Augustan "Golden Age" lauded the legislation more extensively. For example, Horace, in a poem written

during Augustus' absence from Rome after the legislation was enacted, extolled the purification of the Roman *domus*:

> The chaste family (*domus*) is polluted by no adulteries (*stu-*
> *prum*/sexual misconduct): morality and the law have got the
> better of that foul crime; the child-bearing women are com-
> mended for an offspring resembling [the father; and] punish-
> ment presses as a companion upon guilt. (*Odes* 4.5)[2]

Horace bemoaned the absence of Augustus professedly to subdue
Gaul and Spain. Cassius Dio interpreted his absence as "skipping
town" after aggravating the populous with this legislation and its
capricious enforcement. He also noted suspicions that Augustus' departure had been motivated by his desire to violate his own legislation in an adulterous liaison with Terentia, the wife of his close friend
and political advisor Maecenas.[3] Not everyone was convinced of the
benefits of the legislation.

Augustus apparently made a first failed attempt at legislation on
marriage and adultery in 29 BCE shortly after his victory at Actium.[4]
Writers who supported Augustus' efforts beat the drum to bewail
Rome's declining moral state and promoted action to "return"
Rome to its "traditional" values. For example, in his introduction
to his account of Rome's history, an account intended to elevate its
readers' morals with tales of Rome's glorious origins, Livy laments
its moral decline:

> Here are the questions to which I would have every reader give
> his close attention—what life and morals were like; through
> what men and by what policies, in peace and in war, empire was
> established and enlarged; then let him note how, with the grad-
> ual relaxation of discipline, morals first gave way, as it were, then
> sank lower and lower, and finally began the downward plunge
> which has brought us to the present time, when we can endure
> neither our vices nor their cure.[5]

Like the republic that Augustus supposedly restored, the values he
promoted as traditional were his own version of a Roman Strict
Father family that was also the Roman state. Augustus succeeded
in his second effort to pass his "family values" legislation regulating

sexual activity with new laws on marriage and adultery enacted in 18 BCE and later modified in 9 CE. In his own account, he instead passed morality legislation at the request of the Senate using his tribunician powers, by the affirmation of the common people.[6]

To celebrate the advent of the new Golden Age and the enactment of the family legislation, in 17 BCE Augustus revived the Secular Games, traditionally an event held once a century to mark a new era.[7] The days of festivities included sacrifices to Greek and Roman deities, theatrical performances, and chariot races. Horace wrote his "Secular Hymn" (*Carmen Saeculare*) to be sung by choirs of children at this event, including stanzas asking the goddess to bring the decrees of the family legislation to fruition with children:

> Goddess, bring forth our young and
> prosper the decrees of the fathers concerning marriage
> with women and the nuptial law productive
> of new life.
>
> So that the certain cycle through ten times eleven years
> will bring back songs and games
> crowded in for three clear days and as many times
> in welcome night.[8]

The family legislation was of central importance in the Augustan vision of an enduring regeneration and restoration of traditional virtues that would bring peace and prosperity.[9] "Make Rome Great Again," could have been his slogan.

Provisions of the Legislation

The content of the legislation has been reassembled from references to the laws by writers of the time and from later legal digests that incorporate provisions in the legislation, and from records of case law.[10]

Law on Adultery
(*Lex Julia de adulteriis coercendis & Lex Poppia Poppaea*)

The new law criminalized adultery and established a legal procedure for prosecuting adultery similar to criminal proceedings for violent crimes.[11] The double standard in Roman sexual mores described in chapter 6 were given the force of law in the definition of adultery.

Adultery was defined as sexual intercourse between a married woman and a man who was not her husband. A married man committed adultery only in intercourse with a married woman. He could legally have intercourse with any male who was not freeborn, with any woman who was not married or a concubine of another man, or with a woman who ran a business or shop.[12] The law required a husband to divorce an adulterous wife, but the wife of an adulterous husband had no legal recourse under the laws of the Augustan era.[13] The husband, or his wife's father, had sixty days to bring a formal accusation of adultery, first against the man involved, and if he was convicted, against the wife.[14] A husband who did not divorce and prosecute an adulterous wife was liable for charges of pimping.[15]

The law also delineated the circumstances in which it was legal for a father or husband to kill an adulterer. The pair had to be found in the act and in the home of the husband or the father. The woman's father was permitted to kill them both but was required to kill both or neither. The woman's husband could kill her paramour but not his own wife.[16] Punishments were also specified in the law, including exile to separate islands and large financial penalties. The law prohibited a woman convicted from remarrying a freeborn Roman.[17] Women convicted of adultery could no longer wear the *stola* that signified their status as a Roman matron but were obliged to wear the *toga* of a prostitute.[18]

With the law on adultery, an offense against Roman *mores* previously addressed within the household at the discretion of the *paterfamilias* now became a matter of public law with a prescribed procedure known as a *quaestio perpetua*. What had been a matter for a family council now became a concern of state institutions.

Law on Marriage
(Lex Julia de maritandis ordinibus)

A law on marriage was enacted along with the law on adultery. Just as the new legislation introduced the criminalization of adultery, the marriage legislation introduced unprecedented legal inducements for marriage and legitimate procreation.

For the unmarried and childless, the law instituted restrictions on inheriting and bequeathing wealth and excluded them from public festivals.[19] For freeborn parents of three or more children, the law provided privileges, known as the *ius trium liberorum*. The fathers were given easier access to political offices while the mothers attained more autonomy.[20] Those who were married with children sat in the best seats at public events.[21] Freed people benefited from having children as well. A freedman with two or more legitimate children could be released from obligations he had sworn to his patron, and a freedwoman could gain release from her patron's guardianship and manage her own financial affairs after she bore a fourth legitimate child.[22]

Marriage became mandatory. This requirement applied to men between the ages of twenty-five and sixty and women between twenty and fifty. Men were required to remarry within six months after a divorce or widowhood, women within a year.[23] For women this contradicted the traditional ideal of marriage to only one husband in a lifetime, the *univira*. Financial sanctions in the form of restrictions on inheritances enforced compliance.

The law also delineated how members of each class could or could not form a legal marriage. Members of senatorial families could not marry freedmen or freedwomen, for example.[24] Freeborn males could not form a legal marriage with

[... a prostitute,] a procuress, a woman manumitted by a procurer or procuress, a woman taken in adultery, a woman condemned in a public court, and any woman who has formerly practiced the stage profession. ...[25]

Marriage below one's rank was discouraged, and the legislation enforced a distinction between women who could legally marry and women who could not.

Compliance was enforced by rewards for reporting violations. Snitches could receive a quarter of the inheritance of the person they accused.[26] Getting the population to control one another's moral behavior appears to have been one of the purposes of the legislation.

Purposes of the Legislation

Other motivations have been discerned. Tacitus indicates that the failed purpose of the legislation was to increase the rates of marriage and childbearing.[27] Encouragement of larger families, especially among the upper classes, remained a governmental concern, and the legislation remained in place.[28] The family legislation also helped Augustus gain greater control of the elites, subjecting them to greater state control by making love affairs into public crimes and transferring these family matters into public jurisdiction.[29]

The main purpose lay in the overall program of moral and cultural renewal for the Golden Age. Augustus and his supporters promoted the legislation to address the declining moral state of Rome, its immoral decadence. Among the Roman upper classes in the last generation of the republic, a new set of values focused on pleasure and cultural sophistication had developed, characterized as "a certain flamboyance of behavior."[30] Divorce, adultery, and choosing not to have children were accepted aspects of this new way of life among the urban elites.[31] The Augustan family legislation was promoted as an effort to get these "Dionysian" members of the elite to be more Apollonian and responsible.[32]

For men, the Augustan program emphasized the importance of marriage and the value of having children and paying attention to family life, a kind of Roman "Promise-Keepers" movement, if you will. Men were encouraged to live for more than their own pleasure and to instead take social responsibility for families and children. The legislation was intended to restore the moral fiber of elite Roman men.

The legislation also targeted women for control. One factor may have been the age difference at marriage that meant both that adolescent women were married to older men and that they attained an adult status at a young age. The atmosphere of sexual freedom in the last generation of the republic may have given more active outlets for the natural interest in sexual exploration characteristic of such young women, and marriage gave them more adult freedoms and access to social settings in which to pursue their interests.[33] Criminalizing adultery endeavored to control Roman wives' sexuality just as giving benefits for having children was an effort to gain state control of their reproductive capabilities.

The legislation helped to implement the Augustan vision of a Roman moral revival, part of the imperial ideology of Roman moral superiority and its attendant obligation and responsibility to rule the world.

Results of the Legislation

The legislation met with opposition. Ovid, as the "teacher of hideous adultery," mocked the legislation and the ideal image of the chaste Roman wife, and he ended up in exile.[34] Suetonius noted the general outrage, that the people were completely against submitting to the laws and described a scene the equestrian order made in the theater to agitate for complete abolition of the laws. Augustus had responded by making a display of his family as an example, with Augustus and his son Germanicus holding the grandchildren on their laps.[35]

Many of Augustus' contemporaries and later commentators perceived the legislation as a state intrusion into domestic life. A century later, Tacitus described its effects:

> Meanwhile there was an increase in the number of persons imperiled, for every household was undermined by the insinuations of informers; and now the country suffered from its laws, as it had hitherto suffered from its vices.[36]

The legislation made Romans fear their neighbors. We saw in chapter 3 that the Roman *domus* was becoming a public space and a place of display, a display not only of prosperity and luxury but also of virtue. Under the public scrutiny instigated by the family legislation, the display of virtue became even more important. The display included the male virtues, the *virtus* and *auctoritas* of the *paterfamilias*, and the female virtues, the *pudicitia* of his wife and daughters.

The virtue of the elite women was key. The focus on adultery as *scelus*, as sin that affects the body politic, made elite women's bodies a state religious issue. Their sexual purity was needed to maintain the Roman people's good relationship with their deities and thus to maintain the peace and prosperity of the empire. *Pudicitia* was in some senses a privilege of elite women, but their privilege was also a sign of their status as an extension of their husband. Their sexual loyalty to their husbands was required not just for the sake of their marriages and their self-preservation from dire consequences but also for the sake of the well-being of the Roman family empire. Their virtue was on display not only for their neighbors but for the deities.

Other women's lack of *pudicitia* was just as important. The legislation also encoded a category of non-elite women as not subject to the laws of adultery, women with whom men could have sexual relations without committing a sexual offense defined by the law, but women who could not be legally married. This meant that there were two categories of women, one pure and the other, presumably, polluted.

Some women of the upper classes actively resisted this categorization by enrolling as prostitutes.[37] Tacitus relates that the Senate responded by making this option illegal for women of the senatorial classes, and gives the example of Vistilia who was banished to an island for her action.[38] This practice of resistance apparently continued into the reign of Tiberius as well.[39]

Augustus' own daughter Julia provided the most prominent resistance, however, with her blatant adulterous affairs during the marriages her father arranged for her, most notably to his close confidant Agrippa and to Tiberius who would succeed him as emperor. The record hints at a counter-ideology behind Julia's affairs, a movement of resistance to Augustus' moral vision.[40] She was, in any case, flamingly unexemplary of her father's moral vision. In 2 BCE, Augustus exiled Julia to show that his own family was not above the law he had instituted. Her defiant wit in opposition to her father and his moral vision was remembered sympathetically, however. An early fifth-century author tells about her response to those who marveled that her sons resembled her husband Agrippa despite her well-known adulteries, "Why, I never take on passengers until the hold is full," she reportedly quipped.[41] The preserved image of Julia is one of her wittily defiant sexuality.

Julia and the elite women who resisted the restrictions on their sexuality broke one of the boundaries that the Augustan program was attempting to enforce between marriageable women and sexually available, non-marriageable women—a boundary more difficult to break from the other direction, of course. The encoding of such categories was a significant aspect of the program to bring an Augustan vision of order to the family empire.

Yet the legislation also provided new benefits for elite women. Women whose financial resources were being managed by a guardian (*tutela*) could gain control of their wealth by having three children or by an individual dispensation from the emperor. This created a significant group of wealthy widows who used their wealth to project their own identities in public life by sponsoring temples and public works and associations, with the accompanying inscriptions to laud their generosity.[42]

Rules for Displaying Social Stratification

Along with the family legislation came stricter enforcement and new standards in the Roman "dress code." For male citizens, increasingly elaborate white togas became required apparel at the Roman forum and in the theater. Putting on the toga was a laborious procedure, and the garment was uncomfortable and hard to keep clean, but the toga was a sign of *Romanitas*. Augustus himself is said to have publicly shamed citizens wearing their dark everyday clothing at a public event, quoting Vergil: "Look, the Romans, masters of the world, people of the toga."[43] Roman male citizens were strongly encouraged and even required to wear the toga to display both their own citizenship and Roman superiority.

Upstanding Roman matrons were entitled to wear the *stola*, a modest outer garment with wide straps at the shoulder for "protection from unwanted attentions."[44] The plain stola and the woolen fillet wound in the hair symbolized modesty unlike the "elegant gowns of transparent fabric" that were the preferred fashion of elite women.[45]

The toga and stola were signs of social rank, however, and the enforced change of fashion was intended to display the coming of a new age of Roman morality.[46]

The social stratification that was part of the family legislation was also reflected in the building of theaters and arenas for public spectacles, as well as in legislation specifying the seating to be constructed and arrangements for orders and tribes in theaters and

arenas. Suetonius offered a detailed description of the effort to correct the "confusion and disorder" of seating in the stands at public
events.[47] An incident in which no one would yield a theater seat for a
senator instigated a decree from the Senate that required seats to be
left empty for senators. Another incident that indicates some intentional subversion, slaves impersonating foreign dignitaries, justified
the exclusion even of distinguished foreign visitors from senatorial
seating. The additional specifications created new seating arrangements that marginalized and excluded women and displayed the entire social order:

> He separated the soldiery from the rest of the people, and as-
> signed to married plebeians their particular rows of seats. To
> the boys he assigned their own benches, and to their tutors the
> seats which were nearest it; ordering that none clothed in black
> should sit in the centre of the circle. Nor would he allow any
> women to witness the combats of the gladiators, except from
> the upper part of the theatre, although they formerly used to
> take their places promiscuously with the rest of the spectators.
> To the vestal virgins he granted seats in the theatre, reserved for
> them only, opposite the praetor's bench. He excluded however,
> the whole female sex from seeing the wrestlers: so that in the
> games which he exhibited upon his accession to the office of
> high-priest, he deferred producing a pair of combatants which
> the people called for, until the next morning; and intimated by
> proclamation, "his pleasure that no woman should appear in the
> theatre before five o'clock."[48]

The building program made social stratification more visible than
it had been. Traditional family values meant getting everyone "back"
into their places. When members of Roman society, from the senators to the slaves, attended spectacles, they knew their assigned place
and the structure of society was visibly arrayed. The seating structure
in the amphitheaters constructed across the empire for the distinctively Roman spectacles that included gladiatorial combat cast this
societal hierarchy in stone.[49]

The largest of these arenas for the bloody Roman spectacles,
the Flavian amphitheater referred to as the Colosseum, for exam-

ple, architecturally manifested on a gigantic scale the stratification that Augustus had envisioned as the Roman order of the world, the Roman family. A box for the emperor and his family had a central place, and front-row seating was established for senators, with a special section for the Vestal Virgins. The next rows belonged to the equestrian order with stands for men in various social categories behind. Slaves and women had their places in the uppermost seating areas. In the stands of the arena, then, the Roman Strict Father family empire was displayed.

A podium wall divided the spectacle on the sands from the spectators. The spectacle was the distinctively Roman form that began in the morning with the display and mass killing of wild animals, followed by a program of imaginatively cruel modes of killing convicted criminals and captives from Rome's conquests, culminating in the afternoon program of gladiatorial combat. Viewing the violent display on the sands united the spectators above the wall with the re-enactment of Roman victory taking place before them. From the white rows of togas in the seats at the front to the slaves far up in the "nosebleed" seating, they were all part of the Roman family household in seeing the destruction of threats to their world order. The ritual of the Roman arena enacted a "public cognitive system," the populus contemplating and uniting in their Roman imperial identity.

The victory enacted in the arena was repeated for public consumption on coins and on monumental public art across the empire, as well as in the triumph parades that followed each Roman victory over newly subjugated peoples.[50] The Roman versions appropriated visual themes from previous monumental depictions of civilization defeating the forces of chaos on, for example, the Athenian Parthenon and Pergamon Altar.

Conclusion

The victorious Roman family empire displayed in the arena is the same one portrayed on the *Gemma Augustea*. On the sands, the defeat of the barbarian threat in the lower register of the *Gemma*, the defeat of chaos, is enacted. Above the line, above the podium wall, the forces of order can congratulate themselves as they view the destruction of threats to their order. They can identify with the

Roman victory and the victor Augustus and participate in the divine
blessings bestowed on them as Romans, the natural rulers of the
world. As we have seen, the moral ordering of the society above the
line was also a part of victory, a moral ordering that displayed the
honor of the *paterfamilias* and his household. The imperial cults
offered another way for them to participate in Roman victory and
commune with its celestial sponsors, the members of the Roman
family of deities.

9

Inclusion in
the Family Empire

"The family that prays together stays together."

From Christian martyr stories, we may be accustomed to understanding the imperial cult, in the singular, as a loyalty test enforced from the top down: "Sacrifice to the Emperor, or else!" Yet the cult was really cults, as local elites initiated their own ways to pay homage to the emperor in worship. The cults functioned as a complex and evolving synthesis of local and central initiatives and offered opportunities for a significant number of people to connect to the emperor and his family and his successors. Participation in the imperial cults was a way to be included in the imperial family and in the power of Rome, in a familial imperial relationship.

The imperial cults were widespread, more expansive than other ruler cults had been, and permeated the cultural life of the empire, at least in the Hellenized or Romanized urbanized areas.[1] Cult temples appeared in prominent locations in cities across the empire. Eighty are counted in sixty cities in Asia Minor, for example.[2] Devotion to the cult appeared in daily life even far from Rome in shrines in the *gymnasia,* in private homes and associations, and even in curses to protect graves.[3]

The imperial cults took hold by a process that was much more complex than mere projection of propaganda, a process that incorporated local traditions and welcomed local initiatives. The cult at

Rome developed as an extended domestic cult, in the model of the Strict Father *domus*. Before discussing that development more extensively, however, we should note that in Asia Minor, it developed as a ruler cult.[4] Augustus' male family members who commanded armies in the western provinces also transferred the eastern ruler cult form there, where it took on a more militarized aspect.[5]

Ruler cults had emerged in the Greek cities of Asia Minor as a means for Greek citizens to cope with subjection to external powers.[6] The ruler cults were modeled on cults of deities rather than the Greek cults of deceased heroes. Using the model of the deities meant that rulers were worshipped not as citizens elevated to hero status after death but as living deities who were more present and accessible than the celestial ones.[7] As deities, the rulers became approachable in worship and ritual.

A variety of cults of Roman power also emerged in the eastern provinces before the imperial cult. Cults to Roma as a deity were widespread in Greece and Asia Minor, and cults to the "People of the Romans," to "universal Roman benefactors" collectively, and to individual Roman officials were known.[8] Explicit household imagery was associated with a cult at Athens where there was a "priestess of the Hearth of the Romans."[9]

In the development of the cults, aspects of the Roman household, eastern ruler cults, and western military piety intermingled as the family model of the empire spread more widely and members of the imperial family were offered devotion as well. The imperial cults formed an empire-wide family.

In Rome and Italy, the ruler cult form seemed to be more problematic initially. Worship of Augustus as a deity did not fit well in his program of restoration of the republic or with his identity as "first citizen." He could be the son of a god, yet he refused direct worship as a deity at Rome.[10] Just as his role as *Pater Patriae* allowed him to become the sole monarchic ruler of the family empire without assuming a monarchical title, assuming the priestly role of the *paterfamilias* of the empire allowed him, primarily in the form of his *genius*, to be the central focus of the family empire's worship. He was a monarch without being a king, and he was divine and a focus of cult worship without being precisely a god. Just as the assembly of the members of the *domus* to offer devotions to the *genius* of the *paterfamilias* expressed a "public cognitive system" of relationships and power dynamics in the household, the imperial cult wrote that "public cognitive system" large as the family system of the empire.

Augustus as the Focus of the Imperial Cult
Paterfamilias and Priest

As the *pater patriae* of the Roman family empire, Augustus was the focus of the Roman family empire's cult. When he became Rome's chief priest as the *pontifex maximus* in 12 BCE, Augustus gained powers over the Roman religious apparatus. By 16 BCE he already held office in all of Rome's priestly colleges, a first since it had been unusual for anyone to hold more than one priesthood.[11]

By this time, men other than the emperor were rarely portrayed on a Roman public monument as a priest offering sacrifice.[12] The image of Augustus wearing a toga with his head covered, in the posture of sacrificing, now became ubiquitous, however. This image of his *genius* was the image he preferred be spread.[13] In this posture of the *genius,* he displayed the core traditional family value of *pietas,* showing obedience and devotion to the deities above him as a demonstration of how each member of the societal family should act toward those above them. Augustus' *genius* thus became the guardian spirit, the mysterious power (*numen*) of the Roman family empire, and like the *genius* in the household shrine, the image took its place with other deities in shrines and temples across the empire. The whole Empire could thus show devotion to this *genius* of the *Pater Patriae,* the father of the fatherland, and imitate his *pietas.* All of them could now look to his *genius* as their own father and thus be united as a family in their devotion. Elite male heads of household would also look to his *genius* and see their own *genius* images writ large. Through this image, they would identify themselves as little emperors in their own households, aspiring to emulate his *auctoritas.* The empire was one family made of many smaller families in the imperial pattern, and the empire was a family in the pattern of those smaller families—macrocosm and microcosm unified in symbiosis.

Imperial Cults as Domestic Religion
Writ Large and Small

The formation of the imperial cults in Rome and Italy was patterned after and connected to household worship, based on Augustus' priestly role as Rome's *paterfamilias.*

Roman Religion and Imperial Cults
in the Pattern of Worship in the *Domus*

The domestic religion at the household shrine and the hearth was already writ large in Roman public religious observance. In the temple of Vesta, select daughters of Rome's elites tended her fire, Rome's hearth, as the Vestal Virgins. In the forum, the ancient shrine of Janus, the deity of the doors to the house, held special significance for Rome. The doors of the shrine of Janus were symbolically left open when Rome was at war and closed when Rome was at peace, a rare occurrence. By his own account, Augustus closed the doors three times "when victories had secured peace by land and sea through the whole empire of the Roman people."[14]

The Roman state had its own *Penates* and *Lares* as well. The Dioscuri, the twin deities Castor and Pollux, were the *Penates* of the state and "protected the hegemony of Rome" just as their domestic counterparts protected the household storeroom.[15] The state had *Lares* as guardians as well, the *Lares praestites*, who oversaw the maintenance of the imperial cult.[16]

The addition of the imperial cults created a public observance of the devotion of each *paterfamilias* and his household to his *genius.* In the imperial cult, the Roman citizenry gave devotion to the *genius* of the Father of the Fatherland.

Imperial Cult as Cult of Augustus' Own Family

Not only were the cults modeled after Roman household devotions, they were structured as extensions of the domestic cult of Augustus' own household. Through the cult, Romans quite literally became part of Augustus' own Strict Father family household.

When Augustus became *pontifex maximus*, he did not move his residence to the one near the temple of Vesta reserved for this officeholder. Instead he established a shrine of Vesta as a public space within his own residence on the Palatine hill and placed his own family deities there. He also moved the deities that were believed to have been brought from Troy from the temple of Vesta to the hearth in his home. His home's hearth fire thus became the hearth fire of Rome.[17]

Augustus restructured the city of Rome into fourteen districts and 265 wards. The wards had cult organizations with shrines at the crossroads, a revived and revised cult of the *Lares Compitales.* Formerly a location for social unrest, the ward organizations now became a stabilizing force as extensions of Augustus' own domestic cult, with images of the *Lares Augusti*, the deities known from the household shrines, perhaps best understood as his ancestors, and the image of his *genius*.[18] The cults also had altars dedicated "to the August Lares and the genius of Caesar [Augustus]."[19] Rituals depicted are mostly rituals associated with domestic cults, with the exception of the addition of blood sacrifices of bulls, indicating the intertwining of family and state religious forms.[20]

These cults were one of the avenues for inclusion that the imperial cults offered, in this case to well-off freedmen. Many of the local leaders (*magistri*) were freedmen, assisted by slaves in cult roles.[21] With this innovation, Augustus not only created a new and attractive social position for these freedmen but made himself their patron and thus put himself in direct competition with their former masters.[22] For these freedmen, the imperial cults offered status, advancement, and a measure of relative independence.

Augustus also expanded other cult opportunities. The Arval Brotherhood, twelve men responsible for rituals associated with agricultural productivity, rituals much like the family rituals of Roman farmers, were given a higher profile.[23] Outside Rome, primarily in Italy and the western provinces, the Augustales also provided hundreds of cult organizations (*collegia*) in which wealthy freedmen participated.[24] In the east, priesthoods offered high-status civic roles to both men and women.[25] Such cult organizations opened participation in Augustus' family cult to new social sectors.

The *genius* of Augustus thus became accessible to the general population for devotion and appeals for protection in every

neighborhood of Rome and in temples and shrines across the empire.
Many Romans did not even need to leave the *domus* to participate
in the cult as figurines of Augustus' *genius* were included in their
household shrines.[26] They poured libations to him at both public and
private banquets.[27] The imperial cults were everywhere, and everyone became part of the *domus* of Augustus in devotion to his *genius*.

The Roman sacred calendar began to reflect days important for
Augustus' own family cult, and events on the state calendar became merged with events important for his own family celebrations.
Inscribed calendars from towns in Italy show this, listing anniversary
dates of important events in the life of Augustus and his family to
be celebrated with a specified ritual prayer (*supplication*) as a family ritual rather than a public one.[28] Changes in the calendar across
the empire reflected this incorporation of religious practice into
Augustus' own domestic cult.

Rather than coming from a central authority, the transformation
of the calendar was often initiated by cult participants, often provincial elites. One example is a decree from 9 CE from the provincial
council of the province of Asia that reorders the calendar itself to
start the year on Augustus' birthday. An excerpt is telling:

> Decree of the Greek Assembly in the province of Asia, on mo-
> tion of the High Priest Apollonios, son of Menophilos, of
> Aizanoi:
>
> WHEREAS Providence that orders all our lives has in her display of
> concern and generosity in our behalf adorned our lives with the
> highest good:
>
> AUGUSTUS, whom she has filled with virtue for the benefit of
> humanity, and has in her beneficence granted us and those who
> will come after us [a Savior] who has made war to cease and who
> shall put everything [in peaceful] order; and whereas Caesar,
> [when he was manifest], transcended the expectations of [all
> who had anticipated the good news], not only by surpassing the
> benefits conferred by his predecessors but by leaving no expecta-
> tion of surpassing him to those who would come after him, with
> the result that the birthday of our God signaled the beginning of
> Good News for the world because of him . . .[29]

Such local initiatives were a major aspect of the cults especially in the eastern provinces. Far from being imposed from the top down, the cults made room for initiatives from provincial elites and socially aspiring sectors of the population to create monuments and rituals to honor the emperor.[30]

Inclusion in Augustus' family cult also meant the inclusion of members of Augustus' family as recipients of devotion in the cult. Augustus' wife Livia was especially important both before and after his death. Just as the presentation of Augustus in the form of his *genius* was the ideal of the *paterfamilias*, the ideal of the Roman matron appeared in the form of his wife Livia, honored with statues, temples, and birthday celebrations.[31] Other family members received devotion as well as the "Augustan gods" (*Divi Augusti* or the *Theoi Sebastoi*).[32]

The marriage of Augustus and Livia "renowned for its affectionate quality and for their political partnership"[33] also became a matter for religious devotion in the shrine of Concordia. As a concept, Concordia included both marital and civic harmony. As we have seen above, the ideology that promoted Augustus' family legislation assumed that the peace and prosperity of the Roman people depended on upholding marriage and that marital and civic harmony were inseparable.

In honor of their harmonious marriage, Livia built a shrine dedicated to Concordia to present to her husband. The shrine stood on the grounds of what had been a huge luxurious private residence bequeathed to Augustus.[34] The destruction of the luxurious home to build the shrine to marital and civic harmony displayed their marital virtues as well. With this shrine, Livia connected what had traditionally been a public, "political object of worship," civic Concordia, with the previously more private matter of marriage.[35]

Temple-Building
Augustus and the Celestial Family

For Augustus, restoration of the republic and of traditional family values also meant a religious revival. Even though domestic devotions were maintained, public religion had been neglected during the time of the civil wars.[36] Many of the public temples had fallen into disrepair, and Augustus engaged in a program of rebuilding and restoration of the physical abodes of the deities. His attention to the deities showed his *pietas*.

In his account of his many building projects, Augustus names fourteen of the temples he restored or built and mentions a count of eighty-two restored in his sixth consulship alone.[37] Augustus took charge of what had previously been an opportunity for senators to display their wealth and piety. Now only Augustus and his family constructed temples at Rome and thus displayed "a unique relationship with the gods."[38]

This special relationship stands out as well in the temples constructed. During the Augustan period and just after, all the state temples referred to the emperor. Temples to the God Julius and the God Augustus attested to the imperial family's familial divinity. Temples to Apollo, Neptune, and Mars Ultor celebrated the emperor's military victories. Temples to Concordia and Iustitia emphasized imperial virtues, and the temple of Jupiter Tonans was a thank-offering for Augustus' escape from a thunderbolt.[39]

New imperial associations were added to older temples that were restored or built at new locations. Temples for Mars and Apollo were constructed within Rome's sacred boundary for the first time. A temple of Mars the Avenger that visually dominated the new Augustan forum completed Augustus' vow upon the defeat of his father's assassins and commemorated the retrieval of Roman standards from the Parthians, avenging Rome's honor. The whole forum displayed Augustus' piety and his relationship to the deities through the ancestors, Romulus and Aeneas.[40] Near his home on the Palatine, Augustus also built a new temple to Apollo adjacent to his own residence, bringing the god within Rome's sacred boundary for the first time. Reliefs on the temple show Apollo's role in the defeat of Mark Antony and Cleopatra.

Augustus twice rebuilt the temple of the Magna Mater (the Great Mother, Cybele), the imported Phrygian goddess credited with the salvation of Rome in the second Punic war (218 to 201 BCE), whose cults will be discussed in chapter 12. Her temple on the Palatine Hill near Augustus' own residence was rebuilt in tufa, the soft stone used for Rome's early temples, to emphasize her ancient origins.

Augustan era poets Ovid and Vergil associated her Phrygian origins
and the legend of the Trojan origins of Rome so she became symbolic of Rome's proud ancestry.[41]

On the Palatine, then, Augustus resided amidst the celestial family. Vesta was present in Rome's hearth fire inside his home. Apollo
had a home in an adjacent temple, and the Magna Mater was also
close by.

Augustus displayed his piety and renewed the image of the deities
at Rome as part of the entire building project. His unique relationship with the deities was familial. As the son of a god with a *genius*
receiving devotion among the deities, Augustus took his place in the
celestial Strict Father family headed by Jupiter/Zeus as the *paterfamilias*. As the earthly *pater patriae*, he was the stand-in for Jupiter.
The representation in the *Gemma Augustae* shows this equation. Yet
at Rome, he displayed his *pietas* as a dutiful son in the celestial family,
showing honor to the deities above him in the hierarchical order by
building temples to them.

The Roman celestial family was large and inclusive. Romans offered devotion to a wide variety of divine beings, from the great gods
associated with the Greek Olympian deities to the spirits of various
places, virtues, and abstract qualities. Over the course of the next
centuries, temples of deities from the territories Rome conquered
joined the Roman deities with temples in the city, and temples to
deified emperors and members of the imperial family joined the array
at Rome and across the empire.

The arrangement of temples and the placement of deities within
temples expressed familial relationships in the celestial family. These
varied from place to place, but the inclusion of statues of the emperor and his family and shrines to them in temples to other deities
across the empire indicates their inclusion in the celestial family in
a complex web of relationship among deities with distinct roles and
virtues centered on the divine *paterfamilias*, Jupiter/Zeus. For example, the temple to the Mother of the Gods at Olympia in Greece
was filled with imperial cult images.[42]

An example of the empire's projection of the relationship of the
imperial family and the celestial one in Roman victory can be found
in the relief on the Antonine altar at Ephesus, a monument which

"encapsulates ... many themes of empire," including "the centrality of the emperor and his family, the importance of warfare and victory for the whole empire, and the intimacy between members of the imperial house and the gods."[43] The emperor's final destination after death was also portrayed as enthronement in heaven.[44]

Conclusion

In the Augustan era, then, the Roman Empire became a family as a sacral unit as the introduction of the imperial cults created a means of inclusion.

Conclusion to Part III

Augustus became the sole ruler of the Roman Empire based on his role as Rome's *pater pateriae*, Father of the Fatherland. In the process, he also reshaped the empire as a Roman Strict Father family, a model he also promoted. His strategy went beyond the use of the family model as a metaphor, however. His own family, his own *domus*, became the Roman state. He became a *paterfamilias* to all of Rome's population not just figuratively, not just as a root metaphor, but literally as his *domus*.

In Part 3 we have seen that Augustus' ascent to his fatherly role in the empire and his shaping of the empire as his family were part and parcel of the same process. His responsibility for family discipline in his fatherly role was also part of his strategy for repairing relations with the deities the family honored. We have seen as well that his role as the family's priest shaped the Roman family empire's religious life in imperial cults that offered a means of inclusion to unite the family empire, like the family in the Roman *domus*, in devotion to his *genius*.

Emotional relationships in this family empire were as complex as those of the *domus*, and even more multi-layered. While Augustus and his successors shaped the Roman Empire as a household, we would be incorrect in envisioning it as "one big happy family."

Part IV

Movements of Resistance and Endurance

Chapter 2 introduced the notion of the public and the hidden transcript and the variety of strategies that subordinated people use to resist in situations of disproportionate power. In chapter 3 we saw some images of family groupings from Phrygia in what would be an involuntarily hidden transcript had there not been materials and an artisan who could preserve their images. We also saw people in the Roman Strict Father family model who would not necessarily have been enthused about playing their roles to support the honor of the *paterfamilias* and his *domus*, the script that was the public transcript of the household. Mention was made of the power such people had to withhold their willing obedience and thus expose the *paterfamilias* and the household to shame, because part of what upheld his honor was the willing obedience of everyone under his domain. We saw evidence of slaves maintaining close relationships and of women moving beyond prescribed roles.

Chapter 8 offered some hints of opposition to Augustus and his program, most prominently in opposition to his family legislation. Some elite women made public protest actions, and the general displeasure the legislation provoked was well known to historians in subsequent generations. Part 3 might have left the impression of the inevitability of Augustus' rule and of a *Pax Romana* that was actual peace and harmony throughout the Roman Empire. That image of inevitability and harmony was indeed what Augustus and his supporters projected. Yet people who did not subscribe to the Augustan vision or to the Roman Strict Father family model on which it was based opposed, criticized, resisted, and rebelled against it. Conquered peoples did not readily assent to the Roman Empire's

rule. Some rebelled and some negotiated an array of survival strategies. Members of Strict Father families resisted being controlled and
dehumanized.

In Part 4, we will see a smattering of the resistance to and criticism of the Roman family empire. This is not intended to be a comprehensive study of resistance to the Roman Empire or the family
model on which it was built. We will not, for example, address the
opposition to Augustus among the political elites at Rome.[1] Before
turning in Part 5 to an initial look at one early Christian community's response to the Roman Strict Father family empire, and to additional responses and strategies of resistance in volume 2, however,
it is important to realize that the Christians were not exceptional.
Instead we must see them in a context of a variety of responses to
Roman domination. The preservation of early Christian texts gives
us access to discussion closer to the hidden transcript than what is
available for the study of many other groups, but this does not mean
that the early Christians were unique in their resistance.

Social Space for Hidden Transcripts
(Reviewing the Work of James C. Scott)[2]

Preceding chapters have offered glimpses of locations where hidden transcripts could develop within the Roman Empire and in the
Roman Strict Father family on which it was based. As we turn to
explore some of the responses to Roman domination, additional understanding of the social locations where we can expect to find hidden transcripts will be helpful.

To understand the presence of hidden transcripts, we need to recognize that while dominating by coercion may well produce compliance, force also produces a negative reaction. People will comply
positively only if they believe they are complying willingly.[3] The
Roman imperial strategy of using the Roman Strict Father family
model as a structure of inclusion was a double-edged sword on this
point. There is every indication that members of provincial elites
willingly involved themselves in the imperial cults and initiated the
offering of various honors to the emperor uncoerced.[4] Elite men
who headed households would identify with and assimilate to the
image of the *genius* of the emperor as their own *genius* writ large.

Roman power did not depend entirely on military coercion, and constructing the empire as a Roman Strict Father family made that possible, as we have seen. Yet the Roman Strict Father family model required that subordinates constantly promote the honor of the *paterfamilias* by displaying willing submission to his ostensibly morally superior *auctoritas*. Some may have sincerely complied willingly, but such an attitude was hardly universal.

The economy of honor is a key factor in subordinates' need to create a space for a hidden transcript in situations of domination. In the economy of honor and shame, a social superior's honor requires an inferior's shame. The performance of willing submission takes a toll on the social inferior's dignity. Subordinates seek an audience in a social circle of their peers where they can recover some measure of dignity. In this refuge from the humiliation, they can negate the indignities they have suffered in the public transcript and continue to accept them without risking open rebellion.[5]

Hidden transcripts are more than survival strategies, however. Using hidden transcripts, subordinate groups also develop their own ideologies to counter the ideologies that justify domination. Ideologies of power are shaped "in the form of a metaphysics, a religion, a worldview,"[6] and counter-ideologies form alternative metaphysical, religious, and world-shaping perspectives.

Development of counter-ideologies requires a hard-won development of a relatively autonomous social space where the hidden transcript can be "practiced, articulated, enacted, and disseminated," a social space that itself involves power relationships and group norms.[7] The hidden transcript can develop in "a sequestered social site where the control, surveillance, and repression of the dominant are least able to reach" in groups "composed entirely of close confidants who share similar experiences of domination."[8] Such social spaces can be physical, in locations out of earshot of the dominant, but they can also be "linguistic codes, dialects, and gestures."[9]

Leaders have a role in shaping and disseminating alternative ideologies. Such leaders are most likely to be found in the margins of society and among itinerants, especially people who "depend directly on the patronage of a lower-class public to make their living."[10] In early modern Europe, human agents for hidden transcripts were found

among itinerant entertainers, such as actors, acrobats, jugglers and
bards, and travelling craftspeople, including tinkers, petty traders,
shoemakers, and healers.[11] We can expect to find the same sectors
carrying hidden transcripts in the Greco-Roman world as well.[12]

Dominant groups attempt to prohibit the development of hidden
transcripts by controlling and eliminating the social spaces in which
they can develop and by containing the human agents who shape
and disseminate them.[13] Subordinate groups resist. Often, they must
informally enforce conformity to their violation of the dominant
group's norms as part of their means of resistance. They may single
out "anyone who attempts to put on airs, who denies his [or her]
origins, who seems aloof, who attempts to hobknob with elites."[14]
Andalusian laborers, for example, would show respect to their land-
lords in public encounters but heap abuse on them using derisive
nicknames among themselves and would spread slanderous stories
about police and priests.[15] Subordinate groups enforce conformity
using similar tactics to retaliate against those who break rank.[16]

Strong barriers between elites and subordinates provide favorable
conditions for the development of hidden transcripts. The more that
elites require deference, the thicker the mask that subordinates wear.
The more impermeable the elite culture is to those below, the opa-
quer the subordinate culture is to those above. Subordinates can
create power in their feigned ignorance and aggressive use of sub-
missiveness. A grandfather's advice in Ralph Ellison's *Invisible Man*
illustrates this: "Live with your head in the lion's mouth. I want you
to overcome 'em with yesses, undermine 'em with grins, agree 'em
to death and destruction, let 'em soller you till they vomit or bust
wide open. ... Learn it to the young'uns."[17]

Subordinate groups adopt a variety of strategies as the "arts of political disguise."[18] Basic strategies disguise the message or the messenger. Anonymity can be achieved in spirit possession, for example,
which allows a speaker to attribute a veiled message to a deity or
spirit. Gossip, rumor, anonymous letters and threats, and magic can
all function anonymously. Coded language and metaphors can disguise the message, and generalized grumbling to express wide-rang-
ing dissatisfaction without making an open or specific complaint can
also disguise both message and messenger.[19] More elaborate forms

of disguise can also smuggle the hidden transcript into public view without a frontal confrontation with the public transcript. Religious worldviews that envision a reversal offer ways to speak obliquely of present realities of domination. Oral art forms can be impermanent and anonymous and thus allow for a complex disguise. Folk-tales and dramatic forms as well as rituals and carnivals can articulate the hidden transcript for those in the know.[20]

In what follows, then, as we consider resistance to the Roman Empire, we will note settings where hidden transcripts could be developed and some strategies of political disguise subordinate groups could be using. While not all resistance was hidden, we can learn from the open resistance what historical memories may have found their way into hidden transcripts.

Elements of Alternatives to the Roman Strict Father Family Model

We have seen that the dominant ideology of the Roman Empire was propagated using the Roman Strict Father family model as its root metaphor. We can expect that counter-ideologies would offer some alternatives to this root metaphor, including elements of the family model. Questions based on aspects of the family model will be considered: How do family forms vary from the Roman household with its differentiated roles of *paterfamilias*, legitimate wife, sons, daughters, slaves in various roles, freed persons, and clients? How pronounced is the role division? Are values and virtues expressed as generalized expectations of all the members in the family model or are they specified by role?

Other questions have less explicit answers here, but are nevertheless worth mentioning. Some of these will be touched on in Part 5 as well as in the second volume: Can we detect conceptions of moral order that will provide insights into alternative family models? Is the moral order and the role division in the family understood or projected as natural and timeless? What is the purpose for raising children and what is the image of character to be cultivated in citizens or members of the group? Character in the Strict Father model is an individual moral essence as *virtus* for elite men and *pudicitia* for elite women. In alternative family models, do we see conceptions of

moral essence as communal? How is the role of government understood, both internally and externally?

These will be questions to consider as we explore some of the
resistance to Roman imperial rule and the family model on which it
was based.

10

Armed Resistance

Conquered Territories, Revolts, and National Resistance to Roman Domination

Rome's conquest of territories began long before Augustus, and even in the halcyon days of Rome's ostensible moral vigor, the conquered peoples were not convinced of Rome's superiority and moral right to rule them. Roman conquest required military might, and many nations and tribes resisted Roman domination.

Mithradates VI

In one of the most successful efforts to resist Rome, Mithradates VI of Pontus ruled a vast and shifting territory in Asia Minor and along the coast of the Black Sea that for a few years included Greece. During the first of three Mithradatic wars, he ordered an enormous mass killing carried out on a single day in 88 BCE. Local leaders in most of the cities in the Roman province of Asia on the western coast of Asia Minor participated in the conspiracy against Roman rule, and this large number of participants kept the plan a secret for at least a month. On the appointed day, mobs composed of all sectors of the population reportedly slaughtered eighty thousand, perhaps one hundred and fifty thousand, Romans and Italians—men, women, and children. Mithradates' ability to carry out this bloodbath indicates his grassroots support among the populations of those cities and their widespread and intense hatred of the Roman population of merchants and colonists who had come to take advantage of opportunities in Rome's newly conquered province. Whatever the precise numbers, they were wiped out, and symbols of Roman rule were destroyed.[1]

The massive mobs of people who participated in the killing included indigenous Anatolians, Greeks, and Jews of all classes. They were reacting to harsh Roman rule with its ruthless and corrupt taxation that left the land of the native people in the hands of the new settlers. Slavery was also an issue. The Greeks who dominated the territory kept some slaves, and the religious laws of their Persian predecessors may have limited slavery to some degree.[2] The Romans, however, required staggering numbers of slaves, with as many as ten thousand captives from the Black Sea region and Asia Minor being traded *daily* at the market on the Aegean island of Delos. The Romans had offended the population at Ephesus a few years before the massacre by punishing them for their defense of a slave who had taken refuge in a temple. After the massacre, six thousand freed slaves joined Mithradates' army. The mercenaries in the rank and file of the Roman army in the east defected and the Greek sailors manning Rome's ships in the Black Sea brought that navy to Mithradates' side.[3] His forces then liberated Greece where he was hailed as a savior foretold in oracles, and he restored Athenian democracy for its last swan song until the Roman general Sulla reconquered Greece in 85 BCE.[4]

The military history of Rome's three attempts to defeat Mithradates over the following three decades shows his ruthless military brilliance and also his ability to inspire confidence and unite many sectors opposed to Roman domination.[5] His forces included freed slaves and loyal recruits intent on defeating Roman incursion. Rebel leaders from across Rome's empire allied with him: Spartacus of the famous gladiator slave rebellion, insurgent leaders in Italy and Spain, admirals of the pirate navies in the Mediterranean, and tribal chiefs from the Danube to Central Asia.[6] Alliances with Armenia and Scythia also extended his reach. Supporters hailed him as a savior-king, "King of Kings" in Asia, and his birth was associated in popular lore with the arrival of a spectacular comet.[7]

Mithradates' effort to form his new version of Alexander's Greco-Persian empire as a "co-prosperity zone" to challenge Roman expansion left a legacy into the Augustan era and after.[8] Elements that challenge aspects of the Roman Strict Father family model can be detected in his mission. The basic model he appears to have assumed was that of the "good king" with an authentic royal pedigree.[9] As a "good king," he merged highly developed intellectual and scientific skills drawn from both classical Greek education and Persian "Zoroastrian ideals of free will, responsibility and honesty."[10] His contrast between the model of the legitimate king who owns and responsibly manages the resources of his territory and the Roman model of banditry is expressed in a letter he reportedly sent to seek the support of the Parthians:

> From their very origins, Romans have possessed only what they could steal from others—their homes, their wives, their lands, their empire—all stolen! Nothing prevents them from attacking and destroying allies and friends alike, weak and powerful, near and far. Rome is viciously hostile to every government not subject to Rome—especially monarchies.[11]

Later he cast himself and his potential Parthian ally as the legitimate monarchs hated by the Romans as "the avengers of all those [the Romans] subjugate."[12] If there is a "family" model as a root metaphor for his concept or rule, it would appear to be one that assumes a neighborhood where families work together for the common defense against bullying thieves and invading marauders and where the head of the family is responsible for the welfare of its member subjects. The model is a monarchy, but not necessarily the same as the Roman version of the Strict Father model that would emerge as the model of empire under Augustus. Mithradates promoted a vision of legitimate kingship as the very form of leadership so odious to the republican Romans, as a counter to their rapacious ambitions for conquest.

Mithradates also drew on the legacy of the utopian experiment that took place during his infant years, the "City of the Sun" in the Anatolian interior. In 133 BCE, after Attalus III of Pergamon willed his kingdom to Rome to establish what became its province of Asia, his stepbrother Aristonicus launched a popular rebellion. Numerous cities on the western coast of Asia Minor joined the uprising, but the

Roman army prevailed. Aristonicus and his supporters retreated to the highlands in the Anatolian interior and established Heliopolis, the "City of the Sun," as a utopia where citizens were free and equal, slaves were liberated, debts were cancelled, "eradicating evils that were particularly identified with Rome."[13]

Heliopolis was conceived as a democratic kingdom. The exiled Stoic philosopher Blossius, former tutor of the Gracchi at Rome, also joined the cause. From the diverse inhabitants of the highlands, Aristonicus drew an army named the "Citizens of the Sun," evoking the Armenian Zoroastrian tribe of "Children of the Sun," who refused to submit to tyrants, as well as the Persian sun god, Mithra. Their name indicates a fight for Light and Truth against the forces of Darkness. These Heliopolitans held off the Romans for four years, even after Aristonicus was killed in 128 BCE, until the Romans poisoned the water supplies of their cities, indiscriminately killing all the inhabitants.[14]

The success and the values of the Citizens of the Sun, and the Romans' brutality in suppressing them, influenced Mithradates' vision and indicates the aspirations of the population he mobilized. While he did not establish a utopian democratic kingdom, he did free slaves, cancel debts, grant broad citizenship rights, and share his royal treasure with his soldiers.[15] Their success also reveals a hidden transcript of anti-Roman aspirations and a counter-ideology that had emerged publicly in a rebellion.

In the tradition of royal courts of the east, Mithradates also had a series of wives and concubines, and his daughters' marriages were part of his strategy of diplomatic alliances. He was a Strict Father king in this regard. Hypsicratea, his last wife, stands out, however, as a romantic figure and a different model of womanhood. Mithradates met her during his last effort to raise an army in the Caucasus, where men and women alike trained to fight on horseback and were viewed as equals. To join him in the battles of his last years, fought using strategies of nomadic warfare, she dressed in male attire and fought alongside him, and he called her "Hypsicrates," the masculine version of her name. She became an example of a wife loyal to her husband, and their story became a romantic adventure told in later generations in the Roman Empire.[16] It is plausible that she survived after Mithradates' mysterious suicide and re-emerged as the historian Hypsicrates.[17]

While Mithradates can hardly be characterized as a champion of egalitarianism or a defender of human rights, his decades of successful resistance to Rome and his identification as a "liberator" and "savior" would have lingered in the popular imagination of the peoples Rome conquered. We can guess that memories of his victories became part of the hidden transcripts in a later century along with popular recollections of the short-lived City of the Sun.

Other Examples of National Resistance

Uprisings against Roman rule were hardly uncommon.[18] Students of Jewish and Christian history are familiar with a succession of revolts in Judaea and Galilee. For example, revolts occurred in 4 BCE after the death of Herod the Great. Rebels seized the Galilean district capital of Sepphoris, and when Roman forces took it back, they destroyed it and sold its population into slavery.[19] A decade later, after the Romans had deposed Herod the Great's son from his rule of Idumaea, Judaea, and Samaria, Judas the Galilean led an uprising against the taxation the Romans instituted. Josephus characterized his movement as a fourth sect of Jewish philosophy, after the Pharisees, Sadducees, and Essenes, a sect with an almost unconquerable passion for liberty and a belief that "God alone is their leader (*hēgemōn*) and master (*despotēs*)."[20] The rebellion was suppressed but its counter-ideology persisted.[21] This belief articulates an alternative to the Roman emperor, but what it implies for a family model is unclear.

Evidence also remains of a series of at least seven popular protests between 4 BCE and 65 CE. Ancient historians record impressive displays of nonviolent mass action, including a large contingent who laid down surrounding Pilate's house for five days and nights without moving. Most of these protests addressed either taxation or Roman insults to Jewish religious laws, particularly the introduction of images of the emperor as an affront to their proscription against graven images. Some of these actions achieved results.[22] The protestors' willingness to resist unarmed and to risk martyrdom indicates that they did not recognize the ultimate power or authority of the

Roman emperor and his imperial forces. The unity of their actions indicates a developed critique in a hidden transcript, but any content of their discussion that would offer clues to a root family metaphor for their alternative vision remains opaque to us, except, perhaps, what we can learn from the teachings of the Jesus movement.

An urban movement of assassins known as *sicarii*, and bands and even armies of bandits in the rural areas also posed an ongoing threat to the Roman occupiers and their Jewish sympathizers.[23] Bandit leaders appear to have initiated a widespread peasant revolt in 52 CE,[24] although it is difficult to determine their specific role in the extensive unrest that culminated in the major Jewish rebellions against Roman occupation in 66–73 CE, during which the Romans destroyed Jerusalem and the Jewish temple there.

The history of conflict and resistance against Roman occupation in Palestine is too complex and varied to describe in detail here. Of note, however, are images of the role of high priest and king in parts of the resistance. Josephus records that the rebels he names Zealots, having killed the lineage of the high priests, elected one of their own from peasant stock to be high priest.[25] Their actions not only indicate their general antipathy to the urban elites but also offer clues to their alternative organizational model. By electing one of their own to be high priest, they reveal an understanding of their direct connection to their deity, a connection that did not necessitate mediation by a hereditary priest. By killing the hereditary priesthood and electing their own priests, they reveal a belief that their deity would endorse their community authority rather than an inherited authority and that their deity would recognize their elected priestly intermediary. Theirs is a deity who acts from within the community rather than through powers set at the top of or above the community.

While this conflict took place within their own religious culture, their practice would critique the imperial cult and the priesthood of the *paterfamilias* in the Roman Strict Father family model as well. The image of the king is characterized in the term "messianic claimant." The claim evokes David as the ideal king who "was nondynastic, was popularly acclaimed, and had used a base in banditry from which to achieve the kingship."[26] Such claims of kingship expressed a national aspiration to counter Roman domination and to preserve their culture and monotheistic religious practices. Evidence of any understanding of kingship that posed a contrast to the Roman Strict Father family model is scant among the messianic claimants. Uprisings elsewhere in the empire offer hints of a variety of differences.

In 52 BCE, a few years after Mithradates' final defeat, the Celts or Gauls in what is now France revolted, led by Vercingetorix. The Gauls had a tradition of decision-making in a national assembly, and this tradition was a factor in their unifying to revolt as well as in their discussions of strategy, although Vercingetorix was an iron-fisted leader who demanded extreme measures in the campaign to defeat Roman domination.[27] Julius Caesar's defeat of the rebellion in 46 BCE was a major factor in his rise to power. In this last of the Gallic wars, a million Gauls were killed and another million enslaved, two thirds of the population.[28] The uprising, however, appears to have been the Gauls' attempt to maintain aspects of their culture.

Half a century later, the revolt of Arminius at the end of Augustus' reign delivered Rome its greatest defeat. Arminius' forces slaughtered three Roman legions in the Teutoburg Forest in 9 CE and permanently checked the Romans' northern expansion. The revolt also indicates an effort to preserve their culture.[29]

In the parts of Britain conquered by the Romans, the revolt led by Queen Boudicca in 60 CE offers an intriguing example for a contrast of family models. One major provocation of the uprising occurred when Roman officials flogged Queen Boudicca and raped her daughters, another when they destroyed a sacred Druid center on the island of Mona off the coast of Wales, and yet another when they constructed a temple of the imperial cult.[30] Women's leadership in the British tribes was not unknown. Yet as a warrior queen, Boudicca cut an especially striking figure as a tall woman with fiery eyes and a mass of waist-length red or gold hair, a multicolored tunic and a mantle, carrying a spear. She commanded an enormous army, numbering one hundred and twenty thousand to two hundred and thirty thousand according to ancient reports.[31]

Boudicca's speech to her people as reported by Cassius Dio includes several elements of interest for considering alternative models of family and nation at the time. The speech draws contrasts between

the freedom of her people's traditional way of life and Roman en-
slavement and includes an analysis of how the Roman tax system
enslaves them. She also juxtaposes the Romans' fortifications, body
armor, and decadent lifestyle with the Britons' simpler mode of
life and warfare embedded close to their land and relying on their
own bravery. She describes the Romans' need for a thick protective
boundary for their bodies and their towns in a way consistent with
the emphasis on strong boundaries in a Strict Father family model.
In contrast, Dio's Boudicca describes the Britons as integrated into
and unified with their land for protection. Instead of requiring the
armor and fortresses, the Britons conceal themselves for protection
in natural features of the territory they know well, hiding in swamps
and mountains; they rely directly on natural resources for food, unlike the Romans who need refined foods, yeast bread, and olive oil;
and they swim the rivers naked rather than relying on boats.[32]

She also describes the Britons as a family, as kin because they in-
habit the same land and have the same name.[33] These criteria for defining family are notably different from the Roman family defined by
relationship to or ownership by the same *paterfamilias* or *pater patriae*. She even defines her people's relationship to her as their queen
in terms distinct from the Roman model, commending the Britons
not for obedience or personal loyalty but for cooperating with her
and with each other.[34] At least as Cassius Dio presents them, then,
Boudicca and the Britons assume a model of the nation as a family
that was distinctly different from the Roman Strict Father model in
the macrocosm.

Dio's Boudicca also reports a family and community model in the
microcosm among the Britons in which everything was held in common, including wives and children, and where women were as courageous as men.[35] In his description, Dio betrays assumptions about
male ownership that the Britons themselves may not have shared.
Dio assumes that men are the owners and women and children are
the possessions held in common. The Britons appear to have viewed
all the members of the clan and tribal organization, not just the men,
as common owners.[36] In any case, their model of family and nation
plainly differed from the Roman Strict Father model.

This was a problem for the Romans, signified for them by a woman's leadership. Dio introduced his account of the disaster for the Romans in Britain with a summary of the achievement of Boudicca's massive army: "Two cities were sacked, eighty thousand of the Romans and of their allies perished, and the island was lost to Rome. Moreover, all this ruin was brought upon the Romans by a woman, a fact which in itself caused them the greatest shame."[37]

We can comprehend the Romans' fear of being put to shame by a woman leader when we consider how prominently their need to project their victory as *male* victory features in their visual propaganda. Reliefs at the temple of the imperial cult at Aphrodisias in western Asia Minor offer examples. The imperial cult temple complex under construction that so offended the Britons would have included some iconography like that found at Aphrodisias. At Aphrodisias, statues portraying the conquered nations as women line the lowest story of the three-level north portico, each identified with an inscription on the statue base.[38] One of the reliefs from the upper level portrays the initial Roman victory over Britain as the masculine emperor Claudius subduing the female figure of Britannia.[39]

Portraying a conquered nation as a woman, often a grieving woman, was a standard visual trope in the Romans' projection of their victory and their imperial domination as inevitable. A single image represents the subjugation of women and the conquering of the nations. The earth itself could also be portrayed as a female deity suffering defeat.[40] We should also remember that the defeat of Cleopatra was as important as the defeat of Mark Antony in Octavian's victory, and that before the Romans, Greek portrayals feminized their eastern "barbarian" enemies.[41] Feminizing the enemy as a taunt used in warfare hardly originates with the Romans. Battle is where men in military cultures prove their manliness. Roman iconography made this explicit by portraying the victor as a man and the vanquished nation as a woman, the male defeating the female.

Yet with Boudicca, at least as her speech is related by Dio, we have traces of not just the feminized enemy, now led by an actual woman, but another model of social organization and another root family metaphor for a nation as well. This is not a family contained in a Roman *domus* house with thick walls and tightly controlled entries, ruled by a *paterfamilias* whose rule of the household displays his manly *virtus* and *auctoritas*, nor is it the family displayed in the arena where the program begins with a spectacle of the domination of nature in a massive slaughter of wild animals. This is a family living as part of their land, a nation with no need for expansion beyond a territory defined by an ocean that surrounds them.[42] This is a family where the women themselves rise in fury in response to rape. They are not defended by males as their property or honor. They defend themselves. They do not follow the moral example of Roman womanhood presented in the tale of the Roman Lucretia by committing an honorable suicide but instead defend themselves as women and as human beings.[43] This was a threat to the Roman Strict Father family model, and the Romans' determination to defeat Boudicca, Britannia, Judaea, and all the feminized nations was part of a defense of their Strict Father family as superior and "natural."

Lest we oversimplify the conquests as a Roman "patriarchy" suppressing egalitarian goddess-worshipping tribal peoples, however, two items are of note. The Roman people themselves were represented as the goddess Roma, and she and other goddesses form part of the iconography of Roman victory. Boudicca's army was also reported to have singled out Roman women for particularly brutal ritualized and sexualized killing. While ancient historians offer graphic reports, we are not privy to the Britons' interpretation.[44] Yet the rebellion led by Boudicca was hardly in defense of women's solidarity. As we recall the image on the *Gemma Augustea*, however, we can recognize the Roman Strict Father family, with goddesses present among its celestial supporters looking toward the empire's *paterfamilias* portrayed as the head of the divine household. In the lower register, we can see among the defeated nations some glimpses of a way of life that did not endorse the Roman Strict Father way.

Slave Rebellions and Resistance

Many of the people represented in the *Gemma's* lower register became slaves if they were not slaughtered. As slaves, they also rebelled. Three major slave uprisings, known as the "Servile Wars," occurred before the imperial era. The first two were in Sicily, where large numbers of slaves had been imported and were exceptionally mistreated, according to the ancient report of Diodorus Siculus.[45]

Diodorus reports that the first rebellion (probably 135–132 BCE) started when some slaves killed their abusive owners, and it spread under a leader named Eunus who had provided something of a comedy routine for his owner and his friends who mocked him for reporting a vision in which he saw himself as a king. The slave population had apparently formed channels of communication for decision-making among themselves, and they chose the Syrian slave Eunus to lead as a king and general as the rebellion grew. Eunus was a prophet devoted to the Syrian goddess Atargatis, and waved his long hair in the style of the devotees of the Anatolian Mother of the Gods to be discussed in chapter 12.[46] As a prophet, magician, and accomplished juggler, he fit the profile of a leader emerging from the hidden transcript. The rebellion held cities and killed many slaveholders for three years until Roman forces regained control.[47] Sporadic uprisings continued until a second massive rebellion emerged under another leader who took the role of king (probably 104–100 BCE).[48] The length and size of these rebellions indicate military prowess with limited resources, and the emergence of two leaders reported to have the trappings of Hellenistic kings indicates some aspirations for self-government, but evidence for their plans and discussions is slim.

The slave gladiator Spartacus led the third rebellion in 73–71 BCE, and he supported Rome's opponent Mithradates VI, as has been mentioned. With an army numbering some ninety thousand, he defeated several Roman armies and devastated southern Italy. His goal was to reach the Celtic territory in northern Italy, Cisalpine Gaul, and disperse everyone to their own homes there, but his troops preferred plundering Italy. He died in battle when Crassus defeated him and crucified massive numbers of his captured followers.[49] His success loomed large in Roman memory, and the brutal suppression of the rebellion would loom large in the memory of those who might rise again. Crucifixions that were a staple of the mid-day program of executions in the arenas in subsequent centuries reinforced this memory of the ruthlessness of Roman victory over rebellion.

In the imperial era, slaves resisted in more subtle forms using "weapons of the weak." Plutarch, a moralist of the first century CE, related an example:

> Pupius Piso, the orator, not wishing to be troubled, ordered his slaves to speak only in answer to questions and not a word more. Subsequently, wishing to pay honour to Clodius when he was a magistrate, Piso gave orders that he be invited to dinner and prepared what was, we may suppose, a sumptuous banquet. When the hour came, the other guests were present, but Clodius was still expected, and Piso repeatedly sent the slave who regularly carried invitations to see if Clodius was approaching. And when evening came and he was finally despaired of, Piso said to the slave, 'See here, did you give him the invitation?' 'I did,' said the slave. 'Why hasn't he come then?' 'Because he declined.' 'Then why didn't you tell me at once?' 'Because you didn't ask me that.'[50]

This clever slave's action illustrates the creativity and the constant struggle of slaves to maintain their dignity and humanity in a system that viewed them as objects. As the imperial era continued, resistance moved increasingly to hidden transcripts, below the surface, not always in open rebellion but present nevertheless as an ongoing threat to the dominion of the Roman elites, always remaining the "enemy within."[51]

Conclusion

From these examples of resistance, we should note a few key elements. First, Rome was not invincible. From the vantage point of our era, Roman domination seems a foregone conclusion. Yet Roman control was far more tenuous than we imagine. Rome projected itself as inevitable and divinely ordained, as if repeating the dictum of Star Trek's Borg empire: "Resistance is futile." We should not let ourselves be duped by Roman imperial propaganda, however. Rome was continually endeavoring to establish and maintain control. At the level of the empire, Rome strove to forestall and quell rebellion. and at the level of the *domus*, elites struggled to maintain control of slaves.

Secondly, the population of Judaea was notable but not exceptional in its national resistance. The nations that Rome conquered resisted in unique ways based on their own cultures and traditions.

We have seen, thirdly, some hints of elements of alternatives to the Roman Strict Father family model in groups who raised armed resistance to Rome. Mithradates challenged Rome not only militarily but ideologically. He took up some aspects of the utopian "City of the Sun" by freeing slaves and cancelling debts. He also saw his project as establishing a "co-prosperity zone" as a neighborhood of nations ruled by "legitimate kings" for their common benefit, a neighborhood resisting the pillage and plunder of Roman desperados. The legacy of counter-ideology that remained from his decades-long struggle included the romantic saga of Mithradates and his wife Hypsicratea riding together into battle in his last years and the image of her as his equal.

The image of kings emerged as part of the counter-ideology in national rebellions in Judaea, some unarmed, and in slave rebellions in Sicily. Unlike Mithradates, who claimed legitimacy based on heredity, these kings claimed authority based on a combination of their own prophetic visions and their election by the insurgents they led.

Boudicca's monarchical legitimacy appears as a combination of inheriting the role from her husband and a groundswell of support for the rebellion she led as queen and general. A woman's leadership of this massive rebellion that delivered such substantial blows to the Roman occupation offers an element of contrast to the Roman Strict Father family model. Reports of Boudicca's rebellion also hint at elements of a family model significantly different from the family of the Roman *domus*, starting with a strikingly different image of the house in which a family and nation dwells. Rather than a house with thick walls and controlled entrances, she reportedly envisioned a family dwelling in unity with the land and an army taking its strength from its homeland as a nation contained by the natural boundary of the sea. Rather than a household defined as the property of a *paterfamilias*, we can see hints of a family relationship based on common ownership.

We can see a different view of property, too, in Boudicca's response to being flogged and her daughters being raped. She claimed herself as her own property in a response that fused with her people's outrage as the Romans seized their land and enslaved their leaders. She and her daughters and her people all claimed themselves, with their land, as their own property. For them, the offense of rape was an offense against them as women who owned themselves, not against the honor of a husband or father who headed the family. Likewise, the Romans' offense in invading the Britons' territory was not against a monarch who owned the land but against the people themselves. Considering her reported description of her army and her people in intimate relationship with their land, it may not stretch too far to envision their response as the land claiming itself as well, as its people defending much more than "property."

In armed resistance to Rome, then, we can see hints of alternatives and counter-ideologies but no single alternative family model.

11

Intellectual Resistance

Utopian Community Visions and Philosophical Movements

Not all resistance to the Roman Empire and its Strict Father family model was armed. Resistance also took intellectual forms, including utopian visions that imagined different worlds and different ways of organizing societies. Some philosophers also took up ways of life that resisted from within. This chapter will first review some of the utopian visions circulating in the Greco-Roman era and utopian community experiments. Then we will consider one of the prominent active philosophical movements, the Cynics, and the challenges they posed for Strict Father family models in the Greco-Roman era.

Utopias[1]

Propaganda extolling the Augustan Golden Age appealed to utopian aspirations, as we saw in chapter 7. Around 40 BCE, even before the ascendancy of Augustus, Vergil hailed a new age as a return of the age of Saturn, evoking the time of the first generation of the deities when work was unnecessary for abundant life.[2] Vergil extolled Caesar Augustus as the one who would bring the Golden Age and return the Latin lands to the reign of Saturn.[3] The promotion of Augustus as the founder of the new age of Saturn omitted the symbolic inversion associated with the festival of Saturnalia and instead emphasized prosperity and the abundance of the earth as fruits of Roman pacification.[4]

The winter solstice festival of Saturnalia celebrated by Romans and Greeks enacted a symbolic social inversion with masters waiting on tables where their slaves reclined to eat. By the imperial era, however, the ritual celebration appears to have been confined to homes, excluding the population of the poor.[5] Literary descriptions preserved a utopian critique in a symbolic inversion, but the celebrations do not appear to have enacted much role reversal or to have included all sectors of society. Imperial propaganda had appropriated the image of the Golden Age, and elites had domesticated the festival for their own purposes.[6]

Ancient authors described other utopian paradises, however, and some people in the Greco-Roman era established intentional utopian communities that were more counter-cultural. The "City of the Sun" founded by Aristonicus has already been mentioned as an influence on Mithradates VI. As a utopian community, this effort raised a direct ideological and military challenge to the imperial designs of Rome during the time of the republic. Not all the literary descriptions and utopian community experiments were as pointed as this example, but other utopian efforts indicate forms of critique and an underlying aspiration for alternative models of social organization.

Utopias as Mental Experiments

As a form of mental experimentation, some ancient authors described mythic utopias, ideal societies from the dim mists of the past. Plato described Atlantis as a prosperous land destroyed due to the decline of the population's virtue.[7] Utopian romances depicted other ideal societies. In Panchaïa, the priests and artisans were in charge and somewhat better off than the other two castes, the farmers and the soldier-shepherds. Slaves are not mentioned.[8] In Hyperborea, a land beyond the north wind, and in Ethiopia to the south, the population lived without agricultural labor.[9] The physically unique inhabitants of the Islands of the Sun, a utopia which may have inspired the naming of Heliopolis, also maintained themselves simply from the readily available food in their tropical paradise. Diodorus Siculus, a Greek historian writing at the time of Augustus' rise, provides a noteworthy description of their social organization: They lived in groups of about four hundred, led by the eldest male who, due to their excessive longevity, killed himself at the age of one hundred and fifty to yield to the next eldest.[10] Of family organization, Diodorus reports:

> They do not marry, we are told, but possess their children in common, and maintaining the children who are born as if they belonged to all, they love them equally; and while the children are infants those who suckle the babes often change them around in order that not even the mothers may know their own offspring. Consequently, since there is no rivalry among them, they never experience civil disorders and they never cease placing the highest value upon internal harmony.[11]

The critique implies that marriage and the exclusive association of children with their biological mothers causes civil strife. Earlier Greek thinkers had experimented with this notion. Plato's *Republic* presents a vision of a much more controlled society where the property relationship of marriage and child-rearing is abolished.[12] Aristotle critiqued this aspect of the *Republic* as impractical and not clearly designed, probably as part of his understanding of his version of social hierarchy as "natural." Both Plato and Aristotle assumed women and children were part of the property owned by male citizens whether individually or in common.[13] Before these philosophers, Aristophanes had presented an imaginary city where women were in charge and all property was held in common in his comic play *Ecclesiazusae* ("Women of the Assembly").[14] Some early Greek city-states were also idealized: Sparta with its intensely class-stratified military society, early Athenian democracy, and the possible utopian experiment of Ouranopolis, the "City of Heaven."[15]

Utopias as Social Experiments

Except for Heliopolis, the utopian experiment of Aristonicus in Asia Minor, evidence of Jewish efforts to establish utopian communities during the Roman era is better attested than for other communities. The two notable examples are the Therapeutai in Egypt and the Essenes, who were probably the community represented in the Dead Sea Scrolls. Accounts of both show influence of Hellenistic utopian ideas.[16]

Philo of Alexandria described a community of Jewish *therapeutai* and *therapeutrides*, male and female "God-servers" or "Soul-Healers."[17] Members of this community at Lake Mareotis in Egypt were ascetics devoted to study and contemplation and to worship activities that Philo compares to those in the Jerusalem Temple.[18] Philo describes women in the community as "having the same feelings of admiration as the men, and having adopted the same sect with equal deliberation and decision."[19]

Seating at their Sabbath services was ordered by age, with men and women in separate chambers in the same hall.[20] Every seventh week at their festal meal, they were also divided with men on the right, women on the left, arranged in the order of their tenure in the community.[21] At their banquet, they drank cold water rather than wine and ate simple bread.[22] Young men of the community, pointedly dressed as free men, voluntarily served them at these meals, regarding their elders as their parents even though there was no biological relationship.[23] These free members of the communities served because, in a notable critique of the family models that include slaves:

> ... they do not use the ministrations of slaves, looking upon
> the possession of servants or slaves to be a thing absolutely and
> wholly contrary to nature, for nature has created all men free,
> but the injustice and covetousness of some men who prefer in-
> equality, that cause of all evil, having subdued some, has given to
> the more powerful authority over those who are weaker.[24]

Everyone present, including the young men serving the meal, listened to a sober reading and explanation of scripture, and then they all applauded and began a ritual of singing hymns that started with individuals in order and then included male and female choruses in joint harmony.[25]

In these communities, we see an alternative family model without slaves, where men and women apparently participated almost equally, although separately. It is unclear whether women spoke before the assembly. Membership and service to their deity and to one another was voluntary and ranked by tenure in the community, with junior members doing the labor required for the community's simple sustenance.[26] Community members appear to have come from educated Jewish elites at Alexandria and to have left their families and possessions behind to join the community, but it is unclear whether property was owned in common.[27] Without marrying or having children, they relied on voluntary recruits to continue their community. Their family model thus relied on a wider community for continuation, yet aspects of it formed a critique of the prevailing model that relied on slavery and male primacy.[28]

Another Jewish group, the Essenes, formed intentional communities of adult men from Palestinian villages who lived in voluntary pacifist communities, also not based on biological family connections, where everything was owned in common. There were no slaves, and life in the communities was characterized by hard work on the part of all able-bodied members. Older members were cared for. There were no women, either, and the male community members repudiated marriage and practiced continence. Philo attributes their opposition to marriage to the vices of women, a topic on which he often waxed eloquent, depicting women as selfish, jealous, and deceitful.[29] The celibate Essenes were praised for their ethical lifestyle.[30]

The Qumran community that left the documents known as the Dead Sea Scrolls may have been Essenes, although the identification is disputed. Documents from Qumran indicate an attempt to found a utopian community on a blueprint drawn from Hebrew scriptures, particularly the prophet Ezekiel, Deuteronomy, and Leviticus, and influenced by Hellenistic utopias. They saw themselves as preservers of community purity waiting to re-establish a Jerusalem with temple worship freed from its current corruption.[31] The community's rules indicate an elaborate pecking order, renewed annually, with members making decisions for the community. One document also indicates communities that included women.[32] Whether or not these were the Essenes known from ancient authors, their presence indicates an effort to establish an alternative social order based on religious purity.

In these examples of literary and community utopian experiments, we can see a critique of several of the core assumptions of the Roman Strict Father family model and its Greek antecedents. Many of the utopias offer alternatives to traditional assumptions.

Both the utopian thought experiments and the lived communities undermined the notion of traditional Strict Father family forms of marriage and child-rearing and gender relations, and repudiated the notion of slavery as natural. Utopian visions expressed some of the issues philosophers addressed in other forms of resistance. Other philosophers lived out similar critiques in more individual forms.

Alternative Family Metaphors in the Cynic Movement

As early as 155 BCE Athenian philosophers arrived in Rome as ambassadors. One of them gave a well-received speech on justice followed the next day by one on injustice as the basis of Roman rule.[33] Traditionalists, notably Cato the Elder, moved to have them banned, and although he was not successful on this occasion, philosophers were expelled from Rome at other times.[34] At Rome, aristocratic philosophers participated in conspiracies against emperors, notably the Pisonian conspiracy in 65 CE that unsuccessfully attempted to replace Nero with Gaius Calpurnius Piso as emperor.[35] Many were executed and exiled following the conspiracy and in subsequent decades for speaking openly.[36] Philosophers were categorically exiled from Rome during the rules of Vespasian (69–79 CE) and Domitian (81–96 CE).[37]

Yet philosophy and philosophers were part of life at Rome. In the upper classes, Stoicism predominated, and in the age of Augustus their philosophic reasoning supported an individualist and passive response to public life under one-man rule. When action was considered futile, withdrawal into private life was the reasonable and virtuous response.[38] Yet withdrawal could offer a time for philosophers to prepare for metaphorical combat in public life, philosophers training for rhetorical engagement just as gladiators and soldiers prepared for the arena and battlefield.[39] However, the metaphorical battlefield could also be trivialized as after-dinner entertainments for the elites, just as literal gladiatorial combat was. Debates provided the spoken version of the physical gladiatorial dinner party diversions.[40] Philosophers could also be domesticated members of the households and part of the entourage of the *paterfamilias*, as was mentioned in chapter 3.

Other philosophers were less tamed. Historians of the time re-count individual philosophers' protest actions. For example, two Cynics entered a theatrical performance in succession to denounce the Emperor Titus and his mistress Berenice to their faces. After the first was flogged, the second did the same and was beheaded.[41] Such incidents indicate that, emboldened by philosophy, individuals could reveal hidden transcripts even to the emperor himself. This tale also hints at an organized movement planning for a succession of truth-tellers to address the emperor. Was there an alternative vision or a counter-ideology in a hidden transcript that emboldened these two Cynics and others? If nothing else, these two truth-tellers reveal an assumption that the emperor was a human being whose personal behavior could be held to the same standard as others. Their ac-tion also reveals a belief in their own right and obligation to speak truth to power despite the consequences. This counter-ideology had deeper roots.

Cosmopolitanism and Exile

Philosophers of all stripes suffered exile. Some associated their physi-cal dislocation with metaphorical notions of exile that reveal an alter-native family model and metaphor. These philosophers understood themselves as dislocated not only geographically but also from "the norms and conventions of regular society."[42] Their exile made them cosmopolitans, citizens of the universe, and their cosmopolitanism in turn made them exiles.

As an exile from the city of his origin, the Cynic philosopher Diogenes of Sinope articulated the principle explicitly when some-one asked him where he was from. He replied, "I am a citizen of the world (*kosmopolitēs*)."[43] From this the notion of "cosmopolitanism" takes its name. At its core, cosmopolitanism sees all human beings as citizens in a single community.[44]

Diogenes, considered the first of the Cynics, lived at the same time as Alexander the Great. Anecdotes about Diogenes relate his encounters with Alexander. The best known tale recounts that Alexander came to Diogenes where he was sunning himself and of-fered any favor of Diogenes' choosing, to which the Cynic replied,

"Stand out of my light."[45] The notion of cosmopolitanism was emerging in their generation, in contrast to the thought of Plato and Aristotle (Alexander's teacher) who assumed that citizens owed allegiance to their own city and had no obligations to foreigners.[46] Both Alexander and Diogenes can be considered cosmopolitans, but with radically different understandings of the nature of the cosmos.

Imperial Cosmopolitanism
The Cosmos Is the Empire

According to Plutarch, philosophy only imagined an ideal commonwealth where all people participate as one community, not differentiated by local citizenship and laws. Plutarch credited Alexander with enacting it. Alexander, he says, ignored Aristotle's advice and instead treated Greeks and non-Greeks equally and "brought together into one body all people everywhere, uniting and mixing in one great loving-cup, as it were, people's lives, their characters, their marriages, their very habits of life."[47] Plutarch offered a suspiciously rosy picture of one big happy family created by Alexander's conquests and the cultural imperialism, however syncretistic, of his Greek effort to "civilize" the "barbarians." Plutarch, writing in the late first and early second century CE, did articulate the imperial cosmopolitan vision that Rome had appropriated from Alexander, however. What came under Alexander's and later Rome's dominion became the cosmopolis. The empire was the cosmos.

The Roman Empire continued Alexander's cosmopolitan Hellenizing project. Provincial elites across the empire became part of a cosmopolitan identity based on a Greek education that became a sign of their inclusion in high culture and civilization also as *Romanitas*.[48] Rome appropriated Greek cultural forms, architectural styles, and intellectual traditions to create a common culture of the elites and a common architectural appearance in civic centers. Rome's cosmopolis became this network of the educated elites who were willingly included in the apparatus of ruling the empire.

In this context, Stoics developed a notion of the cosmos itself as a polis governed by perfect order and right reason. Stoics advocated direct political engagement as a mode of service to other human beings.[49] Some of the Roman Stoics viewed the Roman *patria* itself as the cosmopolis.[50] For them, cosmopolitanism supported the empire as "a single 'city' that mirrored the completeness and self-sufficiency of the universe."[51]

Others viewed the cosmopolis as larger than the empire. One of the aristocratic philosophers exiled in the first century CE, the Stoic Musonius Rufus, for example, viewed the world, the cosmos, as "the common fatherland of all human beings." He articulated this cosmopolitan perspective as a way for philosophers to view their exile with equanimity, relying on internal strength rather than any specific location for happiness. Philosophers could thus anchor their well-being in a knowledge of their identity as citizens "of the city of Zeus which is populated by human beings and gods."[52] This view of their citizenship beyond the Roman cosmopolis allowed them a perspective outside it.

In the context of an empire under the one-man rule of an emperor as "Father of the Fatherland," the language of a more universal "Fatherland" with Zeus as a divine ruler could evoke a contrast, a power superseding the emperor who rules a country larger than the Roman Empire and holds it to a higher standard. Envisioning the cosmopolis as the city belonging to Zeus as the Father-Ruler, however, easily assumed a Roman Strict Father family model as its root metaphor. While a vision of a cosmos beyond Rome could bring a critique, divine fatherly rule readily maintained the imperial family model, as it would in the triumphant cosmopolitanism of Christianity in subsequent centuries. The cosmopolitanism of the Cynics offered a more radical basis of critique.

Cosmopolitanism in Cynic Resistance

The Cosmos Is Nature

Cynic philosophical critique and counter-cultural witness flourished in the context of this imperial cosmopolitan reality.[53] Theirs was not an imperial cosmopolitanism, however, but a radical alternative. Diogenes' self-identification as a citizen of the world (*kosmopolitēs*) has often been understood as intended primarily to negate any claims of the local polis on him,[54] but the term points to a positive alternative. He did not respond negatively, that is, that he was not a citizen of any polis (*apolis*); rather he positively stated his citizenship in the cosmos.[55] Diogenes may have elaborated a clear alternative in a *Republic* mentioned in ancient sources but now lost.[56] The Cynic vision of the cosmos can be discerned, however, in their view of the polis as "against nature," and world citizenship as life in accord with nature.[57] Nature provided their positive vision of the cosmos.

The Cynics' view of nature takes its place in an ongoing philosophical discussion that counterposed custom (*nomos*) and nature (*physis*). A key discussion question about any given item was, "Does *x* exist by custom or by nature?"[58] The Cynics opposed custom and affirmed nature as the grounding of their way of life. Their view of nature differed from the view of other philosophies in its simplicity. Rather than considering theories of nature or study of the natural world, their emphasis was on training oneself to live in the immediate presence of nature. Life in accord with nature required learning physical disciplines to survive and thrive without the protections that the life of custom in the polis had created: houses, layers of clothing, shoes, and other comforts. The life of custom that the Cynics opposed had to be unlearned to recondition oneself to the natural and virtuous life. Cynic disciplines also cultivated pleasure in their open-air life focused in the here and now. For them, nature was not a battlefield for the survival of the fittest but a trustworthy source of all that is needed for life, without the cultivation of food or livestock.[59] The Cynic life required a mental discipline of presence as well as physical discipline.

The Cynic Cosmopolitan Missionary Movement versus the Strict Father Empire

During the Roman era, mendicant philosophers appeared throughout the empire, especially in the east, recognizable by their long hair, bare feet, and generally scruffy appearance, and often identified as Cynics.[60] Cynicism became a more widespread, diverse, and eclectic movement with adherents in a variety of nationalities in the empire and with its own cosmopolitanism.[61]

These street philosophers also had their critics. Some professed admiration for the "true Cynics" of an earlier era who had practiced "Cynic ideals of self-sufficiency, superiority to fortune, the natural life, [free speech], freedom from false conventions and liberation from all hopes and fears."[62] Critics portrayed the current generation as charlatans without real ideals, leaving their work to live on handouts and imitating Cynic speeches and actions to gain advantages for their own pleasure.[63]

While these homeless philosophers were not part of an organizationally disciplined movement and many may have fit the critique, we should not discount them as a movement. We can see in them the loose organization necessary for a public revelation of some hidden transcripts. They did, after all, attract audiences to their speeches. They developed distinct styles and genres for their speeches, using satire and diatribe, in simplified yet creative language intelligible on the street.[64] They had a consistent message and culture of resistance, and they fit the description of itinerant leaders who promulgate hidden transcripts.

Defacing the Currency and Destroying the House

"Deface the currency" was a famous Cynic slogan, associated with the crime of mutilating coins that originally drove Diogenes from Sinope.[65] The word for "currency" in Greek is *nomisma*, etymologically related and a near-synonym for *nomos*, custom or law. While the word means "coins" and "coinage," it also refers to anything in common usage, including customs and institutions.[66] The slogan thus referred on one level to money, or the love of it, which Diogenes reportedly branded the "mother-city" (*metropolis*) of all evil.[67] On another level, the call is to "deface custom," the larger Cynic project of critiquing the dominant culture, the public transcript of their day. Their lifestyle both embodied their denunciation and freed them to speak it openly. Seen as an expression of a root family metaphor, their lived project of "defacing the currency" also aimed at destroying the house and family model that was the metaphorical foundation of polis and empire.

A Lifestyle in Accord with Nature
as a Lifestyle for Free Speech

Cynicism was first and foremost a way of life in accord with nature. Cynics valued practice more than theory, and practice meant training and discipline (*askēsis*) for an outdoor life of poverty. Some Cynics embraced the lifestyle fully while others admired them from a distance, incorporating their ideas into their writings.[68] The Cynics adopted a frugal and self-sufficient lifestyle in order to be unhindered by societal obligations, to be free to critique the rich and powerful.

The Cynics' "uniform" was an indictment of the wealthy and their ostentatious attire. To critique clothing used as a display, the bearded Cynics went barefoot and wore only a worn thin cloak and carried only a staff and a travelling bag.[69] Their diet emphasized less cultivated food like wild lentils, and they were averse to cooking because fire was the "primal evil" that separated humans from nature.[70] They drank water, disdaining wine as a luxury.[71] As a denunciation of wealth, the Cynics renounced possessions and did not engage in regular work to support themselves. Yet theirs was "a cheerful and hedonistic, not a world-denying, asceticism."[72] It centered on discipline yet was more playful than grim and determined. Humor, from farts to paradoxical satire, was at the heart of their critique.

Like the animals for whom they were named, these Dog-philosophers could be biting as well as playful.[73] Cynics reserved their most intense invectives for the wealthy and their money. They criticized the wealthy for their arrogance and the delusion that their finery improved them as people, as well as for the violence and oppression they caused.[74] Bitter scenes in second-century CE satirist Lucian's dramas reveal the rage in the hidden transcripts into which the Cynics must have been tapping. In one, an assembly of the dead decrees that in punishment for their crimes, the rich should be returned to live as donkeys to bear the burdens of the poor for two hundred and fifty thousand years.[75]

The Cynics opposed not only luxury but owning property, the use of money, and the accumulation of wealth. This precluded owning slaves as well. The Cynics did not accept being labeled slaves, either, and held that humans were innately free regardless of any circumstances imposed upon them.[76]

Athletic events and religious practices also received their mockery. The Cynics joined other philosophers in mocking Greek athletic events, yet they appear to have gone where the crowds were to stage their critiques. They compared their own discipline to that of the athletes, favorably of course, and contrasted the virtue that was their prize with the fleeting honor sought in athletic competition.[77] They also mocked religious practices and held that all places are sacred, obliterating distinctions between sacred and profane.[78]

The Cynics' homelessness, however, most directly revealed their opposition to the most basic aspect of the root family metaphor undergirding Greek and Roman understandings of the state. Rejection of home and hearth, the basic unit of the state, expressed the Cynics' citizenship in the cosmos. The whole earth was their hearth and they lived without houses and walls. Without walls, they defaced the currency of the physical expression of the boundaries emphasized in the Strict Father family model. Without the central hearth of a house, they denied the civic and religious centers of the polis and the capital at the center of the imperial version of the cosmopolis.[79] This lack of center and boundaries broke down traditional customs demarking public and private. They enacted this lack of boundaries by eating and having sex outdoors and performing bodily functions, including defecation and masturbation, in public view. Their routine defacing of the customary divisions of public and private not only performed contempt for custom but also enacted a radical alternative family model and metaphor rooted in nature as their home.

Sexuality and Marriage
Relationships without Family

While sexual activity in public was part of their performance, sexual morality for the Cynics was more complex. They opposed using prostitutes as costly, adultery as a stimulation of sexual appetites, and "Greek love" (adult male sexual liaisons with attractive younger males) as part of a decadent lifestyle of the wealthy.[80] Their emphasis on self-sufficiency would appear to undergird their sexual *mores* as well as their negative attitude toward traditional marriage.[81] They opposed Aristotle's view of marriage as natural and instead viewed marriage as a breeding-ground for "attachments, quarrels, trivial worries" and the disparaged "conventional happiness."[82] In their mostly male-centered negative view of marriage, they viewed women as an impediment to their freedom.[83]

The notable exception was the "dog-marriage" of Crates and Hipparchia, two influential Cynic philosophers, credited as the teachers of Zeno, the founder of Stoicism.[84] Around 300 BCE in a city in Thrace, a young woman named Hipparchia, having chosen to live as a Cynic philosopher herself, defied her family's expectations and threatened suicide if she was not allowed to marry the much older philosopher Crates. Her parents relented, and they were married and lived a public life as Cynics, Hipparchia in the same garb as Crates and exemplifying the Cynic virtue of shamelessness (*anaideia*). They also attended dinner parties where philosophical discussions occurred, known as *symposia*, where later reports portray her as clearly holding her own. One report indicates that Hipparchia was identified as the one who abandoned the womanly virtue of wool-working, choosing to spend her time being educated in philosophy instead.[85]

The threat of women abandoning their virtuous wool-working continued to be an argument against their involvement in philosophy. The aristocratic Stoic Musonius Rufus refuted this perspective in the late first century CE.[86] He argued that women should study philosophy and that daughters as well as sons should receive an education, articulating a view of women as full human beings. He pointed to the basic similarity of men and women, that both have equal reasoning power, senses, an equal number of body parts, and a natural desire and affinity for virtue.[87] He asserted that both men and women should also aspire to the same virtues of good sense, justice, self-control, and courage, yet he held to the traditional division of women working at wool indoors and men being outdoors and going to the gymnasium.[88]

Musonius assumed a family model a little looser in its role definition but mostly conforming to the Roman Strict Father model. He did not expect educated women to depart from their role and appointed tasks. He portrayed a woman who would study philosophy as a wife managing an estate in the traditional role of the Roman matron. Such a woman would study philosophy to enhance her ability to assume her wifely role and to exhibit traditional wifely virtues, free from sexual improprieties, displaying the Stoic virtue of self-control. She would bring honor to her husband's and father's households.[89] Such a wife would study a Stoicism that upholds convention, apparently, not Cynicism.

In Hipparchia, who continued to provide an example throughout the Greco-Roman era, we see a woman taking charge of her own life, defying expectations of her as a woman and rejecting wool-working, a central female virtue, to adopt a counter-cultural Cynic lifestyle. Crates and Hipparchia demonstrated a different model of marriage, apparently as equals, with Hipparchia openly taking the initiative in deciding whom to marry, not allowing her marriage to be used for her family's gain. The couple reportedly had a son and possibly other children and raised them in their Cynic lifestyle.[90] Other reports indicate that some Cynics formed polygamous and polyandrous groups who raised children together.[91] Cynic views defaced the cultural currency of marriage, and the image of the one well-known Cynic woman defied the prescribed role of a woman in the traditional Strict Father family model.

Table 3 summarizes some elements of family models found in Cynic resistance and the Britons' resistance to Rome led by Boudicca.

The Cynic Family Model, Home, and Form of Government

In place of traditional marriage and family, the Cynics recognized a broad web of kinship. This web of relationship included the animals who modeled a life according to nature and the deities who modeled self-sufficiency. The Cynics participated as members of the "community of the wise" and with missionary fervor invited others to join them. The community of the wise shared the cosmos as their common home in kinship with the deities as well, and its members saw themselves as godlike mediators between the deities and humans.[92] Some evidence suggests that they perceived that "everything is full of the divine" and saw no distinction between the sacred and profane because the divine is everywhere.[93]

Whether the Cynics envisioned a form of government based on this expansively defined family model is a more complicated question. The Cynics did not speak of themselves as anarchists or democrats in the sense of those terms in their day, but they did give a lot of attention to the topic of kingship.[94] Cynics used Hellenistic era notions of the ideal king as a standard to address actual rulers, much in the manner of one of the weapons of the weak,[95] that is, ideal kings were depicted as representatives of the deities, "as 'living

Table 3
Elements in Several Forms of Resistance to Roman Empire and Its Strict Father Family Model

ROMAN STRICT FATHER	BOUDICCA/BRITONS	CYNICS
■ Form		
Roman Household in the *Domus*— *Paterfamilias*, son(s), legitimate wife, daughters, slaves, freed persons, clients, others (humans as the household)	United with "our land" as longstanding way of life Humans not envisioned as divided from natural world by walls of houses or fortresses*	Radical choice for life in accord with nature
■ Roles & Responsibilities		
Paterfamilias Sons Mother Daughters Slaves Freed persons Clients	Leadership: Monarch as military leader (male or female) Membership: Roles less differentiated with common child-rearing	No role differentiation: All can be "kings" as the best and most virtuous
■ Priority Childrearing Mission		
Prepare male heirs for survival in competitive world; Prepare female heirs for supportive roles; Prepare all others for assigned social station	Children raised by community to live as part of it in accord with traditional social organization, and to defend community when it is attacked	Children raised by groups of parents to live with them in accord with nature
■ Moral Priorities		
(Virtues determined by status)	*Minimal information* Women's self-defense against rape a virtue	Virtues same for all, living in accord with nature

*See also Table 4 and chapter 12 on *Anatolian Cult of the Mountain Mother*—Deity as the mountain, not confined in Temple, and life under her gaze in accord with her.

ROMAN STRICT FATHER	BOUDICCA/BRITONS	CYNICS

Conception of Moral Order

A natural and timeless order of role division within the household, the natural and entitled rule of Rome over the known world, and a just (Roman) system of reward & punishment in both	Moral order of people living within natural boundaries, defending against invasion; no other power has natural entitlement to invade or rule	Moral order of life in accord with nature, no role divisions and no households; all are "kings" who live according to this virtue

Conception of Character

Roman *virtus/pudicitia* as an individual moral essence established by adulthood	*Minimal information*	Virtues may be acquired at any time in life by choice to live in accord with nature; most people are unvirtuous by participation in "civilization"

Internal Role of Government

Uphold moral order in the nation-family	*Minimal information*	No government

External Role of Government

Protect Rome from barbarians and citizen-family from external evils	Protection from invaders	Cosmopolis means no boundaries

law,' 'benefactors,' 'saviours,' and 'liberators,'" strong and virtuous guarantors of "justice, prosperity and freedom for their subjects."[96] On the flip side were popular tales of tyrant-killing and truth-telling to rulers who were hardly ideal, resulting in heroic deaths of the truth-tellers.[97]

The Cynics also viewed themselves as kings in the Greek philosophic tradition of rule by the "best" and most virtuous.[98] In their understanding of themselves as kings and as mediators between the deities and humanity, they also participated in the kingly virtue of *philanthropia*, love for the people.[99] This virtue allowed them to include the unenlightened majority of humanity in their understanding of the cosmos as the beneficiaries of their missionary zeal while holding themselves apart in the virtuous community of the wise, a community that the rest of humanity could join by living as the Cynics did.[100] Those still deluded to participate in the polis and its allures were the Cynics' potential kin. The Cynics viewed themselves as benefactors in calling others to discard their delusions and live in accord with nature. Some writings hint that frugal and hard-working rural people, fisher-folk, and peasants were already included in the community of the wise as well.[101]

Summary

Family Metaphors in Cynic Resistance

The Cynics, then, represented a radical alternative to the Strict Father family model. Instead of a house with walls that defined a family unit, their family unit was nature itself. To live in unity with nature meant to live without walls and divisions at a radical level. They recognized no spatial distinctions between public and private or sacred and profane, and no wall to divide one family unit or city-state from another. While they had human relationships and some had children, the family model they appear to have assumed was the individual living in accord with nature—without set forms of human organization.

Yet the accounts of their activities do not portray them as hermits living apart from the civic life they denounced, seeking peace and silence in the natural world. Nor did they found separated communities of the wise away from the civic life they denounced. The nebulous community of these radical individuals was formed, paradoxically, precisely by their individuation, setting themselves apart as individuals, without leaving their social context. As the wise, they individuated themselves from civic life or any family model that assumed a house. They lived, each one, as a king in a kinship unity with and dependence on nature and yet understanding themselves as part of a community with others doing the same. The Cynics intentionally lived their "life in accord with nature" as a direct indictment of what they held in contempt and a call to others to their life of virtue on their terms. In their reliance on nature, they sought self-sufficiency that allowed them freedom to denounce custom. They maintained a close but adversarial relationship with the currency of custom even in defacing it, embodying an alternative family model in close connection with the dominant model.

Conclusion

In the previous chapter, we saw that the many movements of armed and national resistance to Rome's imperial domination showed that the empire was not as invincible as it projected itself to be. In this chapter, we have seen a variety of forms of intellectual resistance that demonstrate that major elements of the Roman Strict Father family model and its antecedents could not be assumed as "natural." Utopian visions and communal experiments challenged the notion that slavery was natural and inevitable, and undercut some assumed notions of property and inheritance lines so essential for the Roman Strict Father family. Some notions challenged conventional views of women. We also saw that throughout the Greco-Roman era mendicant Cynic philosophers brought a lived philosophical critique to urban areas to challenge the hegemony of the notion of the inevitability of the polis and state and the Strict Father family metaphor that grounded it at its very foundations, seen perhaps most graphically in their challenge to the very notion of walls for the family's house.

We have also seen themes in the thought of the Cynics that echo some challenges to the Roman Strict Father family model found in some of the national and slave resistance movements discussed in the previous chapter. We saw various forms of the notion of legitimate kings in the slave rebellions and national resistance to Rome. In the Cynics, we see another, in the notion that their version of the virtuous life can make anyone into a king, and a mediator between the human and the divine. Their view of life in accord with nature has some similarities to the notion of the intimacy of the Britons with their land articulated in the speech attributed to Boudicca. These and other themes emerge in popular religious movements as well. Some of the elements of these various forms of resistance are summarized in Table 3.

12

Ritual Resistance and Endurance

Popular Religiosity and Mystery Cults

Religious activity and organization could provide another social location for the development of hidden transcripts both as counter-ideologies of resistance and as modes of self-preservation. In religious activity, members of the population forged a meaningful connection to the ruling powers of their world, deities and their divinized human counterparts. Religious activity offered ways to resist as well as means to endure and to process the experience of being under Roman imperial domination.

While imperial cults were taking hold as a way of incorporating the population of the empire, especially local elites and urbanized populations, into a single Roman Strict Father family with one *Pater Patriae*, other religious practices were also flourishing. Other cults honored other deities and connected devotees in their experiences and narratives. Some of these cults have been called "mystery cults" and others were local and civic cults.

Many of the "mysteries" were connected to cults and religious institutions sanctioned and sponsored by Roman institutions. Others were not. Some were geographically removed from imperial influence. While the imperial cults permeated the urban areas of the empire, in the countryside and areas that remained un-Hellenized and un-Romanized, they remained alien.[1] Some rural cults on the

Anatolian plateau, for example, show no contact with the emperor.[2] In such areas, other cultic activity held sway, and rural populations maintained public cognitive systems not tied to the empire and often tied to features of the landscape of their own homelands. When they were dislocated into urban areas, people from these rural areas could also maintain and develop their cultic practices and cognitive systems as they gathered with others of their ethnicity.

Such cult associations and ritual practices could provide a social location for the development of hidden transcripts to create what can be termed "hidden communal cognitive systems," and could include people of different ethnicities. While their rituals might be associated with sanctioned cults and could occur in plain view, such cultic activities could also function as code language by using "linguistic codes, dialects, and gestures" to create social space for hidden transcripts, "zones of freedom" in the language of a hermeneutics of hunger.[3] In plain view, the ritual activity would be more likely to draw on the "public cognitive system" and its sanctioned activities both to critique and to provide a smokescreen to make the activity appear innocuous. The rubric of popular religiosity will be helpful in what follows to provide a way to understand such religious activity.

Popular Religiosity, Hidden Transcripts, and Hidden Communal Cognitive Systems

The imperial cults functioned as a "public cognitive system" that both projected Roman imperial power and included participants in the Roman family empire, an empire modeled as a Roman Strict Father family. Along with other state-sanctioned cults, the imperial cults articulated the public official transcript in both verbal and ritual expressions of imperial power. The public transcript projected a celestial Strict Father family headed by Jupiter/Zeus as the *paterfamilias* with deities identified by their familial relationships to him and to one another.

This celestial family pantheon was a complex web of relationship, even among the better known "great gods." Myriad deities populated Rome and its empire. These included the *Lares* and *Penates* of the household already mentioned. Natural places had deities associated with them as well. Festivals celebrated an array of deities with various functions. The late summer festival of Consualia, for example, celebrated Consus, the god of grain storage, and the Opiconsiva festival followed for Ops, the goddess of abundance. Deities presided over just about everything of any importance in daily as well as civic life. Each stage of agricultural production had its own specialist deity. Sarritor presided over the weeding, for example, and Convector over carting the harvest. Each step in a new husband's advances toward his bride on their wedding night also had an individual deity, beginning with Virginensis presiding over the loosening of her belt.[4] Deities personified everything from truth (Veritas) to Rome's grain supply (Annona). As many other peoples came under Roman domination, their deities also joined this vast celestial family, and narratives developed to describe their relationships.[5] As a "public cognitive system," the ritual activities associated with these many deities allowed for a complex web of connection and cognition indeed.

This broad array of deities in the familial pantheon allowed an array of options for worshippers to express their relationship to the family empire. They used a variety of religious and ritual expressions characteristic of popular religiosity. They could use worship of a deity that was recognized as part of the imperial-celestial family to create and preserve social spaces where they could express their experience in ritual and create their own communal cognitive systems as hidden transcripts. Popular religiosity created another social location for the hidden transcript, a location for what we will call a "hidden communal cognitive system."

Popular Religiosity

Central and Subsidiary Zones

Popular religiosity can be defined most simply as religious expression controlled by the common people rather than religious officials.[6] The concept of popular religiosity provides a way of understanding the distinction once made too starkly between "official" and "popular (or persecuted)" religion while also recognizing that these are part of "a *continuum* of religious institutions and practices."[7] Rather than proposing distinct "religions," the study of popular religiosity considers the creative processes that common people use on their own initiative to find meaning and connection both within and apart from official religious institutions.

Another definition of popular religiosity relies on the concept of a "central zone" that resembles the public transcript and the public cognitive system as "the order of symbols, of values and beliefs, which govern the society."[8] In the periphery, removed from the centers of power either territorially or hierarchically, attachment to the central zone weakens. There may be active rejection of the central value system, but intermittent and partial affirmation of the central zone is more common.[9] "Subsidiary zones" may also exist where populations possess their own value systems, occasionally and fragmentarily articulated within the central zone."[10] Popular religiosity is the dynamic process of ordinary people drawing on the central zone and on subsidiary zones to "erect for themselves worlds of meaning" and "create identities for themselves" and "make sense out of their lives."[11] The subsidiary zone is another way of describing the array of social locations where hidden transcripts develop. The term "subsidiary zone" acknowledges that these hidden transcripts are not necessarily completely counter to the "central zone." People have a remarkably flexible ability to resist and adapt simultaneously.

What distinguishes popular religiosity is a lack of "the drive for conceptual coherence that marks established religious traditions and institutions." Instead, the effort is to "gain access to the realm of power [represented by the central zone] and to use that power to benefit the individual," to give the person a sense of control.[12] In popular religiosity, then, we can find hidden transcripts that create alternative connections to the deities and powers that form the center of the public cognitive system of the cults in the official transcript.

Popular Religiosity in the Roman Era

In the Roman era, the central zone was defined by geography, with Rome as the center, but more importantly by Rome as the common ideal of *Romanitas*. Popular religiosity can be difficult to delineate in this era because its expressions were so abundant and intertwined with the religious activities of civic life. The celestial family provided various avenues of connection to the central zone as well as social and ritual locations for the creation of "hidden cognitive systems" in ritual expressions of hidden transcripts. These social locations were not necessarily separate from the public cults but functioned as social and ritual spaces in and related to them.

Popular Religious Initiatives Involving Individuals and Small Groups

Popular religiosity includes a variety of expressions that could provide locations for hidden transcripts. Individuals placed votive offerings and curse tablets in the civic-sponsored temples as well as in rustic shrines or near graves or in other "peripheral" locations. These could be expressions of personal need but could also function as "weapons of the weak." Curses, for example, could provide a means to denounce the actions of the powerful.

People formed associations that related closely to official cults. Associations could provide a location for the development of hidden transcripts, as will be discussed in the next chapter. Groups of women held their own meals in banquet rooms that were part of temple complexes. Yet their conversations over meals could create a discourse of resistance. Groups dislocated from conquered territories formed to continue the worship of their own deities, and those deities became part of the central pantheon, members of the celestial family. Their discourse of resistance could take shape in narratives, fashioned creatively in myths to explain the relationships of their deities and claim a place for their deities in the dominant celestial family. Yet their continued worship of their own deities maintained elements of their non-Roman culture, paradoxically hidden in plain sight.

Marginalization of Popular Religiosity

Religio and *Superstitio*

Yet the central zone defined the periphery by labeling some religious expressions as foreign and marginal. *Romanitas* was defined in terms of religious behavior. Romans described themselves as exhibiting proper religious behavior, *religio*, while *superstitio* was a derogatory term for the improper religious behavior of others seen as marginal, including women.[13] In the second century CE, the term *superstitio* was increasingly used to describe religious practices associated with certain foreign peoples, including Galatian, Egyptian, and Jewish people. The distinction between *religio* and *superstitio* was not so much in the content of any belief or in the choice of deities to be revered but in the form of the relationship with them, as Seneca summarized: "*religio* honors the gods, *superstitio* wrongs them."[14] *Religio* was as much about observing customary rituals as about belief. Excessive devotion and "irregular" religious practices were labeled *superstitio*.[15]

Many practices described as popular religiosity were considered *superstitio*. Such foreign innovations, sorcery, and magic posed a threat in the eyes of the Roman powers. Cassius Dio exemplifies this distaste for purveyors of such practices, complaining that those "who introduce new deities persuade many people to change their ways, leading to conspiracies, revolts and factions."[16] To name a practice *superstitio* was not to discount its power but to label it marginal and dangerous. Magic was *superstitio* and feared, for example, but not viewed as foolish delusion.[17] Prophecy not associated with the official augury of the Roman state could also pose a threat, as did Druidic prophecy interpreting the fire at Rome in 69 CE as a sign of the Roman Empire's impending end. Narrating the events of the war waged by the Gauls and Germans at a time of crisis in Rome, Tacitus dismissed the prediction as "an empty *superstitio*," yet palpable in his account is a mood of threat from the religious authorities of a conquered but rebellious people who could use prophecy and rumors as weapons of the weak.[18] *Superstitio* conveys the threat posed by transcripts latent in the religious practices of conquered peoples. "Foreign" practices also threatened the purity of Roman *religio* and the "public value system, centred on the official cults of Rome."[19] Imperial orders expelled and restricted practitioners of such *superstitio* and foreign practices, including magic and astrology as well as cult rituals, from the city of Rome.[20]

The distinction of *religio* and *superstitio* applied particularly to women in characterizations of their virtues or vices. Women were thought to be particularly susceptible to the lack of control associated with *superstitio*.[21] Plutarch, for example, advises the good wife to worship the deities her husband accepts and to "shut the door to excessive rituals and foreign 'superstitions.'"[22] In addition to the virtues mentioned in chapter 4, the *Laudatio Turiae* notes "*religio* without *superstitio*" among Turia's many virtues.[23] The emphasis in the public transcript on *religio* as a wifely virtue points toward a counterargument about how activities designated as *superstitio* could create social spaces for women's development of hidden transcripts. Women gathered for rituals that excluded men, some that were connected to events in women's life cycles, although not much evidence survives that offers much detail of their activities.[24]

Mystery Cults as Popular Religiosity

Some of the "mysteries" were also defined as foreign and marginal. Even though mystery initiations were part of the religious practices of cults that had festivals with public events on the civic calendars, many were considered foreign.[25] Cults of many deities included mysteries. The mysteries were not the cults themselves but initiation rituals that offered initiates "a special opportunity for dealing with the gods within the multifarious framework of polytheistic polis religion."[26] The initiation experience allowed the initiate to share the experience of a suffering deity. The Eleusinian mysteries, for example, presented the experiences of Persephone, abducted into the underworld by Hades to become his wife, and of her grieving mother Demeter. While the myth and mysteries had multiple meanings, the relevance for an adolescent girl processing the experience of marriage at a young age to an older man chosen by her family or for her mother relinquishing her daughter into that marriage is hardly difficult to fathom.

Initiations could include several ritual components. Recitations or re-enactments of myths of the cult's deities or ritual words were known as the *legomena*, the things spoken. These words could also be a commentary on another component, the *deikymena*, the things shown. These could be cult objects hidden in a basket. Dramatic enactments and ritual actions known as *dromena*, the things performed, could also be part of the initiations. The content of these components was secret, a "mystery" from the Greek word for "close," *myein*. The initiate's eyes were closed and later opened in the ritual to see what was revealed. Afterward the initiate's mouth was kept closed as well in secrecy about the ritual.[27]

The many cults with their mystery initiations, as well as public ritual activities, offered participants an emotive and cultural connection to deities in the celestial family. The cults were a venue for people from a wide range of social sectors to connect and emotionally process their relationship to the Roman imperial pantheon and their own position in the Strict Father family structure upon which Rome was founded. The many venues of cult activity offered opportunities not only for individuals to accommodate to their lot in life via identification with the experiences of a deity, but also for conversations that could form the hidden transcript. Associations, often formed to manage a part of the logistical details of cult activities, shared an organizational life and communal meals where cult ritual as public transcript could intersect with reflection on those rituals as the hidden one.

An Example
The Cults of Cybele and Attis

The cults of Cybele and Attis, which were among the non-Roman cults that found a place in the city of Rome and spread across the empire, offer an illustration of how, on the one hand, spaces for hidden transcripts could emerge in cults as they developed in the context of changing empires and, on the other, how the Roman central zone used inclusion to manage such popular religious movements—that is, how the hidden transcripts of a cult become part of the public transcript.

Movement from Phrygia into the Greek Central Zone

The cult known as the "Cult of Cybele and Attis" first appears in the historical record as a cult of the central deity in the Phrygian kingdom that dominated central Anatolia for centuries and was most prominent in the eighth century BCE. The Phrygians worshiped her as Matar Kubileya, Phrygian for "Mother of the Mountain," the source of the deity's name "Cybele."[28] She was identified as the local mountain in locations across the rest of central Anatolia as well.

Matar Kubileya was the only deity represented in icons in the Phrygian kingdom.[29] Attributes in her images include a bird of prey and other predatory animals, symbols of her great power, with iconography showing very little emphasis on maternal or fertility aspects.[30] Evidence remains of worship sites away from urban centers. These sites feature images of the Matar carved directly into rock formations.[31] The Arslan Kaya, a major rock-cut image of her from the sixth century BCE in Phrygia, portrays her flanked by an imposing pair of lions standing on either side of her with their front paws on her shoulders, as a formidable deity allied with the power of wild beasts.[32]

The Mountain Mother continued to be the principal deity in central Anatolia, where she was a guardian of law and an enforcer deity well after the Phrygian kingdom there was no longer independent.[33] Her Anatolian identity fused the power of nature and the force of the law in her overseeing presence as the mountain.[34]

Her cult moved into Greek colonies on the Black Sea and in Sicily, and then to the Greek mainland between the sixth and fifth centuries BCE, appearing as private ecstatic nocturnal rituals enacted in wild spaces outside of towns and not well received by local authorities.[35] The raucous and lively rituals worshipped a deity said to be "well-pleased with the sound of rattles and of timbrels, with the voice of flutes and the outcry of wolves and bright-eyed lions, with echoing hills and wooded [hollows]."[36] Later, as the contest with Persia became the focal point of Greek identity, these activities were portrayed as "foreign."

"In" but Not "Of"

Hellenizing a Foreign Deity

In the early stages, Greeks connected the Anatolian Mother with imagery of familiar goddesses. They found a place for her in the Olympic pantheon by conflating her with Rhea, the Mother of the Gods. They also exchanged her attributes with those of Demeter without merging the goddesses' identities. Yet while the Greeks Hellenized her image and made a place for her in relationship to the Olympian pantheon, she was not "in" precisely, even as their Mother. She was accounted for as a deity of the wild, wild places and wild expressions of emotion, and then as a deity that represented the "foreign" and the "oriental" from a Greek perspective.

In Greece, the Mother acquired the image which was to become the standard presentation of her throughout the remainder of the Greco-Roman era. The Hellenized image portrayed her seated and wearing a crown made of the walls of a mountain fortress, a "mural crown." She held the *tympanum* and *patera*, the large drum and the shallow libation bowl, which were part of the equipment for her rituals. She was usually accompanied by lions sitting at her feet or on her lap, portrayed more as a domesticator of the wild forces of nature than as a part of it.[37]

In the fifth century BCE, the Mother of the Gods took her place in the civic life of some Greek cities as well, most prominently at Athens where her temple was built adjacent to the Council of the Five Hundred (*bouleterion*). Her temple at Athens housed the official legal records and civic archives, and she was "intimately linked to the social and political institutions at the heart of the Athenian democratic government."[38] As the protector of the written records, she thus assumed the role as the legal guardian and enforcer deity that she also had in Anatolia.[39]

Including a Foreign Deity at Athens

How did this cult come to be included in the central zone? Following the work of Lynn E. Roller[40] it's possible to see how the Athenians shifted the narrative toward acceptability. The legend told of the founding of the Athenian temple of the Mother of the Gods (*mētrōon*) illustrates the tension between her civic role and the rituals of her cult. Popular religious initiatives create both a social location for hidden transcripts in the raucous nocturnal rituals outside the city and a connection for the cult at the staid heart of civic life. The outlines of the legend parallel the plot of Euripides' *Bacchae*.

First the outsider comes into town, in this case a *mētragyrtēs*, one of the cultic functionaries who went around gathering collections for the Mother of the Gods. These "Mother-beggars," known later as *galli*, made their appearance on the Greek mainland at about this time. Several ancient sources ridicule them as disreputable charlatans.[41]

The outsider succeeds in promoting devotion to a new deity, the Mother of the Gods, primarily among the women. Greek women and immigrants assist in the introduction of a new deity and join in creative interaction in ritual activities. The immigrants preserve their practices, the Greeks appropriate them, and both groups adapt them to changing circumstances.

In a pattern seen in the introduction of other foreign cults, civic religious authorities perceive the new cult as a threat and react violently, killing the outsider. The new deity is not amused and takes revenge. In this instance, the Mother of the Gods unleashes a plague in retaliation. Then the civic authorities repent and recognize the new deity's power. The authorities build the temple of the Mother of the Gods adjacent to the *bouleutērion*, and her temple becomes the public archive for Athenian legal documents. Later a public festival, the Galaxia, was added, and sacrifice to the Mother became a standard religious obligation of the young citizen males (*ephebes*).[42]

The "weapons of the weak" thus succeeded and achieved connection to the central zone sought by popular religiosity. The mystery aspects and the "mother-beggars" continued to be associated with the "foreign," however, and rituals outside of civic life offered an opportunity for expression of the wild power of nature in a hidden transcript.

Ecstatic rituals also created alternatives to the social boundary definitions expressed in the rituals of the formal civic cults. While the formal civic cults created social boundaries between insiders and outsiders, for example, the ecstatic cults "cut across boundaries of family group, gender, and political affiliation."[43] At night, in rituals outside the city, participants could experiment beyond these social boundaries and move their bodies more freely in ways that did not conform to social conventions, in dances and raucous ritual activity. While no alternative family model remains clearly articulated from their secret nocturnal activities, their rituals were redefining boundaries.

Integrating Cult Organizations

The development of an organization of associates for performing rituals (*orgeones*) in the Piraeus, the Athenian port city where many immigrants lived, parallels the course of development described in the narrative of the Mother's acceptance.[44] An association of alien ritual participants (*thiasotai*), probably Phrygians, worshipped the

Mother of the Gods in a private *mētroon* there. These "outsiders" thus developed their own subsidiary zone in the social periphery. By the third century BCE, however, control had been transferred to ritual association members (*orgeones*) who were Athenian citizens, although aliens were still included. With the shift to citizen control came a shift also to citizen women in the central cult positions.[45] The roles in the organization were the same as those of the Thracian cult of Bendis, and included a committee in charge (*epimeletai*), a treasurer, a secretary, and a priestess (no priest) elected annually by lot from the women of the association.

While the identification of the founding group as alien *thiasotai* could suggest the practice of some form of ecstatic ritual, we have no direct evidence of mystery initiations or ecstatic ritual under the auspices of these particular associations. Provisions were made only for sacrifices and processions, public activities. Yet there is evidence of continuing concern for the lower classes, even as the leadership was taken over by people of more elevated status, and the shrine was open to those who sought to make votive offerings to Anatolian deities other than the Mother of the Gods.[46]

These associations apparently provided a means for aliens to preserve their own cultural heritage while also connecting to the central zone. Yet this connection and acceptability meant that their cult was appropriated by citizens as a location where citizen women could exercise power. In this instance, we see the organizational development of the cult over time in one location, from the periphery into connection to the central zone.

At this point, someone might wonder, "but what about Attis?" Attis as a deity is a late Greek development. In Anatolia, the Attis was a priest-king. The first representation of him as a deity occurs on a votive relief from the Piraeus, dedicated to Angdistis, the Mother's Phrygian name, and to Attis.[47] The use of the goddess' Phrygian name also suggests the maintenance of some aspects of Phrygian cultural identity. Attis appears seated, receiving a small jug from the standing goddess. He is dressed in the Persian dress used in Greek art to depict "Orientals" generally, and he holds a shepherd's crook.[48] This relief shows the emergence of Attis as a deity from the

image of the Anatolian priest-king and the Greek portrayal of the
cult as foreign in its own stereotype of the "foreign" *par excellence*,
that is, as a Persian. Ironically, in the same era the Persian administration in Lydia in Anatolia also considered the same mysteries out
of bounds.[49]

What we see in Greece, then, is the outlines of a pattern that begins when an external influence enters into the periphery, inspiring a
popular religious initiative and leading to the creation of a subsidiary
zone of meaning where hidden transcripts could develop. In this
new zone, participants could experience and develop rituals that allowed unregulated direct contact with the divine. This popular initiative assumed organizational forms that were more adapted to the
Greek setting than those of the Anatolian homeland.

So even though the cult offered a social location for the development of hidden transcripts, there is a constant motion toward connection to the central zone. This motion results both from popular
initiatives seeking validation and from the need of the representatives
of the official religion to establish forms of control and regulation
over the cult. That pressure for control, of course, indicates that the
cult had some powerful appeal among the people.

So it is that the Mother of the Gods could be the guardian of the
law with a temple at the heart of civic life as well as the deity who
inspired ecstatic nocturnal rituals in secluded ravines outside the city,
where the boundaries and conventions that structure that same civic
life did not apply.

Movement into the Roman Central Zone

At Rome the Mother of the Gods was placed at the city's heart as
she had been at Athens, except the narrative of her entry into the city
begins not in clandestine ritual in the periphery but with the Roman
elite giving her a civic welcome. The introduction of the Mother of
the Gods into the city was part of Roman diplomacy, a geo-political
and diplomatic event as much as a religious one.

In a time of crisis at the end of the Second Punic War (218–
201 BCE), as the official story is told, Hannibal's forces were present in southern Italy and ominous meteor showers incited fear in

the populus. A prophecy was discovered in the Sibylline oracular books, which declared that, "whenever an enemy from abroad had carried war into the land of Italy, he can be driven out and defeated if the Idaean Mother had been brought from Pessinus to Rome."[50] This was one of several times that consulting the Sibylline books had yielded a prescription for the introduction of an Eastern or Greek cult or custom as a solution for a crisis.[51] The Romans thus arranged to bring the Mother of the Gods to Rome and sent a delegation to fetch her in the form of a black meteoric stone. On the way, they also called on the oracle of Apollo at Delphi, which had already predicted Roman victory three years earlier. Having received confirmation at Delphi, they obtained the assistance of King Attalus of Pergamon in securing the stone.[52]

The Mother of the Gods arrived in Rome on April 4 in 204 BCE, and members of the Roman ruling elite received the stone at the harbor in Ostia. The matrons of the senatorial elite reportedly formed a line from the harbor to the Palatine hill and passed the stone hand to hand so that each woman touched the deity as she traveled through their line to arrive in her new home in the Temple of Victory there. She became a protector of the Roman state, credited with Rome's victory over Hannibal.

The deity's placement in the Temple of Victory was temporary, however. A few years after her arrival, now as the Magna Mater, the Great Mother, of Rome, she was placed in her own temple nearby on the Palatine, next to the hut of Romulus, Rome's founder. This location associated her with the very foundation of Rome.[53] Later the houses of Augustus and Livia were constructed close by.[54]

As Romans elaborated the narrative of their Trojan origins, a narrative that emerged most prominently in the propaganda of the Augustan era, the Mother became identified more specifically as the Idaean Mother, Mount Ida towering above Troy.[55] Vergil's *Aeneid* features her as Aeneas', and thus Rome's, protector.[56]

The Mother of the Gods also figures in imperial visual propaganda, both in propaganda the Romans produced and in imperial propaganda they appropriated. For example, she appears on the Pergamon altar at the beginning of the battle scene where the

Olympian deities fight to conquer the serpent-legged children of Gaia, a primordial version of the battle of the "civilized" to conquer the "barbarians," a standard aspect of imperial ideology, both Greek and Roman. She rides into battle mounted on one of her lions to fight on the side of "civilization."[57]

Throughout the Roman era, coins displayed the image of the Mother of the Gods. In the imperial era, images often associate her with the divinized women of the imperial household, beginning with Livia.[58] Livia's assimilation to Cybele is noteworthy. She ordered cameo-cutters to portray the deity with her own likeness, and her face also appears on statues of the Mother of the Gods.[59]

Roman propaganda clearly associated the Mother of the Gods with their ideology of the inevitability of Roman world domination. As a major deity of Asia Minor, her endorsement mattered. By incorporating her at the center of Rome, recognizing her as the Mother of the deities of the entire Greco-Roman celestial family, and appropriating her as the Magna Mater of Rome, the deity who had once been central in the Phrygian kingdom was now portrayed as a supporter of Roman domination over her own homeland. When images assimilated Livia, the human *materfamilias* of the empire, to Cybele as the divine Magna Mater, the images also incorporated the Mother of the Gods into the imperial celestial family, pressing the Anatolian Mother into service as the Mother of the Roman Empire.

As part of the Roman celestial family, the Magna Mater assumed a prominent place on the festival calendar as well, with the seven-day *Megalesia* in April. The celebration was of the magnitude characteristic of civic cults and included public games, dramas, and lavish banquets in elite households.[60] As a civic cult, this festival was reserved for Roman citizens.

The Mother of the Gods thus joined the Roman imperial pantheon as a member of the Greco-Roman celestial family, a deity credited with protecting Rome's ancestor Aeneas on his journey from Asia Minor and with saving Rome from Hannibal's invasion. As a member of the Greco-Roman celestial family, she participated in the archetypical cosmic battle of the "civilized" to conquer the "barbarians." As the Magna Mater, she figured in Rome's self-presentation of its inevitable rule.

As the imperial period began, then, we might assume that the Magna Mater with her temple adjacent to the palace of Augustus became completely unified with the Roman central zone and even the Roman state. The complexity of the presence of the Mother of the Gods at Rome's heart illustrates the multifaceted religious dynamics of Rome's empire. What entered Rome was not only a cult object that could be nicely housed in a temple museum, but also a human cult organization. Attis accompanied the Mother as the god who castrated himself in loyalty to her, as well as members of the cult organization, the *galli*, who assimilated themselves to Attis in a ritual of self-castration in their initiation mystery.[61]

In addition to the civic cult of the *Megalesia*, a cycle of rituals for Attis was also introduced for a week in March. These "Phrygian" rituals became part of the official calendar during the reign of Claudius (41–54 CE).[62] During this festival, raucous and ecstatic parades featured Cybele on her lion-drawn chariot accompanied by her colorfully clad gyrating servants, the *galli*.[63] Spectators scattered coins along the parade route to offer a major collection for the cult.

During this festival, some young men joined the ranks of the Mother's cultic servants, the *galli*, in a ritual of self-castration. This reportedly involved an altered state of consciousness in which the initiate castrated himself while possessed by the *mania*, the madness, of the deity. The knife or potsherd in his hand was said to move at her direction, and this self-castration was indelible evidence that the *gallus* was possessed by the Mother of the Gods and spoke for her. After the ritual, the new *gallus* donned ritual attire interpreted in the Roman era as feminine, colorful flowing robes, long hair, and face powder. Roman citizens were banned, however, from participation in these "Phrygian" rituals.[64]

The cult had undergone a transformation in the Hellenistic era. Attis, for example, became prominent as the deity he had not previously been as a priest-king in Anatolia. Evidence from Rome indicates lower class devotion to Attis as a deity already in the era of the republic.[65] With the cult's entry into Rome, the *galli* took on a new role related to the cult's mystery aspects. The castration of the *galli*, their assimilation to Attis, and their ambiguous gender status became more central to the cult.

The goddess' eunuch cult staff also gained a base in a temple on the Palatine Hill at the very heart of Rome. Nothing of the sort had ever occurred in Greece. As the "Mother's beggars," the *mētragyrtai* wandered as itinerant collection agents. In Anatolia, they were part of temple state organizations and appeared in leadership, for example as negotiators with Roman forces, apparently allying themselves with Rome and negotiating a place for themselves in Roman expansion.[66] In the Roman era, traveling bands of *galli* appeared in Anatolia for fund-raising tours that involved performing blood-letting rituals under the possession of the deity. They would enter a village, for example, accompanied by an intoxicating rhythm beat on their large cult drum. During the ritual performance, they beat themselves with a whip of bones and slashed their arms with long knives until they bled. Then they splattered their fresh blood on an image of the deity. After the ritual, they circulated with baskets to take up a collection for their temple.[67]

Some of this temple staff, including *galli*, took up residence in the Magna Mater's temple at the heart of Rome. The Roman elite made every effort to keep the colorful eunuchs carefully contained in their precincts in the Palatine, however. They emerged into the streets only during specific festivals to produce their spectacle and take up their collection from the crowds.

Here we see the tension again between the cult's foreign, mystery aspects and its role in the central zone. From the Roman point of view, the image of the *galli* played a role in Roman self-definition during changing social circumstances. When the cult entered Rome during the republican era, Romans portrayed the *galli* and their flamboyant ritual frenzy as "foreign" and "not Roman." The Romans used the contrast as part of their self-definition as properly behaved Romans. Later, as elite Roman males were redefining their manhood during the transition under Augustus, the image of the *galli* as "not men" provided a contrast for their self-definition as male.[68] Many of the literary descriptions of the *galli* are part of this Roman male self-definition.

Even as the *galli* figured in the elite Roman males' definition of their masculinity, however, it is the *galli*'s own self-definition that offers glimpses of resistance to the Roman Strict Father family model. As issues of gender identity and the defense of Roman masculinity came to the fore in the early imperial era, the *galli* were also projecting their own identity. Images on funerary and other honorific monuments portrayed the *galli* unapologetically in the full regalia of their cultic identity, with the very elements that Roman authors mocked as feminine, in cultic garb with earrings and long hair, and wearing icons across their chests.[69] Rituals that had been performed only inside the sanctuary began to be performed publicly by freed persons of the imperial household.[70] This increased public presence also triggered Roman anxieties about the cult and provoked a backlash and polemics against the *galli* in increasingly graphic sexualized terms.[71]

The presence of the *galli* and their colorful spectacles appealed, however, to popular religiosity, exciting the popular imagination. While spectacle for the sake of popular appeal was not extraordinary in the Roman way of governing, the *galli* formed a direct contrast to the priests of the civic cults. The flamboyant and colorful gender-ambiguous *galli* with their religious frenzies would take up collections from the people while the plainly dressed priests of the traditional civic cults undertook cult activities as a benefaction for the people.[72] The *galli* also offered a means of direct access to divine power in their frenzy and trance, also in contrast to the staid civic cults which decorously mediated with the divine for the people at a relative distance.[73] The visible evidence of their possession by the deity, in their self-castration and in their subsequent frenzied bloody embodiment of the deity in rituals, also gave the *galli* indelible authority to speak for her.[74]

Here we have the alternative access to divine power that popular religiosity seeks, yet already connected as well to the central zone of meaning. In the array of cult organizations that produced the festivals, in which people from all sectors of Roman society participated, we can see opportunities for vicarious participation in the *gallis*' direct divine connection. We do not have much record of the content of their shrill cries and prophecies while in their ecstatic state, but their credibility as the voice of the Mother would certainly afford them an opportunity to speak words from a hidden transcript and attribute them to the deity, using spirit possession as a classic "weapon of the weak."

What we are seeing here is not an accidental introduction of wild foreign rituals into respectable, well-regulated Roman society but a more complex phenomenon in the development of the Roman Empire itself, a development that is very much part of the imperial genius of Rome. The Roman central zone of symbols and values incorporated subsidiary zones so that popular religiosity became, for the most part, integrally connected with it. Members of the elite may have needed to elevate their aristocratic noses and cast a condescending gaze on the ecstatic and flamboyant cultic activities as the foolish excesses of foreigners. Yet there they were, right at the heart of Rome, exciting a popular devotion in rituals that the Roman state acknowledged and even sponsored.

Later, in the second century CE, members of the elites found ways to participate in the devotion. An *archigallus*, a Roman citizen, appeared as the high priest of the cult, perhaps a sign of the elite's need to assert some management of a cult that had gained influence among the people. The *taurobolium* was introduced as an initiation ritual for elite individuals.[75] In this ritual, the initiate was placed in a pit and a bull was sacrificed above a perforated board or plate so that the initiate was showered in the bull's blood. This was "an aristocratic ritual whose purpose was to guarantee the health and wellbeing of the imperial house and city" and was "both a political and mystical alternative for citizens who could not participate in the castration reserved for the *galli*."[76] Over time, then, Roman elites and citizens assumed more influential roles in a cult once controlled by imported leadership defined as quintessentially "non-Roman."

In this cult at the heart of Rome, we see the creation of a social location not only for a hidden transcript of a foreign Phrygian tradition but also for a transgendered reality. The central ritual of the Phrygian festival days was a bloody gender transformation. Young men castrated themselves and became a cultic form of female, dressing not in women's clothing but in cultic garb now interpreted as feminine. The Romans' preoccupation with gender identification during the early empire brought the transgendered characteristic of their cultic identity more to the fore.

Their rituals offered a means to develop a distinctive counter-imperial ideology in rituals that could develop a transgendered cognitive system. In the context of the Roman Strict Father family empire, the *galli* became a distinctive transgender as a radical alternative to Roman hyper-masculinity, and they performed flamboyantly colorful and frenzied rituals as an alternative to the ever-appropriate socially prescribed behavior of Roman *pietas* in the civic cults. They served a celestial *materfamilias* who was, on the one hand, impressed into service as the Mother of the Roman imperial celestial family and yet, on the other hand, as the Great Mother, was not under the domination of a *paterfamilias*.

The gender-ambiguous *galli*, as the representatives of a cult that spread across the empire, formed a base for the development of hidden transcripts in the Roman era. Membership in the *galli*, specifically, offered a socially acknowledged form of transgendered life for those born male who did not fit in the Roman Strict Father family system with its rigid gender expectations. This social location embodied a ritual cognitive system that was an alternative to the public masculine cognitive system of the imperial cult with its focus on the image of the *genius* of the *paterfamilias*. In their bloody gender transformation and in their subsequent frenzied rituals, they "put on the mind" not of that *genius* but of the Mother of the Gods. They assimilated not to a divine image of masculine *virtus* and *auctoritas* but to Attis, a divine image of total devotion to a powerful Mother, and to the Mother of the Gods herself. Yet they also connected to the Roman central zone in devotion to its Magna Mater, guardian now of the Roman state and emperor. They forged a place for themselves to both participate in and display a critique of the Roman Family Empire.

In the family model of the cult, the *galli* were slaves of the Mother of the Gods. Yet as slaves, they were her agents and extensions, and they spoke for her. As slaves of a deity, they had authority. As trans-gendered slaves of a divine *materfamilias*, they embodied a challenge to the masculine-focused Strict Father family model. While the cult was well-ensconced in Roman civic life as part of the cultic fabric of the empire, it also provided an alternative ritual cognitive system to the public cognitive system of imperial cult. Here we see the intersection of the hidden transcript and the connection to the centers of power that popular religiosity seeks, hence the wide popular appeal of the cult across the empire.

Movement Back to Anatolia

Rome's eastern imperial expansion brought a Romanized version of the goddess back to her Anatolian homeland. The Roman model of the cults of the Magna Mater that had spread to all parts of the empire now encountered the Hellenized version of the Phrygian goddess in her Anatolian homeland.[77] Two changes in the cults in Asia Minor during this time can be traced to Roman influence. One was the increased prominence of Attis. With this there are also indications that the *galli* were becoming increasingly visible in Anatolia.[78] The other change was that the stature of the Mother of the Gods was somewhat reduced as she "lost ground to the civic cults of the established Greek gods and to the Roman Imperial cult" in Anatolia.[79] This weakening indicates a repositioning of the goddess in civic life with the increasing role of the imperial cults and other deities. Yet she continued to enjoy widespread popularity. While she was rarely the most important civic deity, her worship continued to proliferate in Anatolia, especially in the countryside and on mountain shrines.[80]

Abundant evidence attests to widespread popular dedication to the Mother of the Gods in Anatolia during this period, including small statuettes of her seated on her throne between her lions, as well as many small altars, *stelai*, and plaques dedicated to her.[81] Roman coins from this period issued at "virtually every city in western and central Asia Minor" depict her as a civic protective deity in the Roman image.[82]

The Mother's cult shrines are even more abundant in rural areas and in the interior.[83] In these rural areas, remains of worship

of the local Meter and of other local deities show a notable lack
of reference to the emperor or the imperial cult.[84] Local designations of the Mother in Anatolia proliferated during the Roman era,
named for the local mountain. She was Meter Dindymenê, Meter
Zizimmenê, Meter Imruragenê, Meter Silandenê, Meter Andeirenê,
Meter Sipylenê, to name just a few.[85] These many local identifications result from a popular aspiration as

> worshippers tried to pin the goddess down to a specific commu-
> nity in order to stress her connection with their particular locale.
> As a result, the goddess's topographical epithets in Anatolia, al-
> ways numerous, mushroomed during the first two centuries CE,
> to the point where every little town and village claimed its own
> individual form of Meter.[86]

The local cults appear to have provided a location for cultural
preservation. Consistent with popular religious strategies for negotiating imperial encroachment, local cults continued to assert the
dominion of the local Mountain Mother and other local deities, providing a location for hidden transcripts of cultural resistance in rural
areas.

In these rural areas, we can discern another contrast in the family
models. It is important to note that an essential difference for the
worship of the deity in the Anatolian rural interior was not only the
proliferation of her local identifications but also her identification as
the local mountain. As the Mountain Mother, she was for them both
the source of life, providing the water and the forests that sustained
them, and the guardian presence of their territory, as her overseeing
eye regulated their conduct.

As a metaphorical family or household model for the nation, we
can see the cult in its rural Anatolian home as occupying a much
larger "house" than any temple. At the heart of Athens and of Rome,
the deity was honored with a temple where she was "housed." The
cult image that was copied in replicas found across the expanse of
the Roman Empire was the one created for the temple at Athens
and portrays her seated with her tamed lions at her feet. We can see
the effort at Rome to contain the ecstatic "Phrygian" cult elements

within the temple walls, only allowing public displays during a confined set of days on the annual festival calendar. Honoring her with a "house" and with specified days on the festival calendar provided a benign means to confine her.

In Anatolia, by contrast, her body was not a portable stone but a mountain, the local mountain that dominated the landscape. The deity herself was the "house" both sustaining and overseeing all within her view from her mountain height.

With Roman imperial expansion in Anatolia, then, the Mother of the Gods figured as a powerful indigenous deity and as a deity with power in association with the foreign regime. Especially in the countryside "where local traditions remained stronger" she continued to be a guardian deity as a local Mountain Mother.[87] For more urban and Hellenized populations, she was a universalized Mother of the Gods and a civic protector in the Roman image, the Magna Mater who bestowed her favor on Roman dominion. In the hidden transcript in the countryside, we can suspect that there may well have been social pressures to exclude references to Rome, yet such a counter-ideology was not necessarily hermetically sealed. Aspirations expressed in popular religiosity can simultaneously seek a religious connection with the dominating power and a means to resist it by preserving traditions and cultural institutions. As Roman influence increased, the Mother of the Gods became a both a means of cultural resistance with the emphasis on the localized deity and a means of cultural inclusion with devotion to a deity closely related to the current power. She remained a deity capable of more than one identification.

Table 4 summarizes some elements of a family model found in the cult of the Mother of the Gods.

Conclusion

We can see, then, that ritual resistance is a pliable instrument in the toolbox of subjugated peoples. Such resistance allows for both accommodation and affiliation. Ritual also offers opportunities both to create social spaces to articulate discontent and to embody counterideologies as "hidden communal cognitive systems." This chapter

Table 4
Family Model in the Cult of the Mother of the Gods

CULT OF THE MOTHER OF THE GODS

▦ Form

Mother of the Gods; (King); Cultic Servants; Population

▦ Roles & Responsibilities

Mother of the Gods:
Provides sustenance for the people; Enforces rules & guidelines;
Administers rewards & punishment
King/Royal Family (Phrygia) (Midas/Attis as king):
Rule the territory;
Show devotion to the Mother
Attis (later, as deity):
Show total devotion to the Mother by self-castration
Galli (Transgendered):
Show total devotion to the Mother by self-castration as images of Attis;
"Slaves" of the Mother;
Mediate between Mother of the Gods and the people;
Speak for the deity;
Mediate between external power (e.g. Roman army) and people
People/Children of the Mother:
Show devotion by donating to temple and to *galli*;
Obey laws
(Some or all?) Participate in ecstatic ritual experiences

▦ Priority Childrearing Mission

Galli (Roman era) have no children, "childrearing" is inclusion in cult

▦ Moral Priorities
(Virtues determined by status)

Unity with deity

▦ Conception of Moral Order

Life sustained and regulated by the power of nature represented in the
Mountain;
Unifying with will of the deity is part of the moral order but may take the
form of wild and ecstatic behavior
The deity who inspires ecstatic behavior is also Law

CULT OF THE MOTHER OF THE GODS

Conception of Character

Character is formed in alignment with divine power of Mother

Internal Role of Government

Deity provides sustenance and regulation

External Role of Government

Representatives of deities mediate for people with foreign powers

has traced the complexity of such developments in the worship of the Mother of the Gods and her companion deity Attis.

The cult offered opportunities to develop not only accommodation and locations of power in relation to the Roman Empire but also social locations for resistance to the empire and the Roman Strict Father family model on which it was based. This can be seen especially in devotees' creation of a social location for a transgendered hidden transcript in Romanized areas and in the assertion of the Mother's presence in Anatolian rural areas as a social location for cultural preservation and maintenance of her identification with nature itself, present in local mountains.

13

Convivial Resistance and Endurance

Associations and Meals

Associations and the form of meals they shared became a widespread phenomenon in the Greco-Roman era. The meals and associations that have been mentioned in connection with organized ritual and cultic activity in the previous chapter provided some initial examples. As the rise of empires in the time from Alexander the Great to the Roman imperial era brought social dislocation for much of the population, associations and communal meals provided connections and a location for the emergence of hidden transcripts. In the associations and meals, participants not only formed and maintained social connections but also preserved and developed relational patterns that differed from the Roman Strict Father family. The importance of the associations and meals for understanding early Christianities has been demonstrated by studies in recent decades.[1]

Here I will discuss meals and associations together, but these are overlapping rather than contiguous categories. Associations had business meetings without meals to accomplish purposes in addition to the regular sharing of a meal, and many meals were shared in settings apart from the associations. Here a description of the communal meals will precede a discussion of the associations. Then we will consider the associations and meals as an intersection of the public and hidden transcript and a location for experimentation with alternative relational patterns.

Greco-Roman Communal Meals

Communal meals, or "banquets," were a common feature of social life in the Greco-Roman world. These meals were held in private homes, in the *triclinium* we saw in chapter 3 and in similar rooms in temple complexes, rented banquet rooms, and in club houses owned or leased by various forms of associations.

Referring to these communal meals as "banquets" appropriately calls to mind luxury and leisure, but "banquet" may also evoke a picture very different from the Greco-Roman meals.[2] These meals were not held in a large hall with tables and chairs. We should not imagine a large room with a head table and other tables spread with cloths and decorated with candelabra and colorful flower arrangements, with a place setting of shining plates and silverware and goblets at each seat. "Banquet" evokes the image of dozens, if not hundreds, of seated guests and a din of chatting interrupted when the formal speech-making program begins. The Greco-Roman communal meals as a social institution were much smaller gatherings, usually including nine to twelve guests who reclined on couches arranged in a conversational pattern. Couches lined three sides of the room, the fourth side open, around an open center, the three couches of a *triclinium*. If more space was needed to accommodate diners, additional *triclinia* would be added so that an appropriate size for discussion was maintained.[3]

Communal meals were something apart from everyday consumption of food and were characterized by consistent features. The two basic components were the main meal (*deipnon* in Greek, *cena* in Latin) followed by the *symposion/convivium*, a drinking party as an extended time of discussion and entertainment accompanied by wine-drinking and a dessert of fruits and nuts with salt to promote thirst.[4] The pouring of libations to the deities defined the transition between these two elements.[5] The "bread" and "wine" of Christian Eucharistic practice reflects its origins in these standard components of Greco-Roman communal meals.[6]

Other elements consistently framed this basic structure of the *deipnon*-libations-*symposion*. A host sent written or oral invitations a day or two before the event, and thus made choices about who would be included. Uninvited guests could be a challenge to negotiate, if the stock characters in literary descriptions are any indication.[7] Communal meals were held in the late afternoon or evening and lasted about two and a half hours.[8] When guests arrived, slaves assisted them in washing up, hands or feet or both, following various cultural norms.[9] Then they entered the room where the communal meal was to be held.

Reclining, Postures and Social Positions

Diners reclined on the couches provided. Reclining was a sign of elevated social status, and as a practicality, reclining to eat required being served. Traditionally only free male citizens could recline. Women who were present as part of the entertainment might also recline with them, but if wives attended, they sat at their husbands' feet. As customs changed in the Roman era, wives were more likely to recline with their husbands at banquets. At most meals, children and slaves also sat when they were not serving the reclining guests, although slaves reclined at some agricultural festival meals and in some of the mystery cults as well.[10] The posture of those present, in addition to the free male citizen diners, displayed their social status.[11]

The placement of the reclining guests relative to the guest of honor in the most favorable place displayed a pecking order. Some locations on the couches were more favorable than others, and diners were socially ranked by their placement. Usually the host determined the diners' positions, and placement depended on who was present at the meal and their social positions relative to one another in the group. The ranking was defined for each meal and could change depending on who was present and on changes in a diner's relative status.[12]

The first part of the communal meal, the *deipnon* or *cena*, was a hearty spread of cuisine served by slaves on portable tables or trays. Diners used their hands to eat from the dishes on these tables set next to the couches and used pieces of bread as napkins to wipe their hands during the meal. They threw the bread scraps on the floor

for the dogs. After the meal, slaves cleared away the tables and trays
and swept the floor. Then water was passed so the guests could wash
their hands.[13]

After these rituals concluded the meal, libations were poured to
the deities honored by the diners as an invocation. Libations most
often involved either pouring out a cup of unmixed wine onto the
floor or into the hearth or passing the cup around for each of the
diners to share in drinking it.[14] Diners were said to greet an unmixed
cup of wine saying "To the Good Deity! (*Agathou Daimonos*)" and
a subsequent cup dedicated at the mixing of the wine, "To Zeus
Savior (*Dios Sōterōs*)."[15] The libation was accompanied by a prayer.

For the Romans, the libation and prayer were associated with
household rituals. The Romans might include a short prayer to the
Lares used in private household meals, using the simple formula, *dii
propitii*, "May the gods be gracious!"[16] Cato the Elder gives instructions for a formula prayer over a libation to Jupiter Dapalis (Jupiter
of the Feast) in a meal in a rural household context, indicating that
wine is poured to honor the deity, and that Vesta may also be honored in the same fashion.[17] The Greeks recited or sang a prayer in
unison, a *paean*, accompanied by a female flute player.[18]

The libations are one indication of the importance of the deities
in the communal life represented in the meals and associations.[19]
In chapter 4, we saw the role of the deities in the Roman Strict
Father family. Participants in communal meals also honored the deities as patrons of their common life not only in the libations at the
meals but also in many other activities from sacrifices to singing.[20]
Diners could also welcome the deities themselves to be present at
their meals. For example, the god Sarapis was said to take his place
as host and *symposiarch* at his devotees' banquets.[21] Participants both
honored and communed with deities at the meals, and libations at
communal meals helped those present to maintain their relationship
to the deities and in some form invited the deities' presence for the
remainder of the festivities.

The choice of deities and the content of the prayers could reveal
familial, social and political allegiances as well.[22] Just as mystery initiations and cultic participation offered participants a way to connect
to the celestial family by experiencing the trials and tribulations of

one of its deities, the libation offered a way to show connection to one or more of those celestial family members and thus to place themselves in relation to the imperial reality that the pantheon oversaw and to express connections with broader civic life.

One telling choice at the libation related to the imperial cult. In chapter 9, we saw the importance of the imperial cults for establishing the empire as a family. As part of the promulgation of the imperial cults that started during the rise of Augustus, a libation to the *genius* of the emperor came to be expected in communal meals. The decision of a group to offer this honor or not, and the way the libation was offered, the facial expressions and whispered responses of participants to those nearby on the couches could signal an opening for the hidden transcript to emerge in the subsequent discussion, or that such discussion would be unwelcome.[23]

Following the libation, participants joined in a drinking party (*symposion/ convivium*) that could include a variety of group activities. They often selected a symposiarch from among them to conduct the festivities, set rules for the activities that followed, and decide on the amount of water to be added to the wine.[24] Conversation was a major element, along with musical entertainment, songs, and drinking games. Each participant was expected to offer some form of entertainment for the others' enjoyment. Group enjoyment was emphasized rather than individual pleasure. Activities could also include dramatic presentations, recitations, and speeches. Both competition and camaraderie were part of the mix.[25]

Communal meals, especially those hosted in houses, could also be sexually charged events, with slave servers selected for their attractiveness, not only women and girls but also attractive young men and especially young boys who served as cupbearers. The sexually attractive slaves were part of the host's display to enhance the atmosphere and opulence of the affair. Overt sexual activity was not generally accepted in the dining room itself and would take place in a nearby bedroom if at all.[26] As we saw in chapter 3, access to one of these more private areas of the *domus* meant closer proximity to the *paterfamilias* and hence a more elevated status. Such sexual contact with one of the household's slaves or an entertainer hired for the occasion, also most probably a slave, would thus indicate a closer relationship

to the host. Many communal meals took place as an activity of voluntary associations in locations other than homes, but there is no reason to believe that such meals did not also include sexually attractive
slave attendants as part of the ambience and entertainment. As we
consider early Christianities forming as house churches, as voluntary
associations, and as associations meeting in houses, this is an aspect
of the communal meals that should not be forgotten.

Meals at Family Occasions and Ritual Gatherings

The communal meal in the form described, including a *symposion*,
has been a major focus of recent research, yet other communal meals
also inform the context for meals shared by early Christian groups.
In chapter 3, we saw that the *paterfamilias* of a Roman *domus* regu-
larly invited guests for a meal in the *triclinium* and that members
of the elite hosted meals as part of their social obligations and their
household display, with household members playing their specific
roles.

Communal meals were part of the commemorations of events in
family life as well. In addition to rituals around the birth and development of the children of the Roman *paterfamilias*, families of many
social sectors in the Greco-Roman world shared communal meals,
most notably for weddings and funerary commemorations. Meals
were a major element in these events, and women were commonly
present at these gatherings, which could be larger than a communal
meal in a *triclinium*.[27]

Weddings were an occasion to invite all the family's connections
to avoid the embarrassment of someone knowing they had been left
out.[28] Women were invited, and some evidence suggests separate
tables for men and women.[29] Women sometimes hosted wedding
feasts for their children.[30] These familial occasions find a place in
early Christian texts as images that raise questions of inclusion and
exclusion in the community of Christ, depicted as an eschatological
banquet.

Chapter 4 mentioned the importance of the presence of the dead
in the life of the Roman *domus*. Greco-Roman funerary rituals, both
at the time of death and in subsequent commemorations, were, as
many other aspects of family life, more than private familial affairs,

with public processions to the tomb and often broad community participation.[31] Women's laments were a major element and could express more than raw grief. Laments afforded an opportunity for voicing hidden transcripts such as calls for revenge and various forms of protest as well as creating "a sense of continuity with the dead."[32]

Communal meals were also part of funerary practices and cults of the dead, with the deceased possibly considered to be present at the meal. A series of meals could be held at the tomb or at the home of the departed, at the time of interment, at intervals during the mourning period and at its conclusion.[33] Some portrayals suggest a communal meal with diners seated or with men reclining and women seated.[34]

In addition to these communal meals directly related to events in family life, women participated in meals in ritual and cultic contexts, as has been mentioned in connection with cults that included mysteries. Some of the rituals of the mysteries included men and women equally.[35] Women also held their own communal meals in the context of their own religious rituals.[36] A prominent example was the Thesmophoria, a state-sponsored autumn festival at Athens where the women gathered and elected their own leadership to preside over a women-only three-day feast.[37] Other women's festivals, some on the official calendar and some not, included feasting and ritual lamentations for the deities. Some meals took place in banquet rooms that have been excavated at sites of women's worship.[38] Women also organized their own visits to religious sanctuaries, visits that could include a communal meal.[39] Men were included in some communal meals led by women as well.[40]

In the context of religious rituals, priestesses also offered libations and blood sacrifices, and women worshippers shared in meals that included meat from the sacrifices.[41] Portrayals of women participating in the festive joy of a communal meal may also depict this activity as a womanly virtue. Such depictions indicate the relation between cult service and social status.[42] Images of cult association meals also depict women in prominent roles.[43]

Along with the communal meals of the voluntary associations to be discussed shortly, meals at family and ritual occasions form a part of the context for the development of early Christianities. When we consider meals as an intersection of the hidden and public transcript later in this chapter, we must remember that both women and slaves gathered in settings that could allow them extended conversation not only as diners in some cases but also in the preparation and serving of the meal. Such gatherings would give them an opportunity to forge a variety of strategies of resistance to oppressive aspects of relationships in the Strict Father family. These locations for hidden transcripts are relevant for understanding the development of early Christianities as house churches, some led by women. First, however, some basic understanding of the role of voluntary associations will be helpful.

Voluntary Associations

Various terms were used for voluntary associations, clubs, and guilds.[44] In Latin, they were most often called *collegia*, and in Greek, *thiasoi, koina,* and *eranoi*, as well as other terms.[45] Many groups had a monthly business meeting and a monthly meal, at separate times. People from a variety of social sectors, especially non-elite sectors, formed these associations for various purposes. For example, associations could function as a family for funerary rituals when members died, members who found themselves isolated from biological family members.[46] Associations might also take a particular logistical task in festivals for one of the deities. For example, the *cannophori*, the "reed-carriers," and the *dendrophori*, the "guys who carry in the big log," in the processions during the annual festivals of Attis, formed associations (*collegia*) based on their respective roles.[47] The associations served social purposes and often a specific mission or task as well.[48]

An association's purpose could be expressed in the term *koinonia*, the Greek term for the Latin legal term *societas*. *Koinonia* is a term with multiple meanings, however, and not confined to the notion of purpose. For example, *koinonia* could mean "community" to express a social value, one of the virtues expressed in the meals. It was also a term for the community formed and could specify the entity defined in Roman law as a *societas*, a voluntary partnership for a specific common purpose. In this usage, the common purpose defined the *societas/koinonia*. No written contract was necessary if the group of people was united in their common purpose. As long as each person upheld that common purpose, there was a *societas/koinonia*, and the relationship had legally binding status. When individual partners undertook action for the common purpose of the *societas/koinonia*, they were obligated to consider the other parties in the agreement, and when they undertook work for the common goal, they could legitimately expect compensation for their expenses. The *koinonia* was dissolved if the common purpose that brought them together was completed, or if there was fraud or deceit on the part of one member. A lawsuit by one party to the agreement against another also dissolved the partnership. The *koinonia/societas* continued as long as the relationship of good faith and trust continued. Voluntary associations organized around a shared purpose would form such a *koinonia/societas*.[49]

Membership criteria for the voluntary associations was determined by the group itself. Some included women and slaves as well as free citizen males. Social networks provided the basis for the formation of voluntary associations. These networks could be based on family or household ties, ethnic identity, neighborhood, occupation, or cultic activity.[50] One example of a household association was founded by a man named Dionysios, the head of a household in Philadelphia in Lydia in Asia Minor. An inscription establishing a cult association in a room in his home reports that the impetus for its establishment was a dream given by Zeus. The association was open to "men and women, free people and household slaves," and membership does not appear to have been limited to the household.[51] Immigrant groups also formed associations based on their ethnicities. These could include freed persons and slaves, and neighborhood associations could include women.[52] People formed associations based on their occupations and trades as well. Associations related to cultic activities, including those formed by mystery initiates, could include children as well as both men and women and slaves.[53]

Financial sponsors, both male and female, provided resources for associations' communal meals and other activities.[54] In turn, associations honored their sponsors in laudatory inscriptions and other public acknowledgements, and some could provide a "cheering section" at the arena to chant a slogan on behalf of their patron.[55] Specified dues and required contributions for the meals and other purposes also provided self-funding for associations. Associations provided public benefactions for their cities as well, many of which honored prominent citizens and officials, including imperial officials.[56] Such financial support formed connections based on honor, and associations were part of the social networks in civic life established by benefactions.[57]

Voluntary associations organized in a form analogous to a *polis*, as little city-states that afforded their members the experience of democratic participation. Each association managed its own finances and property, elected its own officers, and admitted members according to its own constitution and structure.[58] Yet the associations could also use familial language and function as fictive families as well. In addition to the familial funerary role many associations played, some used familial terms with members referring to one another as "brothers" and sometimes "sisters," and to their leaders and financial supporters as "fathers" and "mothers."[59] As organizational forms, voluntary associations might be seen as shape-shifting, morphing from social to political groups and back.[60] As both social and political organizations, associations were similar to elite families of the time. As organizations that exhibited aspects of both *polis* and family, the associations could also provide an intersection where participants could experience and experiment with alternative family and organizational models as a root metaphor for the state.

Meals and Associations as an Intersection of Public and Hidden Transcripts

In the associations and communal meals, the public and hidden transcripts intersected. Associations offered members a sense of group identity, and communal meals confirmed their belonging by defining insiders who shared the food and drink and conviviality over against outsiders not invited to partake. At the same time, associations functioned to integrate members into civic life beyond the group itself, helping them find their place in the society and cosmos being established by the Roman Empire.[61] This included connecting to Roman imperial power by honoring the emperors at several levels, from libations to monuments and civic projects. Roman imperial ideology could also visually surround the diners, as frescoes on the walls of banquet rooms depicted scenes of Rome's ideology of victory and its myths of origins.[62]

When non-elites gathered for communal meals, they were not necessarily anti-Roman or counter-imperial. The associations' communal meals offered a potential intersection of the public and hidden transcript, a potential not always realized. Yet the historical record more readily preserves the public transcript, and we must use informed imagination to see how the hidden transcript could be present. For example, while frescoes would impose formidable images of Roman victory at the meal, they could also offer a topic for criticism in discussion or sidebar conversations. We should not simply assume that diners, or those who served them, agreed with such visual presentations. We do have some evidence of social experimentation in the meal settings that suggests critical thinking about such aspects of the meal, especially among philosophers whose conversations are not lost to history.

Values and Virtues in the Communal Meal

Meals in the associations could be a location for social experimentation particularly around a set of values and virtues that emphasized community. In the communal meals, participants could communicate with more mutuality than was expected in social relations dominated by the metaphor of the Roman Strict Father family. Communal meals thus experimented with utopia and enacted aspects of the utopias described in chapter 11. Utopic aspirations can be seen in the effort to eliminate or mitigate social divisions and to display abundance in the provision of food and drink.[63] How and whether the utopian experimentation affected relationships beyond the meal context is an open question, however. While there were some occasions when slaves and slaveholders reclined at meals together, for example, this momentary equality at the meal did not appear to change the relationship.[64] Yet at some communal meals diners attempted alternatives to the values and virtues emphasized in the hierarchy of the Roman Strict Father family model and the empire based on it.

Rather than virtues being assigned by social position, according to the role one had in the Strict Father family, common values for all the participants applied in what has been termed the "ethics of the meal."[65] These community-oriented virtues can be summarized as:

- sharing in community (*koinonia*)
- equality and friendship (*isonomia* and *philia*)
- pleasure (*hēdonē*) and festive joy (*euphrosyne*)
- a combination of grace, joyful festivity, reflection, and godliness summed up in the Greek term *charis* as the spirit of the meal[66]

The meals also provided a location for a difficult negotiation between competing sets of values. The communal virtues were expressed in a context that also included jockeying for social prestige in seating arrangements and leadership positions as well as for a superior portion of the food. The meals expressed a form of relationship grounded in sibling solidarity, and the emphasis on equality was expressed in a standard adage, "Make no differences!"[67]

The values and virtues indicate a relationship of the participants in familial terms as brothers, expressing the ideal virtues of friendship (*philia*) and equality (*isonomia*) and broadly accepted family values of "solidarity, goodwill, affection, friendship, protection, glory, and honor."[68] The meals and the associations offered a form of fictive family that emphasized the sibling relationship rather than the central role of the *paterfamilias*.[69] Rivalry for positions, while in tension with a pure ideal of equality, exhibits an aspect of the sibling relationship, a characteristic of a "band of brothers."

The ethics of the meal were a frequent topic of discussion at meals recorded in philosophical texts, and especially in the meals of Epicureans.[70] They discussed whether guests should be placed according to rank or allowed to place themselves, as well as whether portions of food should be equal or differentiated by rank.[71] Philosophical discussion reflects a view of the meal as a community functioning by "its own rules and not those of society-at-large."[72] One of the rules, however, was the priority of "good order" at the meals, manifested in accepting the couch placements assigned by the host. When total equality was impossible, good order was to prevail.[73]

Table 5 summarizes elements of the Greco-Roman meal as a family model.

Associations, Meals, and the Hidden Transcript

While they functioned for social integration in civic life under Roman domination, the associations and meals also offered a location for subversion. Roman authorities recognized the threat and imposed some legal restrictions and controls on them.[74] The benefactions from elites that formed stabilizing social networks were not entirely motivated by civic responsibility and good feeling. The threat of social unrest and rioting was also an impetus to provide funding.[75] The tacit threat of unrest gave association members some power and influence in relation to the elites.

The ritual setting of the communal meals offered a location for the delicate power negotiation of hidden and public transcripts. Participants could, as part of the content of the libations and *symposion* and with some protection in numbers for plausible deniability, allude to subversion without making it explicit. This undertone of threat would allow them to exercise some power in relation to the elites.[76]

Meals were private in the sense that they were hosted by private individuals, but architectural choices in banquet locations afforded public viewing and access.[77] The meals created a public-private space for "the imagination of alternative worlds" as well as the exercise of communal values and virtues.[78] The content of the activities at the *symposion/convivium* could express notions and visions that challenged power relationships, subtly or openly mocked local civic leaders, lampooned social conventions, and much more. Drinking songs, humorous skits, and story-telling could all convey hidden transcripts in a semi-public venue. Drink could provide some cover for pushing at some boundaries of convention and edging toward offending the powerful. Physical proximity of the diners to one another would also empower "under-the-breath" commentary where such views could be expressed. Exposure of hidden transcripts always involves some

Table 5
Family Model Expressed in Associations and Meals

SOCIAL ORGANIZATION OF ASSOCIATIONS AND MEALS

▧ Form

Organization of equals with rotating leadership and shifting social stratification; "Sibling Solidarity" as underlying assumption

▧ Roles & Responsibilities

Leadership: *Symposiarch*, President, Fathers & Mothers of associations. Most leadership roles term-limited. Responsibilities for chairing business meetings and conducting affairs of association; hosting responsibilities for meals
Membership: Participate and pay dues; contribute to the "festive joy" of the meals
Servants and Attendants (Slaves):
Table service and entertainment functions at meals
Patron (usually not a member): provides resources, receives honors
Varying influence of gender, slave, and other status designations external to group

▧ Priority Childrearing Mission

Participants prepared for joyful participation in the meal
Happiness as a priority
(Presence of children as participants and/or servants or entertainment varies)

▧ Moral Priorities (Virtues determined by status)

(Generalized virtues, not specified by role)
    Community (*Koinonia*)
    Equality (*Isonomia & philia*)
    Pleasure (*Hēdonē*)
    Grace/Generosity/Beauty (*Charis*) expressed as utopian political values

▧ Conception of Moral Order

Joy as moral order?
System of reward and punishment specified in fines for violation of order of banquet & other offenses against community

▧ Conception of Character

Character of the gathering as joyful as priority?
Maintain the order of the meal

▓ **Internal Role of Government**

Maintain the purposes of the association

▓ **External Role of Government**

Accomplish outward purposes of the association

---

risk, but the communal meal as a social institution provided a venue with a modicum of safety, especially when diners maintained an atmosphere of good humor, conviviality, and festive joy.

Conclusion

Associations and communal meals were major social institutions that provided a context for the development of a variety of counter-ideologies including early Christianities, as we shall see in Part 5 and in volume 2. These social institutions also offered a venue for experimentation with forms of social organization that represented alternatives to the Roman Strict Father family on which the empire was founded. These are summarized in Table 5.

Conclusion to Part IV

The Roman Empire projected itself as inevitable and omnipotent, based on a family model portrayed as natural. In these chapters in Part 4, we have seen that resistance was not nearly as futile as the empire would have its inhabitants believe and that resistance came in many forms, from military resistance to table talk. Military resistance was successful in limiting the empire's expansion to the north and east and nearly successful in many instances. Military resistance and the threat of it kept the Roman army busy. Resistance took intellectual forms as well. Some intellectual resistance envisioned alternative forms of social organization that critiqued aspects of the empire and its purported inevitability. Some resisted intellectually by living in communities that embodied alternatives. Examples include the social experiments of Aristonicus at Heliopolis, the *therapeutai* described by Philo, the pacifist Essene communities, and the communities who wrote the Dead Sea Scrolls. Others resisted by embodying and proclaiming a critique in a less defined community as Cynics. Ritual and cult organization provided another form of resistance. In just one cult we saw a variety of forms of resistance, including rural people maintaining their cultural heritage by recognizing the unconfined identity of their deity as a local mountain mother and transgendered cultic representatives forming a location to resist the hyper-masculinity of the Roman Strict Father family model. Finally, we saw that in the seemingly simple form of communal meals, various forms of resistance were possible.

All of these forms of resistance created social spaces for the development of hidden transcripts that could challenge the assumed inevitability of Roman imperial domination and the claims of the Roman Strict Father family model on which that domination was founded was the natural form of family. While most of the content of those hidden transcripts is lost in the victors' writing of history, we have caught a few glimpses and hints peeking through. Several common themes can be detected.

One theme or metaphor that emerges in disparate forms of resistance is the notion of kingship. Mithradates VI emphasized legitimate kingship as an image of resistance partly because the republican Romans, whose impulse to imperial conquest he and the kings who joined with him opposed, so despised the image of kings. For his military resistance movement, the image of the king portrayed legitimate rule of a territory in a community of kings of other territories, and legitimate kingship countered what he portrayed as Roman banditry, illegitimate seizure of the property and territory of others. Leaders of various uprisings also adopted the trappings and language of kingship, and in many cases the image of kingship indicated not only the personal aspirations of the leader but also the national aspirations of the participants in the movement. In one rebellion in Palestine, participants killed the hereditary priesthood and elected one of their own as high priest. While the title and position was priest, not king, the notion of election reveals an alternative view of the divine source of power residing in the community that could also apply to kingship. In quite a different form of resistance, the Cynics used kingship as a core image, relying on the Greek philosophic tradition of rulers as the most virtuous. They viewed themselves as the "best" and "most virtuous" and thus as mediators between the deities and humanity, as legitimate kings. Their view did not, however, assume that one-person rule of a territory was an inherent aspect of kingship. Theirs was a more communal notion of kingship that did not imply national aspirations but instead incorporated their cosmopolitan view. All were citizens of the cosmos of nature, and all could be its kings by living virtuously in accord with nature. Ritual resistance could also be centered around deities with kingly origins. For example, Attis, who became the deity to whom the *galli* assimilated themselves, was originally the title of kings.

Critiques of slavery emerge as a theme in many of the resistance movements. Mithradates' allies included Spartacus, the leader of a slave rebellion, and his armies included large contingents of freed slaves. The Heliopolitan social experiment that was one of his inspirations also opposed slavery. Some utopic visions imagined social organizations without slavery, and the banquets of the *therapeutai* displayed the absence of slavery in their community. Some cult organizations, communal meals, and voluntary associations included slaves as members and as equal participants in some activities although this was hardly the prevailing norm.

Alternative aspects of family models have been seen as a theme as well and we have seen indications of alternatives to the model of the Roman Strict Father family. Boudicca, for example, at least as presented by Cassius Dio, describes the Britons as a nation based on their common territory and name. She emphasizes their cooperation with one another and reports family relationships with common ownership. The definition of family assumed in her speech does not focus on a *paterfamilias* at the head but on commonality and relationship among the family's members. The Cynics, too, conveyed an alternative to the family centered on the *paterfamilias*. Their alternative was primarily centered in the individual, but they also formed groupings that relied on relationship to other individuals with children sometimes in the mix. Rituals in popular religious cultic formations could critique as well as cope with the Strict Father family model of the Greco-Roman era. The transgendered family formation of the *galli* in the cult of the Mother of the Gods offered one example. In the camaraderie of the Greco-Roman communal meals and voluntary associations, we also saw an emphasis on a fictive family structure centered on the sibling relationship that could offer an alternative definition of family.

In Part 5 and in volume 2, we will see how these themes emerge in early Christian resistance to the Roman Strict Father family model and the empire founded on it.

Part V

A Community of Resistance and Endurance

Early Christians Meeting in the House of a Slaveholder

In the preceding chapters, we have seen the Roman Strict Father Family model as it came to dominance in the Roman Empire. We have seen it in the microcosm as a social reality in the Roman *domus*. The Roman Strict Father family model, as the form of family of the Roman elites, was a dominant family model as the provinces Romanized. We have also seen that the model dominated the macrocosm, as the empire became a Roman Strict Father family metaphorically and literally. This family model made one-man rule viable in the Roman Empire without needing the title of "king" for the one man who ruled.

This family empire met with resistance, however, in a variety of forms as we have also seen. We saw open and armed resistance as conquered territories refused to accept Roman rule. We saw intellectual resistance that included public displays as well as thought experiments in alternatives. We saw resistance in rituals and religious expressions that offered common people alternative connections to power and created social locations for the preservation and development of alternative world views. Finally, we considered the associations and meals that offered social locations for experimentation with alternatives. Hidden transcripts could develop in many of these

231

locations, and some elements of alternative family models were visible in many of them.

The Roman family empire may have proclaimed its own inevitability, but the acquiescence of those they ruled was hardly universal.

A brief letter preserved among Christian texts offers a glimpse of a community grappling at several levels with the dominant Roman Strict Father Family model of the empire. A close examination of this short letter can afford us an opportunity to bring many of these elements together using informed imagination to perceive a community developing a counter-ideology in a social location where hidden transcripts could develop.

As was mentioned in the introduction, here we will shift gears to move toward the second volume of this project. Part 5 will look at one text in the relational context of the Roman Strict Father family model and the empire. Individual scholars will be mentioned more extensively in this part in order to acknowledge the groundbreaking work of a group of African American scholars on the letter to Philemon. Chapter 15 will also include a verse-by-verse review of the letter. Responses from discussion groups who have made use of earlier versions of this material indicate that hearing and discussing the letter at this level of detail makes the relational issues in the family and household models and life in the empire more vivid and understandable. Not every aspect of the preceding discussion will come into play, of course, but an intense focus on one letter to one community can give us one picture.

14

Paul's Letter to Philemon

Preparing to Hear the Letter

A brief letter to Philemon can be found among the letters of Paul, one of the early organizers of communities that would later be identified as Christian. The letter is twenty-five verses long, easy to flip past while paging through the New Testament. In the letter, we see Paul negotiating his way through something of a prickly relational problem. Using informed imagination to consider this letter, we can gain some insight into the web of relationship in an early Christian community meeting, in a household centered on a *paterfamilias* who owned slaves.

In an initial reading, the situation is this: Paul, mentioning Timothy, writes from imprisonment. Previously, Paul had brought Philemon into the community of Christ, and a Christian assembly was meeting in his home.[1] Philemon is a *paterfamilias* of enough means to have a house that will accommodate the meeting of an assembly (*ekklesia*) and to have guest rooms. This may not necessarily mean an enormous elite household, but the size indicates a household with slaves. While imprisoned, Paul has met up with Onesimus, a slave from Philemon's household. In prison, Onesimus has apparently become a member of the Christian community by being baptized by Paul.[2] Paul sends Onesimus back to the household of Philemon with the letter we have preserved in the New Testament. In it he seeks Philemon's assent to some form of change in his relationship with Onesimus.

The Letter to Philemon and Slavery
Highlights in the History of Interpretation

In the early centuries of the Christian era, some theologians argued that the letter to Philemon should not be included in the canon of the New Testament because it was too mundane. John Chrysostom and others argued for its inclusion precisely because it provided ammunition in defense of Christian slave-holders. His and others' arguments in the late fourth and early fifth centuries indicate that there was also a current of opinion that Christians should not hold slaves.[3] The letter to Philemon was included in the canon as a text useful for advocates of slave-holding.[4]

We can see this same tension about the purpose of the letter and its place in the canon from an incident in the United States antebellum South where Philemon was a chestnut for the advocates of slavery. A circuit-riding evangelist during the years of slavery records his experience with this text. In 1833, Charles Colcock Jones relates:

> I was preaching to a large congregation on the Epistle to Philemon: and when I insisted on fidelity and obedience as Christian virtues in servants, and upon the authority of Paul, condemned the practice of running away, one-half of my audience deliberately rose up and walked off with themselves; and those who remained looked anything but satisfied with the preacher or his doctrine. After dismission, there was no small stir among them; some solemnly declared that there was no such Epistle in the Bible; others that it was not the Gospel; others, that I preached to please the masters; others that they did not care if they ever heard me preach again! ... There were some too, who had strong objections against me as a Preacher, because I was a master, and said, 'his people have to work as well as we.'[5]

These slaves did not hear this as a liberating text. Consider this: *slaves* in 1833 not only got up and left a sermon but also claimed their own right to determine what is and is not in the Bible. While most current interpreters do not use the letter to defend slavery, and some even see it as anti-slavery, the slaves' verdict is something to reckon with in our interpretation. Here we can glimpse the hidden transcript from the era of slavery in the United States and the critical thinking happening in discussions among forcibly illiterate slaves. Later as we examine the letter in the context of Philemon's household, we should imagine these slaves present with us as well.

Interpreters have also seen Paul as demonstrating the meaning of his message of world transformation by advocating for some form of equality for Onesimus. One such optimistic view names what happens in the letter "a rupture in the normal reality of slavery" that requires the community meeting in Philemon's house to confront the question of slavery.[6] Many current interpretations, as well as abolitionist interpretations in the nineteenth century, assume the portrait of a "radical Paul" challenging slavery on some level.[7]

With an awareness of how the letter has been used in controversies over slavery, let us turn to examine the situation of the letter in more detail. What occasioned the meeting of Onesimus and Paul in these circumstances? A variety of explanations are debated.[8]

Allen Callahan revives an abolitionist interpretation to contend that Onesimus may not have been a slave at all but Philemon's estranged blood brother. He argues that the identification of Onesimus as a slave is metaphorical.[9] Without modification, this explanation is less plausible than other possibilities and has generally been found thought-provoking but not persuasive. Here I will assume that Onesimus was, indeed, a slave. He could very well have been both Philemon's slave and his blood brother, as Demetrius K. Williams points out.[10]

The traditional interpretation, still often uncritically assumed, portrays Onesimus as a runaway slave. John Chrysostom presented this explanation in the late fourth century in arguing for the inclusion of Philemon in the canon of the New Testament.[11] If Onesimus was a runaway slave, however, the letter gives us little indication of the severe legal consequences for both Onesimus as a fugitive and Paul for assisting him. This interpretation must also explain how Onesimus happened to end up in prison with Paul and why Paul can send him to Philemon. A captured runaway would fall under the control of legal authorities, not another prisoner. In addition, the assumption that Onesimus was some form of "bad slave" shares a legacy of interpretation from perspectives that justify the slaveholder. Whatever the circumstances, I would join Matthew Johnson in starting from the assumption that whatever caused Onesimus to leave, he was *justified*.[12]

Onesimus may have come to Paul to ask for his intervention as an *amicus domini* (friend of the master) due to some difficulty with his master Philemon. This option is the most probable. A slave who had a complaint could appeal to the master's friend, usually someone higher in rank, as Paul was in the Christian community. The friend would assist in resolving the matter.[13] Such a slave would not be considered a runaway.

It is also possible that Philemon may have sent Onesimus as a messenger to Paul, probably with financial assistance from the community.[14] In this case, the letter still hints that there were difficulties between Onesimus and Philemon.[15]

Philemon may have sent Onesimus as a gift to Paul in prison, thus assuming the role of Paul's patron. In this case, Paul sends Onesimus back with the letter in order to refuse the gift and to clarify that he does not accept a status as Philemon's client.[16] While this proposal presents several difficulties, it reveals the status negotiation at work in the letter.

Another plausible reading of the situation of the letter does not specify how or why Onesimus met up with Paul in prison, but sees the language of "usefulness" at verse 11 as a reference to Onesimus' sexual usefulness.[17] This reading accounts for the ubiquitous "usefulness" of slaves to satisfy their masters' sexual urges and refuses to sanitize Paul to conform to the sexual mores of later centuries. In this reading, Paul's request has more to do with Onesimus' usefulness to Paul—and perhaps his restored usefulness to Philemon—as a sexual object than with a change of status that would benefit Onesimus.[18] Although this reading founders at some other points in the letter, it will provide some useful insight for the verse-by-verse reading in chapter 15.

In any case, once he arrived in the prison, Onesimus got to talking with Paul and probably Timothy and the others listed in verses 23–24. Perhaps matters were discussed that indicated some difficulty between Onesimus and his master. In any case, Paul accepted some form of parental responsibility for Onesimus as his "child" (*teknon*). The usual assumption, accepted here, is that Onesimus decided to join the community, and Paul baptized him. If this reading is correct, we learn something about baptism in the assembly. By baptism, Paul metaphorically adopts or "begets" Onesimus and takes a new role as his father (v. 10). Paul accepts fatherly financial responsibility for Onesimus as well (vv. 18–19). While we cannot assume that Paul claims the same relationship with all the others he probably baptized there, he does make a claim that Philemon owes him his life (v. 19), a status like Onesimus' having been begotten by Paul. Paul appears in the letter as both brother and father to members of the community.

We also learn from Onesimus' baptism that not all members of Philemon's household had been baptized together with Philemon. Apparently, members of his household, at least the slaves, decided as individuals whether to join the community of Christ meeting in his home. We cannot determine whether other slaves were members of the *ekklesia*.

Shifts in Vision

Before looking at the letter in any more detail, however, we need to shift our vision. Many contemporary scholars and interpreters throughout the course of Christian history have read the letter to Philemon to understand what *Paul* is saying to a community in Philemon's house. Many contemporary interpreters congratulate him for his skillful rhetoric and his radical counter-cultural message. Some scholars point to the limitations of Paul's vision.[19] The focus generally remains on what Paul intends, however, and how Philemon would receive it. Most interpreters tend to empathize with the prisoner Paul as the speaker in absentia or with the initial addressee of the letter, the community's patron, the slaveholder Philemon.[20]

What is missing from this discussion?

First, we need to imagine the audience of the community meeting in the house of Philemon, probably at a meal.[21] We need to visualize them not just as recipients of Paul's message or as onlookers whose presence can intimidate Philemon to do what Paul wants. We need to perceive them also as members of a community who are themselves defining the values to which Paul appeals. Their gathering would provide a social location for members to develop a hidden transcript, a counter-ideology to the Roman ideology of divine authorization of the rule of the Roman emperor. Paul's version of a counter-ideology centered on a different emperor, the divinely authorized Christ (the Anointed). What that means for how they function as a community and relate to one another and their neighbors is still under discussion. We would be mistaken to envision them as unanimous in their opinions or in lockstep agreement with Paul.

In the letter, Paul appeals to the common values that are emerging in the community, or at least the values he chooses to reinforce. Some of these are values characteristic of the communal meal groupings discussed in chapter 13. Among those present there may be some who seek a more radical transformation, and certainly there were those like Philemon for whom any substantive transformation could mean a painful loss of privilege and honor.

With a potentially diverse audience in view, we can also start to see the real elephant in the room, the subject matter of the letter, Onesimus, perhaps standing among slaves on the sidelines.[22] We may wonder whether any of those other slaves are members of the *ekklesia*. Perhaps they are continuing with their work to serve and clean up from the meal and can only overhear the letter being read.

What would happen, however, if Onesimus were the starting point? A group of mostly African American scholars from the United States have written a book of essays that begin to address this question.[23] As the contributing scholars point out, we must reckon with Onesimus' silence. His silence bears witness to the entire question of what "family" relationships ought to be. Paul's words struggle around the point, but Onesimus' silence is the starting-point for really grappling with the truth. Matthew V. Johnson states this eloquently:

> Onesimus represents the terrible and earth-shattering silences, the disruptive spaces buried beneath the grand narratives of oppressive elites. Beneath these surfaces, the un-integrated voices, the trauma of histories unwritten and unworked through, remain, straining through broken sibilants, interspersed with dashes and blank spaces in the repetitive rhythms of the mad and

the maddeningly marginalized to be heard. Onesimus's voice, like the unintegrated inertness of trauma, disturbs the comfort zone of the text and like a pregnant silence impinges upon our cultural and spiritual imaginations. The gravitas of the slaves' silence refracts the passing of all other light, including Paul's glowing recommendations for brotherhood and acceptance on the part of slaveholding Philemon.[24]

Without using the terms, interpreters who congratulate Paul for his radical slavery-challenging message tend to read the letter as part of the hidden transcript in the context of the public transcript of the Roman Empire. There are more layers to both the public and the hidden transcripts, however. The Roman Empire had a public transcript at the level of the macrocosm, as we have seen in Part 3. As we saw in Part 2, each Roman household (*domus*) had a public transcript as well, one that upheld the honor and domination of the *paterfamilias*. Such a householder might participate in a hidden transcript in opposition to Rome while the slaves and underlings in his own household had their own hidden transcript about him.

As we turn to look at the letter in more detail, we will read it first as the *public* transcript in the household of Philemon, in the sense of preserving the slaveholder's view of his domain and upholding his honor. Yet if we stand with Onesimus and with the slaves and others in the household, we can catch glimpses of hidden transcripts beneath the surface. In addition to Philemon, Paul names two other leaders in the community whose presence and opinion we should take into account: a woman, Apphia, and a man, Archippus. Others are unnamed but also merit consideration: the other members of the assembly, slave servers, and children of the household. Other members of the household who may or may not be members of the assembly could be present in the background, perhaps Philemon's wife and his legitimate sons or daughters. Neighbors could also be within earshot.

Let us revisit the possibility that Onesimus has fled to Paul to seek his intervention as an *amicus domini*, a friend of the master. This would mean that Philemon has done something to Onesimus severe enough to warrant the risk of flight. Given our knowledge

of the Roman household, we can speculate about what Philemon
may have done. He may have had Onesimus beaten one too many
times, or he may have sexually used Onesimus or someone he cared
about, or something else. Given Paul's use of language often associated with sexual use of slaves, we can plausibly imagine that the
issue is related to sexual use.[25] Whatever the story, we can assume
that other slaves in the household know it. We can also assume that
Paul has impressed Onesimus as someone who will be sympathetic
to his complaint, that Paul's message has offered Onesimus hope.
Paul also knows the real story. From what he says about Onesimus,
we can guess that Paul might see the conflict from the slave's side yet
he never challenges the master's behavior. Paul keeps the household
public transcript intact.

Knowing the real story, Paul addresses Philemon as a *paterfamilias* whose powers are very much intact and probably as someone
with the presumptions that those who hold absolute power tend to
exhibit, primarily the presumption that his will is to be intuited and
obeyed by subordinates. Yet Philemon is also a member of the community of the Anointed (Christ) and is thus committed to the common values the new community espouses. In the new community,
Paul is his superior. In the next chapter, as we listen to the letter with
Onesimus and the slaves, we can hear at least two levels of hidden
transcript.

15

Layers of Resistance and Endurance in a Community

Reading for Layers of Hidden Transcripts in the Letter to Philemon

Imagine the *triclinium* where members of the assembly are reclining. The assembly may be visible from the street, and neighbors and passersby may be able to hear. Slaves have attended to the members as guests and washed their feet as they entered and assisted them to their assigned places on the couches. Slaves have served the meal, supervised, perhaps, by Philemon's wife. The members of the assembly have eaten. The slaves have cleared the remains of the meal and swept up. Some of those who have assisted with the meal may still be in earshot, perhaps loitering near the door to the *triclinium* to listen. Others may be attending to tasks farther away and awaiting the latest word about what is in the letter that Onesimus has brought from Paul. The member designated to lead the gathering, perhaps Apphia or Archippus, has poured a libation and perhaps the assembly has joined in singing a hymn. Then comes the time for a letter from Paul to be read. One of the members who can read opens the papyrus that Onesimus has carried from Paul and reads the letter aloud to the assembly.[1]

Verse 1a: Sender[a]

Paul, a prisoner because I serve the Anointed Jesus, and
Timothy my associate [*adelphos*, brother],[2] (SV)

The assembly hears Paul identifying himself and Timothy as the
senders. Paul states as his credential that he is a prisoner for the
cause, for the Anointed (Christ) Jesus.[3] This functions on one level
as a reminder: "I'm paying the price. Don't you be selfish, now."
Four more times he will repeat that he is in prison for the cause.
His imprisonment probably indicates that the community of the
Anointed is making a counter-imperial message from the hidden
transcript publicly visible and paying the price. At another level, Paul
uses his imprisonment for the cause of the Anointed/Christ as a credential in a way that appeals to basic Roman values, displaying the
virtus (manliness, courage, self-sacrifice) that was an essential part of
Roman identity and a virtue expected of a *paterfamilias,* as we saw
in chapter 4.

The letter also begins with the sibling relationship that will be
of critical importance in the letter. Timothy is identified as the co-
sender in familial terms as Paul's "brother," a leader in the community along with Paul.

Verses 1b–2: Recipients

to Philemon our dear colleague [beloved "co-worker" (*syner-
gos*)], [2]also to Apphia our sister, to Archippus who joined up
with us ["fellow-soldier" (*synstratiotos*)] and to the Anointed's
people who meet [the "*ekklesia*" (assembly)] in your house:[b]

Philemon, Apphia, and Archippus could be family members at
the core of the household where the assembly meets, but this is
hardly clear from the letter. The language Paul uses indicates that it
is more likely that they are the leaders of the assembly. As they hear

---

a. The verse-by-verse analysis here is structured according to the form of Paul's
letters, based on the family letter form used in the Greco-Roman era. This will be
explained in more detail in volume 2.

b. Several Greek terms will be rendered in the Greek on the first use in this
chapter and subsequently in an unaccented transliterated form in place of an English
translation. The transliterated form is used for readers unfamiliar with Greek
characters.

Paul identify the recipients of the letter, we can see members of the assembly turning their gaze toward each named recipient in turn: Philemon, Apphia, Archippus. The assembly's eyes are upon them.

Paul addresses Philemon using a warm term to remind him of their relationship: "To our beloved co-worker Philemon." We may well wonder, however, whether there is also an initial distancing here. He does not identify Philemon as "brother," having just referred to Timothy in those terms and referring immediately after to Apphia as a sister. The term "co-worker" emphasizes the relationship that will undergird Paul's claims on Philemon, their united work for a common purpose. Philemon is the patron who provides the community's meeting place and the head of a household (v. 2).

Next, Paul addresses Apphia as "our sister," as the second of the three community leaders he names. Apphia is often identified as Philemon's wife, but if Paul were addressing her in this capacity, the reference would be to the two of them together.[4] Even if she is Philemon's wife, the fact that Paul mentions her individually among the addressees, as "our sister Apphia," indicates her position of respect and is an acknowledgement of her leadership role in the community.[5]

We do not know precisely what that role was. She may have been a sponsor of the association, as Philemon was, or one of the leaders. If the assembly in Philemon's house met in one of the Romanized cities where Paul organized assemblies, the image of the *matrona* or *materfamilias* or widow portrayed in chapter 4 might fit her, or perhaps she was a business owner, a woman not "marriageable" under Augustan family law.[6] As a business owner, she might seek a position of dignity in a leadership role in the assembly. Paul's address to her as "sister" could mean that she was a "mother" of the association as a female counterpart to Paul's paternal role, and in a leadership role found in other associations.[7] The role as "mother" of an association afforded some non-elite women a position of honor.[8]

While we cannot precisely determine her status in broader society or within the assembly, one plausible choice among several is to imagine her as an independent business woman of some means, accomplished and savvy. Yet as a woman in her position she is not perceived, at least legally and by men of rank, as having the privilege of sexual integrity. In the assembly of the Anointed, Apphia has earned the respect of her peers. We can plausibly imagine that she may aspire to recognition for traditional virtues of a Roman matron, especially *pudicitia* as well as acknowledgement for her leadership. On the other hand, we could imagine her as a woman who embraces the sexual freedom of her "non-marriageable" status. She could also be a wife, a *matrona*, whose husband is not a member of the *ekklesia*, or a widow.

Once we acknowledge that Apphia is probably not Philemon's wife, we can also plausibly imagine that his wife may be present as well. As the *materfamilias* of the household, she may be busy supervising the serving and cleanup of the meal but positioning herself to overhear the conversation. We can imagine her as at least dutifully supportive of the assembly because her husband is a sponsor. She may well be privy to the story of why Onesimus sought Paul's help as well.

Archippus is also addressed as a community leader, as a "fellow-soldier." Family language and military language intersect in Paul's metaphor here and elsewhere much as they do in Roman imperial language. We have here an indication of the alternative empire Paul envisions as both family and army. As another leader in the assembly, Archippus may have motivations like those of Apphia. He may be a worker or a freedman who has achieved some level of financial stability as a business owner, and like our plausibly imagined Apphia, seeks respect he does not receive in his daily life.

To say, however, that Apphia and Archippus seek dignity and respect as leaders in the assembly of the Anointed in no way denies their serious commitment to the cause. Paul addresses Philemon and Archippus as co-worker and co-soldier, emphasizing their sharing in the cause. He uses words with a prefix in Greek (*syn*) that means "with," one of his favorite modes of expression, to indicate his emphasis on shared purpose. Throughout the letter, the shared purpose that has landed Paul and Timothy in prison will be the basis for claims on Philemon.

Finally, Paul addresses the letter to the assembly (*ekklesia*) meeting in Philemon's house.[9] This is not a private letter for Philemon alone or even for the three individuals named. It is to be read in the presence of the whole community, a community that may include members who are not part of Philemon's own household. The identification of at least one woman among the addresses suggests that other women may be present as community members. Slaves may be present as well, but we cannot determine whether any of them are members of the community. Even if all the members are also members of Philemon's household, members are present by their own choice and continued commitment to the cause. Again, the fact that Onesimus had not been baptized before his encounter with Paul in prison indicates that some members of the household, at least the slaves, had not been baptized with Philemon.

The eyes of this assembly are watching. Paul intends to bring community opinion to bear on Philemon.[10] Consider this enlistment of the assembly's opinion. The letter places the relationship of Philemon and Onesimus before the assembly as their proper concern.[11] Paul assumes the weight of their presence and their opinions as he presses Philemon for a decision. This family model does not assume the authority of the *paterfamilias* as an "absolute monarch"[12] but places authority in the community assembly as well. The assembly hears the letter, and Paul trusts that their presence will represent common values and a common vision that Philemon will uphold in his decision about Onesimus. (No pressure here, of course!) We can glimpse the content of these common values in what follows.

Verse 3: Greeting

[3]May you have favor and peace from God, our creator and benefactor [*pater* (father)] and from our lord [*kyrios* (master/head of the household)] Jesus, God's anointed.

Paul's usual greeting offers evidence of his counter-imperial understanding of the celestial family. "Grace to you and peace from God *our* Father [that is OUR father of OUR metaphorical fatherland, not the father-emperor of the Roman Imperial fatherland] and [our or the] *kyrios* Jesus Christ [the true ruler Jesus Christ]."[13]

Verses 4–7: Thanksgiving / *Exordium*

[4]I always thank my God when I remember you, Philemon, in my prayers, [5]because I keep hearing about the confidence [*pistis*

(relationship of fidelity/trust/loyalty/faith)] you have with regard to the lord Jesus and your love for all God's people. [6]I pray
that the sharing [*koinonia* (association/partnership)] of your
confident trust [*pistis*] in God will result in a recognition of all
the good that we are capable of in the service of the Anointed.
[7]Your love has brought me great joy and encouragement because the hearts of God's people have been refreshed because of
you, my dear friend [*adelphos* (brother)].

The thanksgiving in the letter is intended to flatter Philemon, but
the content of the flattery is significant. The thanksgiving functions
rhetorically as an *exordium* that introduces the themes of the letter/
speech. It is noteworthy in verse 5 that Paul flatters Philemon for his
love (*agape*) and faith (*pistis*) as core values.[14] Lost in the translation
that emphasizes Philemon's actions is the phrase that emphasizes
these as values: Hearing about your love (*agape*) and faith (*pistis*).
Here Paul brings the community's shared values to mind.

The value of *pistis* is also attached to the theme of "partnership"
in verse 6, a verse not easily translated.[15] The phrase translated as
"the sharing of your confident trust..." is something closer to a
clumsier rendition: "the *koinonia* (partnership) of your *pistis* (trust
relationship)."[16]

To understand this verse and the concept of shared purpose on
which Paul's appeal to Philemon depends, the explanation of *koinonia* in chapter 13 will be helpful. When Paul greets Philemon as a
"beloved one" and specifically as a "co-worker" and then reminds
him in flattering fashion of "how the *koinonia* of your trust relationship is becoming effective," Paul is assuming a *koinonia* partnership
relationship for a purpose related to Christ. Their joint participation
in a larger mission is assumed. Paul deliberately frames his request
concerning Onesimus with a reminder to Philemon of their larger
purpose—and what is at stake in a breach of that trust relationship.[17]

The usual translations of *koinonia* as "fellowship" or "sharing"
and of *pistis* as "faith" or "belief" or even "confident trust" mask the
relational and corporate aspect of the words in modern individualist assumptions. For the phrase "the *koinonia* (partnership) of your
pistis (trust relationship)" we need to think in terms of a group of

people joined together in a relationship of trust for a common purpose and intention, something more than a sharing of individual belief understood as intellectual assent. Faith is a trust relationship in the context of a mutual community of common purpose.[18]

Paul evokes this purpose-driven relationship when he reminds Philemon of their shared values of *agape* and *pistis* and affirms Philemon's personal contribution for the larger cause. Paul closes the thanksgiving with a flattering reminder of Philemon's beneficial role in the community framed in terms of warmth, ending now by addressing Philemon as "brother" (v. 7). They are siblings in the fictive family of the *koinonia*.

Note that Paul appeals to Philemon based on community-oriented moral priorities, not based on values that inhere in Philemon as an individual. This is significant for understanding the family model that Paul and the community are assuming. By contrast, in Pliny's letters to Sabianus, addressed to a similar situation, we can see an appeal to a patron based on a Roman Strict Father family model. The letter to Philemon is frequently compared to this correspondence in which Pliny appeals to Sabianus for clemency for one of his young freedmen. The unnamed freedman has come to Pliny for assistance after angering Sabianus. See Box 4, p. XXX.[19]

A brief examination of that correspondence reveals that it maintains the assumption of a Roman Strict Father family model. Pliny's appeal acknowledges no equality between the freedman and his social superior. While Pliny is at pains not to seem to condescend toward Sabianus, there is no hint that the freedman is anything but a social inferior to be indulged for his youth. Pliny advocates granting pardon based on the freedman's self-abasing display of penitence to show that he knows his place.

Pliny's larger purpose is to counsel Sabianus in the proper management of his subordinates, not to recognize them as equals but to keep them in their proper places. Pliny also appeals to Sabianus' own need to develop his individual moral essence, affirming his ability to dominate his own anger and emotion. These are moral values inhering in the individual. Pliny emphasizes the personal self-control that is part of *virtus*, the Roman manly virtues that establish a *paterfamilias'* commanding *auctoritas*, as was discussed in chapter 4. The

Letters of Pliny the Younger to Sabianus

C. Pliny to Sabinianus, G(reetings).

Your freedman, whom you had mentioned as having displeased you, has come to me; he threw himself at my feet and clung to them as he could have to yours. He cried much, begged constantly, even with much silence; in short, he has convinced me that he repents of what he did. I truly believe that he is reformed, because he recognizes that he has been delinquent.

You are angry, I know, and rightly so, as I also recognize; but clemency wins the highest praise when the reason for anger is most righteous. You once had affection for (this) human being, and, I hope, you will have it again. Meanwhile it suffices that you let me prevail upon you. Should he again incur your displeasure, you will have so much more reason to be angry, as you give in now. Allow somewhat for his youth, for his tears, and for your own indulgent conduct. Do not antagonize him, lest you antagonize yourself at the same time; for when a man of your mildness is angry, you will be antagonizing yourself.

I fear that, in joining my entreaties to his, I may seem rather to compel than to request (you to forgive him). Nevertheless, I shall join them so much more fully and unreservedly, because I have sharply and severely reproved him, positively threatening never to entreat again on his behalf. Although I said this to him, who should become more fearful (of offending), I do not say it to you. I may perhaps have occasion to entreat you again and obtain your forgiveness, but may it be such that it will be proper for me to intercede and you to pardon. Farewell.

—*Ep.* 9.21

C. Pliny to Sabinianus, G(reetings).

You have done well, on the receipt of my letter, to welcome back into your house and your affection the freedman who was once so dear to you. This will help you greatly; it certainly

> helps me, first of all, when I see that you are pliant enough
> to be governed in your anger. Then too that you grant me so
> much, either in seeming to yield to my authority or in giving
> way to my entreaties. I praise you, then, and thank you; at the
> same time, I counsel you for the future that you show yourself
> tolerant of the mistakes of your (slaves), even if there be no one
> to intervene on their behalf. Farewell.
> —*Ep.* 9.24

emphasis on moral priorities as individual qualities is consistent with
the Roman Strict Father family model.

Paul, by contrast, grounds his appeal to Philemon in relational
values located in the community. As an individual, the value Paul
holds up for Philemon is not one that inheres in him personally but
in his ability to "refresh the hearts" of others in the community. The
entire thanksgiving flatters Philemon for demonstrating community-
based values in relationships of trust and love, indicating that his
values are based in a different family model, one more consistent
with the social institution of the meal and the associations described
in chapter 13.[20]

A major difference can also be seen in the addressees. Where Pliny
addresses Sabianus as an individual with total authority in his household, Paul addresses Philemon in the presence of the entire assembly that meets in his household. Where Pliny assumes the unilateral
authority of the individual Strict Father, Paul assumes a communal
authority that resides in the *ekklesia*. Paul does not base his appeal in
the question, "Do you want to be a good *paterfamilias*, Philemon?"
but "Will you continue to be part of the *koinonia*?"

How might this sound if we listen as the slaves and Onesimus? We
can guess that some would probably be nodding for the values Paul
is expressing, but they may not be as enthusiastic about considering
Philemon to be someone who models those values. They might be
nodding in agreement to Philemon's face, but saying something else

amongst themselves. They may also be wondering to what extent they are included in "God's people."

Still others among the slaves might not affirm the values of *agape* and *pistis* and instead harbor values rooted in the anger and desire for revenge that are part of being subordinated. Taking a dim view of both Paul and Philemon and the whole dinner party, they might collaborate in strategies of the "weapons of the weak" in a hidden transcript completely out of view in the letter.

Apphia and Archippus might have some conflicted responses at this point. As leaders named as recipients, they would recognize that Paul expects them to be part of holding Philemon accountable to the community's values. This could be a difficult task if Philemon is bred to the assumptions of privilege that are common to his role as the *paterfamilias*.

Verses 8–20: Body

[8]So, although in my capacity as an envoy of the Anointed I could order you to do what is fitting,[21] I would rather appeal to you out of love[9]—just as I am, Paul, an old man and now even a prisoner because of the Anointed Jesus.

After the flattering introduction, Paul begins to get to the point, indicating that he is about to ask Philemon to do something. Paul asserts his right to give Philemon an order and states his credential as a *presbyter*, an "old man" or "elder." This may indicate his advanced age or his position in the community or both. He is pulling rank in any case and adds a second reminder that he is in prison for the cause.

Yet he states his reluctance to command, much in the attitude of Pliny's expression of concern that he "may seem rather to compel than to request" Sabianus to pardon his unnamed freedman.[22] We could read Paul's stated preference to appeal to Philemon out of love as a sincere expression, or more likely as a rhetorical maneuver that allows Philemon as a *paterfamilias* to obey an order without being forced to acknowledge that it is, in fact, an order. Here Paul allows Philemon to save face by appealing to the value of love that he and Philemon hold in common as members in the assembly (v.8). If Philemon does what Paul wants him to, he can be seen to be upholding the community's values and the *koinonia*. Paul has thus enlisted the authority of the community's purpose in place of his personal authority. Here and at verse 14, Paul also demonstrates that he functions as an individual partner in the *koinonia*. Inasmuch as the changed situation of Onesimus represents an action for the common purpose of the *koinonia*, he is considering Philemon as another party to their agreement and therefore is not acting without the other party's assent.

We may surmise that the community and perhaps the slaves overhearing are aware of the maneuver. For them, Paul's authority may be useful as a "weapon of the weak" to give them some leverage to undermine Philemon's absolute authority as a patron and *paterfamilias*. Even without Paul's personal authority to give an order that would limit Philemon's absolute power, they can still appeal to the common values of the *koinonia*, particularly love, to persuade him to mitigate the use of that power. While Paul may be simply offering Philemon a way to save face, his choice to use community values rather than a value associated with Philemon's status as a *paterfamilias* offers members of the community and the slaves an opportunity to empower themselves. They also can strategize based on the agreement of the *koinonia*.

> [10]I appeal to you on behalf of my child [*teknon*], the one whose father I became [whom I begot] while I was in prison, Onesimus.

In verse 10 Paul introduces the subject matter of the letter: Onesimus. Paul describes his relationship with Onesimus in a way that is in keeping with the community value of love. He also does not miss a third opportunity to repeat that he is imprisoned for the cause. Paul also stakes a claim in describing himself as Onesimus' father and claiming him as "my child," using the term *teknon*, a term not used for slaves.[23] Paul's claim challenges Philemon's ownership of Onesimus.[24] If Paul is Onesimus' father, how can Philemon claim to own him?

We can imagine the slaves' ears perking up at this, and everyone in the room is probably watching to see how Philemon reacts. This might also give the other slaves a different view of Onesimus. Some

might look to him as a model for themselves, as a way they could improve their position or condition. They might think to themselves or
discuss out of earshot later how they could be baptized and included
in the brother/sisterhood. Other slaves who might view the whole
assembly with contempt could view Onesimus resentfully as some
form of brown-noser, expecting him to take advantage of his new
position. They might anticipate his condescension towards them and
already resent it.

> [11]At one time he was "Useless" (*achrēstos*) to you, but now he
> has become "Useful" (*euchrēstos*) both to you and to me.

Paul immediately follows his challenge to Philemon's ownership
with a reminder, using a pun on Onesimus' name, of his previous
"uselessness" to Philemon. While we do not know the content of
the issue, it indicates some conflict that probably caused Onesimus
to flee to Paul to seek his protection. The language of usefulness that
Paul uses was applied to many expectations of slaves, including sexual
use. If Onesimus was previously "useless," he may, for example, have
in some way resisted Philemon's sexual use of him. For Onesimus
to resist would be an affront to Philemon's honor that would undermine his *auctoritas* in the household.[25] Paul refers to Onesimus
as "useless" to remind Philemon, "You didn't want him anyway."[26]
Then Paul quickly offers a description of joint "ownership" or joint
usefulness because of Onesimus' "usefulness" to Paul and Philemon
in their common purpose as members of the *koinonia*.[27]

The concept underlying this pun on Onesimus' name as "useless"
and "useful" also tells us something about the family model Paul assumes. Paul assumes that Onesimus is more "useful" in his new relationship than he was as Philemon's slave. "Usefulness," a slave's very
purpose, is being redefined. The core assumption of slave systems,
including the Roman one, is that the very utility of the slave lies in
his or her subjection to the master, usefulness created by behavior
and *pietas* appropriate to his or her station.[28] An aphorism quoted by
Cicero indicates a common conception among masters about how to
improve a slave's value: "A Phrygian [slave] usually becomes better
because of a whipping."[29]

The slave is useful as an extension of the master, as a part of his body or a tool.[30] Paul articulates a different concept of usefulness: that Onesimus is of greater service to the purposes of the *koinonia* as Paul's child than he is as Philemon's slave. Paul asks Philemon to measure "usefulness" by what serves the *koinonia*, not by what is useful to him personally as a master.[31]

What might Onesimus hear, though? While there is a shift in relationship, Onesimus still hears himself described in terms of usefulness to Paul and Philemon as members of the *koinonia*. He might feel pride in his usefulness to the *koinonia* as acceptance of his full humanity and as a member himself. He and the other slaves might also hear this description as joint ownership, as Paul and Philemon now jointly owning Onesimus, or as the *koinonia* now owning him.

If we consider the language of "useless" and "useful" in a more hidden transcript, we can consider "uselessness" as a description of a variety of possible weapons of the weak. Perhaps Onesimus had been adept at undermining Philemon's authority or at any number of strategies slaves would use to assert their humanity without being in open defiance of the master. Perhaps this is what got him into trouble. Perhaps he was Philemon's half-brother, the son of his father by a slave mother, and this put him in a position to be more audacious than other slaves—and posed other threats to Philemon in the emotional undertow of the household. Perhaps when he was with Paul in prison he chose Paul's offer of inclusion in the community as a more effective means to claim his humanity. From this change of relationship, Philemon is promised that Onesimus will be more "useful" and perhaps stir up less trouble in the household. This is speculation, to be sure, but in the realm of possibility. "Usefulness" is still a trait of "good" slaves, however, defined from the master's perspective.

[12]In sending him back to you I am sending my own heart.[32]

This statement elevates Onesimus to a position as Paul's agent. Yet it could also, from the slaves' perspective, continue this problematic notion of usefulness. Paul evokes warm emotion, both to ask Philemon to view Onesimus warmly and to remind Philemon of sharing in a bond of love. Yet in this statement Paul also uses

Onesimus as an extension of his own body. Instead of being the master's hands, Onesimus is an extension of Paul's "heart," the internal organs (*splankhna*) where emotions were understood to reside. In this image, Onesimus is still a form of tool in the relationship between Paul and Philemon, even though he is included in the emotion of the relationship and is elevated within his slave status to a position as Paul's agent.[33]

Onesimus and the slaves could have an ambivalent response to this description. Onesimus might feel honored in his new status as the agent of the community leader, and more fully alive as others perceive him not as an object or tool but as an extension of their leader's very self. Some of the other slaves might see him as a turncoat. All of the ambivalence of the language of "useful" and "useless" would continue here.

> [13]I really wanted to keep him with me, so that he could assist me on your behalf while I am in prison for proclaiming God's world-transforming message; [14]but I did not wish to do anything without your consent, so your good deed would not be done out of coercion but of your own free will.

Here Paul arrives at his request, still without being completely direct. Paul would like to have Onesimus with him to assist him in prison in Philemon's place.[34] Paul reminds Philemon a fourth time that he is in prison for their shared cause.

Yet Paul's statement of what he wants assumes that Onesimus would have remained the slave of Philemon and would have functioned as his agent in assisting Paul. This appears to be the order that Paul would give if he gave orders. Note that the request is about what *Paul* wants for the sake of serving the larger cause. The request is not about the status of Onesimus. In his request, in fact, he now appears to concede Philemon's ownership of Onesimus. Onesimus may now be Paul's child, but Philemon still owns him. Paul must consult him if their partnership in the *koinonia* is to be maintained.

Paul sends Onesimus back to Philemon, to obtain Philemon's consent. There is a difficulty here for Paul and his status in relation to Philemon. If Onesimus assists Paul as Philemon's slave agent or as a slave "gift," then Paul accepts patronage from Philemon. Paul would then be subordinating himself to Philemon in a problematic way.[35]

To get what he wants, Paul needs to placate Philemon without subordinating himself. Just as in verses 8–9, in verse 14 Paul again offers Philemon a way to comply with his request while saving face by acting, ostensibly, of his own free will and for the common cause. Paul addresses Philemon as his superior in the matter of ownership of Onesimus, but Paul makes the request using the authority of his superior suffering for the cause.

We should note that there is no mention of any consultation with the *ekklesia* meeting in Philemon's house about the admission of Onesimus into membership. Perhaps we can presume that Paul has baptized him into the wider fellowship or into the community near him in prison. This appears to be something Paul is authorized to do, however, without consultation.

How might the slaves and Onesimus hear this? For Onesimus, it would depend on whether he wanted to stay with Paul and assist him. We might guess that this would be the best option he had. Yet Onesimus is silent and is not the one making any choices. Onesimus has no public voice here. For the slaves, this would probably sound like a negotiation between masters. Here they may well perceive that no actual change has taken place. Alternatively, they may suppose that Paul is simply placating Philemon to accomplish a real change in relationship. They may well hold both possibilities in mind to wait and see what happens.

> [15]Perhaps the reason that Onesimus was separated from [went away from][36] you for a while is so that you could have him back forever, [16]no longer as your slave but more than a slave, a beloved friend [*adelphos*, brother]. He is that special to me, but even more to you, both as a man [*en sarki* (in the flesh)] and as one who belongs to our Lord.

These verses introduce the notion of a change in the relationship between Philemon and Onesimus. Paul suggests that Onesimus is no longer a slave.[37] He would have remained a slave had he continued to serve him on Philemon's behalf, as Paul says he would have preferred. Paul sends him back to Philemon, however, as his child and agent, and now a "brother" to Philemon. We do not know what the concrete implications would be for Onesimus if he were received by Philemon "as a beloved brother." Yet Paul describes a changed relationship. A brother is not a slave.

There is a continuing debate about whether Paul is asking Philemon for the literal manumission of Onesimus.[38] This is unclear given the evidence we have, and it is a question focused on slavery more as a status than as a relationship. By manumission, Onesimus and Philemon would not relate to one another as brothers or peers. Onesimus' status would be improved as a *libertus*, a freedman, but he would hardly be viewed as an equal to Philemon. Philemon would still be the patron and Onesimus one of his client freedmen, continuing a vertical relationship.[39] Pliny's correspondence with Sabianus about his unnamed freedman shows the sniveling subservience expected of the freedman in that relationship. By asking that Philemon relate to Onesimus as a *brother*, Paul encourages a new and more mutual relationship. The expectation that Philemon will do so indicates the values commonly held in the *koinonia*. While exactly what Paul is requesting is unclear and disputed,[40] the expectation that Onesimus be accepted as a brother is no small thing.

The brotherly relationship between Philemon and Onesimus can have its basis in their joint membership in the *koinonia*, yet they are also "brothers" because they are both Paul's (spiritual) children.[41] The mention in verse 16b of being a brother "in the flesh and in the Lord" indicates another possible wrinkle in the situation. It is quite possible that Philemon and Onesimus are biological half-brothers, "brothers in the flesh," Philemon by the legitimate wife of their father and Onesimus by one of his slaves. This could be in the emotional undertow of the situation, as has been mentioned. Yet being "brothers in the Lord" introduces a new relationship.

Yet from the standpoint of Onesimus, we need to question what is missing from this picture. If we assume provisionally that Onesimus sought Paul's intercession due to Philemon's mistreatment, we do not see Paul addressing this.[42] This could mean, among other possibilities, that Paul is walking on eggshells to appease a slaveholder. In most relationships of disproportionate power, those in superior positions are rarely challenged to acknowledge their abusive behavior, and those in inferior positions are routinely expected to continue as if nothing has happened. We have no reason to believe this situation would be any different. We do not have any indication in the letter what level of truth-telling the relationship of "brotherhood" will require in the public transcript of Philemon's household. The slaves who know the story may be skeptical about how much real reconciliation can happen.

How might Apphia or Archippus hear all this? What, they might wonder, is Onesimus' position in the community to be now? As the extension of Paul, will he have authority? Will he be in a new leadership position that would in any way compete with theirs? Or will they be glad to have another "hand on deck" for the work and mission of the community? Either of them, and other community and household members, if they know the reason that Onesimus ran away, might have empathy for him or might judge him. An array of responses is possible.

[17]So if you consider me your partner [(if you have *koinonia* with me)], welcome him as you would me.

Paul refers to the relationship that he and Philemon share as members of the *koinonia*, clarifying the basis for the sibling relationship of Onesimus and Philemon in the previous verse. Based on his relationship to Philemon in the *koinonia*, Paul also asks Philemon to accept Onesimus as a stand-in for him. Onesimus is still Paul's agent, an extension of Paul, but he is included in a peer relationship grounded in the *koinonia*. This appears to render the three of them coequal partners,[43] expressing the new relationship that all of them have under the "lordship" of Christ.[44]

Yet it could also indicate that Paul, by claiming Onesimus as his child, is assuming a form of ownership of him and sending him as his envoy. He could have in mind something more like an ownership transfer—from being the slave of Philemon to being the child of Paul. In this case, Onesimus relates to Philemon as a brother because he is a stand-in for Paul.

For Onesimus, the change in relationship would surely be a new and positive experience. Yet he and the other slaves would probably also view this with the array of ambivalent reactions proposed for previous verses, some viewing Onesimus with suspicion and resentment, others glad to see Onesimus in a better position and perhaps wondering if they might be included, too.

> [18]And if he has wronged you in any way or owes you anything, charge that to my account. [19]I, Paul, am putting this in my own handwriting: I will pay you back, in order to avoid saying to you that you owe me your life.

Paul's conditional statement at verse 18 could well be an echo of a conventional stereotype of slaves as thieves and not an indication of anything Onesimus has actually done.[45] The statement nevertheless hints at a difficulty between Philemon and Onesimus. Paul pays obeisance to Philemon's honor by allowing him to maintain the necessary household public transcript that Onesimus was somehow at fault. In the public transcript, the slave is by definition at fault. Yet Paul also reiterates his acceptance of responsibility as Onesimus' father by accepting financial responsibility for him.[46] Paul re-stakes his claim from verse 10 and effectively challenges Philemon's ownership of Onesimus. What Onesimus owes, if nothing else, is his price as a slave.

Paul implicitly offers to buy Onesimus, but we can see by the dose of guilt Paul includes that he wants Philemon to write off the debt. Paul asserts his authority as Philemon's "spiritual patron"[47] or "spiritual father." With the strategic reminder that he owes Paul his life, Philemon would hardly be in a position to refuse.

How might Onesimus and the slaves hear this? They would probably understand that Paul is just allowing Philemon to save face over whatever the difficulty may have been. They are familiar with the terms of the public transcript. For Onesimus, the lack of acknowledgement of being wronged would likely still sting, but we may surmise that he has been heard and believed by Paul and the others in prison. It could still be emotionally confusing for Onesimus if he believed that he was in a different and more equal relationship due to his membership in the *koinonia* now to hear what sounds like an offer to purchase him. Yet when Paul reminds Philemon that Paul also "begot" him, Onesimus might feel some vindication as he hears Paul pull rank.

[20]Yes, my friend [*adelphos* (brother)], I am asking you for something "useful" in the service of our lord. Refresh my heart as one who belongs to the Anointed.

Now Paul addresses Philemon again as his brother to ask for "a benefit"—that he release Onesimus to him—invoking the larger purpose of the *koinonia*. The Greek does not objectify Onesimus quite as much as the English translation does here. Paul says something closer in the vernacular to "Help me out." Paul makes it personal, with an emotive appeal, but still in the context of the common cause.

Onesimus and the slaves are now overhearing the relationship of Paul and Philemon. Whether they hear themselves included in the common cause or not depends on their attitudes.

Verses 21–22: Closing

[21]I am writing like this to you because I am confident that you will comply with my wishes. I know that you will do even more than I am asking. [22]And, by the way, prepare a guest room for me, because I am hoping that, through your prayers, I will be restored to you.

Paul reiterates his request, now more boldly using the language of obedience. Paul defines the common cause by what he wants. Just in case, though, he lets Philemon know that he plans a visit. Philemon can anticipate shame if he does not obey Paul. Philemon is to pray for Paul's release, and now the community will expect him to do so. They are also on notice that Paul is coming as well, and they can probably expect to speak to Paul during his visit to let him know out about Philemon and the whole situation, out of his earshot, of course.

Onesimus, and possibly the other slaves, might strategize about how to appeal to Paul during his visit for other strategies that are "weapons of the weak." Paul's warning to Philemon of his impending visit can also be an alert that empowers them.

Verses 23–25: Greetings and Farewell

[23]Epaphras, who is imprisoned with me because of his service to the Anointed Jesus, sends greetings to you, [24]as do Mark, Aristarchus, Demas, and Luke, my fellow workers. [25]May all of

you be conscious that the gracious favor of the lord Jesus, God's
Anointed, is present among you.

In the added greetings, Paul reminds Philemon for a fifth time
of what others are sacrificing by being imprisoned for the cause. He
adds their names as part of a normal letter-writing function, adding
simple greetings to maintain relationships. The list adds to the letter's audience, however, and not only reminds Philemon of others'
superior sacrifices but also that others know the contents of the letter
and will be watching to see what he does.

Paul closes with a farewell to the whole community, reminding
Philemon that they are all witnesses to uphold the community's values as Philemon makes a decision about how to respond, and they
will report to Paul when he visits. The farewell also reminds them of
the wider purpose that they have committed themselves to serve and
promises the benefit of divine favor.

How Onesimus and the slaves would hear this closing depends on
how they understand themselves in relation to the *koinonia*. If they
feel included, they would accept the blessing offered. If not, they
would view it as more of the same.

Family Models Discerned
in the Letter and Its Hearers

Table 6 below, along with Table 2, summarize the layers of family
models in Paul's letter to Philemon. Table 2 provides a description
of the Roman Strict Father Family model, which is the model for
Philemon's household as it would present itself both to the outside
world and within the household. The letter indicates that the household probably conforms to this expectation. Philemon has at least
one slave, probably more given that the house also has more than
one guest room and is large enough to accommodate a community
assembly.

Table 6 outlines the layers of the public and hidden transcripts
identified in the letter to Philemon to discern elements of the family models being assumed in each layer. The first column identifies
the elements of Paul's acknowledgement of the Roman Strict Father

Family model as the public transcript in Philemon's household. In the middle column are elements of Paul's acknowledgement and re-inforcement of the values of the community of the Anointed/Christ. The column on the right shows the elements of the metaphorical family model assumed by the community as these elements can be discerned from the letter.[48] The elements of the family model on the right resemble other community formations in the Roman Empire that have been discussed in chapter 13 above. There is no reason to assume that the communities Paul organized were utterly unique or exceptionally radical counter-cultural formations.[49]

All along, I have been mentioning how slaves who were skeptical of the community meeting in Philemon's house might respond. No column is included on the chart to indicate a family model for this level because it is, in fact, so hidden.

Table 6 indicates that Paul frames his own role as a *paterfamilias* to the community. To challenge Philemon, he claims authority in a superior role in the *koinonia*. In this letter, he bases this author-ity on his fatherly role of bringing community members, including Philemon, into a new life; his superior sacrifice as a prisoner for the cause, thus demonstrating the *virtus* that is the core of Roman iden-tity and a value for a *paterfamilias*; and his age and tenure in the community, as a *presbyter* or "old man." Worth noting is the absence of an explicit reference found in other letters to his superior status as an agent of the Anointed/Christ.[50] Here he roots his authority more in his relationship with Philemon and members of the community than in external authorization.

As we have seen in the discussion of Paul's language, he upholds Philemon's position as a head of household and a slave-holder in several instances. Paul carefully couches challenges to Philemon in warm emotions. He acknowledges Philemon's role without subordi-nating himself to Philemon. He implies at several turns, in fact, that Philemon is obligated to obey him and owes *pietas* to him.

The family model that emerges in the middle column of Table 6 both upholds and challenges the Roman Strict Father model. Paul upholds the model by presenting himself as a *paterfamilias*. Some challenges to Rome's domination are at the level of the macrocosm,

Table 6
Family Models in the Letter to Philemon

PUBLIC TRANSCRIPT	HIDDEN TRANSCRIPT	
Paul Addressing Roman Strict Father Values	Paul Appealing to Shared Community Values	Audience Values

▦ Form

Paul as *paterfamilias*, superior to Philemon in community, father to Philemon Local leadership as Paul's siblings & fellow soldier & co-worker Philemon as patron to the community and owner of Onesimus Members as Paul's adult children, siblings to one another (and voluntary slaves to serve the purpose?) Onesimus as slave owned by Philemon, child of Paul, agent & bodily extension of Paul (high status slave), member of community, brother to Philemon	*Koinonia* as metaphorical household (and army), relating as siblings Local leaders recognized by Paul: Philemon – householder (patron) Apphia – woman Archippus – man Paul as *paterfamilias* presents himself as a leader able to act unilaterally but instead seeking consensus (not as a monarchical role)	*Koinonia* as an association of fictive siblings (and metaphorical army?) Local leaders: Philemon, Apphia, Archippus? (and/or alternative leadership in the hidden transcript?) (Recognition of Paul's self-defined role & authority may not be a consensus)

▦ Roles & Responsibilities

(Paul's) Leadership authority based on: • originating the community/baptizing new members (fatherhood), • sacrifice for the community (Roman *virtus*), • age/tenure in community (*presbyter*)	Community Authority resides in: • community members • community PURPOSE (Anointed/Christ) Philemon, Apphia, Archippus & all the members of the *ekklesia* have important opinions and are in some way involved in decision-making	Community Authority resides in: • community members • community PURPOSE (Anointed/Christ) Philemon, Apphia, Archippus & all the members of the *ekklesia* have important opinions and are in some way involved in decision-making

▨ Roles & Responsibilities *continued*

Philemon owns Onesimus and is the decision-maker about him, but owes *pietas* to Paul in community matters Onesimus as extension of Paul (heart) has responsibility to represent Paul Members: *pistis/fides* used to expect obedience (*pietas*); credibility created by sacrifice for the cause (similar to Roman military values)	No unilateral decision-makers, relationship as siblings A slave (Onesimus) is visible as a human being (not speaking, but named and identified as an agent of Paul)	No unilateral decision-makers, relationship as siblings Unacknowledged alternative leadership in the hidden transcript may influence decision-making (*Koinonia* and household response to Onesimus' new position cannot be determined)

▨ Priority Childrearing Mission

Prepare child (slave) for usefulness to cause	Prepare "children" and new members for participation in and usefulness to the *koinonia*'s purpose of world transformation (or replacement of Roman emperor with God/Christ) Prepare members to relate with love and trustworthiness as siblings

▨ Moral Priorities

Paul: *Virtus:* sacrifice on behalf of the community purpose *Pietas* to God & Anointed/Christ Philemon: *pietas* to Paul, couched as *pistis/fides* to community purpose; usefulness?	Values for all community members *Pistis/fides:* Faith, trust, trustworthiness, trust relationship *Agape:* love, affection, sibling bonds of love, love in community, divine love, loving concern

▨ Conception of Moral Order

PUBLIC TRANSCRIPT	HIDDEN TRANSCRIPT
Onesimus: usefulness Members of community: *Pistis/fides* & *agape*; Usefulness? Vs. Roman Strict Father (The natural rule of Rome is implicitly questioned, v. 3. Philemon's monarchical authority as *paterfamilias* is challenged.)	*Pistis/fides:* Faith, trust, trustworthiness, trust relationship *Agape:* love, affection, sibling bonds of love, love in community, divine love, loving concern

▨ Conception of Character

Vs. Roman Strict Father (*Virtus* as sacrifice on behalf of the community, but no appeal to values that inhere in the individual)	Values inhere in the community (*pistis, agape*)

▨ Internal Role of Government

Vs. Roman Strict Father No stress on reward & punishment or discipline	Upholding moral order of *pistis* and *agape*

▨ External Role of Government

Vs. Roman Strict Father
God (with Christ) as real ruler, not Roman Emperor and pantheon
(not much information in letter beyond this)

---

proclaiming an opposing emperor in the Anointed/Christ and a God to oppose the Roman pantheon. Other challenges are in the microcosm. Most telling, perhaps, is the element of the conception of character. Paul does not appeal to Philemon based on values that inhere in him as an individual.

This column reveals the assumption of a family model that is not fully the Roman Strict Father model but includes role divisions based on it, but redefined. Paul's claims to a desire that Philemon make his own decision, even as rhetorical devices to allow him to save face, indicate a style of fatherhood that has a lot in common with the Nurturant Parent model.

What metaphorical family model is assumed in the hidden transcript of the community meeting in Philemon's house? On the chart, a majority of the elements in the columns on the right are the same, so they have been merged in most instances. Just as Paul is responding to the Roman Strict Father family model, he is also responding to and upholding the values that the community/*koinonia* holds and the model they are assuming as well. A look at the right-hand column will show what we can discover from the letter about the model and values they probably assume.

Rather than the elaborate role division of the Roman Strict Father family focused on the *paterfamilias,* the *koinonia* in Philemon's household shows very few role divisions and the evidence in the letter indicates that they relate to one another as an association of fictive siblings. They may also consider themselves a metaphorical army, or that could be Paul's image.

Three local leaders are mentioned, not just one, and a woman is among them. Apphia and Archippus appear to be local leaders that the community expects would be acknowledged in addition to the patron, Philemon. Other leaders may exercise influence, including some who function in the hidden transcript. Paul may not have mentioned others to whom he would rather not lend credibility. Leadership appears to be shared in any case. The community may also view Paul with respect without necessarily acknowledging him as their *paterfamilias.*

They also distinguish themselves from the Roman Strict Father family model in their decision-making. From the mention of local leadership and inclusion of the community as recipients of the letter, we can gather that decisions are not made unilaterally or at least not in private. Here a matter involving a new community member, Onesimus, is brought before the community even though the issue at hand would appear to be the decision of Philemon alone. This indicates that the community will not accept having such a decision made in private, even by their patron. Paul has also made a unilateral decision to accept Onesimus into their community, so the decision now affects them as well and is no longer a private matter. A decision made in front of the community will not be fully unilateral, even if there is no discussion, since the community's opinion must be considered if they are present.

We can also assume that the purpose of the community in the Anointed/Christ is a major factor in decision-making. This purpose is what ties them together, and service to this purpose trumps individual interests. From the letter we can determine little information about the common purpose as it relates to their conception of moral order in the world at large. From the emphasis on community-oriented moral priorities, *pistis* and *agape*, we might be tempted to assume that they hold a view of an interdependent world consistent with a Nurturant Parent model family. This cannot be determined. They could, in fact, place a strong priority on their common bond internally as a metaphorical army intent on conquest externally. The community prepares new members as metaphorical children, possibly as soldiers, for usefulness in the community's purpose and to relate to one another in *pistis* and *agape*.

The community's view is visible only as Paul addresses them. For the most part, he reflects and affirms their values, as can be seen on the chart. We do not know whether they would endorse his view of himself and his role in the community as *paterfamilias*. We may also wonder whether the address to one of their leaders as a "fellow soldier" indicates a shared understanding of the community as a metaphorical army. We also cannot know whether they share Paul's view and presentation of Onesimus or of Philemon.

Conclusion to Part V

In the short letter to Philemon, we can see that the family model that emerges for one of the early Christian communities differs from the Roman Strict Father form. Leadership is shared, not monarchical. Authority resides in the community and its purpose, not in a *paterfamilias.* Values and virtues inhere in the community, not the individual. All the members of the community are expected to exhibit the same community virtues of *pistis* and *agape.* Virtues are not specific to roles in the family or to status. The authority of a *paterfamilias* and his ownership of one of his slaves can be challenged. A slave is presented by name and as a human being who can share full membership in the community, even if his legal status is unclear. A slave is his own agent in deciding to be baptized, even though he is not viewed as his own agent with his own voice in the matter of the letter. Within the community, he is now his owner's brother. What this means beyond the community is to be determined.

Epilogue

Family Empires and Current Culture Wars

When I began this project as lectures at a liberal church in 2004, a large chasm separated two perspectives in the culture wars in the United States. While extra effort was required, the two viewpoints were audible across the gulf, and bridges were imaginable. As I complete this volume following the 2016 United States election, state power at the national level has passed entirely into the hands of a more extreme version of a Strict Father family model than liberals ever imagined just over a decade ago. Other liberal democracies are seeing similar movements gaining ground. On the other side of what now seems to be a bottomless abyss between competing root metaphors, a well-fortified and purposively deaf version of reality based on that Strict Father family model is being constructed.

Some modern commentators are comparing the current shift to the time of transition in the Roman era addressed in this book, the transition from a contentious republic to an empire under one-man rule.[1] Readers will surely have noticed many parallels. I hope, dear reader, that you will find useful ways to connect the dots for yourself as you decide how to address the new reality we share.

I also hope against hope that you draw two essential perspectives from this book. One is the awareness that absolute power does not exist and that such power is only an empire's projection of what they want those subjected to believe. Inevitability is just propaganda. A second element is that we can learn from history. We are not required to repeat it. Various forms of resistance in the Roman era never coalesced around a family model as an alternative to the Roman Strict Father as a root metaphor.

In our time, we have access to tools of communication that can empower new options. Movements are already coalescing around indigenous understandings of our connection to the earth. Some of these understandings have commonalities with some of the notions mentioned in movements of resistance to the Roman Strict Father model and the empire founded on it. In a time when the fate of our species is in doubt due to climate change, articulating a new and ancient family model that, at its core, assumes that all life and all creatures are our relatives and that we are not and never were separate from "nature" can offer hope.

Notes

Preface

1. Roman cameo, onyx, 9–12 CE, H. 19 cm, W. 23 cm, Vienna, Kunsthistorisches Museum http://www.khm.at/en/objektdb/detail/59171.

2. The interpretation of the image here relies on Zanker, *The Power of Images*, 230–38; and Galinsky, *Augustan Culture*, 120–21.

Introduction

1. Lakoff, *Moral Politics*.

2. Steven Newcomb has used Lakoff's work on root metaphor to analyze US Supreme Court decisions that are the basis for seizure of native peoples' lands. He demonstrates that these decisions rely on the concept of the "Doctrine of Christian Discovery" and that these decisions are based on Christian religious assumptions rather than secular legal principles. In volume 2, I will analyze the roots of Christian imperialism in the Roman Empire and add another understanding of the foundation of the Christian sense of entitlement to seize the lands and lives of people defined as pagan and barbarian. See Newcomb, *Pagans in the Promised Land*.

Part I, Chapter 1

1. Lakoff and Johnson, *Metaphors*, 5. In his study of sibling language in Paul, Reidar Aasgaard also uses Lakoff's notion of root metaphor and cites this description of metaphor. Aasgaard, *My Beloved*, 23.

2. Noyes, *Collected Poems*. The first stanza: "The wind was a torrent of darkness among the gusty trees, | The moon was a ghostly galleon tossed upon cloudy seas, | The road was a ribbon of moonlight over the purple moor, | And the highwayman came riding— Riding—riding— The highwayman came riding, up to the old inn-door."

3. William Shakespeare, *As You Like It*, Act II, Scene VII.

4. See Lakoff and Johnson, *Metaphors*; Lakoff, *Women*; Lakoff, *Moral Politics*.

5. Lakoff, *Women*, xi.

6. Lakoff, *Moral Politics*, 33.

7. Lakoff, *Moral Politics*, 35.

8. Lakoff, *Moral Politics*, 87.

9. Lakoff, *Moral Politics*, 163.

10. Lakoff, *Moral Politics*, 163.

11. Lakoff, *Moral Politics*, 33–34.

Part I, Chapter 2

1. The phrase is the title of a volume in Douglas Adams' series *The Hitchhiker's Guide to the Galaxy*.

2. Bradley, ed., *Discovering*, 5.

3. Severy, *Augustus and the Family*.

4. See, for example, the early collection of essays they edited: Balch and Carolyn, eds., *Early Christian Families* and Osiek and Balch, *Families in the New Testament World*.

271

5. Many scholars of early Christianity in the Roman era after the first century have also been producing a large body of work on the family. They will be mentioned around specific topics in subsequent chapters and in volume 2.

6. I am indebted to a lucid summary by Halvor Moxnes in his introduction to a volume of essays by Nordic, Scottish, and one Spanish scholar on the topic. See the introduction and his opening essay, Moxnes, "What is Family?" 13–41. His summary is still one of the most useful introductions available.

7. Moxnes, "What is Family?" 15. Moxnes defines the context as "Mediterranean society and culture in antiquity" (19). In this project, the context will be defined more specifically in terms of the coming of Roman domination.

8. Moxnes, "What is Family?" 20.

9. Moxnes, "What is Family?" 17. The term "task-oriented residence units" is drawn from work on analysis of contemporary family that distinguishes the household so defined from "family" as a kinship unit. See Netting, Wilk, and Arnould, eds., *Households*.

10. Many of these studies focus on cultural anthropological categories that may mask the other aspects of the context, especially power relations. For example, to analyze family systems as "patrilineal" can be a way to look at family systems without looking at them as patriarchal. One example is Hellerman, *The Ancient Church As Family*, although his work does focus on fictive sibling relationships as an effort toward more equal relationships among early Christians. The group of scholars who have developed social scientific criticism have focused on kinship, mostly using a broadly defined "circum-Mediterranean culture." For a collection of articles by scholars of social scientific criticism, see a festschrift for John Pilch, one of the founders of this approach, along with Bruce J. Malina, John H. Elliott, Jerome H. Neyrey and others: Campbell and Hartin, eds., *Exploring Biblical Kinship*.

11. Moxnes, "What is Family?," 29–30.

12. Moxnes, "What is Family?," 31.

13. Patterson, *Slavery and Social Death*.

14. Collins, "It's All in the Family," 63.

15. Collins, "It's All in the Family," 63.

16. Collins, "It's All in the Family," 63.

17. Collins, "It's All in the Family," 64–67. Collins uses the work of MacClintock, *Imperial Leather,* who points to the "metaphoric afterimage" of the family in the European imperialist ideologies of the nineteenth and twentieth centuries and the use of the family metaphor to naturalize hierarchy (45).

18. Collins, "It's All in the Family," 67–77.

19. Collins, "It's All in the Family," 78.

20. This work benefits greatly from discussions among the scholars that Richard A. Horsley gathered in those years, including Brigitte Kahl, Davina Lopez, Mark Nanos, Luise Schottroff, Noelle Damico, Angela Standhartinger, Steven Friesen, David Lull, Joseph Marchal, Raymond Pickett, Neil Elliott, William Herzog, James Walters, John Lanci, and others. Those discussions were also part of framing the first volume of the Fortress Press series, Horsley, ed, *A People's History of Christianity: Christian Origins.*

21. A substantial body of scholarship has assumed that religion and politics are discrete categories. For a survey of the issue with relevant citations, see Harland, "Imperial," 88–89.

22. Horsley, *Paul and Empire,* 3.

23. Burkert, *Ancient Mystery Cults,* 3–4. The use of the plural begins with a clarification that "there is no such thing as 'the imperial cult'" in Beard, North, and Price, *Religions of Rome,* used by Karl Galinsky in a paper to launch an interdisciplinary discussion of "the imperial cult": Galinsky, "The Cult of the Roman Emperor," 3.

Most of the respondents refer to this caution, and Steven J. Friesen suggests converting our references to the plural (Friesen, "Normal Religion," 24). The same caution needs to be applied to the mystery cults.

24. Price, *Rituals and Power*, 9.

25. Price, *Rituals and Power*, 9.

26. Friesen, "Normal Religion," 25, discussing Price, *Rituals and Power* points to the influence of anthropologists Victor Turner and Clifford Geertz on Price's concepts.

27. Price clarifies that the type of knowledge that ritual contains is "symbolic knowledge," following Dan Sperber's early work in cognitive science. Sperber distinguishes symbolic knowledge from semantic knowledge as a knowledge of categories and encyclopaedic knowledge as knowledge of facts about the world. Symbolic knowledge "offers a crucial way for people to handle types of knowledge that do not fit into either the semantic or the encyclopaedic categories." Price, *Rituals and Power*, 8–9, following Sperber, *Rethinking Symbolism*. The notion of "symbolic knowledge" is similar to the concept of "root metaphor."

28. Scott, *Weapons of the Weak* and *Domination*.

29. Scott, *Domination*, 2.

30. Scott, *Domination*, 4.

31. Scott, *Domination*, 3.

32. For an explanation of people's history and its application in New Testament Studies, see Horsley, "Unearthing," 1–20.

33. For an outline of the distinction between people's history and standard history, see Horsley's charts: Horsley, "Unearthing," 5. The bias for oral communication is based on evidence for the importance of oral communication and performance of written texts in the Greco-Roman world and on the general prominence of story-telling and oral transmission among sectors of society without access to literacy. This will be discussed further in volume 2.

34. Translation of "*Er betrachtet es als seine Aufgabe, die Geschichte gegen den Strich zu bürsten*" in Benjamin, "Theses on the Philosophy of History," Thesis VII, 256–57.

35. Horsley, "Unearthing," 1.

36. Vander Stichele and Penner, "Mastering," 9. They most extensively analyze the biases of Adolf Von Harnack and Ernst Troeltsch and their influence on historical critical method. Harnack is cited as assuming a unity of human experience in history that can be accessed "objectively." Troeltsch, in particular, assumed the superiority of Christianity as a European religion, for example, and reveals his bias for the white race and Germanic culture as well as his masculinist biases, among other issues. Insights from Audre Lorde, an African American lesbian poet and writer who has critiqued mainstream feminist theorists, are counter-posed to the male Germans' perspective, indicating the importance of recognizing *difference* as a strength. Lorde's critique of universalizing was mostly directed at the tendency of white feminist thinkers to universalize the category of "women." For another summary see Johnson, Noel, and Williams, *Onesimus*, 2–5.

37. Benjamin, Theses on the Philosophy of History," Thesis VII, 256–57.

38. Vander Stichele and Penner, "Mastering," 1–2, cite Lorde, "The Master's Tools," 98–99.

39. Schneiders, *The Revelatory Text*, Kindle Locations 3471–73.

40. Paul Ricœur introduced the term "hermeneutic of suspicion" to describe the ideological criticism of religion current in the nineteenth and early twentieth century, particularly in the work of Karl Marx, Friedrich Nietzsche, and Sigmund Freud. Sölle, *The Silent Cry*, 46–47, adds feminist criticism to this list of "masters of suspicion."

41. Schneiders, *The Revelatory Text*, Kindle location 3493.

42. Sandra Schneiders, for example, seeks to move beyond the potential dismissal of biblical texts by a hermeneutics of suspicion and into a "hermeneutics of retrieval." Schneiders, *The Revelatory Text*, Kindle location 3511. In her book on hermeneutical method, she provides an example of this retrieval using feminist criticism to interpret the narrative of the Samaritan woman in John 4. She chooses a stance within the tradition and makes a credible case for the woman in the narrative as a positive and powerful image of a woman and as figure with a positive symbolic role. (Kindle locations 3553–897.) Schneiders does not invalidate the choice some feminists make to repudiate the biblical text.

43. Wire, *The Corinthian Women Prophets.*

44. Schüssler Fiorenza, *The Power of the Word*, 31.

45. Schüssler Fiorenza, "What She Has Done," 6.

46. On the disputes around this question, see Beavis, "Christian Origins," 27–49. She offers a cogent analysis of John Elliott's efforts to dismiss the work of "egalitarian theorists." His critique focuses especially on Schüssler Fiorenza and other feminists, but also includes others: John Dominic Crossan, Gerd Theissen, and Annette Merz. See Elliott, "Jesus Was Not an Egalitarian," 75–91; and "The Jesus Movement," 173–210. As Beavis points out, Elliott misrepresents his opponents' positions and inaccurately assumes that there were no utopian movements in the Greco-Roman world. Her work on these movements will be discussed in chapter 11. Elliott does, however, tellingly attempt to counter-pose "egalitarian" and "family-oriented." His view that the early Christian movement was restructuring the family rather than establishing an egalitarian social structure is similar in some ways to some of what will be examined in volume 2.

47. Schüssler Fiorenza, "What She Has Done," 8.

48. Sölle, *The Silent Cry*. Kathleen M. O'Connor advocated this hermeneutic in her presidential address to the Catholic Biblical Association in 2009. The Feminist Biblical Hermeneutics Task Force of the Catholic Biblical Association has since explored this hermeneutic in its ongoing work. A first volume of essays using a hermeneutic of hunger includes O'Connor's address. (O'Connor, "Let All the People Praise You".)

49. Sölle, *The Silent Cry*, 46.

50. Sölle, *The Silent Cry*, 46.

51. Sölle, *The Silent Cry*, 48.

52. Sölle, *The Silent Cry*, 48.

53. For a lucid discussion of the efforts of feminist scholars to create such myths of origin and critiques by other feminist scholars, see Beavis, "Christian Origins," 29–30.

Part II, Introduction

1. See the summary of Moxnes, "What is Family?" in the section on "Family Studies" in ch. 2.

2. Among these are funerary reliefs portraying family groupings of wealthy freedmen and women. The most common is a portrayal of a freed couple. For a discussion of the implications of these reliefs in understanding the importance of family connections to former slaves, see George, "Family Values," 37–66.

3. Drew-Bear, Thomas, and Yildizturan, *Phrygian Votive Steles*. A variety of family configurations of slave families also appear in funerary inscriptions from Asia Minor assembled in Martin, "Slave Families."

4. Drew-Bear, Thomas, and Yildizturan, *Phrygian Votive Steles*, 87–112, nos. 70–123 (men) and 151–72, nos. 197–241 (women).

5. Portrayals on funerary reliefs of Roman freed persons also include a variety of family configurations. See George, "Family Values," 51–52. For a set of provincial reliefs portraying family configurations, see Boatwright, "Children and Parents," 287–318.

6. Drew-Bear, Thomas, and Yildizturan, *Phrygian Votive Steles*, 114–20, nos. 125–39.

7. Drew-Bear, Thomas, and Yildizturan, *Phrygian Votive Steles*, 123–50, nos. 144–45, 147, 149, 152–55, 158, 161, 163, 175, 180, 184, 186–87, and 189–92. The clearest example of a probably married couple includes an inscription from Alexander and Tateis, 125, no. 127. Another may be a mother and son, 121, no. 140.

8. Drew-Bear, Thomas, and Yildizturan, *Phrygian Votive Steles*, 122, nos. 141 and 142; 132, no. 159; 140, no. 170; and 144, no. 181 (also includes two animals); 145, no. 183.

9. Drew-Bear, Thomas, and Yildizturan, *Phrygian Votive Steles*, 124, no. 146; 131, no. 157; 141, no. 171; 143, no. 177; 144, no. 182; 145, no. 185; and 149, no. 194.

10. Drew-Bear, Thomas, and Yildizturan, *Phrygian Votive Steles*, 140, no. 169.

11. Drew-Bear, Thomas, and Yildizturan, *Phrygian Votive Steles*, 137, no. 167. See *LSJ*, s.v. "*dómos*," 444. "*Doumos*" is a misspelling.

12. Drew-Bear, Thomas, and Yildizturan, *Phrygian Votive Steles*, 127, no. 150.

13. Lefkowitz and Fant, *Women's Life*, 190, no. 254, Posilla Senenia. Monteleone Sabino, first century BCE = ILLRP 971.L.

14. On their role as "public benefactresses," see Cooper, "Closely Watched Households," 6 and n. 12. On priestesses, see Connelly, *Portrait of a Priestess*. On the issues surrounding the difficulties in assuming women were confined to a "domestic" sphere in the early imperial era in Rome, see Milnor, *Gender, Domesticity*, 1–2. On women's public roles, see Ramsay MacMullen, "Woman in Public," 208–18.

15. See Lefkowitz and Fant, *Women's Life*, for a few examples of women as philosophers (167–70, nos. 216–18, 221–22, and 225) and as gladiators (214, no. 296.) Women enrolled themselves in defiance of the Augustan family legislation to be discussed in chapter 8. Winter, *Roman Wives*, 46, cites Raditsa, "Augustus' Legislation," 318, who cites Suetonius, *Tiberius*, 35; Tacitus, *Annals*, 2.85; and Cassius Dio, *Roman History*, 48.5.11, 20.

16. Lefkowitz and Fant, *Women's Life*, 168, no. 219. A learned woman. first century CE = *The Suda. Fragmenta Historicorum Graecorum 3.520. G.*

Part II, Chapter 3

1. On terminology, see: Saller, "Familia, Domus," 36–55; "Slavery and the Roman Family," 67; Dixon, *The Roman Family*, 1–11; and *The Roman Mother*, 13–21; Moxnes, "What is Family?," 20–21; Bender, "A Refinement"; Rawson, "The Roman Family," 7–8; Aasgaard, *My Beloved*, 40–41; Severy, *Augustus and the Family*, 5–8. For a discussion of historians' focus on "family" and archaeologists' focus on "household" and its application to interpretations of excavations of Roman era housing in Egypt see Nevett, "Family and Household," 15–31.

2. Moxnes, "What is Family?," 20.

3. Hatlen, "Honour and Domestic Violence," 49–51.

4. Moxnes, "What is Family?," 23.

5. Gardner and Wiedemann, *The Roman Household*, 3–4, no. 2, Ulpian, *Digest*, 50, 16.195.

6. For a discussion of this issue and the evidence of various family forms across

the empire, see Huebner, "Household and Family," 73–91.

    7. Changes and alterations continued. For example, archaeological reports from the port city of Ostia near Rome indicate that the "Pompeiian" model to be discussed in this chapter was transformed during the first century ce and that many of these houses were demolished to make way for other forms in subsequent centuries. See Bakker, *Living and Working*.

    8. Bergmann, "The Roman House," 225.

    9. Wallace-Hadrill, "The Social Structure," 44. The luxury of houses and villas was part of the aristocratic competition that characterized the late Republican era. See Hales, *The Roman House*, 20–23.

    10. Wallace-Hadrill, "The Social Structure," 44–45.

    11. Wallace-Hadrill, "The Social Structure," 72.

    12. Wallace-Hadrill, "The Social Structure," 73.

    13. For discussions of a conversation during the Republican era recorded around 30 ce by Velleius Paterculus between Livius Drusus and the architect he had engaged to design his house on the Palatine at Rome, see Cooper, "Closely Watched Households," 9–11; Wallace-Hadrill, "The Social Structure," 46. The architect suggests that privacy is a sign of means and privilege, but Drusus chooses as much exposure as possible. He wants to be on display. On the importance of the location of the house in order to maximize the view, see Hales, *The Roman House*, 44–46.

    14. Wallace-Hadrill, "The Social Structure," 46.

    15. For discussion of this issue, see Cooper, "Closely Watched Households," and Hales, *The Roman House*.

    16. For a discussion of the Romanization of houses in the provinces, see chapters on houses in the western and eastern provinces in Hales, *The Roman House*, 167–243.

    17. Hales, *The Roman House*.

    18. For a review of the issues around these terms as applied to the ancient world, see Milnor, *Gender, Domesticity*, 16–27. The recommended use of locks and doorkeepers indicates that the houses were not entirely open, even during the day. See Hales, *The Roman House*, 36–39, and 132–34.

    19. Meyers, "The Problems," 44–72; Trümper, "Material and Social Environment," 19–43. For a useful brief summary of the issue, see Peskowitz, "'Family/ies' in Antiquity," 9–36 (24–28).

    20. Milnor, *Gender, Domesticity*, 105–6.

    21. Cooper, "Closely Watched Households," 12, citing Vitruvius, *The Ten Books on Architecture*, 6.5.1. The "private life" associated in modern times with one's home as a retreat was the *otium* or relaxation associated with the villa, the luxurious country houses that the elites used for their retreat, where they sought *otium* in contrast to *negotium*, the civic duties and responsibilities managed in the urban *domus*. See Zanker, *The Power of Images*, 25–31.

    22. Cooper, "Closely Watched Households," 12. Wallace-Hadrill, 54.

    23. Vitruvius, *The Ten Books on Architecture*, 6.5.1.

    24. Rutland et al., *A Roman Town*, 10–11.

    25. Métraux, "Ancient Housing," 395–96.

    26. Wallace-Hadrill, "The Social Structure," 59–60, 68–69.

    27. Wallace-Hadrill, "The Social Structure," 68–71. For a detailed description of the Pompeiian houses, see Hales, *The Roman House*, 97–163.

    28. Harrill, "The Domestic Enemy," 235, mentions that slaves often slept in the storerooms.

    29. See, for example, reports from Ostia in Bakker, *Living and Working*, 32–41.

    30. Evidence for the household rituals is slim. On this issue, see Schultz, *Women's Religious Activity*, Kindle Locations 2136–60.

31. For illustrations, see Connolly and Dodge, *The Ancient City*, 51.

32. "Salutatio," Smith, Wayte, and Marindin, *A Dictionary*.

33. On the importance of this display as a projection of the prestige of the house-hold's lineage in the identity of the householder in the community, see Hales, *The Roman House*, 47–50; and Bergmann, "The Roman House."

34. Langlands, *Sexual Morality*, 17. Bronze plaques indicating the owner's patron-age of organizations and other civic honors were also displayed. Starr, "Augustus as 'Pater patriae.'"

35. Hales, *The Roman House*, 2.

36. Milnor, *Gender, Domesticity*, 108–9.

37. Milnor, *Gender, Domesticity*, 109.

38. Wallace-Hadrill, "The Social Structure," 75.

39. Wallace-Hadrill, "The Social Structure," 59.

40. For a discussion of this distinction of these "axes of differentiation" and the absence in the Roman house of distinction of space by gender and age, see Wallace-Hadrill, "The Social Structure," 50–54.

41. Wallace-Hadrill, "The Social Structure," 55.

42. Andrew Wallace-Hadrill, for example, has re-evaluated data from Rome and concluded that we should "think about Rome not so much as an undifferentiated sea of distinct units of housing, be they *domus* or *insulae* flowing around the great public monuments, but as a series of cellular neighborhoods." See Wallace-Hadrill, "*Domus* and *Insulae*," 13.

Part II, Chapter 4

1. Orr, "Roman Domestic Religion," 1559. Roman households observed devo-tion to the *Lares, Penates,* and Vesta, the goddess of the hearth, while Zeus and Hestia received worship in Greek households. Aasgaard, *My Beloved*, 47.

2. Dolansky, "Honouring," 138.

3. Dolansky, "Honouring," 139.

4. Orr, "Roman Domestic Religion," 1560.

5. Orr, "Roman Domestic Religion," 1561–62.

6. On the types of these shrines and altars, see Orr, "Roman Domestic Religion," 1576–85.

7. Orr, "Roman Domestic Religion," 1567.

8. Orr, "Roman Domestic Religion," 1573.

9. Orr, "Roman Domestic Religion," 1569–70.

10. Orr, "Roman Domestic Religion," 1571.

11. Schultz, *Women's Religious Activity*, Kindle Locations 2197–2212.

12. Richard Saller argues that the term *paterfamilias* was used most frequently in legal texts and indicates a "head of household" who may be female (Saller, "Pater Familias," 182–97). His survey of the use of the term in ancient literature indicates that it primarily denoted an estate owner rather than the image constructed in con-temporary scholarship of "a severe, patriarchal male head of household" (192).

13. Lassen, "The Roman Family," 109.

14. For an extended discussion of the scrutiny he was under, see Cooper, "Closely Watched Households."

15. Cooper, "Closely Watched Households," 5. For additional discussions of *patria potestas*, see Lacey, "Patria Potestas"; Saller, "*Patria Potestas*"; and Crook, "Patria Potestas."

16. Saller, "Corporal Punishment"; "Pietas."

17. Eva Marie Lassen discusses the mitigating factors. See Lassen, "The Roman Family," 106–7.

18. Gardner and Wiedemann, *The Roman Household*, 5, no. 3 = Gaius, *Institutes*, I.55.

19. Saller, "*Patria Potestas*," 7–8; Lassen, "The Roman Family," 104–6; Rawson, "The Roman Family," 16–17.

20. Rawson, "The Roman Family," 17.

21. Harris, "The Roman Father's"; Connolly and Dodge, *The Ancient City*, 82–85.

22. Harris, "The Roman Father's," 87–88.

23. Livy, *History of Rome*, 39.18. Rawson, "The Roman Family," 16.

24. Harris, "The Roman Father's," 93–95.

25. Brent Shaw contends that little evidence exists for the ritual known as the *tollere liberos* in which the newborn is placed on the floor before the father and he either picks the child up or leaves the child on the floor to be consigned to exposure. His analysis of the texts used indicates that *tollere*, the term for "raise" instead means "rear." He also disputes the extent of the legal rights of the *paterfamilias* to have his children killed. Yet he acknowledges that "no sensible historian of antiquity has ever sought to deny the pervasive reality of infanticide or, more commonly, the exposure or setting out of unwanted newborns." Shaw, "Raising and Killing," 31. He disputes the relevance of the usual literary citations that have been assumed to refer to the ritual. On these see "Appendix I: *Tollere Liberos:* The Birth of a Roman Child" in Dixon, *The Roman Mother*, 237–40. See also Bakke, *When Children*, 28–33; Cameron, "The Exposure," 105–14.

26. Lefkowitz and Fant, *Women's Life*, 187, no. 249. Exposure of a Female Child, Oxyrynchus, Egypt, first century BCE = POxy 744 G.

27. For a discussion of evidence of exposed infants' changes for retrieval or death, see Harris, "Child-Exposure," 3–11.

28. Veyne, *The Roman Empire*, 9; Osiek, MacDonald, and Tulloch, *A Woman's Place*, 52–53 and 267, n. 6, 7. On the Jewish practice of raising all their children, i.e. not practicing infanticide, see Ilan, *Jewish Women*, 46–47.

29. The late age of men at first marriage, in their mid-to-late twenties, meant that they were significantly older than their children. Saller, "Men's Age."

30. Rawson, "The Roman Family," 18.

31. Cooper, "Closely Watched Households," 7.

32. Cooper, "Closely Watched Households," 7.

33. Cooper, "Closely Watched Households," 8. She points out that this was the danger that voluntary associations, including Christian ones, posed for the Roman social order. They allowed a discussion that could breed a different interpretation of household relationships. See also the discussion of associations and meals in chapter 13.

34. Cooper, "Closely Watched Households," 9.

35. Galinsky, *Augustan Culture*, 84

36. Wallace-Hadrill, "The Emperor," 298–323. He discusses the distinctions and permutations of these conventional virtues and the ones listed on the shield and provides an extensive resource on the development of imperial virtues on coinage.

37. Wallace-Hadrill, "The Emperor," 300–301.

38. Galinsky, *Augustan Culture*, 84.

39. Aasgaard, *My Beloved*, 51.

40. Galinsky, *Augustan Culture*, 86.

41. Galinsky, *Augustan Culture*, 86, 88.

42. Galinsky, *Augustan Culture*, 88.

43. Severy, *Augustus and the Family*, 11, characterizes the attitude of the other members of the household expressing *pietas* at the shrine as "an honored if dutiful devotion."

44. Seneca (*De providentia*, 2.5) draws a contrast between the highly disciplined love of fathers and the more protective and tender love of mothers. Eyben, "Fathers and Sons," 117.

45. For a thorough description, see Dixon, *The Roman Mother*. For a discussion of the term *mater familias or materfamilias*, see Saller, "Pater Familias."

46. For an extensive discussion of the image and role of the Roman mother, see Dixon, *The Roman Mother*.

47. Other forms in which the wife came under the authority of her husband continued but were rare. Certain religious office-holders had to be born from one of these forms of union so there is evidence that some marriages were not *sine manu*. Rawson, "The Roman Family," 20.

48. Rawson, "The Roman Family," 19.

49. Dio Chrysostom, *Discourses*, 33.48–49. For other references, see MacMullen, "Women in Public," 208 and n. 4.

50. Bradley, "Wet-Nursing," 201–29, and "The Social Role," 13–36.

51. Dixon, *The Roman Mother*, xiv, 28.

52. Dixon, *The Roman Mother*, 28–9, cites Tacitus, *Dialogus*, 29.1–2.

53. Suzanne Dixon details the role of the economic power in the Roman mother's relationships as a central argument in Dixon *The Roman Mother*. Widows in classical Athens had a similar status and also frequently outlived their husbands. See Hunter, "The Athenian Widow," 291–311.

54. Dixon, *The Roman Mother*, 47–51.

55. Dixon, *The Roman Mother*, 63–64.

56. Dixon, *The Roman Mother*, 61.

57. Dixon, *The Roman Mother*, 61 cites Seneca, *ad Helviam*, 16.3; Favorinus (Aulus Gellius, *The Attic Nights*, 12.1.8) and Juvenal, *Satires*, 6.595–97.

58. Dixon, *The Roman Mother*, 62–63.

59. Dixon, *The Roman Mother*, 227.

60. Dixon, *The Roman Mother*, 227–28. See her chapter on "Mothers and Daughters," 210–32.

61. Dixon, *The Roman Mother*, 211, 223–27.

62. Dixon, *The Roman Mother*, 202.

63. Dixon, *The Roman Mother*, 202.

64. Aulus Gellius, *The Attic Nights*, 1.23 as summarized in Dixon, *The Roman Mother*, 181.

65. MacMullen, "Woman in Public," 209 and n. 5.

66. MacMullen, "Woman in Public," 209, lists many other forms of involvement. See also, for example, Schultz, *Women's Religious Activity*, Kindle locations 2431–626; Forbis, "Women's Public Image"; Hemelrijk, "Local Empresses," "Patronesses," and "Public Roles"; and Cotter, "Women's Authority Roles." For women in prominent roles as priestesses in Greece, see Connelly, *Portrait of a Priestess*.

67. ...*uxor enim dignitatis nomen est, non voluptatis* cited in Laes, "Desperately Different?," 321. Laes cites *Scriptores Historiae Augustae*, 5.11, but the reference is not at this location in the edition I have consulted.

68. Cassius Dio, *Roman History*, 56.3.3. Translation from Dixon, "The Sentimental Ideal," 100.

69. Elizabeth P. Forbis lists them as: *pudicitia, modestia, probitas, pudicitia, obsequium, lanificium, diligentia*, and *fides*, but this does not match the text of the inscription (Forbis, "Women's Public Image," 494). For a translation, see Lefkowitz and Fant, *Women's Life*, 136–39, no. 168. Most of the Latin text is found in CIL VI 1527 and LS 8393.

70. Lefkowitz and Fant, *Women's Life*, 136.

71. Parker, "Loyal Slaves and Loyal Wives," 168–74.

72. Jan F. Hatlen defines this as "gendered honor" because the husband's masculinity is defined by his control of his wife and daughters' sexuality (Hatlen, "Honour and Domestic Violence," 24).

73. Rawson, "The Roman Family," 31–32.

74. Hatlen, "Honour and Domestic Violence," 23–25. He comments on reasons not to apply the term "shame" as the antonym of this use of the term "honor."

75. Hatlen, "Honour and Domestic Violence," 25.

76. Dixon, *The Roman Mother*, 24.

77. Forbis, "Women's Public Image,"499.

78. For a discussion of this image and its importance, see Milnor, *Gender, Domesticity*, 99–101. The poem concludes, *"tristis inest cum pietate pudor"* ("there is sad modesty in her along with piety") (100).

79. A woman who aborted might be subject to some disapproval for a selfish action, but did nothing illegal or meriting religious disapproval. Rawson, "Adult-Child Relationships," 9. In debates about abortion, the main issue was the rights of the father. Abortion was seen by traditionalists as a sign of decadence. Criminalization of abortion to protect the father's interests began in the second century CE. See Bakke, *When Children*, 26–28.

80. Bakke, *When Children*, 26.

81. Rawson, "Adult-Child Relationships," 11, 13.

82. Rawson, "Adult-Child Relationships," 13.

83. Rawson, "Adult-Child Relationships," 14.

84. For an extended discussion of the causes of child mortality and parents' efforts to keep their children alive, see Bradley, "The Roman Child," 67–92. See also Horn and Martens, *"Let the Little Children Come to Me,"* 21–22. On funerary commemorations of children of elite families, see Rawson, "Death, Burial," 277–97.

85. For a delineation of the stages of life in Jewish and Greco-Roman sources, see Horn and Martens, *"Let the Little Children Come to Me,"* 6–37.

86. Rawson, "Death, Burial," 20; Horn and Martens, *"Let the Little Children Come to Me,"* 24–25. On the role of dolls in the development of girls, see Dolansky, "Playing with Gender."

87. Rawson, "Adult-Child Relationships,"17.

88. Bakke, *When Children*, 47–51; Horn and Martens, *"Let the Little Children Come to Me,"* 33–34.

89. Quintilian, *Institutio Oratoria*, 1.1.5, 8. See the discussions of Quintilian in Osiek, MacDonald, and Tulloch, *A Woman's Place*, 84–85; and Rawson, "Adult-Child Relationships," 20–21.

90. Quintilian, *Institutio Oratoria*, 1.1.6.

91. Quintilian, *Institutio Oratoria*, 1.1.15–19.

92. Quintilian, *Institutio Oratoria*, 1.2.

93. Osiek, MacDonald, and Tulloch, *A Woman's Place*, 85–7; Rawson, "The Roman Family," 40; and Rawson, "Adult-Child Relationships," 20.

94. Osiek, MacDonald, and Tulloch, *A Woman's Place*, 87.

95. Rawson, "The Roman Family," 38–39; Horn and Martens, *"Let the Little Children Come to Me,"* 29.

96. Rawson, "The Roman Family," 39.

97. Rawson, "The Roman Family," 39; Bakke, *When Children*, 20–21.

98. Bakke, *When Children*, 20.

99. Horn and Martens, *"Let the Little Children Come to Me,"* 32–33.

100. Rawson, "Adult-Child Relationships," 27–28; Horn and Martens, *"Let the Little Children Come to Me,"* 17; Dixon, *The Roman Mother,* 170.
101. Rawson, "The Roman Family," 40–41.
102. Rawson, "Adult-Child Relationships," 28.
103. Horn and Martens, *"Let the Little Children Come to Me,"* 16, 25–27.
104. For a discussion of non-elite children working outside the home, based on Egyptian papyri evidence from the first to eighth centuries CE, see Vuolanto, "Children and Work," 97–111; and Bradley, "Child Labor," 103–24.
105. Bakke, *When Children,* 15, 21–22.
106. Plato, *Republic* 4.431b–c. Golden, "Pais, 'Child' and 'Slave,'" 100; Bakke, *When Children,* 16.
107. Plato, *Laws,* 7.808d. Bakke, *When Children,* 16; and Golden "Pais, 'Child' and 'Slave,'" 100.
108. Bakke, *When Children,* 18.
109. Golden, "Pais, 'Child' and 'Slave,'" 92, 97.
110. Golden, "Pais, 'Child' and 'Slave,'" 101.
111. Golden, "Pais, 'Child' and 'Slave,'" 101–2; Horn and Martens, *"Let the Little Children Come to Me,"* 30–32.
112. *Pietas* was not listed as one of the four for the *materfamilias,* but it applies to her role as well as to the others.
113. This view of *pietas* follows Saller, "Pietas, Obligation, and Corporal Punishment."

Part II, Chapter 5
1. Columella, *On Agriculture,* 1.8.16.
2. Saller, "Symbols," 89–90; Harrill, "The Domestic Enemy," 236.
3. Patterson, *Slavery and Social Death,* 12–13.
4. Patterson, *Slavery and Social Death,* 5.
5. For a discussion of the numbers and changes over the course of the Roman era, see Scheidel, "The Roman Slave Supply," 7–9.
6. Dionysus of Halicarnassus, *Roman Antiquities,* 2.27.1–2 indicates that this was a right of fathers granted by Romulus at the founding of Rome.
7. Osiek, MacDonald, and Tulloch, *A Woman's Place,* 99.
8. Osiek, MacDonald, and Tulloch, *A Woman's Place,* 100.
9. Osiek, MacDonald, and Tulloch, *A Woman's Place,* 103.
10. Patterson, *Slavery and Social Death,* 1–2.
11. Beryl Rawson presents an optimistic estimate of a household slave's chances of manumission. See Rawson, "The Roman Family," 12–13.
12. Rawson, "The Roman Family," 13.
13. Rawson, "The Roman Family," 13.
14. Rawson, "Children in the Roman Familia," 186.
15. Bradley, "Wet-Nursing," 209–11.
16. Young, "Paidogogus," 152 and n. 21.
17. Young, "The Figure," 82.
18. Young, "The Figure," 80; "Paidogogus," 162–63.
19. Gardner and Wiedemann, *The Roman Household,* 24–26, no. 2 = *Année Epigraphique,* 1971, no. 88 (Puteoli).
20. Roman, fourth–sixth century CE, Rome, Terme Diocleziano, (National Museums). http://www.vroma.org/cgi-bin/mfs/var/www/html/images?link=/mcmanus_images/index13.html&file=/var/www/html/images/mcmanus_images/index13.html&line=694#mfs. For an example of such a collar from the later

imperial era, placed by a Christian archdeacon around the neck of one of his slaves, see Glancy, *Slavery in Early Christianity*, 9.

21. Mayor, *The Poison King*, 8 and 379, n. 12.

22. Bradley, "Wet-Nursing," 211. See also Osiek, MacDonald, and Tulloch, *A Woman's Place*, 99; Glancy, *Slavery in Early Christianity*, 18–21.

23. Bradley, "Wet-Nursing," 211–12. House-born slaves (*vernae*) were more desirable than slaves purchased from a dealer, so such reproduction was encouraged and part of maintaining the slave supply at Rome in the early empire.

24. Aulus Gellius, *The Attic Nights*, 4.2.9–10, cited in Rawson in Rawson, 50–51, n. 64.

25. Columella, *On Agriculture*, 1.8.19.

26. See the discussion in Marchal, "The Usefulness of an Onesimus," 757–60.

27. For an extensive discussion, see Laes, "Desperately Different?," 296–326. For a summary of the slavery and the sex trade in the Greco-Roman world, see Daniels-Hughes, "The Sex Trade," 165–67.

28. Rousselle, "Personal Status," 313–14; Walters, "Invading the Roman Body," 31, citing Seneca *Epistulae* 122.7.

29. For a discussion of the lack of moral judgment about this in anecdotes told by Valerius Maximus, see Langlands, *Sexual Morality*, 10–12. On female slaves and the issue of *porneia* in early Christian writings, see Osiek, "Female Slaves."

30. Rawson, "The Roman Family," 22. Another example is a marble gravestone of a couple, an older freedman and younger freedwoman in the marriage pose, inscribed with their full freed names, Amphio and Fausta Melior, from the family of Publius Aiedius, found on the Via Appia, Rome, ca. 30 BCE, now in the Pergamon Museum at Berlin. See http://www.vroma.org/images/raia_images/index4.html.

31. Gardner and Wiedemann, *The Roman Household*, 43, no. 46 = ILS 8432 = CIL VI, 22355a (Rome)

32. For this view, see, for example, Aristotle, *Politics*, 1253b–55b; Plato. *Laws* III.690A–D. For additional references on the perception of slaves as animals, see Bradley, "Animalizing the Slave."

33. Bradley, *Slaves and Masters*, 28.

34. Glancy, *Slavery in Early Christianity*, 133–34, 138.

35. George, "Family Values," 42.

36. Glancy, *Slavery in Early Christianity*, 138.

37. Glancy, *Slavery in Early Christianity*, 136. Slave gladiators made themselves exceptions to this expectation. On this, see Elliott, "Gladiators and Martyrs."

38. For an extended discussion of this aspect of slavery, see Harrill, "The Domestic Enemy."

39. George, "Family Values," 42–43.

40. Parker, "Loyal Slaves," 161–68. Many of the tales take place during the civil wars at the end of the Roman republic.

41. Bradley, *Slaves and Masters*, 33.

42. See Parker, "Loyal Slaves," 162.

43. Valerius Maximus, *Memorable Doings and Sayings*, 6.8 cited in Bradley, *Slaves and Masters*, 36.

44. Glancy, *Slavery in Early Christianity*, 134.

45. Athenaeus, *The Deipnosophists* 6.81 discussed in Glancy, *Slavery in Early Christianity*, 135.

46. Glancy, *Slavery in Early Christianity*, 135.

Part II, Chapter 6

1. Dixon, *The Roman Mother*, 30–34.

2. Aasgaard, *My Beloved*, 40.

3. These could include the *peculium* mentioned above and the size of an inheritance. Aasgaard, *My Beloved*, 50.

4. Aasgaard, *My Beloved*, 37.

5. Aasgaard, *My Beloved*, 39.

6. Aasgaard, *My Beloved*, 59.

7. Aasgaard, *My Beloved*, 62–70. He outlines sibling relationships in Roman household and points to variations in Greek and Jewish relationships.

8. Aasgaard, *My Beloved*, 71–75, and 94–99 on the expression of the ideal in Plutarch, *On Brotherly Love*.

9. Aasgaard, *My Beloved*, 75, 99–102.

10. Aasgaard, *My Beloved*, 76.

11. Aasgaard, *My Beloved*, 77–90, 102–5.

12. Frier, McGinn, and McGinn, *Casebook on Roman Family Law*, 45, 56 (Cases 15 and 20).

13. For a brief summary of the range of views on affection in Roman marriage, see Dixon, "The Sentimental Ideal," 102–3.

14. This is the view of Bradley, ed., *Discovering the Roman Family*, 6–8.

15. Bradley, *Discovering the Roman Family*, 8, and 12, n.18.

16. Tacitus, *Annals* 3.33–34.

17. Rawson, "The Roman Family," 27–28; Dixon, "The Sentimental Ideal," 101, and additional examples, 105–6.

18. Cassius Dio, *Roman History*, 56.3.3.

19. Dixon, "The Sentimental Ideal," 103.

20. Dixon, "The Sentimental Ideal," 106.

21. Dixon, "The Sentimental Ideal," 106–7.

22. Dixon, "The Sentimental Ideal," 110–11.

23. Bradley, *Discovering the Roman Family*, 7.

24. Bradley, *Discovering the Roman Family*, 7.

25. Rawson, "The Roman Family," 21. Shaw, "The Age," 30–46. The legal age for marriage was twelve for girls and fourteen for boys, Horn and Martens, *"Let the Little Children Come to Me,"* 15.

26. Saller, "Men's Age."

27. Rawson, "The Roman Family," 21; Dixon, *The Roman Mother*, 27.

28. Plutarch, *Advice to Bride and Groom*.

29. Plutarch, *Advice to Bride and Groom*, 47–48, 29.

30. Plutarch, *Advice to Bride and Groom*, 8.

31. Plutarch, *Advice to Bride and Groom*, 11.

32. Plutarch, *Advice to Bride and Groom*, 9.

33. Plutarch, *Advice to Bride and Groom*, 14.

34. Plutarch, *Advice to Bride and Groom*, 19, 35–36.

35. Plutarch, *Advice to Bride and Groom*, 30.

36. Plutarch, *Advice to Bride and Groom*, 32–33.

37. Plutarch, *Advice to Bride and Groom*, 20.

38. Rawson, "The Roman Family," 32–33.

39. Rawson, "The Roman Family," 36.

40. Rawson, "The Roman Family," 35–36.

41. Bradley, "Remarriage," 156–76. Bradley, *Discovering the Roman Family*.

42. Rawson, "The Roman Family," 33–34.

43. Rawson, "The Roman Family," 14–15.

44. See the discussion of the results of the Augustan family legislation in chapter 8 below.

45. Plutarch, *Advice to Bride and Groom*, 10, 16.

46. Langlands, *Sexual Morality*, 6.

47. Daniels-Hughes, "The Sex Trade," 169; Walters, "Invading the Roman Body," 30.

48. For a chart and discussion, see Parker, "The Teratogenic Grid." See also Marchal, "The Usefulness of an Onesimus."

49. George, "Family Values and Family Imagery," 50.

50. Langlands, *Sexual Morality*, 6–7.

51. Langlands, *Sexual Morality*, 21.

52. Langlands, *Sexual Morality*, 2.

53. Langlands, *Sexual Morality*, 30.

54. Langlands, *Sexual Morality*, 2. *Pudicitia* was also worshipped in personified form as a goddess, 39–49.

55. Langlands, *Sexual Morality*, 17.

56. Langlands, *Sexual Morality*, 23.

57. Langlands, *Sexual Morality*, 17–18, 37–38.

Part III, Introduction

1. Hales, *The Roman House*, 241–42, citing Aelius Aristides, *Orations* 26 and 26.102. The quotations are Hales' paraphrases.

2. Hales, *The Roman House*, 205.

3. Lacey, "Patria Potestas," 125–30, on the symbolic familial unity created by the cult of Vesta and other cults that were writ small in each household and large in the city of Rome.

4. *Rerum gestarum divi Augusti, quibus orbem terrarum imperio populi Romani subiecit ... Res Gestae*, 19–20.

Part III, Chapter 7

1. Edward Gibbons begins with this insight in his *History of the Decline and Fall of the Roman Empire*, published in 1776, and it is a commonplace in discussions of Augustus and the empire. See Ando, *Imperial*, Kindle Locations 455–459.

2. *Res Gestae*, 4.4. The *Res Gestae Divi Augusti*, Augustus' records of his life accomplishments, was inscribed after his death at his tomb and on walls in huge panels in temples of the imperial cult across the empire. Augustus left it with other documents with the Vestal Virgins for safe keeping, with instructions, as Suetonius reports, that it be "inscribed on bronze tablets and set up in front of his mausoleum." Brunt and Moore, *Res Gestae*, 1, citing Suetonius, *Augustus*, 101.4. The document was inscribed and displayed in other locations as well, and the surviving versions are in central Turkey. The best preserved one at Ankara offers a view of the importance of the document as ongoing imperial propaganda. The text is inscribed in Latin with a Greek paraphrase on walls of the Temple of Rome and Augustus, in six pages each 2.7 meters high and 4 meters wide. Shipley, *Velleius Paterculus*, 333–34.

3. McManus, "Augustus, the Principate, and Propaganda," Online: http://www.vroma.org/~bmcmanus/augustus2.html; *OCD*, s.v "Tribuni Plebis," 1092. For more detail on Augustus' use of his powers to enact legislation, see Tuori, "Augustus, Legislative Power," 938–45.

4. Brunt and Moore, *Res Gestae*, 11–12.

5. Galsterer, "A Man, a Book," 14.

6. *Res Gestae*, 6.1. Translation Brunt and Moore, *Res Gestae*, 21.

7. Suetonius, *Augustus* 27; Cassius Dio, *Roman History*, 54.10.5.

8. Galsterer, "A Man, a Book," 15.

9. See *OCD*, s.v. "Names, Personal, II, Italian," 720–21.

10. *Res Gestae,* 4.1.

11. *Res Gestae,* 4.3, Brunt and Moore, *Res Gestae,* 21.

12. Lendering, "Imperator-Livius." Online: http://www.livius.org/articles/concept/imperator/.

13. Zanker, *The Power of Images,* 34–35; Galinsky, *Augustan Culture,* 17 and 395, n. 29.

14. Zanker, *The Power of Images,* 35.

15. Eder, "Augustus and the Power of Tradition," 72. On the images of Octavian as a deity see Zanker, *The Power of Images,* 37–43. See Galinsky, "Memory and Forgetting in the Age of Augustus," 5, on Augustus' "memory management and redirection."

16. On the contrast of the crueler Octavian and the more benevolent Augustus, see Yavetz, "The Personality of Augustus," 33. The proscriptions were ordered to remove opposition to the triumvirate of Antony, Octavian, and Lepidus who took power after the assassination of Julius Caesar. To be proscribed meant to have one's name posted as "fair game" to be killed, with the reward of being able to purchase the property of the one killed. This was a means of removing opposition as well as increasing the coffers of the state. Proscription was rare, used once previously by the dictator Sulla. See *OCD,* s. v. "Proscriptio," 888.

17. Zanker, *The Power of Images,* 98–99.

18. Beard, North, and Price, *Religions of Rome,* 182.

19. Severy, *Augustus and the Family,* 98.

20. *Res Gestae,* 34. Brunt and Moore, *Res Gestae,* 35–37.

21. Karl Galinsky provides an extended description of *auctoritas* as the "essential characteristic of his rule" (10) and as a key element in Augustan culture. See Galinsky, *Augustan Culture,* 10–20. The description of *auctorias* here follows his.

22. Galinsky, *Augustan Culture,* 12–13.

23. Galinsky, *Augustan Culture,* 14.

24. Galinsky, *Augustan Culture,* 14–20, using categories found in Burns, *Leadership.*

25. *Res Gestae,* 34.3.

26. Galinsky, *Augustan Culture,* 13.

27. *Auctoritas* also incorporates other virtues, including *fides,* a concept of trust and protection equated with the Greek word usually translated as "faith," (*pistis*). Galinsky, *Augustan Culture,* 15. He names *fides, dignitas, gravitas,* and *libertas.* He associates *fides* with qualities of a guarantor implied in the root of *auctoritas* in *auctor.*

28. *Res Gestae,* 10.2. See also Bowerstock, "The Pontificate of Augustus," 380–94.

29. Severy, *Augustus and the Family,* 99–100; *OCD,* s. v. "Pontifex, Pontifices," 860.

30. Stevenson, "Roman Coins," 121.

31. *Res Gestae,* 35.1.

32. For an extended discussion, see Galinsky, 197–213. For a clear summary description, see Barbara McManus, "Plan of the Forum of Augustus." Online: http://www.vroma.org/~bmcmanus/forumaugplan.html.

33. Starr, "Augustus as 'Pater patriae,'" 296–97.

34. Stevenson, "Roman Coins," 120. Cassius Dio, *Roman History,* 55.10.10.

35. "The point that a Roma *pater* had *auctoritas* needs no elaboration." Galinsky, *Augustan Culture,* 16.

36. Galinsky makes this observation. See Galinsky, *Augustan Culture,* 18 and 395, n. 30.

37. Zanker, *The Power of Images*, 57.

38. Zanker, *The Power of Images*, 50.

39. Zanker, *The Power of Images*, 49.

40. Zanker, *The Power of Images*, 49.

41. Wallace-Hadrill, 6–7.

42. This section relies on Severy, *Augustus and the Family*, ch. 6, "The *Familia* of Augustus," 140–57.

43. Severy, *Augustus and the Family*, 142.

44. Severy, *Augustus and the Family*, 142.

45. Severy, *Augustus and the Family*, 143.

46. Severy, *Augustus and the Family*, 144.

47. Severy, *Augustus and the Family*, 144–45.

48. Severy, *Augustus and the Family*, 145–46.

49. Severy, *Augustus and the Family*, 146.

50. Severy, *Augustus and the Family*, 146, citing Suetonius, *De Grammaticus*, 21, and Wallace-Hadrill, "*Mutatio morum.*"

51. Severy, *Augustus and the Family*, 148–49.

52. Severy, *Augustus and the Family*, 149–50.

53. Severy, *Augustus and the Family*, 80–81.

54. *Res Gestae*, 24; Zanker, *The Power of Images*, 85–89.

55. *Res Gestae*, 12.2.

56. Zanker, *The Power of Images*, 173–75.

57. See Zanker, *The Power of Images*, 175–76 on the identification of the deity as Pax.

58. Severy, *Augustus and the Family*, 104.

59. Severy, *Augustus and the Family*, 104. The identification of Aeneas is not without dispute, and the image of Romulus and Remus is reconstructed from other sculptures and reliefs.

60. Severy, *Augustus and the Family*, 104–12.

61. Wallace-Hadrill, "The Golden Age," 24–25.

62. Wallace-Hadrill, "The Golden Age," 26, relying on Horace, *Odes*.

63. Dixon, *The Roman Mother*, 72.

64. For an overview of scholars' interpretations of the purpose of the Augustan family legislation, see Raditsa, "Augustus' Legislation," 280–90.

Part III, Chapter 8

1. *Res Gestae*, 8.5. Some scholars see the *Res Gestae* as intentionally omitting extended mention of the family legislation due to its failure. For references, see Reid, "Law Reform," 182, and notes 147, 148, and 149.

2. *nullis polluitur casta domus stupris,* | *mos et lex maculosum edomuit nefas,* | *laudantur simili prole puerperae,* | *culpam poena premit comes.* Horace, *Odes*, 4.5.21–24. Literal prose translation from Smart and Buckley, *The Works of Horace*, 35–36. On Horace's other odes on this theme and other poetic support for the legislation, see Williams, "Poetry in the Moral Climate."

3. Cassius Dio, *Roman History*, 54.19, and commentary by Paul Shorey in Shorey and Laing, *Horace. Odes and Epodes*.

4. Frank, "Augustus' Legislation," 43; Raditsa, "Augustus' Legislation," 295–96.

5. Livy, *History of Rome, Praefatio*, 9. Translated by Benjamin Oliver Foster. The final line could imply a first attempt at the legislation: *quibus nec vitia nostra nec remedia patipossumus, perventum est.*

6. *Res Gestae*, 6.2. Frank, "Augustus' Legislation," 47–48.

7. Galinsky, *Augustan Culture*, 100.

8. Horace, *Carmen Saeculare* 17–24: *Diva, producas subolem patrumque | Prosperes decreta super iugandis | Feminis prolisque novae feraci | Lege marita. || Certus undenos deciens per annos | Orbis ut cantus referatque ludos | Ter die claro totiensque grata | Nocte frequentes.* Translation from Milnor, *Gender, Domesticity,* 146–47. At ll. 57–59, Horace names restored virtues as the basis of prosperity: *iam Fides et Pax et Honos Pudorque | Priscus et neglecta redire Virtus | Audet, adparetque beata pleno | Copia cornu.* "Now Faith, Peace, Honor, old-fashioned Shame, and Valor, which had been neglected, dare to return, and Abundance returns, blessed with her full horn." Translation from Galinsky. *Augustan Culture,* 104.

9. Milnor places the family legislation in Augustus' vision of himself as the "new Romulus," a new founder of Rome, restoring Rome with the laws he dispensed. Milnor, *Gender, Domesticity,* 146–48.

10. For an explanation of the sources for the laws on adultery, see Richlin, "Approaches to the Sources," 226–27.

11. Richlin, "Approaches to the Sources," 227. There were some earlier laws that had provided consequences for adultery. See Dixon, *The Roman Mother,* 86.

12. Paulus *Sententiae* 2.26.11 specifies that adultery cannot be committed with a woman who runs a business.

13. The definition here follows Richlin, "Approaches to the Sources," 228.

14. Richlin, "Approaches to the Sources," 227.

15. Richlin, "Approaches to the Sources," 227 (*lenocinium*).

16. Richlin, "Approaches to the Sources," 228.

17. Richlin, "Approaches to the Sources," 228. The penalties are specified in Paulus *Sententiae* 2.26.14.

18. York, "Feminine Resistance," 3.

19. Raditsa, "Augustus' Legislation," 329.

20. This summary follows Dixon, *The Roman Mother,* 72.

21. Raditsa, "Augustus' Legislation," 329.

22. Raditsa, "Augustus' Legislation," 328.

23. Galinsky, *Augustan Culture,* 130; York, "Feminine Resistance," 4.

24. Raditsa, "Augustus' Legislation," 326.

25. Ulpian, *Digest,* 13.2 cited in York, "Feminine Resistance," 4.

26. Raditsa, "Augustus' Legislation," 329.

27. Tacitus, *Annals* 3.25.

28. Rawson, "The Roman Family," 10.

29. Reid, "Law Reform," 165; Raditsa, "Augustus' Legislation," 310.

30. Richlin, "Approaches to the Source," 226.

31. Frank, "Augustus' Legislation," 42–43

32. Zanker, *The Power of Images,* 156–59.

33. Raditsa, "Augustus' Legislation," 318. He cites Carcopino, *Passion et Politique,* 86–90.

34. Ovid, *Tristia,* 2.212, cited in Zanker, *The Power of Images,* 165. He wrote *Tristia* in exile. York, "Feminine Resistance," 5.

35. Suetonius, *Augustus,* 35.

36. Tacitus, *Annals,* 3.25.

37. Raditsa, "Augustus' Legislation," 318; and York, "Feminine Resistance," 5–7.

38. Tacitus, *Annals,* 2.85.

39. Suetonius, *Tiberius,* 35.2.

40. Winter, *Roman Wives,* 51; Raditsa, "Augustus' Legislation," 293–94. Other elements of intrigue and conspiracy against Augustus may also have been factors. See Raaflaub and Samons, "Opposition to Augustus," 430–33.

41. Macrobius, *Saturnalia*, 2.5, cited in York, "Feminine Resistance," 8–10, relying on Richlin, "Julia's Jokes," 65–92. This is one of a series of Julia's quips as related by Macrobius.

42. Cooley, "Women beyond Rome," 27.

43. Suetonius, *Augustus*, 40 citing Vergil, *Aeneid*, 1.282. Cited with translation in Zanker, *The Power of Images*, 163.

44. Zanker, *The Power of Images*, 165. The translation of Zanker puts this phrase in quotation marks but cites no source, presumably as a type of tongue-in-cheek reference.

45. Zanker, *The Power of Images*, 165–66.

46. The standards may have been set more by fashion and imitation of the imperial family than by legislations. See Cooley, "Women beyond Room," 28–31.

47. Suetonius, *Augustus*, 44.

48. Suetonius, *Augustus*, 44

49. For additional description of the arena, the spectacle program, and the role of gladiators, see Elliott, "Gladiators and Martyrs," 2016; "Gladiators and Martyrs," 2017.

50. Ando, *Imperial Ideology*, Kindle Locations 4983–5096.

Part III, Chapter 9

1. Price, *Rituals and Power*, 78.

2. Price, *Rituals and Power*, 135.

3. For examples from Asia Minor, see Price, *Rituals and Power*, 118–20.

4. Price, *Rituals and Power*; Severy, *Augustus and the Family*, 113–16.

5. Severy, *Augustus and the Family*, 116–18.

6. Price, *Rituals and Power*, 29–30.

7. Price, *Rituals and Power*, 32–38.

8. Price, *Rituals and Power*, 41–43.

9. Price, *Rituals and Power*, 41.

10. Cassius Dio, *Roman History*, 53.27.3. For a discussion of this topic and additional references, see Severy, *Augustus and the Family*, 118.

11. A coin was minted to commemorate this accomplishment. See Beard, North, and Price, *Religions of Rome*, 186; Zanker, *The Power of Images*, 126–27. On other positions, see *Res Gestae*, 7.3.

12. Beard, North, and Price, *Religions of Rome*, 186. Recognition of the *genius* of Augustus, in the sacrificing posture, outside his own family began just after Actium. Severy, *Augustus and the Family*, 122.

13. Zanker, *The Power of Images*, 127.

14. *Res Gestae*, 25. Translation Brunt and Moore, *Res Gestae*, 25.

15. Orr, "Roman Domestic Religion," 1562–63.

16. Orr, "Roman Domestic Religion," 1597.

17. Severy, *Augustus and the Family*, 100; Galinsky, 301.

18. Beard, North, and Price, *Religions of Rome*, 184–85; Galinsky, *Augustan Culture*, 300.

19. "*Laribus Augustis et Genio Caesaris.*" For references to the inscriptions, see Severy, *Augustus and the Family*, 125 and 280, n. 134.

20. Severy, *Augustus and the Family*, 126.

21. Severy, *Augustus and the Family*, 127; Zanker, *The Power of Images*, 129–30.

22. Severy, *Augustus and the Family*, 128.

23. Beard, North, and Price, *Religions of Rome*, 194–96; Galinsky, *Augustan Culture*, 292–93.

24. Ostrow, "The *Augustales*," 364–79; Galinsky, *Augustan Culture*, 310–11.

25. For a discussion of the organization of the cult in the province of Asia, see part 1 of Friesen, *Imperial Cults*. He mentions the opportunities for women, 42–43.

26. Severy, *Augustus and the Family*, 123.

27. Beard, North, and Price, *Religions of Rome*, 207 and n. 130.

28. Severy, *Augustus and the Family*, 129–30.

29. From the Letter of Paulus Fabius Maximus and Decrees by Asians Concerning the Provincial Calendar. Translation from Danker, *Benefactor*, 215–17. For another translation with more of the inscription and additional discussion see Friesen, *Imperial Cults*, 32–36.

30. This process is documented in detail in Price, *Rituals and Power*. Galinsky, "The Cult," 3–4.

31. Severy, *Augustus and the Family*, 114. Barbette Spaeth also points to the importance of women in the imperial cults in her study of these cults at Corinth, Spaeth, "Imperial Cult in Roman Corinth," 71.

32. On the distinction between the two terms, see Lozano, "Divi Augusti and Theoi Sebastoi: Roman Initiatives and Greek Answers." On devotions to other family members, see Severy, *Augustus and the Family*, 113–15.

33. Dixon in Rawson 106–7. She cites Suetonius, *Augustus*, 72.2, 99.1; Tacitus, *Annals*, 1.11.

34. Ovid, *Fasti*, 6.637–48. For a more detailed rendering of the events, relying on additional ancient sources, see Severy, *Augustus and the Family*, 131–34.

35. Severy, *Augustus and the Family*, 131–32. See also Dixon, "The Sentimental Ideal," 107.

36. Galinsky. *Augustan Culture*, 291–92.

37. *Res Gestae*, 19–21.

38. Beard, North, and Price, *Religions of Rome*, 196–97.

39. This listing follows Beard, North, and Price, *Religions of Rome*, 197.

40. Beard, North, and Price, *Religions of Rome*, 199–201.

41. Beard, North, and Price, *Religions of Rome*, 197–98.

42. Price, *Rituals and Power*, 160–61.

43. Price, *Rituals and Power*, 159. The altar dates to the mid-second century CE.

44. Price, *Rituals and Power*, 159.

Part IV, Introduction

1. On this, see: Raaflaub and Samons, "Opposition to Augustus," 417–54; MacMullen, *Enemies of the Roman Order*, 1–45.

2. See the section, "People's History and Historical Criticism," in ch. 2 above.

3. Scott, *Domination*, 109.

4. For an extended account, see Ando, *Imperial Ideology*.

5. Scott, *Domination*, 111–15. Scott does not use the language of honor and shame here but describes the honor-shame dynamic in terms of dignity.

6. Scott, *Domination*, 115.

7. Scott, *Domination*, 118–19.

8. Scott, *Domination*, 120.

9. Scott, *Domination*, 121.

10. Scott, *Domination*, 123–24.

11. Scott, *Domination*, 123–24.

12. For a study that includes such religious itinerants under the rubric of "free-lance experts," a category that includes self-authorized religious practitioners from across a wide spectrum, see Wendt, *At the Temple Gates*. Wendt mentions how such figures could at times be perceived by officials as a threat due to their influence in public affairs in everything from divination to influence state decisions to leader-

ship roles in rebellions and slave revolts, 55–62. Wendt's study focuses on these figures as entrepreneurs who emerged in greater numbers during the early empire and provides a helpful reorientation of the image of "religion" in the Greco-Roman era. Her study does not extend to an examination of the communal role of some of these figures in developing "hidden transcripts" or counter-ideologies, or in preserving cultural identities of peoples subjugated by the Romans.

13. Scott, *Domination*, 124–28.
14. Scott, *Domination*, 129–30.
15. Scott, *Domination*, 130.
16. Scott, *Domination*, 130–31.
17. Scott, *Domination*, 132–33. The quotation is from Ellison, *The Invisible Man*, 19.
18. Scott, *Domination*, 136, from his chapter titled, "Voice under Domination: The Art of Political Disguise."
19. Scott, *Domination*, 137–55.
20. Scott, *Domination*, 156–82.

Part IV, Chapter 10
1. For a detailed account, see Mayor, *The Poison King*, 1–6.
2. Mayor, *The Poison King*, 8, claims that "Slavery was forbidden by ancient Persian law and religion." This may be overdrawn, but Persia was not economically dependent on slavery to the extent that Rome was. The cylinder on which Cyrus the Great records his deeds may include a claim to have abolished slavery. http://www.britishmuseum.org/research/collection_online/collection_object_details.aspx?objectId=327188&partId=1.
3. Following Mayor, *The Poison King*, 7–9.
4. Mayor, *The Poison King*, 11.
5. For a detailed historical account, see Mayor, *The Poison King*.
6. Mayor, "Mithradates Scourge of Rome."
7. Mayor, "Mithradates Scourge of Rome," 11–12, 15–16.
8. The term "co-prosperity zone" for Mithradates' vision is used by Mayor, "Mithradates Scourge of Rome," 10.
9. See the paraphrase summary of one of his speeches in Mayor, *The Poison King*, 147–49, relying on Justin, *Epitome of Trogus*, 38.
10. Mayor, "Mithradates Scourge of Rome," 11.
11. Mayor, *The Poison King*, 301. She cites the Letter to Arsaces as preserved in Sallust, *Histories*, 4.69 (4.67 in Rolfe translation).
12. Mayor, *The Poison King*, 302.
13. Mayor, *The Poison King*, 47.
14. Mayor, *The Poison King*, 46–49; *OCD*, "Aristonicus," 112; Strabo, *Geography*, 14.1.38–39.
15. Mayor, *The Poison King*, 11.
16. Mayor, *The Poison King*, 317.
17. Mayor, *The Poison King*, 362–65.
18. The examples cited here are from Dyson, "Native Revolts." He also discusses the Pannonian-Dalmation uprisings (250–53). For a summary of Dyson, see Crossan, *The Historical Jesus*, 208–10.
19. Crossan, *The Historical Jesus*, 17, 198–202.
20. Josephus, *Antiquities of the Jews*, 18.23. For a description of the sect see Crossan, *The Historical Jesus*. 112–17.
21. Crossan, *The Historical Jesus*, 117, describes the activities of his sons who were

crucified under Tiberius Alexander (46–48 BCE); Josephus, *Antiquities of the Jews,* 20.100–102.

22. Crossan, *The Historical Jesus,* 128–36; 451.

23. Crossan, *The Historical Jesus,* 117–23; 174–206.

24. The role of the banditry is the conclusion of Crossan, *The Historical Jesus,* 184.

25. Josephus, *The Wars of the Jews,* 4.147–49. Crossan, *The Historical Jesus,* 195–96.

26. Crossan, *The Historical Jesus,* 198.

27. Dyson, "Native Revolts," 244–45, 247.

28. Kahl, *Galatians Reimagined,* 70.

29. See Dyson, "Native Revolts," 254–58.

30. Tacitus, *Annals,* 14.31, reports the flogging and rape among other seizures of land and insults to the leadership of the Britons as a betrayal of the intent of Boudicca's husband to provide protection for his people by willing his kingdom to the Roman Emperor along with his daughters. On the temple, see Fishwick, "The Provincial Centre at Camulodunum," 34. The temple was at Camulodunum, now Colchester in Essex.

31. Dyson, "Native Revolts," 261–62; Tacitus, *The Life of Cnaeus Julius Agricola.* Cassius Dio *Roman History,* 62.2.2–4, 62.8.2.

32. Cassius Dio, *Roman History,* 62.5.5–6.

33. Cassius Dio, *Roman History,* 62.4.3.

34. Cassius Dio, *Roman History,* 62.5.1.

35. Cassius Dio, *Roman History,* 62.3.

36. Celtic family, clan, and tribal structures and the domestic archaeology of this period in Britain are complex topics well beyond the scope of this project.

37. Cassius Dio, *Roman History,* 62.1.1. A woman also featured prominently in a revolt in Batavia a few years later.

38. See the description in Smith, "Simulcra Gentium."

39. This is a focal image for an extended discussion of gender in Roman imperial visual propaganda in Lopez, *Apostle to the Conquered.*

40. The most prominent image is on the Pergamon altar, an earlier installation appropriated as Roman imperial propaganda. See Kahl, *Galatians Reimagined,* 92–106.

41. Athenians assimilated their Persian enemies to Amazons, as effeminate men rather than masculinized women, Tyrrell, *Amazons,* 63.

42. The massive Celtic migrations show another aspect of the culture not accounted for in the image in the speech of a people contained.

43. On Lucretia, see Livy, *History of Rome,* 1.57–60.

44. Dyson, "Native Revolts," 261, citing Cassius Dio, *Roman History,* 62.7.3 and Tacitus, *Annals,* 14.33.6.

45. Diodorus Siculus, *Library of History,* 34. For an evaluation of the sources and a discussion of whether the slaves in the Sicilian rebellions envisioned a Hellenistic kingdom or just identified the leaders as kings, see Bradley, "Slave Kingdoms."

46. Florus, *Epitome of Roman History,* 2.7.19.

47. Diodorus Siculus, *Library of History,* 34.

48. Diodorus Siculus, *Library of History,* 36.

49. This account follows *OCD,* s.v. "Spartacus," 1008.

50. Plutarch, *Concerning Talkativeness,* 18. See also Bradley, "BBC—History." Online: http://www.bbc.co.uk/history/ancient/romans/slavery_01.shtml.

51. See Harrill. "The Domestic Enemy," and the discussion of vices and virtues of slaves in ch. 5 above.

Part IV, Chapter 11

1. This section relies on the discussion of utopians in Beavis, *Jesus & Utopia*.

2. Vergil, *Eclogue* IV. Beavis, *Jesus & Utopia*, 12–13. Stages of devolution from the golden age were described by Hesiod, *Works and Days*, 106–200. The works of Hesiod are considered to be from roughly the same time as Homer, around 700 BCE.

3. Vergil, *Aeneid*, 6.791–94.

4. Heen, "The Role of Symbolic Inversion," 141.

5. Lucian, *Saturnalia*, 20–23 as cited by Heen, "The Role of Symbolic Inversion," 123, and discussed in the article.

6. For a more extensive discussion of Saturnalia, see Heen, "The Role of Symbolic Inversion."

7. Plato, *Timaeus*, 25a–d; *Critias*, 113c–121c, summarized in Beavis, *Jesus & Utopia*, 14–15.

8. Beavis, *Jesus & Utopia*, 16.

9. Beavis, *Jesus & Utopia*, 16–17.

10. Diodorus Siculus, *Library of History*, 57.1, 58.6.

11. Diodorus Siculus, *Library of History*, 58.1. He describes the report of the journey of Iambulus. For a summary, see Beavis, *Jesus & Utopia*, 18–19.

12. Beavis, *Jesus & Utopia*, 20.

13. Aristotle, *Politics*, 2.1. Beavis, *Jesus & Utopia*, 20–21.

14. Beavis, *Jesus & Utopia*, 23–24.

15. Beavis, *Jesus & Utopia*, 24–28.

16. Beavis, *Jesus & Utopia*, 53.

17. On the term as one generally used for servants of the deities in the Greco-Roman world, see Taylor and Davies, "The So-Called Therapeutae," 5–7.

18. Taylor and Davies, "The So-Called Therapeutae," 10; Philo, *On the Contemplative Life*, 80–81.

19. Philo, *On the Contemplative Life*, 32.

20. Philo, *On the Contemplative Life*, 30–32.

21. Philo, *On the Contemplative Life*, 66–69.

22. Philo, *On the Contemplative Life*, 73.

23. Philo, *On the Contemplative Life*, 71–72.

24. Philo, *On the Contemplative Life*, 70.

25. Philo, *On the Contemplative Life*, 79–89.

26. Taylor and Davies, "The So-Called Therapeutae," 22–24.

27. Taylor and Davies, "The So-Called Therapeutae," 16, 19.

28. For a listing of the similarities and differences between Philo's description of these communities and the description of the Heliopolitan communities in Diodorus Siculus, see Beavis, *Jesus & Utopia*, 61–68.

29. Taylor and Davies, "The So-Called Therapeutae," 14.

30. On the Essene community, see Beavis, *Jesus & Utopia*, 54–55. She cites: Philo, *Every Good Man is Free*, 75–91; *Hypothetica*, 11.1–18. Josephus, *Life* 1.2.10–12; *Jewish War*, 2.8, 2–13, 119–61; *Jewish Antiquities*, 18.1, 2, 5, 11, 18–22. Pliny, *Natural History*, 5.17.4.

31. Beavis, *Jesus & Utopia*, 55–58.

32. For citations and a discussion, see Crawford, "Not According to Rule."

33. Desmond, *Cynics*, 43.

34. Desmond, *Cynics*, 44–45.

35. MacMullen, *Enemies of the Roman Order*, 54.

36. MacMullen, *Enemies of the Roman Order*, 5–8.

37. Whitmarsh, *Greek Literature and the Roman Empire*, 134, n. 5.

38. MacMullen, *Enemies of the Roman Order*, 50–51.

39. MacMullen, *Enemies of the Roman Order*, 51.

40. MacMullen, *Enemies of the Roman Order*, 59, specifically describes Nero's use of philosophers at his dinner parties.

41. Cassius Dio, *Roman History*, 65.15.3–5.

42. Whitmarsh, *Greek Literature and the Roman Empire*, 145.

43. Kleingeld and Brown, "Cosmopolitanism." Diogenes Laertius, *Lives,* 6.2.63: "Asked where he came from, he said, 'I am a citizen of the world.'"

44. Kleingeld and Brown, "Cosmopolitanism."

45. Diogenes Laertius, *Lives,* 6.2.38. The incident also appears in other ancient sources.

46. Kleingeld and Brown, "Cosmopolitanism."

47. Plutarch, *On the Fortune or the Virtue of Alexander*, 1.6. Translation modified from Frank Cole Babbitt. Plutarch attributes the philosophic cosmopolitan vision to Zeno, the founder of Stoicism. Zeno was the student of the Cynic philosopher couple Crates and Hipparchea in the next generation.

48. See Perkins, *Roman Imperial Identities*, 18–28.

49. Kleingeld and Brown, "Cosmopolitanism."

50. Kleingeld and Brown, "Cosmopolitanism."

51. Desmond, *Cynics*, 44.

52. King, *Musonius Rufus*, Kindle Locations 603–608. From Stobaeus, 3.40.9. On this passage, see also Whitmarsh, *Greek Literature and the Roman Empire*, 145–46.

53. Desmond, *Cynics.*

54. Kleingeld and Brown, "Cosmopolitanism."

55. Moles, "Cynic Cosmopolitanism," points this out (109) in making a compelling case for Diogenes and other Cynics' positive vision of the cosmos as nature, a case I will rely on here.

56. Desmond, *Cynics*, 22.

57. Moles, "Cynic Cosmopolitanism," 106–7; Kleingeld and Brown, "Cosmopolitanism."

58. Desmond, *Cynics*, 137.

59. Desmond, *Cynics*, 132–61.

60. MacMullen, *Enemies of the Roman Order*, 59; Desmond, *Cynics*, 53.

61. Desmond, *Cynics*, 11–12.

62. Desmond, *Cynics*, 54.

63. Desmond, *Cynics*, 54–55. An extended example is found in Lucian, *The Runaways.*

64. Desmond, *Cynics*, 121–28; 242–43 ; MacMullen, *Enemies of the Roman Order*, 60–61. A diatribe is a form of speech that takes the form of a conversation where the speaker both asks and answers questions from an imagined interlocutor.

65. Diogenes Laertius, 6.20.1. The verb is *paracharasso*, "re-stamp." The crime was committed by either Diogenes or his father

66. Desmond, *Cynics*, 98. *LSJ*, s.v. *nómisma;* 1179, *nómos*, 1180.

67. Desmond, *Cynics*, 98. Diogenes Laertius, *Lives,* 6.50.

68. Desmond, *Cynics*, 5.

69. Desmond, *Cynics*, 79.

70. Desmond, *Cynics*, 85.

71. Desmond, *Cynics*, 87.

72. Desmond, *Cynics*, 101.

73. The Greek word for dog is *kynos*. In the Greco-Roman world, they were called "Dogs." The transliteration into English sanitizes them with a more respectable and philosophical name.

74. Desmond, *Cynics*, 99–100.

75. Desmond, *Cynics*, 100 citing Lucian, *Menippus* or *The Descent into Hades*, 12.

76. Desmond, *Cynics*, 95–98.

77. Desmond, *Cynics*, 105–7.

78. Desmond, *Cynics*, 117–18; Diogenes Laertius, *Lives*, 6.2.37, 6.2.73.

79. On the Cynics' homelessness in opposition to home as the basis of the state, see Desmond, *Cynics*, 82–83.

80. Desmond, *Cynics*, 88–91.

81. Desmond, *Cynics*, 92.

82. Desmond, *Cynics*, 94.

83. Desmond, 9 *Cynics*, 92.

84. Grams, "Hipparchia (fl. 300 BCE)."

85. Diogenes Laertius, Lives, 6.97.

86. King, *Musonius Rufus*, Kindle Locations 354–358. Musonius Rufus was also part of the so-called "Stoic Opposition" to the one-man rule of the Roman emperors as tyranny. Desmond, *Cynics*, 48–49.

87. King, *Musonius Rufus*, Kindle Locations 324–325.

88. King, *Musonius Rufus*, Kindle Locations 367–421.

89. King, *Musonius Rufus*, Kindle Locations 318–354.

90. Grams "Hipparchia (fl. 300 BCE)."

91. Desmond, *Cynics*, 95.

92. Moles, "Cynic Cosmopolitanism," 113–14 and 118.

93. Moles, "Cynic Cosmopolitanism," 114; Diogenes Laertius, *Lives*, 6.2.37, 6.2.73.

94. Desmond, *Cynics*, 193.

95. Scott, *Domination*, 97–103.

96. Desmond, *Cynics*, 196.

97. MacMullen, *Enemies of the Roman Order*, 70–88.

98. Desmond, *Cynics*, 193.

99. Desmond, *Cynics*, 197–99.

100. Moles, "Cynic Cosmopolitanism," 114–18.

101. Desmond, *Cynics*, 35 on the Cynic-influenced poet Leonidas of Tarentum, and Dio Chrysostom, *Discourses*, 7.

Part IV, Chapter 12

1. Price, *Rituals and Power*, 78–79.

2. Price, *Rituals and Power*, 93–98.

3. Scott, *Domination*, 121. On "zones of freedom," see the discussion of a hermeneutics of hunger in chapter 2 above, and Sölle, *The Silent Cry*.

4. Schilling and Rüpke, "Roman Religion," 7899. On the deities of the wedding night, they cite Augustine, *The City of God*, 6.9.264–65.

5. There were technical terms and processes for such inclusion that changed over time. On this see comments on *evocatio* in Schilling and Rüpke, "Roman Religion," 7904 and Momigliano and Price, "Roman Religion: The Imperial Period," 7911.

6. Wulff, "An Enduring Flame," 480, summarizes popular religiosity in a review of the works on its expression in contemporary Latin America, "Popular religiosity—which the authors emphasize is a complex and changing phenomenon that cannot be adequately understood when it is simply reduced to superstition or false belief—does not necessarily diverge from theological orthodoxy. All that is required is for control to have slipped from the hands of the clergy into those of the common people."

7. Beard, North, and Price, *Religions of Rome*, 247. Raffaele Pettazzoni, one of the early proponents of the historical study of religions, made the distinction between official and persecuted religion in his 1954 article, "Les mystères grecs et les religions à mystères de l'antiquité: Recherches récentes et problèmes nouveaux." His article provides methodological suggestions that continue to be useful for the now widely accepted holistic approach suggested in the language of "continuum." The holistic approach primarily addresses the question of how to understand the "mysteries." Pettazzoni suggested first recognizing that the mysteries are cults with diverse origins, both Greek and Eastern, not "Oriental religions." Second, he proposed viewing the "mysteries" as part of analogous trajectories of historical development that influenced one another as they came into contact during the Greco-Roman era. They are not a single phenomenon with a common origin but similar phenomena with common historical trajectories in a common historical context. Third, the commonality among the mystery cults should be sought in their similar relation to the religion of the state or "official religion." While Pettazzoni overdrew the dichotomy between the "persecuted religions" and the "official state religion," he nevertheless pointed in a useful direction if we consider the *relationship* of the mysteries to "official religion," assuming the relationship to be complex and not readily reducible to one of oppression and persecution by the state. A holistic model for describing the mysteries is widely accepted. Walter Burkert's chapter on the mysteries in *Greek Religion*, for example, proposes for the Greek and Hellenistic eras a holistic model of religion bound to the polis with public and secret expressions. The mysteries, as the secret expressions, were not a separate religion outside or apart, but rather "a special opportunity for dealing with the gods" through an initiation experience that allowed the *mystes* in some way to share the experience of a suffering god, Burkert, *Greek Religion*, 276–67. In another volume in the same series, Robert Turcan also points to a holistic model of transformation, pointing to the Hellenization of cults in the East over the course of centuries before their subsequent Romanization as they spread in the Roman era, Turcan, *The Cults of the Roman Empire*. While the chapters on the individual cults function more as a mini-sourcebooks than coherent accounts of the cults, the introduction articulates an advance in the conceptual model for treating the cults.

8. Charles Lippy uses the concept articulated by Edward Shils, Lippy, *Being Religious, American Style*; Shils, "Centre and Periphery," 117.

9. Shils, "Centre and Periphery," 124.

10. Shils, "Centre and Periphery," 124; Lippy, *Being Religious, American Style*, 10.

11. Lippy, *Being Religious, American Style*, 10. The language of "negotiation" in postcolonial theory is also applicable for this phenomenon. For a description, see Hanges, "To Complicate Encounters," 27–34.

12. Lippy, *Being Religious, American Style*, 10.

13. Beard, North, and Price, *Religions of Rome*, 215, 217.

14. Beard, North, and Price, *Religions of Rome*, 216, citing Seneca, *De Clementia*, 2.5.1, "*religio deos colit, superstitio violat.*"

15. Beard, North, and Price, *Religions of Rome*, 217.

16. Beard, North, and Price, *Religions of Rome*, 214. Cassius Dio, *Roman History*, 52.36.1–3. Writing in the early third century CE, Cassius Dio includes this in his rendition of advice from Maecenas to Augustus.

17. Beard, North, and Price, *Religions of Rome*, 220–21.

18. Tacitus (*Histories*, 4.54) writing about events after the eight-month reign and execution of Vitellius in 69 CE. See Beard, North, and Price, *Religions of Rome*, 221.

19. Beard, North, and Price, *Religions of Rome*, 230.

20. Beard, North, and Price, *Religions of Rome*, 230–36.

21. Beard, North, and Price, *Religions of Rome*, 217.

22. Beard, North, and Price, *Religions of Rome*, 224. The translation is from their citation of Plutarch, *Advice to Bride and Groom*, 19 (or 140d).

23. Beard, North, and Price, *Religions of Rome*, 217. Lefkowitz and Fant, *Women's Life*, 136, no. 168, 30.

24. Dixon, "Sex and the Married Woman," 116–17.

25. This definition was not unique to the Roman imperial authorities. The Persian administration in Lydia in the early fourth century bc viewed the mysteries of Sabazios, Agdistis (the Phrygian name for Cybele), and Mâ as suspect and proscribed participation in these cults by those who served in the cult of Ahuramazda, perhaps to protect the purity of the Persian cult's fire. Sokolowski, "Tὰ Ἔνπυρα: On the Mysteries in the Lydian and Phrygian Cults"; Robert, "Une nouvelle inscription grecque de Sardes"; Vermaseren, *Corpus Cultus Cybelae Attidisque*, I, no. 456. At Athens, the Eleusinian mysteries were considered an exception. Beard, North, and Price, *Religions of Rome*, 223–25.

26. Burkert, *Greek Religion*, 277.

27. Elliott, "Mystery Cults," 931.

28. Roller, "Phrygian Myth and Cult," 43. Kubileya was an epithet in Phrygian attached to Matar as her name.

29. Roller, "Phrygian Myth and Cult," 43.

30. Roller, "Phrygian Myth and Cult," 47.

31. Roller, *In Search*, 79, discusses the paucity of evidence for worship sites or temples to Matar in the cities.

32. For a more complete description, see Roller, *In Search*, 85–90; Haspels, "Lions;" Haspels, *The Highlands of Phrygia*, Figs 186–91.

33. Roller, "Phrygian Myth and Cult," 47; Elliott, *Cutting Too Close*, 120–26.

34. Elliott, "Gladiators and Martyrs"; Elliott, *Cutting Too Close*, 125–26.

35. Roller, *In Search*, 68. When the cult and its private and ecstatic ritual was introduced into Greek colonies on the northern coast of the Black Sea by the sixth century, civic authorities expressed concern and other colonists appear to have damaged altars to Matar. See citations in Johnston, "Cybele and Her Companions," 103–4. At the same time, rock monuments associated with a Greek colony on Sicily may also indicate nocturnal ritual. See Gasparro, "Per la storia," 52–86.

36. Homeric Hymn 14, cited in Roller, "Reflections of the Mother," 306.

37. On the lions in the image of the Arslan Kaya as a contrast to the Greek image of the goddess as the tamer (or "mistress") of beasts, with her domesticated lions, see Haspels, "Lions." For a comprehensive reference on the cult, see Roller, *In Search*.

38. Roller, "Reflections of the Mother," 308.

39. On her enforcer role, see Elliott, "Choose Your Mother," 674–75 and Elliott, *Cutting Too Close*, 120–23.

40. This section follows Lynn Roller's analysis, Roller, *In Search*, 166–67; Roller, "Reflections of the Mother," 305–22, with the addition of notes on the locations for hidden transcripts.

41. Roller, "The Ideology," 546.

42. Roller, *In Search*, 218. See her citations.

43. Roller, "Reflections of the Mother," 309.

44. Ferguson, "The Attic Orgeones," 107–15.

45. A priestess was substituted for a priest, and in the solemn processions in which collections were taken, women, not the (*metragyrtai*) did the collecting.

46. Ferguson lists Mên, Artemis Nana, and Hermes Hegemon, Ferguson, "The Attic Orgeones," 113.

47. Vermaseren, *Corpus Cultus*, II, no. 308.

48. Roller, *In Search*, 179–80.

49. See n. 25 above.

50. Parke, *Sibyls and Sibylline Prophecy*, 201–2, citing Livy, *History of Rome*, 29.10.6; 29.11.5; 29.14.6; Diodorus Siculus, *Library of History*, 34.33.21; Ovid, *Fasti*, 4.253. Turcan, *The Cults of the Roman Empire*, 35–36.

51. Parke, *Sibyls and Sibylline Prophecy*, 191–200.

52. See Roller, *In Search*, 268–69. The object may have been brought from the Mother's cult center at Pessinus or from a location within the Pergamon's domain.

53. The temple was rebuilt at the same location after fires in 111 BCE and twice during the reign of Augustus.

54. Wiseman, "Cybele, Virgil, and Augustus,"124; Roller, *In Search*, 299–304.

55. Roller, *In Search*, 299–300.

56. While Vergil shows contempt for the Mother's *galli* at several points in the narrative, as T. P. Wiseman aptly summarizes, "she is a saviour and miracle-worker, without whom Aeneas' mission could not have been fulfilled." Wiseman, "Cybele, Virgil, and Augustus," 120. He also reviews the Vergil's treatment of the *galli* and the role of the Mother of the Gods, 119–23.

57. For a discussion of the Pergamon altar, see Kahl, *Galatian Reimagined*, 82–127.

58. For a survey, see Bieber, "The Images of Cybele."

59. Lambrechts, "Livie-Cybele." A statue in the Getty Museum at Malibu is the most notable, although it cannot be dated with certainty: *The Statue of Cybele*. For a discussion of examples of Livia's assimilation to Ceres and Magna Mater as well as other deities, see Zanker, *The Power of Images*, 234–36.

60. Roller, *In Search*, 283, 288–90.

61. Some have attributed the presence of the "Phrygian" elements of the cult as the Roman elites getting more than they bargained for. More recently several scholars have challenged this assumption and interpret the cult in the temple on the Palatine as part of Roman imperial culture. For a discussion, see Latham, "'Fabulous Clap-Trap,'" 92–93.

62. Borgeaud, *Mother of the Gods*, 91.

63. Borgeaud, *Mother of the Gods*, 63, citing the major source is Lucretius, *De Rerum Natura*, 2.598–643.

64. Borgeaud, *Mother of the Gods*, 65. The days in March are described as a "Holy Week of Attis" in sources from the late Empire. See Borgeaud's chapter, "Attis in the Imperial Period," 90–119.

65. Latham, "'Fabulous Clap-Trap,'" 95; Beard, North, and Price, *Religions of Rome*, 98.

66. Beginning in the republican era, *galli* of the Mother of the Gods played an important role as civic dignitaries negotiating with Roman forces. We have no details about the negotiations that allowed the stone identified as the goddess to be transported to Rome in 204 BCE, but in scenes in Roman histories a few year later, historians depict *galli* in full regalia coming out to intercede for their cities in the name of the Mother of the Gods as the Roman military was approaching. Polybius, *Histories*, 21.6.7; 21.27.5; Livy, *History of Rome*, 37.9.9; 38.37.9. Roller, "The Ideology," 544; Elliott, *Cutting Too Close*, 165 and 208–10.

67. Elliott, *Cutting Too Close*, 189–93, based on a description of *galli* of the Syrian deity Atargatis in Apuleius, *Metamorphoses*, 8.27–28. Roller, *In Search*, 333.

68. "During the late republic, the *galli* were not Roman; in the empire, they were not men." Latham, "'Fabulous Clap-Trap,'" 86. Latham discussed this use of the *galli* and the cult to negotiate Roman masculine identity over the course of several centuries. He mentions the work of Lynn Roller and Mary Beard on the cult

as a Romanized one that was part of defining *Romanitas* and the significance for
Roman self-definition of the presence of both the staid civic cultic activities associated with the Magna Mater and the more raucous aspects associated with Attis and
the "Phrygian" elements. Roller, *In Search*, 292, n. 34; Beard, "The Roman and
the Foreign." On the elite males' redefinition of their manhood in the transition to
one-man rule, see the work of Carlin Barton, especially, *The Sorrows of the Ancient
Romans* and *Roman Honor*, also summarized in Elliott, "Gladiators and Martyrs."

69. Latham, "'Fabulous Clap-Trap,'" 109.

70. Latham, "'Fabulous Clap-Trap,'" 103.

71. Latham, "'Fabulous Clap-Trap,'" 109–114. Latham indicates that this type of
portrayal faded in the later empire.

72. Beard, "The Roman and the Foreign," 165–66.

73. Beard, "The Roman and the Foreign," 177.

74. Elliott, *Cutting Too Close*, 198–99.

75. The ritual may have ancient origins in Phrygia, derived from Hittite rituals,
but in the Greco-Roman era it first appears in the second century CE. See Özkaya,
"The Shaft Monuments." A ram could be used in place of a bull for a *criobolium*.

76. Borgeaud, *Mother of the Gods*, 92.

77. This section relies on Roller, *In Search*, 327–43.

78. Roller, *In Search*, 333. See also her comment on the public character of the
rituals at Rome that she suggests were more private in Anatolia and Greece (317).

79. Roller, *In Search*, 328.

80. Roller specifies an area that is of interest for the context of Paul's letter to the
Galatians: "It formed a distinctive feature of the religious practices of western and
northwestern Asia Minor, in Ionia, Aeolis, Mysia, and Bithynia. Meter also had a
strong presence in Caria, Lydia, Phrygia, and the older Phrygian heartland, now the
province of Galatia." Roller, *In Search*, 328.

81. Roller, *In Search*, 329.

82. Roller, *In Search*, 330. She refers to Henri Graillot's extensive discussion in
his monumental study of the cult early in the twentieth century: Graillot, *Le culte de
Cybele*, 346–411.

83. Immigrants from the interior appear to have sponsored cult shrines in locations on the coast in at least one instance at Iasos in Ionia, where the first two names
on the subscription are Phrygian and Paphlagonian. Roller, *In Search*, 330.

84. Price, *Rituals and Power*, 94–97.

85. Elliott, *Cutting too Close*, 108–20.

86. Roller, *In Search*, 328.

87. Roller, *In Search*, 330.

Part IV, Chapter 13

1. On associations, see Harland, *Associations, Synagogues, and Congregations*,
and essays collected in Kloppenborg and Wilson, eds., *Voluntary Associations*.
On meals, see Smith, *From Symposium to Eucharist;* Taussig, *In the Beginning*.
Streett, *Subversive Meals* also provides a useful, if simplistic, summary. Taussig and
Streett cite and summarize Klinghardt, *Gemeinschaftsmahl und Mahlgemeinschaft*.
Klinghardt and Smith came to similar conclusions regarding the meals research-
ing independently, and then participated with Taussig and others in the Society of
Biblical Literature Seminar on Meals in the Greco-Roman World. Essays reflecting
the work of the seminar are collected in Smith and Taussig, eds., *Meals in the Early
Christian World*.

2. Smith advocates for the term "banquet," while Klinghardt uses the term
"communal meal." See Smith, "The Greco-Roman Banquet," 23–24; Klinghardt,
"A Typology."

3. Klinghardt, "A Typology," 14; Smith, *From Symposium to Eucharist*, 16–17; Smith, "The Greco-Roman Banquet," 25–26.

4. Smith, *From Symposium to Eucharist*, 30.

5. This is the structure delineated by both Smith and Klinghardt. For their summaries of the typology, see Klinghardt, "A Typology," and Smith, "The Greco-Roman Banquet." Smith discusses the apparent Roman deviations from this form pointed out by Dunbabin, *The Roman Banquet* and Roller, *Dining Posture*. See also Taussig, *In the Beginning*, 24.

6. Klinghardt, "A Typology," 10.

7. Smith, *From Symposium to Eucharist*, 22–25.

8. On the times of meals and variations by season and between Greek and Roman meals, see Smith, *From Symposium to Eucharist*, 20–22.

9. Smith, *From Symposium to Eucharist*, 27–28.

10. Evans, "Evidence for Slaves" and Glancy, "Slaves at Greco-Roman Banquet," 207.

11. Smith, "The Greco-Roman Banquet," 25; Smith, *From Symposium to Eucharist*, 14–20; Standhartinger, "Women in Early Christian Meal Gatherings," 91. For a detailed treatment of postures and social status in the meals, see Roller, *Dining Posture*.

12. Smith, *From Symposium to Eucharist*, 33–34. See also the description and illustration, 16–17, Figs. 3, 4.

13. This description follows Smith, *From Symposium to Eucharist*, 28.

14. Klinghardt, "A Typology," 11–12.

15. Smith, *From Symposium to Eucharist*, 29, citing Diodorus Siculus, *Library of History*, 4.3.4.

16. Klinghardt, "A Typology," 12. Examples of prayers to other deities include the "Good Deity," and "Zeus Savior." Smith also indicates that Greek libations may have originated as honors to household deities. Smith, *From Symposium to Eucharist*, 29.

17. Klinghardt, "A Typology," 12, citing Cato the Elder, *On Agriculture*, 132.

18. Klinghardt, "A Typology," 12; Smith, *From Symposium to Eucharist*, 30.

19. On the importance of the deities in the associations and their meals, contra previous scholars' tendency to downplay religious dimensions in the associations, see Harland, *Associations, Synagogues, and Congregations*, 45–60.

20. Harland, *Associations, Synagogues, and Congregations*, 50–60.

21. Harland, *Associations, Synagogues, and Congregations*, 62.

22. Taussig, *In the Beginning*, 76–79,

23. Taussig repeatedly raises the issue of the libation to the emperor and responses to it, emphasizing early Christian practices as showing resistance in substituting honors to Christ in the libations.

24. Smith, *From Symposium to Eucharist*, 33–34.

25. Klinghardt, "A Typology," 12–13; Smith in Smith and Taussig, 30–31.

26. Daniels, "The Sex Trade," 174.

27. Standhartinger, "Women in Early Christian Meal Gatherings," 98–99; Burton, "Women's Commensality," 158–59.

28. Marks, "Present and Absent," 129, citing Plutarch, *Quaestiones conviviales*, 666f–67a.

29. Marks, "Present and Absent," 129, citing Athenaeus, *Deipnosophists*, 14.644d–f; Smith, *From Symposium to Eucharist*, 40.

30. Marks, "Present and Absent," 130. See also Lefkowitz and Fant, *Women's Life*, 205, no. 271, A Wedding Invitation. Oxyrhynchus, Egypt, third century CE = POxy 111.G.

31. Corley, "Women's Funerary Rituals," 35. See also Smith, *From Symposium to Eucharist*, 40–42.

32. Corley, "Women's Funerary Rituals," 42, referring here specifically to women's laments in Greek literature.

33. Corley, "Women's Funerary Rituals," 39–40, and 44–45.

34. Corley, "Women's Funerary Rituals."

35. Burton, "Women's Commensality," 158.

36. Burton, "Women's Commensality," 151–57.

37. Burton, "Women's Commensality," 151.

38. Burton, "Women's Commensality," 151–52; Corley, "Women's Funerary Rituals," 48–52.

39. Burton, "Women's Commensality," 152.

40. Burton, "Women's Commensality," 154–57.

41. This is documented especially in the Greek east. See Connelly, *Portrait of a Priestess*, 176–79 on priestesses offering libations; 179–91 on women performing animal sacrifice; and 190–92 on women portrayed in ritual feasting.

42. Connelly, *Portrait of a Priestess*, 192.

43. Harland, *Associations, Synagogues, and Congregations*, 45–47.

44. These have been referred to as "voluntary associations" by contemporary researchers although the term is not without difficulties. On the utility of the term, see Wilson, "Voluntary Associations," 1–2; Taussig, *In the Beginning*, 92–93;

45. Kloppenborg, "*Collegia* and *Thiasoi*," 17.

46. For examples of the funerary functions of the associations, see Harland, *Associations, Synagogues, and Congregations*, 67–69.

47. Fishwick, "The Cannophori," 193–202.

48. Attempts to categorize associations founder on the multiple purposes many associations served. Kloppenborg, "*Collegia* and *Thiasoi*," and Harland, *Associations, Synagogues, and Congregations*, 23.

49. The association of *koinonia* and *societas* relies on Sampley, *Pauline Partnership in Christ*. Richard Ascough also indicates "shared purpose" as an assumption in the definition of the associations, Ascough, "Social and Political Characteristics," 59.

50. Harland, *Associations, Synagogues, and Congregations*, 19, 23–42.

51. Harland, *Associations, Synagogues, and Congregations*, 24–25 categorizes this as a family or household cult. Barton and Horsley, "A Hellenistic Cult Group." It is noteworthy that Agdistis, the Phrygian name for the Mother of the Gods, is listed as the overseeing deity.

52. Harland, *Associations, Synagogues, and Congregations*, mentions an association at Pompeii of Phrygians of the imperial household that included freedmen and slaves (27) and gender inclusiveness in neighborhood associations (28).

53. Harland, *Associations, Synagogues, and Congregations*, 33–42.

54. See Hemelrijk, "Patronesses," on women's patronage of associations.

55. Elliott, "Gladiators and Martyrs," 31.

56. Harland, *Associations, Synagogues, and Congregations*, 85–87.

57. Richard Ascough interprets these financial arrangements between elites and associations as crossing boundaries of social class. See Ascough, "Social and Political Characteristics," 65. Here I follow Philip Harland's perspective that interprets the financial and honor exchanges as part of social networking. See Harland *Associations, Synagogues, and Congregations*.

58. Ascough, "Social and Political Characteristics," 59–60; Kloppenborg, "*Collegia* and *Thiasoi*," 18.

59. Harland, "Familial Dimensions of Group Identity: 'Brothers'"; "Familial Dimensions of Group Identity (II): "Mothers" and "Fathers"" and Hemelrijk, "Patronesses."

60. Ascough, "Social and Political Characteristics," 59.

61. Finding a place included "monumental honors for the emperors or imperial family" that show "something about how such groups understood and expressed their own conception of where they fit within society and the cosmos." Harland, *Associations, Synagogues, and Congregations*, 119. On associations providing members with a sense of belonging, see his summary, 69.

62. Streett, *Subversive Meals*, 7, relying on Balch, *Roman Domestic Art*, 202–9.

63. Klinghardt, "A Typology," 16. See also Taussig, *In the Beginning*, 28–29, relying on Klinghardt.

64. Glancy, "Slaves at Greco-Roman Banquets," 208.

65. Taussig, *In the Beginning*, 27–29, 49–53, following Klinghardt; Klinghardt, "A Typology," 13–16.

66. Taussig, *In the Beginning*, 27–29, following Klinghardt. Smith adds pleasure (*hēdonē*) as a "category for defining relationships at a meal." Smith, *From Symposium to Eucharist*, 55. The ethical expectation is "pleasure for all." On "festive joy," Smith, "The Greco-Roman Banquet," 30.

67. Klinghardt, "A Typology," 15.

68. Harland, 513. See also Smith, "The Greco-Roman Banquet," 28, on the tension between social stratification and equality, and Aasgaard, *My Beloved*, 93–106, on Plutarch's discussion of brotherly love.

69. On fictive family language in the associations, see Harland, "Familial Dimensions of Group Identity: 'Brothers'"; and "Familial Dimensions of Group Identity (II): 'Mothers' and 'Fathers.'"

70. Smith, *From Symposium to Eucharist*, 54–62.

71. Smith, *From Symposium to Eucharist*, 55, relying on Plutarch, *Quaestiones Conviviales*.

72. Smith, *From Symposium to Eucharist*, 57, reflecting Plutarch, *Quaestiones Conviviales*, 616F.

73. Klinghardt, "A Typology," 16.

74. Cotter, "The Collegia and Roman Law"; and Beard, North, and Price, *Religions of Rome*, 230.

75. Harland, *Associations, Synagogues, and Congregations*, 80.

76. This could pose a threat as a "rival cognition that could destabilize a social system." Cooper, "Closely Watched Households," 8.

77. Taussig, *In the Beginning*, 35.

78. Taussig, *In the Beginning*, 102.

Part V, Chapter 14

1. I will refer to the addressee of the letter as Philemon, although the addressee may be Archippus, as John Knox and others have argued. The analysis here applies irrespective of the addressee. See Knox, *Philemon Among the Letters of Paul*, 56–70; Winter, "Paul's Letter to Philemon," 2. Winter assumes that Philemon and Apphia are addressed first because they are the church leaders and possibly husband and wife, and that Archippus is the owner of Onesimus and the house where the church meets. Even if Archippus is the one addressed, the issues are the same.

2. While the letter does not specifically state that the action in which Paul "begot" Onesimus was baptism, it is commonly assumed from language in Paul's other letters. The letter indicates a special relationship closer than what might be assumed for every baptism Paul performed. If it was not a baptism, another area of speculation opens that would require a separate investigation.

3. In the second century, the Carpocratians are said to have rejected slavery as well as other legal structures like marriage and private property. The Circumcellion sect of Donatists in fourth century North Africa is also reported to have called for

releasing all slaves. Demetrius Williams mentions these movements in Williams, "'No Longer as a Slave,'" 19.

4. Williams, "'No Longer as a Slave,'" 17.

5. Callahan, "Paul's Epistle to Philemon," 364–65, citing Raboteau, *Slave Religion*, 139. Williams, "'No Longer as a Slave,'" 36.

6. Bieberstein, "Disrupting." Bieberstein also takes an approach rooted in Walter Benjamin to read against the grain, but her approach does not move beyond a focus on Paul's message and the uncritical assumption that he must be saying something radical.

7. For examples intended for popular audiences, see the introduction to the letter in Dewey, Hoover, McGaughy, and Schmidt, *The Authentic Letters*, 153–56; and Crossan, *God and Empire*, 160–65.

8. For a clear exposition of the options in interpretation, see Fitzmeyer, *The Letter to Philemon*, 17–23. For an extensive history of interpretation, see Williams, "'No Longer as a Slave,'"11–46.

9. Callahan, *Embassy of Onesimus*, 5–6 and "Paul's Epistle to Philemon," 362–64.

10. Williams, "'No Longer as a Slave,'" 44–45. He uses the example of Francis James Grimké from the era of slavery and reconstruction in the US.

11. Callahan, "Paul's Epistle to Philemon," 366–68. According to Callahan, Chrysostom introduced the view of the situation of the letter as dealing with a runaway slave, as well as the unsubstantiated notion that Onesimus was a thief, an interpretation that continued to be accepted for centuries (360–61, 374). For a continued discussion of Chrysostom's language, see Mitchell, "John Chrysostom on Philemon: a Second Look," 135–48; and Allen D. Callahan, "John Chrysostom on Philemon: a Response to Margaret M. Mitchell," 149–156.

12. Johnson, "Onesimus Speaks," 95.

13. Peter Lampe first proposed this in Lampe, "Keine Sklavenflucht des Onesimus," 135–37 and Lampe, "Paul, Patrons, and Clients," 501–2. The proposal has been most notably critiqued by James A. Harrill, "Using the Roman Jurists to Interpret Philemon: A Response to Peter Lampe," and Harrill, *Slaves in the New Testament*, Kindle Location 141–91. Lampe responds effectively to Harrill's critique as well as Peter Arzt-Grabner's ("How to Deal with Onesimus?" 124–25) in Lampe, "Affects and Emotion," 61–77. See also Kea, "Paul's Letter to Philemon," 224 and n. 2 for additional citations and Frilingos, "'For My Child, Onesimus,'" 91–104.

14. See White, "Paul and Pater Familias," 469 and 484, n. 65.

15. Bieberstein poses the difficulty with this explanation that it would be unlikely that a slave who was not a member of the *ekklesia* would be given this responsibility. It is not, however, improbable that a slave would be sent as an extension of his master. Bieberstein, "Disrupting," 108–9.

16. Scott S. Elliott makes this argument in "'Thanks, But No Thanks,'" 51–64.

17. Marchal, "The Usefulness of an Onesimus."

18. Marchal, "The Usefulness of an Onesimus." Marchal does not offer a specific re-reading of v. 11 that would explain his previous "uselessness" to Philemon.

19. Without grinding any axes for or against Paul, Kea focuses specifically on the letter to Philemon to show that Paul does not advocate any change in Onesimus' status. He analyzes slavery in terms of status, however. Here we will focus more on slavery as a relationship. Kea, "Paul's Letter to Philemon," 231–32.

20. Williams, "'No Longer A Slave,'" 14.

21. Inclusion of the audience as a consideration in understanding the rhetoric is becoming a more prominent aspect in contemporary scholarship. See, for example, Frilingos, "'For My Child, Onesimus,'" 91–104.

22. I have heard it suggested that perhaps Onesimus reads the letter. This would mean that he was a literate slave secretary. Such a proposal requires another layer of speculative reconstruction.

23. Johnson, Noel, and Williams, *Onesimus, Our Brother*. See also Punt, "Paul, Power, and Philemon," 223–50.

24. Johnson, "Onesimus Speaks," 95.

25. See Marchal, "The Usefulness of an Onesimus," on the vocabulary at v. 11.

Part V, Chapter 15

1. Here I will use the device of listening verse by verse in order to consider their reaction. We can guess that Onesimus already knows the content of the letter before it is read to the community in Philemon's house.

2. The translation used in this chapter is the Scholar's Version with insertions to indicate translation choices that mask familial and military metaphors as well as vocabulary for which no contemporary equivalent is readily available. Dewey, Hoover, McGaughy, and Schmidt, *The Authentic Letters*, 157–58.

3. He does not use the title "Apostle" here. On this see Weima, "Paul's Persuasive Prose," 33.

4. Eduard Lohse, for example, assumes that Apphia is Philemon's wife "since her name follows after Philemon's" (Lohse, *Colossians and Philemon*, 190). The juxtaposition here is hardly determinative, and it would be more likely that a married couple would be addressed together. Paul addresses apparent married couples jointly in Romans 16, for example. On this see Cotter, "Women's Authority Roles," 351. Allen D. Callahan clarifies that the most logical assumption from the text is that the three named addressees are a leadership "triumvirate" in the community. He points out that the assumption that Apphia is Philemon's wife comes from John Chrysostom's commentary in the fourth century and has not been questioned. Callahan, *Embassy of Onesimus*, 25. Jeffrey A. Weima argues that the inclusion of Apphia and Archippus is an aspect of the letter as a public letter, not a private one to Philemon. This would indicate that the three individuals are considered leaders in the *ekklesia*. Weima, "Paul's Persuasive Prose," 38.

5. Bieberstein views Apphia's presence as evidence of "liberating praxis" in the community around Paul (Bieberstein, "Disrupting," 106) but Cotter's investigation indicates that her presence in a leadership role would not have been startling assuming that the community is located in a Romanized city. If Philemon's household was in Colossae and it remained un-Romanized, her leadership role would be a notable departure from cultural assumptions. Cotter, "Women's Authority Roles," 368–69.

6. For the argument that this and other letters were written to communities in Romanized cities and that the women mentioned should be understood in the framework of Roman culture rather than Greek, see Cotter, "Women's Authority Roles." She argues (368) that if the city was Romanized, her leadership role as a woman would not have been counter-cultural.

7. Hemelrijk, "Public Roles," 482–83; Hemelrijk, "Patronesses," and Harland.

8. Hemelrijk, "Public Roles," 482–83.

9. Or the house of Philemon, Apphia, and Archippus.

10. Scott S. Elliott describes this as two conversations taking place simultaneously. Elliott, "'Thanks But No Thanks.'"

11. This poses a difficulty for Marchal's reading. It would seem more likely that Paul would request Onesimus for his personal sexual use in a private letter than in a letter that includes the assembly. See Marchal, "The Usefulness of an Onesimus."

12. Fitzmeyer, *The Letter to Philemon*, 82.

13. This standard greeting will be discussed further in volume 2.

14. The omission of "hope" and the structuring of the sentence draws attention to "love" (*agape*), as F. Forrester Church has pointed out. See his notes for further citations on this: Church, "Rhetorical Structure and Design in Paul's Letter to Philemon," 22.

15. Sara Winter, who argues that the community leadership to whom Paul writes had sent Onesimus to him, says that this phrase "refers to the recipient's partnership with Paul" which "has been given concrete expression in the former's sending Onesimus to Paul." For Winter the recipient is Archippus. See Winter, "Paul's Letter to Philemon," 3. She also points to the importance of Sampley's work on the *societas/koinonia* form of association: Sampley, *Pauline Partnership*.

16. Fitzmeyer enumerates several options for this phrase, preferring the translation "that the participation (of others) in your faith may be(come) effective." Fitzmeyer, *The Letter to Philemon*, 97.

17. So also Martin, "The Rhetorical Function," 329 and n. 3.

18. The relationship of trust indicated in the word *pistis* (*fides*) is not necessarily egalitarian. Peter Lampe, for example, points out that the patron-client relied on this mutual loyalty more than on the power (*potestas*) of the patron. See Lampe, "Paul, Patrons, and Clients," 493. This is consistent with the rhetoric of friendship in the patron-client relationship.

19. The translation is from Fitzmeyer, *The Letter to Philemon*, 21–22. He also discusses the correspondence (20–23) as do numerous other commentators.

20. This family is also consistent with collegial relationships indicated in some of the voluntary associations. There is no reason to believe that the Pauline communities were doing something entirely new.

21. The translators have inferred here that Paul is claiming his authority as an "envoy" of the Anointed (Christ) although this is not explicit in the text. The NRSV, for example, translates: "For this reason, though I am bold enough in Christ to command you to do your duty."

22. See Box 4, p.XXX.

23. Tolmie, "Tendencies," 7, citing Arzt-Grabner, *Philemon*, 202–4. Paul also uses "child" not "son." This language poses a problem for Marchal's reading that he addresses in the general terms of not too readily assuming affection in the term, Marchal, "The Usefulness of an Onesimus," 764. He does not adequately address the change of status that the term implies, however.

24. Kea briefly notes this as a claim on Onesimus, Kea, "Paul's Letter to Philemon," 228. Frilingos mentions this in more detail, "… the apostle's parent-child relationship with Onesimus 'supersedes any slavish role Onesimus may have served in Philemon's household.' In other words, the apostle possesses a greater 'right' to the slave than does the slaveholder." He sees Paul using Onesimus as a tool to undermine Philemon's authority in the household, "to disassemble the structure of Philemon's domestic command." (Frilingos, "'For My Child, Onesimus,'" 101, 102.) The quote he cites is from Hock, "A Support For His Old Age," 81.

25. The use of the terms *achrēstos* and *euchrēstros* to refer to slaves was not uncommon in ancient letters and referred to various forms of work assigned to slaves. See Arzt-Grabner, "How to Deal with Onesimus?," 122–23. See the discussion of the sexual use of slaves in chapter 5, and the need of the *paterfamilias* for the appearance of willing obedience and cooperation from his subordinates as a matter of public honor in chapters 3 and 4, and Marchal, "The Usefulness of an Onesimus," 757–58.

26. Another layer in the pun may indicate that Onesimus was also "without Christ" as a pun on *Christos*, since the pronunciation of *achrēstos* and *euchrēstros*

would be the same in Hellenistic Greek. See Lohse, *Colossians and Philemon*, 200–201. This pun would mean that Onesimus was once "without Christ" but is now "good with Christ." Papyrological evidence casts doubt on this contention: Tolmie, "Tendencies," 7, citing Arzt-Grabner, *Philemon*, 216–14.

27. He is also "good in Christ" if the second layer of a pun is intended.

28. On this see Patterson, *Slavery and Social Death*.

29. *Phrygem plagis fiere solere meliorem* (Cicero, *Pro Flacco* 65). The citation and translation is from Fitzmeyer, *The Letter to Philemon*, 108.

30. Aristotle, *Eudemian Ethics*, 7.1241b.

31. Marchal's reading, however, would indicate that both Paul and Philemon can sexually use Onesimus more easily. Marchal, "The Usefulness of an Onesimus."

32. "Heart" is a translation of the Greek term *splankhna*, a term for "inward parts" that includes the rest of the internal organs and entrails, closer to "guts." "Heart" renders the Greek identification of this anatomical location as the seat of emotions. (*LSJ*, s.v. "*splankhnon*," 1628.) In his analysis of the emotions in the letter, Peter Lampe sees Paul's purpose here as standing in for Onesimus as a replacement object so that Philemon can vent his anger on Paul instead of Onesimus. Lampe, "Affects and Emotion," 67–68.

33. Jeremy Punt also comments on this aspect of slaves as "surrogate bodies" of their owners. Punt, "Paul, Power, and Philemon," 243–44.

34. The phrase translated "on your behalf" (*hyper sou*) poses some problematic although not insurmountable difficulties for Marchal's ("The Usefulness of an Onesimus") reading since it indicates service by Onesimus in place of Philemon, as his agent. See Lohse, *Colossians and Philemon*, 202, n. 48.

35. Scott Elliott points out the problem for Paul of accepting patronage from Philemon, but his analysis of vv. 13–14 does not fully explain why this appears to be Paul's request. Elliott, "'Thanks But No Thanks,'" 56–57.

36. The use of this term in ancient letters indicates that "he went away" would be a more accurate translation. See Arzt-Grabner, "How to Deal with Onesimus?" 124.

37. "Brother" describes what he means by "more than a slave."

38. Several commentators on Philemon indicate a distinction between "literal" and "spiritual" relationships, as if the so-called "spiritual" relationships being established in the communities Paul founded place no effective claim on the actions of the participants. In a footnote to a summary on v. 16, for example, Clarice Martin indicates, aptly, that "The widely held view that v. 16 can refer only to a new relationship of 'spiritual equality' between Onesimus and Philemon is, in this writer's view, very problematic," Martin, "The Rhetorical Function," 328, n. 3. The "spiritual" relationship makes real behavioral claims, as can be seen in Paul's use of his spiritual patronage or fatherhood of Philemon to make real claims on his decision regarding Onesimus. For a summary of opinions on whether Paul is asking for Onesimus' manumission: Wessels, "The Letter to Philemon in the Context of Slavery in Early Christianity," 162–68.

39. See chapter 5. For a useful short summary of the distinction in these relationships, see Lampe, "Paul, Patrons, and Clients," 489–93.

40. Sara Winter argues that the letter is a request *for* Onesimus, that Paul writes because he wants Onesimus to stay with him and assist him in the work of the Christian community. She also argues that the absence of mention of Onesimus' arrival in the thanksgiving in the letter shows that the recipient knew that he was with Paul and most probably sent by the recipients to him. Winter, "Paul's Letter to Philemon," 3–5, 6–7. She also argues (7) on the basis of comparison of Paul's language to legal terminology that v. 12 refers to sending the "case" to a higher

authority rather than sending Onesimus himself back with the letter.

41. In his postcolonial reading, Jeremy Punt contends that their common relationship to Paul is the primary one: Punt, "Paul, Power, and Philemon," 237. For an analysis of how Paul uses Onesimus to place himself at the top of a relational triangle that subordinates Philemon and Onesimus, see Frilingos, "'For My Child, Onesimus,'" 91–104.

42. Margaret B. Wilkerson uses literature about emancipation in the United States to imagine the meeting of Onesimus and Philemon as a moment of engaging the truth of slavery. She is optimistic about Paul's intent, but her work reveals what is absent both in the moment in the letter and in the truth-telling needed to address the US legacy of slavery. See Wilkerson, "Ain't You Marster," 101–20.

43. See Church, "Rhetorical Structure," 29.

44. On similar language in ancient letters that show the language of "accept him as me" in a brotherly or collegial business relationship, see Arzt-Grabner, "How to Deal with Onesimus?" 135–36.

45. Punt, "Paul, Power, and Philemon," 238. For several explanations of the language of debt, see Callahan, "Paul's Epistle to Philemon," 374.

46. Scott Elliott interprets this is a power move on Paul's part as he asserts his role as Philemon's patron. Elliott, "'Thanks But No Thanks,'" 61.

47. L. Michael White uses this term. He suggests that Paul is Philemon's client in matters of financial support and that Paul asserts his own status as patron in his spiritual relationship with Philemon. See White, "Paul and Pater Familias," 469–70.

48. It may be tempting to attribute these values to Paul as the one who has organized this community, but it is hardly likely that he would have had much hearing unless he was connecting to a discussion already occurring in the hidden transcript.

49. Perry Kea suggests that "sub-culture" better characterizes the community's values than "counter-culture." His analysis focuses on the values of the "dominant culture" here described in terms of the public transcript and the Roman Strict Father family model. Analysis of the public and hidden transcript allows us to see Paul addressing the dominant culture and the hidden transcript at the same time. Kea, "Paul's Letter to Philemon," 230–32.

50. The SV translation at v. 8 is a reasonable interpretation, but the language of agency is not explicit in the Greek text. See for example, Galatians 1:1 and 1:10, where Paul bases his authority on his status as one sent by Jesus the Anointed and God, not human authorities (1:1) and as a slave of the Anointed (1:1).

Epilogue
1. Paul Krugman, "How Republics End."

Bibliography

Primary Sources

Aristotle. *Works*. 23 vols. Loeb Classical Library. Trans. H. Rackham. Cambridge, MA: Harvard University Press, 1944.

Augustine. *The City of God*. Trans. Marcus Dods. Lawrence, KS: Digireads.com Pub, 2009.

Athenaeus. *The Deipnosophists*. 7 vols. Loeb Classical Library. Trans. Charles Burton Gulick. Cambridge, MA: Harvard University Press, 1929.

Augustus. *Res Gestae*. P. A. Brunt and J. M. Moore, *Res Gestae Divi Augusti: The Achievements of the Divine Augustus*. Oxford: Oxford University Press, 1967.

Aulus Gellius. *The Attic Nights*. 3 vols. Trans. John C. Rolfe. Cambridge, MA: Harvard University Press, 1927.

Cassius Dio Cocceianus. *Roman History*. 9 vols. Loeb Classical Library. Trans. Earnest Cary and Herbert Baldwin Foster. Cambridge, MA: Harvard University Press, 1914.

Cicero. *Works*. 29 vols. Loeb Classical Library. Cambridge, MA: Harvard University Press, 1976.

Columella, Lucius Junius Moderatus. *On Agriculture*. 2 vols. Trans. Harrison Boyd Ash. Cambridge, MA: Harvard University Press, 1940.

Dio Chrysostom. *Discourses*. 5 vols. Loeb Classical Library. Trans. J. W. Cohoon and H. Lamar Crosby. Cambridge: Harvard University Press, 1932–51.

Diodorus Siculus. *Library of History*. 12 vols. Loeb Classical Library. Trans. C. H. Oldfather. Cambridge, MA: Harvard University Press, 1933.

Diogenes Laertius. *Lives of Eminent Philosophers*. 2 vols. Loeb Classical Library. Trans. R. D. Hicks. Cambridge, MA: Harvard University Press, 1972 (1925).

Dionysius of Halicarnassus. *Roman Antiquities*. 7 vols. Loeb Classical Library. Trans. Earnest Cary. Cambridge, MA: Harvard University Press, 1937.

Florus, Lucius Annaeus. *Epitome of Roman History*. Trans. Edward Seymour Forster. Cambridge, MA: Harvard University Press, 1929.

Fragmenta Historicorum Graecorum. 5 vols. Ed. Karl Wilhelm Ludwig Müller. Paris: Didot, 1841–73. Online: http://www.dfhg-project.org.

Gaius and Ulpian. *The Institutes of Gaius and the Rules of Ulpian*. Trans. James Muirhead. Edinburgh: T & T Clark, 1880.

Hesiod. *The Homeric Hymns, Homerica*, and Hesiod, *Works and Days*. Trans. Hugh G. Evelyn-White. Cambridge, MA: Harvard University Press, 1914.

Horace. *The Works of Horace*. Trans. C. Smart and Theodore A. Buckley. New York: Harper & Brothers, 1863.

Horace, *Odes and Epodes*. Trans. Paul Shorey and Gordon J. Laing. New York: Benjamin H. Sanborn and Co., 1910.

Josephus. *The Works of Flavius Josephus*. Trans. William Whiston A.M. Auburn. Buffalo: John E. Beardsley, 1895.

Justinus, Marcus Junianus. *Epitome of the Philippic History of Pompeius Trogus*. Trans. John Selby Watson. London: Henry G. Bohn, 1853.

Livy. *History of Rome*. 14 vols. Loeb Classical Library. Trans. Benjamin Oliver Foster. Cambridge, MA: Harvard University Press, 1919.

Lucian. *Works*. 8 vols. Loeb Classical Library. Trans. A. M. Harmon. Cambridge, MA: Harvard University Press, 1936.

Lucretius. *De Rerum Natura*. Trans. William Ellery Leonard. New York: E. P. Dutton. 1916.

Ovid. *Fasti*. Loeb Classical Library. Trans. James George Frazer. Cambridge, MA: Harvard University Press, 1933.

————. *Tristia*. Loeb Classical Library. Trans. Arthur Leslie Wheeler. Cambridge, MA: Harvard University Press, 1939,.

Oxyrhynchus Papyri. 53 vols. Greco-Roman Memoirs Series. London: Egypt Exploration Society, 1882–2014. Online: http://www.papyrology.ox.ac.uk/POxy/.

Paulus Prudentissimus, Julius. "Sententiarum receptarum libri quinque qui vulgo Iulio Paulo adhuc tribuntur." *Rivista di Diritto Romano* 1 (2001): 1–34. Online: http://www.ledonline.it/rivistadirittoromano/.

Philo. *The Works of Philo: Complete and Unabridged*. Trans. Charles D. Yonge. Peabody, MA: Hendrickson, 1993.

Plato. *Platonis Opera*. Ed. John Burnet. Oxford: Oxford University Press, 1903.

Pliny the Elder. The Natural History. Trans. John Bostock and H.T. Riley. London: Taylor and Francis, 1855.

Plutarch. *Moralia*. 15 vols. Loeb Classical Library. Trans. Frank Cole Babbitt. Cambridge, MA: Harvard University Press, 1927–36.

Polybius. *Histories*. Trans. Evelyn S. Shuckburgh. New York: Macmillan, 1889. Reprint Bloomington, 1962.

Quintilian. *Institutio Oratoria*. 4 vols. Loeb Classical Library. Trans. Harold Edgeworth Butler. Cambridge, MA: Harvard University Press, 1920.

Sallust. *Works*. Loeb Classical Library. Trans. John Carew Rolfe. Cambridge, MA: Harvard University Press, 1921.

Seneca, Lucius Annaeus. *Moral Essays*. 3. Vols. Loeb Classical Library. Trans. John W. Basore. London: Heinemann, 1928.

Strabo. *Geography*. 8 vols. Loeb Classical Library. Ed. H. L. Jones. Cambridge, MA: Harvard University Press, 1924.

Suetonius. *The Lives of the Twelve Caesars*. Ed. J. Eugene Reed and Alexander Thomson. Philadelphia: Gebbie & Co., 1889.

Tacitus. *Complete Works of Tacitus*. Trans. Alfred John Church, William Jackson Brodribb, and Sara Bryant. New York: Random House, 1942.

Valerius Maximus, *Memorable Doings and Sayings*. 2 vols. Loeb Classical Library. Trans. D. R. Shackleton Bailey. Cambridge, MA: Harvard University Press, 2000.

Velleius Paterculus, Compendium of Roman History and Res Gestae Divi Augusti. Loeb Classical Library. Trans. Frederick W. Shipley. Cambridge, MA: Harvard University Press, 1924.

Vergil. *Aeneid*. Trans. Theodore C. Williams. Boston: Houghton Mifflin, 1910.

————. *Eclogues*. Trans. J. B. Greenough. Boston: Ginn, 1895.

Vitruvius. *The Ten Books on Architecture*. Trans. Morris Hicky Morgan. Cambridge, MA: Harvard University Press, 1914.

Secondary Sources

Aasgaard, Reidar. *My Beloved Brothers and Sisters!: Christian Siblingship in the Apostle Paul*. London: Continuum / T. & T. Clark, 2004.

Ando, Clifford. *Imperial Ideology and Provincial Loyalty in the Roman Empire.* Classics and Contemporary Thought 6. Berkeley, CA: University of California Press, 2000.

Anonymous. *The Homeric Hymns and Homerica.* Cambridge, MA: Harvard University Press, 1914.

Arzt-Grabner, Peter. *Philemon.* Papyrologische Kommentare zum Neuen Testament Band 1. Göttingen: Vandenhoeck & Ruprecht, 2003.

———. "How to Deal with Onesimus?: Paul's Solution within the Frame of Ancient Legal and Documentary Sources." Pp. 113–42 in *Philemon in Perspective: Interpreting a Pauline Letter.* Ed. D. F. Tolmie. Beihefte zur Zeitschrift für die Neutestamentliche Wissenschaft. Berlin: Walter de Gruyter, 2010.

Ascough, Richard. "Social and Political Characteristics of Greco-Roman Association Meals." Pp. 59–72 in *Meals in the Early Christian World: Social Formation, Experimentation, and Conflict at the Table.* Ed. Dennis E. Smith and Hal Taussig. Hampshire, UK: Palgrave, 2012.

Bakke, O. M. *When Children Became People: The Birth of Childhood in Early Christianity.* Minneapolis: Fortress Press, 2005.

Bakker, Jan T. *Living and Working with the Gods: Studies of Evidence for Private Religion and its Material Environment in the City of Ostia : 100–500 AD.* Dutch Monographs on Ancient History and Archaeology 12. Amsterdam: J.C. Gieben, 1994.

Balch, David L. *Roman Domestic Art and Early House Churches.* Wissemschaftlich Untersuchungen Zum Neuen Testament 228. Tübingen: Mohr Siebeck, 2008.

Balch, David L. and Carolyn Osiek, eds. *Early Christian Families in Context: An Interdisciplinary Dialogue.* Grand Rapids, MI: William B. Eerdmans, 2003.

Barton, Carlin A. *The Sorrows of the Ancient Romans: The Gladiator and the Monster.* Princeton, NJ: Princeton University Press, 1993.

———. *Roman Honor: The Fire in the Bones.* Ewing, NJ: University of California Press, 2001.

Barton, Stephen C. and G. H. R. Horsley. "A Hellenistic Cult Group and the New Testament Churches." *Jahrbuch für Antike und Christentum* 24 (1981) 7–41.

Beard, Mary. "The Roman and the Foreign: The Cult of the 'Great Mother' in Imperial Rome." Pp. 164–90 in *Shamanism, History, and the State.* Ed. Nicholas Thomas and Caroline Humphrey. Ann Arbor, MI: University of Michigan Press, 1994.

Beard, Mary, John North, and S. R. F. Price. *Religions of Rome: A History.* 2 vols. Vol. 1. 1st ed. Cambridge: Cambridge University Press, 1998.

Beavis, Mary A. *Jesus & Utopia: Looking for the Kingdom of God in the Roman World.* Minneapolis: Fortress Press, 2006.

———. "Christian Origins, Egalitarianism and Utopia." *Journal of Feminist Studies in Religion* 23 (2007) 27–49.

Bender, Donald R. "A Refinement of the Concept of Household: Families, Co-residence, and Domestic Functions." *American Anthropologist* 69 (1967) 493–504.

Benjamin, Walter. "Theses on the Philosophy of History." Pp. 253–63 in *Illuminations.* Trans. Harry Zohn. New York: Schocken Books, 2011

Bergmann, Bettina. "The Roman House As Memory Theater: The House of the Tragic Poet in Pompeii." *The Art Bulletin* 76 (1994) 225–56.

Bieber, Margarete. *The Statue of Cybele in the J. Paul Getty Museum.* Malibu, California: J. Paul Getty Museum, 1968.

————. "The Images of Cybele in Roman Coins and Sculpture." Pp. 29–40 in *Hommages À Marcel Renard*. Ed. J. Bibauw III. Collection Latomus 103. Brussels, 1969.

Bieberstein, Sabine. "Disrupting the Normal Reality of Slavery: A Feminist Reading of the Letter to Philemon." *Journal for the Study of the New Testament* 79 (2000) 105–16.

Boatwright, Mary T. "Children and Parents on the Tombstones of Pannonia." Pp. 287–318 in *The Roman Family in the Empire: Rome, Italy, and Beyond*. Ed. Michele George. Oxford: Oxford University Press, 2005.

Borgeaud, Philippe. *Mother of the Gods: From Cybele to the Virgin Mary*. Baltimore, MD: Johns Hopkins University Press, 1996.

Bowerstock, G. "The Pontificate of Augustus." Pp. 380–94. in *Between Republic and Empire*. Ed. Kurt A. Raaflaub and Mark Toher. Berkeley, CA: University of California Press, 1990.

Bradley, Keith R. "Slave Kingdoms and Slave Rebellions in Ancient Sicily." *Historical Reflections / Réflexions Historiques* 10 (1983) 435–51.

————. "Wet-Nursing at Rome: A Study in Social Relations." Pp. 201–29 in *The Family in Ancient Rome: New Perspectives*. Ed. Beryl Rawson. Ithaca, NY: Cornell University Press, 1986.

————. *Slaves and Masters in the Roman Empire: A Study in Social Control*. New York: Oxford University Press, 1987.

————. "Child Labor in the Roman World." Pp. 103–24 in *Discovering the Roman Family: Studies in Roman Social History*. Ed. Keith R. Bradley. New York: Oxford University Press, 1991.

————. ed. *Discovering the Roman Family: Studies in Roman Social History*. New York: Oxford University Press, 1991.

————. "Remarriage and the Structure of the Upper-Class Roman Family." Pp. 156–76 in *Discovering the Roman Family: Studies in Roman Social History*. Ed. Keith R. Bradley. New York: Oxford University Press, 1991.

————. "The Social Role of the Nurse in Roman World." Pp. 13–36 in *Discovering the Roman Family: Studies in Roman Social History*. Ed. Keith R. Bradley. New York: Oxford University Press, 1991.

————. "Animalizing the Slave: The Truth of Fiction." *Journal of Roman Studies* 90 (2000) 110–25.

————. "BBC—History—Ancient History in depth: Resisting Slavery in Ancient Rome." Online: http://www.bbc.co.uk/history/ancient/romans/slavery_01. shtml.

————. "The Roman Child in Sickness and in Health." Pp. 67–92 in *The Roman Family in the Empire: Rome, Italy, and Beyond*. Ed. Michele George. Oxford: Oxford University Press, 2005.

Brunt, P. A., and J. M. Moore. *Res Gestae Divi Augusti: The Achievements of the Divine Augustus*. Oxford: Oxford University Press, 1967.

Burkert, Walter. *Greek Religion*. Greek Religion. Cambridge, MA: Harvard University Press, 1985.

————. *Ancient Mystery Cults*. Carl Newell Jackson lectures. Cambridge, MA.: Harvard University Press, 1987.

Burns, James M. *Leadership*. 1st ed. New York: Harper & Row, 1978.

Burton, Joan. "Women's Commensality in the Ancient Greek World." *Greece & Rome* 45 (1998) 143–65.

Callahan, Allen D. "Paul's Epistle to Philemon: Toward an Alternative Argumentum." *Harvard Theological Review* 86 (1993) 357–76.

————. "John Chrysostom on Philemon: A Response to Margaret M. Mitchell." *Harvard Theological Review* 88 (1995) 149–56.

————. *Embassy of Onesimus: The Letter of Paul to Philemon*. Valley Forge, PA: Trinity Press International, 1997.

Cameron, A. "The Exposure of Children and Greek Ethics." *Classical Review* 46 (1932) 105–14.

Campbell, Joan C. and Patrick J. Hartin, eds. *Exploring Biblical Kinship: Festschrift in Honor of John J. Pilch*. The Catholic Biblical Quarterly Monograph Series 55. Washington, DC: The Catholic Biblical Association of America, 2016.

Carcopino, Jerome. *Passion et Politique chez les Césars*. Paris: Hachette, 1958.

Church, F. F. "Rhetorical Structure and Design in Paul's Letter to Philemon." *Harvard Theological Review* 71 (1978) 17–33.

Corpus Inscriptionum Latinarum. 17 vols. Berlin: Berlin-Brandenburg Academy of Sciences and Humanities 1862. Online: http://cil.bbaw.de/cil_en/dateien/datenbank_eng.php.

Collins, Patricia H. "It's All in the Family: Intersections of Gender, Race, and Nation." *Hypatia* 13 (1998) 62–82.

Connelly, Joan B. *Portrait of a Priestess: Women and Ritual in Ancient Greece*. Princeton: Princeton University Press, 2007.

Connolly, Peter, and Hazel Dodge. *The Ancient City: Life in Classical Athens & Rome*. Oxford: Oxford University Press, 1998.

Cooley, Alison E. "Women beyond Rome: Trend-setters or Dedicated Followers of Fashion?" Pp. 23–46 in *Women and the Roman City in the Latin West*. Ed. Emily A. Hemelrijk and Greg Woolf. Mnemosyne. Supplements. History and Archaeology of Classical Antiquity 360. Leiden, Boston: Brill, 2013.

Cooper, Kate. "Closely Watched Households: Visibility, Exposure and Private Power in the Roman Domus." *Past & Present* 197, no. 1 (2007) 3–33.

Corley, Kathleen E. "Women's Funerary Rituals." Pp. 35–87 in Seminar Papers of the Christianity Seminar, Westar Institute, Spring Meeting, 2013, Santa Rosa, California, 2013.

Cotter, Wendy. "Women's Authority Roles in Paul's Churches: Countercultural or Conventional?" *Novum Testamentum* 36 (1994) 350–72.

————. "The Collegia and Roman Law: State Restrictions on Voluntary Associations, 64 BCE–200 CE." Pp. 74–89 in *Voluntary Associations in the Graeco-Roman World*. Ed. John S. Kloppenborg and S. G. Wilson. London: Routledge, 1996.

Crawford, Sidnie W. "Not According to Rule: Women, the Dead Sea Scrolls and Qumran." Pp. 127–50 in *Emanuel: Studies in Hebrew Bible Septuagint and Dead Sea Scrolls in Honor of Emanuel Tov*. Ed. Shalom M. Paul et al. Leiden: Brill, 2003.

————. "Not According to Rule: Women, the Dead Sea Scrolls and Qumran." Online: http://digitalcommons.unl.edu/cgi/viewcontent.cgi?article=1064&context=classicsfacpub.

Crook, J. A. "Patria Potestas." *Classical Quarterly* 17 (1967) 113–22.

Crossan, John D. *The Historical Jesus: The Life of a Mediterranean Jewish Peasant*. Historical Jesus. New York and San Francisco: Harper Collins, 1991.

————. *God and Empire: Jesus Against Rome, Then and Now*. San Francisco: HarperCollins, 2007.

Daniels-Hughes, Carly. "The Sex Trade and Slavery at Meals." Pp. 165–78 in *Meals in the Early Christian World: Social Formation, Experimentation, and Conflict at the Table*. Ed. Dennis E. Smith and Hal Taussig. Hampshire, UK: Palgrave, 2012.

Danker, Frederick. *Benefactor: Epigraphic Study of a Graeco-Roman and New Testament Semantic Field.* St. Louis, Missouri: Clayton Publishing, 1982.

Degrassi, Attilio. *Inscriptiones Latinae Liberae Rei Publicae.* 2 vols. Florence: La Nuova Italia, 1963, 1965.

Dessau, Hermann. *Inscriptiones Latinae Selectae.* 3 vols. Berlin: Weidmann, 1892–1916.

Desmond, William. *Cynics.* Ancient Philosophies. Stocksfield [England]: Acumen, 2008.

Dewey, Arthur J., Roy W. Hoover, Lane C. McGaughy, and Daryl D. Schmidt. *The Authentic Letters of Paul: A New Reading of Paul's Rhetoric and Meaning: The Scholars Version.* Salem, OR: Polebridge Press, 2010.

Dixon, Suzanne. *The Roman Mother.* London: Routledge, 1988.

———. "The Sentimental Ideal of the Roman Family." Pp. 99–113 in *Marriage, Divorce, and Children in Ancient Rome.* Ed. Beryl Rawson. Oxford, Canberra: Clarendon; Humanities Research Center, 1991.

———. *The Roman Family.* Baltimore: Johns Hopkins University Press, 1992.

———. "Sex and the Married Woman in Ancient Rome." Pp. 111–29 in *Early Christian Families in Context: An Interdisciplinary Dialogue.* Ed. David L. Balch and Carolyn Osiek. Grand Rapids, MI: William B. Eerdmans, 2003.

Dolansky, Fanny. "Honouring the Family Dead on the Parentalia: Ceremony, Spectacle, and Memory." *Phoenix* 65 (2011) 125–57.

———. "Playing with Gender: Girls, Dolls, and Adult Ideals in the Roman World." *Classical Antiquity* 31 (2012) 256–92.

Drew-Bear, Thomas, Christine M. Thomas, and Melek Yildizturan. *Phrygian Votive Steles.* Museum of Anatolian Civilizations, General Directorate of Monuments and Museums, Ministry of Culture, Turkish Republic, 1999.

Dunbabin, Katherine M. D. *The Roman Banquet: Images of Conviviality.* Cambridge: Cambridge University Press, 2010.

Dyson, Stephen. "Native Revolts in the Roman Empire." *Historia* 20 (1971) 238–74.

Eder, W. "Augustus and the Power of Tradition: The Augustan Principate as Binding Link between Republic and Empire." Pp. 71–122 in *Between Republic and Empire.* Ed. Kurt A. Raaflaub and Mark Toher. Berkeley, CA: University of California Press, 1990.

Elliott, John. "Jesus Was Not an Egalitarian: A Critique of an Anachronistic and Idealistic Theory." *Biblical Theology Bulletin* 32 (2002) 75–91.

———. "The Jesus Movement Was Not Egalitarian But Family Oriented." *Biblical Interpretation* 11 (2003) 173–210.

Elliott, Scott S. "'Thanks, But No Thanks': Tact, Persuasion, and the Negotiation of Power in Paul's Letter to Philemon." *New Testament Studies* 57 (2011) 51–64.

Elliott, Susan. *Cutting Too Close For Comfort: Paul's Letter to the Galatians in its Anatolian Cultic Context.* Library of New Testament studies 248. London: T & T Clark International, 2003.

———. "Choose Your Mother, Choose Your Master: Galatians 4:21–5:1 in the Shadow of the Anatolian Mother of the Gods." *Journal of Biblical Literature* 118 (1999) 661–83.

———. "Mystery Cults." Pp. 931–32 in *Eerdmans Dictionary of the Bible.* Ed. David N. Freedman, Allen C. Myers and Astrid B. Beck. Grand Rapids, MI.: W.B. Eerdmans, 2000.

————. "Mystery Cults as Expressions of Popular Religiosity." Paper for Greco-
Roman Religions Section, Society of Biblical Literature, Nashville, Tennessee,
November 18, 2000.

————. "Gladiators and Martyrs." *The Fourth R* 29, no. 5 (2016) 3–8, 20.

————. "Gladiators and Martyrs: Icons in the Arena." *Forum 3,6* (2017) 27–55.

Ellison, Ralph. *The Invisible Man*. New York: New American Library, 1952.

Evans, Nancy A. "Evidence for Slaves at the Table in the Ancient Mediterranean:
From Traditional Rural Festivals to Urban Associations." Pp. 149–64 in *Meals
in the Early Christian World: Social Formation, Experimentation, and Conflict
at the Table*. Ed. Dennis E. Smith and Hal Taussig. Hampshire, UK: Palgrave,
2012.

Eyben, Emiel. "Fathers and Sons." Pp. 114–43 in *Marriage, Divorce, and
Children in Ancient Rome*. Ed. Beryl Rawson. Oxford, Canberra: Clarendon;
Humanities Research Center, 1991.

Ferguson, William S. "The Attic Orgeones." *Harvard Theological Review* 37 (1944)
61–140.

Fishwick, Duncan. "The Cannophori and the March Festival of Magna Mater."
Transactions and Proceedings of the American Philological Association 97
(1996) 193–202.

Fishwick, Duncan. "The Provincial Centre at Camulodunum." *Britannia* 28 (1997)
31–50.

Fitzmeyer, Joseph A. *The Letter to Philemon: A New Translation with Introduction
and Commentary*. New York: Doubleday, 2000.

Forbis, Elizabeth P. "Women's Public Image in Italian Honorary Inscriptions." *The
American Journal of Philology* 111, no. 4 (1990) 493–512.

Frank, Richard I. "Augustus' Legislation on Marriage and Children." *California
Studies in Classical Antiquity* 8 (1975) 41–52.

Frier, Bruce W., Thomas A. McGinn, and Thomas A. J. McGinn. *Casebook on
Roman Family Law*. Cary, NC, USA: Oxford University Press, 2003.

Friesen, Steven J. *Imperial Cults and the Apocalypse of John: Reading Revelation in
the Ruins*. Oxford: Oxford University Press, 2001.

————. "Normal Religion, or, Words Fail Us: A Response to Karl Galinsky's 'The
Cult of the Roman Emperor: Uniter or Divider?'" Pp. 23–26 in *Rome and
Religion: A Cross-Disciplinary Dialogue on the Imperial Cult*. Ed. Jeffrey Brodd
and Jonathan Reed. Atlanta, GA: Society of Biblical Literature, 2011.

Frilingos, Chris. "'For My Child, Onesimus': Paul and Domestic Power in
Philemon." *Journal of Biblical Literature* 119 (2000) 91–104.

Galinsky, Karl. *Augustan Culture: An Interpretive Introduction*. Princeton, NJ:
Princeton University Press, 1996.

————. "The Cult of the Roman Emperor: Uniter or Divider?" Pp. 1–21 in *Rome
and Religion: A Cross-Disciplinary Dialogue on the Imperial Cult*. Ed. Jeffrey
Brodd and Jonathan Reed. Atlanta, GA: Society of Biblical Literature, 2011.

————. "Memory and Forgetting in the Age of Augustus." Sidney, Australia,
September 30, 2014; 2016.

Galsterer, H. "A Man, a Book, and a Method: Sir Ronald Syme's Roman Revolution
After Fifty Years." Pp. 1–20 in *Between Republic and Empire*. Ed. Kurt A.
Raaflaub and Mark Toher. Berkeley, CA: University of California Press, 1990.

Gardner, Jane F. and Thomas Wiedemann. *The Roman Household: A Sourcebook*.
London: Routledge, 1991.

Gasparro, Giulia S. "Per la storia del culto di Cibile in Occidente: il santuario rup-
    estre di Akrai." Pp. 51–86 in *Cybele, Attis, and Related Cults: Essays in Memory
    of M.J. Vermaseren*. Ed. Eugene N. Lane. Religions in the Graeco-Roman
    World v. 131. Leiden: E.J. Brill, 1996.
George, Michele. "Family Values and Family Imagery in Roman Italy." Pp. 37–66
    in *The Roman Family in the Empire: Rome, Italy, and Beyond*. Ed. Michele
    George. Oxford: Oxford University Press, 2005.
Glancy, Jennifer. "Slaves at Greco-Roman Banquets: A Response." Pp. 205–13 in
    *Meals in the Early Christian World: Social Formation, Experimentation, and
    Conflict at the Table*. Ed. Dennis E. Smith and Hal Taussig. Hampshire, UK:
    Palgrave, 2012.
————. *Slavery in Early Christianity*. 1st ed. Minneapolis, MN: Fortress Press, 2006.
Golden, Mark. "Pais, 'Child' and 'Slave.'" *L'Antiquité Classique* 54 (1985) 91–104.
Graillot, Henri. *Le culte de Cybele, mère des dieux, á Rome et dans l'Empire romain*.
    Le culte. Paris: Fontemoing, 1912.
Grams, Laura. "Hipparchia (fl. 300 B.C.E.)." in *The Internet Encyclopedia of
    Philosophy: ISSN 2161–0002*, http://www.iep.utm.edu/. Ed. James Fieser and
    Bradley Dowden.
Hales, Shelley. *The Roman House and Social Identity*. Cambridge: Cambridge
    University Press, 2003.
Hammond, N. G. L., and H. H. Scullard. *The Oxford Classical Dictionary*. 2d ed.
    Oxford, UK: Oxford University Press, 1970 (1976).
Hanges, James C. "To Complicate Encounters: A Response to Karl Galinsky's 'The
    Cult of the Roman Emperor: Uniter or Divider?.'" Pp. 27–34 in *Rome and
    Religion: A Cross-Disciplinary Dialogue on the Imperial Cult*. Ed. Jeffrey Brodd
    and Jonathan Reed. Atlanta, GA: Society of Biblical Literature, 2011.
Harland, Philip. "Familial Dimensions of Group Identity (II): 'Mothers' and
    'Fathers' in Associations and Synagogues of the Greek World." *Journal for the
    Study of Judaism* 38 no. 1 (2007) 57–79.
————. "Imperial Cults Within Local Cultural Life: Associations in Roman Asia."
    Ancient History Bulletin / Zeitschrift für Alte Geschichte 17 (2003) 85–107.
————. "Familial Dimensions of Group Identity: 'Brothers' (ΑΔΕΛΦΟΙ) in
    Associations of the Greek East." *Journal of Biblical Literature* 124 (2005)
    491–513.
————. *Associations, Synagogues, and Congregations: Claiming a Place in Ancient
    Mediterranean Society*. 2d ed. Kitchener, Ontario: Philip Harland, 2013.
Harrill, J. A. "Using the Roman Jurists to Interpret Philemon: A Response to Peter
    Lampe." *Zeitschrift für die Neutestamentliche Wissenschaft* 90 (1999) 135–38.
————. "The Domestic Enemy: A Moral Polarity of Household Slaves in Early
    Christian Apologies and Martyrdoms." Pp. 231–54 in *Early Christian Families
    in Context: An Interdisciplinary Dialogue*. Ed. David L. Balch and Carolyn
    Osiek. Grand Rapids, MI: William B. Eerdmans, 2003.
————. *Slaves in the New Testament: Literary, Social, and Moral Dimensions*.
    Minneapolis: Fortress Press, 2006.
Harris, William V. "The Roman Father's Power of Life and Death." Pp. 81–95 in
    Studies in Roman Law in Memory of A. Arthur Schiller. Ed. Roger S. Bagnall
    and William V. Harris. Leiden: E. J. Brill, 1986.
————. "Child-Exposure in the Roman Empire." *Journal of Roman Studies* 84
    (1994) 1–22.
Haspels, C. H. E. "Lions." *Mnemosyne, Bibliotheca Classica Batava* n.v. (1951)
    230–34.

————. *The Highlands of Phrygia: Sites and Monuments.* 2 vols. Highlands. Princeton, NJ: Princeton University Press, 1971.

Hatlen, Jan F. "Honour and Domestic Violence in the Late Roman West C. 300–600 A.D." Ph.D., Norwegian University of Science and Technology, 2015.

Heen, Erik. "The Role of Symbolic Inversion in Utopian Discourse: Apocalyptic Reversal in Paul and in the Festival of the Saturnalia/Kronia." Pp. 123–144 in *Hidden Transcripts and the Arts of Resistance: Applying the Work of James C. Scott to Jesus and Paul.* Ed. Richard A. Horsley. Semeia Studies 48. Atlanta: Society of Biblical Literature, 2004.

Hellerman, Joseph H. *The Ancient Church As Family.* Minneapolis: Fortress Press, 2001.

Hemelrijk, Emily A. "Local Empresses: Priestesses of the Imperial Cult in the Cities of the Latin West." *Phoenix* 61 (2007) 318–49.

————. "Patronesses and "Mothers" of Roman Collegia." *Classical Antiquity* 27 (2008) 115–62.

————. "Public Roles for Women in the Cities of the Latin West." Pp. 478–90 in *A Companion to Women in the Ancient World.* Ed. Sharon L. James and Sheila Dillon. Blackwell Companions to the Ancient World. Chichester, West Sussex: Wiley-Blackwell, 2012.

Hock, Ronald F. "A Support For His Old Age: Paul's Plea on Behalf of Onesimus." Pp. 67–81 in *The Social World of the First Christians: Essays in Honor of Wayne Meeks.* Ed. L. M. White and O. L. Yarbrough. Minneapolis: Fortress Press, 1995.

Horn, Cornelia B. and John W. Martens. *"Let the Little Children Come to Me": Childhood and Children in Early Christianity.* Washington, DC: Catholic University of America Press, 2009.

Horsley, Richard A. *Paul and Empire: Religion and Power in Roman Imperial Society.* Ed. Richard A. Horsley. Harrisburg, Pennsylvania: Trinity Press International, 1997.

————. "Unearthing A People's History." Pp. 1–20 in *Christian Origins.* Ed. Richard A. Horsley. A People's History of Christianity v. 1. Philadelphia, PA: Fortress Press, 2005.

————, ed. *Christian origins.* A People's History of Christianity v. 1. Philadelphia, PA.: Fortress, 2005.

Huebner, Sabine R. "Household and Family in the Roman East and West." Pp. 73–91 in *A Companion to Families in the Greek and Roman Worlds.* Ed. Beryl Rawson. Blackwell Companions to the Ancient World. Malden, MA: Wiley-Blackwell, 2011.

Hunter, Virginia. "The Athenian Widow and Her Kin." *Journal of Family History* 14 (1989) 291–311.

Ilan, Tal. *Jewish Women in Greco-Roman Palestine.* Peabody, MA: Hendrickson Publishers, 1995.

Johnson, Matthew V. "Onesimus Speaks: Diagnosing the Hys/Terror of the Text." Pp. 91–100 in *Onesimus, Our Brother: Reading Religion, Race, and Culture in Philemon.* Ed. Matthew V. Johnson, James A. Noel and Demetrius K. Williams. Paul in Critical Contexts. Minneapolis: Fortress Press, 2012.

Johnson, Matthew V., James A. Noel, and Demetrius K. Williams. *Onesimus, Our Brother: Reading Religion, Race, and Culture in Philemon.* Paul in Critical Contexts. Minneapolis: Fortress Press, 2012.

Johnston, Patricia A. "Cybele and Her Companions on the Northern Littoral of the Black Sea." Pp. 101–16 in *Cybele, Attis, and Related Cults: Essays in Memory of M.J. Vermaseren.* Ed. Eugene N. Lane. Religions in the Graeco-Roman World v. 131. Leiden: E.J. Brill, 1996.

Kahl, Brigitte. *Galatians Reimagined: Reading With the Eyes of the Vanquished.* Paul in Critical Contexts. Minneapolis: Fortress, 2009.

Kea, Perry V. "Paul's Letter to Philemon: A Short Analysis of Its Values." *Perspectives in Religious Studies* 23 (1996) 223–32.

King, Cynthia. *Musonius Rufus: Lectures & Sayings.* [S.l.]: CreateSpace, 2011.

Kleingeld, Pauline, and Eric Brown. "Cosmopolitanism." in *Stanford Encyclopedia of Philosophy.* Ed. Edward N. Zalta. Online: http://plato.stanford.edu/archives/win2012/entries/davidson/.

Klinghardt, Matthias. *Gemeinschaftsmahl und Mahlgemeinschaft: Soziologie und Liturgie frühchristlicher Mahlfeiern.* Tübingen: Francke Verlag, 1996.

———. "A Typology of the Communal Meal." Pp. 9–22 in *Meals in the Early Christian World: Social Formation, Experimentation, and Conflict at the Table.* Ed. Dennis E. Smith and Hal Taussig. Hampshire, UK: Palgrave, 2012.

Kloppenborg, John S. "*Collegia* and *Thiasoi*: Issues in function, taxonomy and membership." Pp. 16–30 in *Voluntary Associations in the Graeco-Roman World.* Ed. John S. Kloppenborg and S. G. Wilson. London: Routledge, 1996.

Kloppenborg, John S., and S. G. Wilson, eds. *Voluntary Associations in the Graeco-Roman World.* London: Routledge, 1996.

Knox, John. *Philemon Among the Letters of Paul.* New York: Abingdon Press, 1935.

Krugman, Paul. "How Republics End." *The New York Times,* New York, December 19, 2016, A21. Online: http://www.nytimes.com/2016/12/19/opinion/how-republics-end.html.

Lacey, W. K. "Patria Potestas." Pp. 121–44 in *The Family in Ancient Rome: New Perspectives.* Ed. Beryl Rawson. Ithaca, NY: Cornell University Press, 1986.

Laes, Christian. "Desperately Different? *Delicia* Children in the Roman Household." Pp. 298–326 in *Early Christian Families in Context: An Interdisciplinary Dialogue.* Ed. David L. Balch and Carolyn Osiek. Grand Rapids, MI: William B. Eerdmans, 2003.

Lakoff, George. *Women, Fire, and Dangerous Things.* Chicago: University of Chicago Press, 1987.

———. *Moral Politics: How Liberals and Conservatives Think.* Chicago: University of Chicago Press, 2002.

———. *Philosophy in the Flesh: The Embodied Mind and Its Challenge to Western Thought.* New York: Basic Books, 1999.

Lakoff, George, and Mark Johnson. *Metaphors We Live By.* Chicago: University of Chicago Press, 1980.

Lambrechts, Pierre. "Livie-Cybele." *La Nouvelle Clio* 4 (1952) 251–59.

Lampe, Peter. "Keine Sklavenflucht des Onesimus." *Zeitschrift für die Neutestamentliche Wissenschaft* 76 (1985) 135–37.

———. "Paul, Patrons, and Clients." Pp. 488–523 in *Paul in the Greco-Roman World: A Handbook.* Ed. J. P. Sampley. Harrisburg, PA: Trinity Press International / Continuum, 2003.

———. "Affects and Emotions in the Rhetoric of Paul's Letter to Philemon: A Rhetorical-Psychological Interpretation." Pp. 61–77 in *Philemon in Perspective: Interpreting a Pauline Letter.* Ed. D. F. Tolmie. Beihefte zur Zeitschrift für die Neutestamentliche Wissenschaft. Berlin: Walter de Gruyter, 2010.

Langlands, Rebecca. *Sexual Morality in Ancient Rome.* Cambridge: Cambridge University Press, 2006.

Lassen, Eva M. "The Roman Family: Ideal and Metaphor." Pp. 103–20 in *Constructing Early Christian Families: Family as Social Reality and Metaphor.* Ed. Halvor Moxnes. London: Routledge, 1997.

Latham, Jacob. "'Fabulous Clap-Trap': Roman Masculinity, the Cult of Magna Mater, and Literary Constructions of the galli at Rome from the Late Republic to Late Antiquity." *The Journal of Religion* 92 (2012) 84–122.

Lefkowitz, Mary R., and Maureen B. Fant. *Women's Life in Greece and Rome: A Source Book in Translation.* 3d ed. Baltimore: Johns Hopkins University Press, 2005.

Lendering, Jona. "Imperator—Livius." Online: http://www.livius.org/articles/concept/imperator/.

Liddell, Henry G., Robert Scott, Henry Stuart Jones, and Roderick McKenzie. *Greek-English Lexicon.* 9th ed. Oxford: Clarendon Press, 1996.

Lippy, Charles H. *Being Religious, American Style: A History of Popular Religiosity in the United States.* Westport: Greenwood Press, 1994.

Lohse, Eduard. *Colossians and Philemon: A Commentary on the Epistles to the Colossians and to Philemon.* Hermeneia—A Critical and Historical Commentary on the Bible. Philadelphia: Fortress Press, 1971.

Lopez, Davina C. *Apostle to the Conquered: Reimagining Paul's Mission.* Paul in Critical Contexts. Minneapolis: Fortress Press, 2008.

Lorde, Audre. "The Master's Tools Will Never Dismantle the Master's House: Comments at 'The Personal and Political Panel' (Second Sex Conference, October 29, 1979)." Pp. 98–101 in *This Bridge Called My Back: Writings by Radical Women of Color,* Ed. Cherríe Moraga and Gloria Anzaldúa. 2d ed. Ed. Cherríe Moraga and Gloria Anzaldúa. New York: Kitchen Table, 1983.

Lozano, Fernando. "Divi Augusti and Theoi Sebastoi: Roman Initiatives and Greek Answers." *Classical Quarterly* New Series 57 (2007) 139–52.

MacClintock, Ann. *Imperial Leather: Race, Gender and Sexuality in Colonial Context.* New York: Routledge, 1995.

MacMullen, Ramsay. *Enemies of the Roman Order: Treason, Unrest, and Alienation in the Empire.* Cambridge, MA: Harvard University Press, 1966a.

MacMullen, Ramsay. "Woman in Public in the Roman Empire." *Historia: Zeitschrift für Alte Geschichte* 29, no. 2 (1980b) 208–18.

Marchal, Joseph A. "The Usefulness of an Onesimus: The Sexual Use of Slaves and Paul's Letter to Philemon." *Journal of Biblical Literature* 130 (2011) 749–70.

Marks, Susan. "Present and Absent: Women at Greco-Roman Meals." Pp. 123–48 in *Meals in the Early Christian World: Social Formation, Experimentation, and Conflict at the Table.* Ed. Dennis E. Smith and Hal Taussig. Hampshire, UK: Palgrave, 2012.

Martin, Clarice. "The Rhetorical Function of Commercial Language in Paul's Letter to Philemon (Verse 18)." Pp. 321–37 in *Persuasive Artistry: Studies in New Testament Rhetoric in Honor of George A. Kennedy.* Ed. Duane F. Watson. Rhetorical Function. Sheffield: Sheffield Academic Press, 1991.

Martin, Dale B. "Slave Families and Slaves in Families." Pp. 207–230 in *Early Christian Families in Context: An Interdisciplinary Dialogue.* Ed. David L. Balch and Carolyn Osiek. Grand Rapids, MI: William B. Eerdmans, 2003.

Mayor, Adrienne. "People Illustrated." *Archaeology* 52 (1999) 54–57.

———. "Mithradates: Scourge of Rome." *History Today* 59 (2009) 10–15.

———. *The Poison King: The Life and Legend of Mithradates, Rome's Deadliest Enemy.* Princeton, NJ: Princeton University Press, 2010.

McManus, Barbara. "Augustus, the Principate, and Propaganda." Online: http://www.vroma.org/~bmcmanus/augustus2.html.

————. "Plan of the Forum of Augustus." Online: http://www.vroma. org/~bmcmanus/forumaugplan.html.

Métraux, Guy P. R. "Ancient Housing: "Oikos" and "Domus" in Greece and Rome." *Journal of the Society of Architectural Historians* 58 (1999/2000) 392–405.

Meyers, Eric M. "The Problems of Gendered Space in Syro-Palestinian Domestic Architecture: the Case of Roman-Period Galilee." Pp. 44–72 in *Early Christian Families in Context: An Interdisciplinary Dialogue.* Ed. David L. Balch and Carolyn Osiek. Grand Rapids, MI: William B. Eerdmans, 2003.

Milnor, Kristina. *Gender, Domesticity, and the Age of Augustus: Inventing Private Life.* Oxford Studies in Classical Literature and Gender Theory. Cary, NC: Oxford University Press, 2006.

Mitchell, Margaret M. "John Chrysostom on Philemon: a Second Look." *Harvard Theological Review* 88 (1995) 135–48.

Moles, John L. "Cynic Cosmopolitanism." Pp. 105–20 in *The Cynics: The Cynic Movement in Antiquity and Its Legacy.* Ed. Robert B. Branham and Marie-Odile Goulet-Cazé. Hellenistic Culture and Society 23. Berkeley, CA: University of California Press, 1996.

Momigliano, Arnaldo and Simon R. F. Price. "Roman Religion: The Imperial Period." Pp. 7911–25 in *Encyclopedia of Religion.* Vol. 12. 2d ed. Ed. Lindsay Jones. Detroit: Macmillan Reference, 2005.

Moxnes, Halvor. "What Is Family?: Problems in Constructing Early Christian Families." Pp. 13–41 in *Constructing Early Christian Families: Family as Social Reality and Metaphor.* Ed. Halvor Moxnes. London: Routledge, 1997.

Netting, R., R. Wilk, and E. Arnould, eds. *Households: Comparative and Historical Studies of the Domestic Group.* Households. Berkeley, CA: University of California Press, 1984.

Nevett, Lisa C. "Family and Household, Ancient History and Archeology: A Case Study from Roman Egypt." Pp. 15–31 in *A Companion to Families in the Greek and Roman Worlds.* Ed. Beryl. Rawson. Blackwell Companions to the Ancient World. Chichester, West Sussex, UK, MA: Wiley-Blackwell, 2011.

Newcomb, Steven T. *Pagans in the Promised Land: Decoding the Doctrine of Christian Discovery.* Golden, CO: Fulcrum Publishing, 2008.

Noyes, Alfred. *Collected Poems.* New York: Frederick A. Stokes Company, 1913.

O'Connor, Kathleen M. "Let All the People Praise You: Biblical Studies and a Hermeneutics of Hunger." Pp. 17–34 in *By Bread Alone: The Bible through the Eyes of the Hungry.* Ed. Sheila E. McGinn, Ngan, Lai Ling Elizabeth, and Ahida C. Pilarski. Minneapolis: Fortress Press, 2014.

Orr, David G. "Roman Domestic Religion: The Evidence of the Household Shrines." *Aufstieg und Niedergang der römischen Welt* II 16.2 (1978) 1559–91.

Osiek, Carolyn. "Female Slaves, Porneia, and the Limits of Obedience." Pp. 255–76 in *Early Christian Families in Context: an Interdisciplinary Dialogue.* Ed. David L. Balch and Carolyn Osiek. Grand Rapids, MI: William B. Eerdmans, 2003.

Osiek, Carolyn, and David L. Balch. *Families in the New Testament World: Households and House Churches.* Families. Louisville, KY: Westminster/John Knox, 1997.

Osiek, Carolyn, Margaret Y. MacDonald, and Janet H. Tulloch. *A Woman's Place: House Churches in Earliest Christianity.* Minneapolis: Fortress Press, 2006.

Ostrow, S. E. "The *Augustales* in the Augustan Scheme." Pp. 364–79 in *Between Republic and Empire*. Ed. Kurt A. Raaflaub and Mark Toher. Berkeley, CA: University of California Press, 1990.

Özkaya, Vecihi. "The Shaft Monuments and the 'Taurobolium' among the Phrygians." *Anatolian Studies* 47 (1997) 89–103.

Parke, H. W. *Sibyls and Sibylline Prophecy in Classical Antiquity*. London: Routledge, 1992.

Parker, Holt N. "The Teratogenic Grid." Pp. 47–65 in *Roman Sexualities*. Ed. Judith P. Hallett. Princeton: Princeton University Press, 1998.

———. "Loyal Slaves and Loyal Wives: The Crisis of the Outsider-Within and Roman Exemplum Literature." Pp. 157–78 in *Women and Slaves in Greco-Roman Culture: Differential Equations*. Ed. Sandra R. Joshel and Sheila Murnaghan. London: Routledge, 2001.

Patterson, Orlando. *Slavery and Social Death: A Comparative Study*. Cambridge, MA: Harvard University Press, 1982.

Perkins, Judith. *Roman Imperial Identities in the Early Christian Era*. London: Routledge, 2009.

Peskowitz, Miriam. "'Family/ies' in Antiquity: Evidence from Tannaitic Literature and Roman Galilean Architecture." Pp. 9–36 in *The Jewish Family in Antiquity*. Ed. Shaye J. D. Cohen. Atlanta: Scholars Press, 1993.

Pettazzoni, Raffaele. "Les mystères grecs et les religions à mystères de l'antiquité: Recherches récentes et problèmes nouveaux." *Cahiers d'histoire mundiale* 2 (1954) 301–12; 661–67.

Price, Simon R. F. *Rituals and Power: The Roman Imperial Cult in Asia Minor*. Cambridge, England: Cambridge University Press, 1984.

Punt, Jeremy. "Paul, Power, and Philemon. 'Knowing Your Place': A Postcolonial Reading." Pp. 223–50 in *Philemon in Perspective: Interpreting a Pauline Letter*. Ed. D. F. Tolmie. Beihefte zur Zeitschrift für die Neutestamentliche Wissenschaft. Berlin: Walter de Gruyter, 2010.

Raaflaub, Kurt A., and L. J. Samons, II. "Opposition to Augustus." Pp. 417–54 in *Between Republic and Empire*. Ed. Kurt A. Raaflaub and Mark Toher. Berkeley, CA: University of California Press, 1990.

Raboteau, Albert. *Slave Religion*. Oxford: Oxford University Press, 1982.

Raditsa, L. F. "Augustus' Legislation concerning Marriage, Procreation, Love Affairs and Adultery." *Aufstieg und Niedergang der römischen Welt* II.13 (1980) 278–339.

Rawson, Beryl. "Children in the Roman Familia." Pp. 170–200 in *The Family in Ancient Rome: New Perspectives*. Ed. Beryl Rawson. Ithaca, NY: Cornell University Press, 1986.

———. "The Roman Family." Pp. 1–57 in *The Family in Ancient Rome: New Perspectives*. Ed. Beryl Rawson. Ithaca, NY: Cornell University Press, 1986.

———. "Adult-Child Relationships in Roman Society." Pp. 7–30 in *Marriage, Divorce, and Children in Ancient Rome*. Ed. Beryl Rawson. Oxford: Clarendon; Humanities Research Center, 1991.

———. "Death, Burial, and Commemoration of Children in Roman Italy." Pp. 277–97 in *Early Christian Families in Context: An Interdisciplinary Dialogue*. Ed. David L. Balch and Carolyn Osiek. Grand Rapids, MI: William B. Eerdmans, 2003.

Reid, Charles J., JR. "Law Reform in the Ancient World: Did the Emperor Augustus Succeed or Fail in His Morals Legislation?" *William & Mary Journal of Women and the Law* 22, no. 2 (2016) 165–202.

Richlin, Amy. "Approaches to the Sources on Adultery at Rome." *Women's Studies* 8
    (1981) 225–50.
————. "Julia's Jokes, Galla Placidia, and the Roman Use of Women as Political
    Icons." Pp. 65–92 in *Stereotypes of Women in Power: Historical Perspectives
    and Revisionist Views*. Ed. Barbara Garlock, Suzanne Dixon and Pauline Allen.
    Westport: Greenwood Publishing Group, Inc., 1992.
Robert, Louis. "Une nouvelle inscription grecque de Sardes: Réglement de
    l'autorite' perse relative à un culte de Zeus." *Comptes rendue de l'Academie des
    Inscriptions et Belles-lettres* (1975) 306–30.
Roller, Lynn E. "Phrygian Myth and Cult." *Source* 7 (1988) 43–50.
————. "Reflections of the Mother of the Gods in Ancient Tragedy." Pp. 305–22
    in *Cybele, Attis, and Related Cults: Essays in Memory of M.J. Vermaseren*. Ed.
    Eugene N. Lane. Religions in the Graeco-Roman World v. 131. Leiden: E.J.
    Brill, 1996.
————. "The Ideology of the Eunuch Priest." *Gender and History* 9 (1997) 542–
    59.
————. *In Search of God the Mother: The Cult of Anatolian Cybele*. Berkeley, CA:
    University of California Press, 1999.
Roller, Matthew B. *Dining Posture in Ancient Rome: Bodies, Values, and Status*.
    Princeton, NJ: Princeton University Press, 2006.
Rousselle, Aline. "Personal Status and Sexual Practice in the Roman Empire." Pp.
    300–33 in *Fragments for a History of the Human Body, Part III*. Ed. Michel
    Feher. New York: Zone Press, 1989.
Rutland, Jonathan, Angus McBride, Bill Stallion, and Bernard Robinson. *See Inside
    A Roman Town*. London: Kingfisher Books, 1986.
Saller, Richard P. "Familia, Domus, and the Roman Conception of the Family."
    Phoenix 38 (1984) 336–55.
————. "*Patria Potestas* and the Stereotype of the Roman Family." *Continuity and
    Change* 1 (1986) 7–22.
————. "Men's Age at Marriage and Its Consequences in the Roman Family."
    Classical Philology 82 (1987) 21–34.
————. "Slavery and the Roman Family." Pp. 65–87 in *Classical Slavery*. Ed. M. I.
    Finley. London: Frank Cass, 1987.
————. "Pietas, Obligation and Authority in the Roman Family." Pp. 393–410 in
    Alte Geschichte und Wissenschaft Geschicthe: Festschrift für Karl Christ. Ed. Peter
    Kneissle and Volker Losemann. Darmstadt: Wissenschaftliche Buchgesellschaft,
    1988.
————. "Corporal Punishment, Authority, and Obedience in the Roman
    Household." Pp. 144–65 in *Marriage, Divorce, and Children in Ancient Rome*.
    Ed. Beryl Rawson. Oxford: Clarendon; Humanities Research Center, 1991.
————. "Pater Familias, Mater Familias, and the Gendered Semantics of the Roman
    Household." *Classical Philology* 94 (1999) 182–97.
————. "Symbols of Gender and Status Hierarchies in the Roman Household." Pp.
    87–93 in *Women and Slaves in Greco-Roman Culture: Differential Equations*.
    Ed. Sandra R. Joshel and Sheila Murnaghan. London: Routledge, 2001.
Sampley, J. P. *Pauline Partnership in Christ: Christian Community and Commitment
    in Light of Roman Law*. Philadelphia: Fortress Press, 1980.
Scheidel, Walter. "The Roman Slave Supply." Princeton/Stanford Working Papers in
    Classics, no. 050704, 2007.
Schilling, Robert and Jörg Rüpke. "Roman Religion: The Early Period." Pp. 7892–
    911 in *Encyclopedia of Religion*. Vol. 12. 2d ed. Ed. Lindsay Jones. Detroit:
    Macmillan Reference, 2005.

Schneiders, Sandra M. *The Revelatory Text: Interpreting the New Testament as Sacred Scripture*. 2d ed. Collegeville, MN: Liturgical Press, 1999.

Schultz, Celia E. *Women's Religious Activity in the Roman Republic*. Studies in the History of Greece and Rome. Chapel Hill, NC: University of North Carolina Press, 2006.

Schüssler Fiorenza, Elisabeth. *The Power of the Word: Scripture and the Rhetoric of Empire*. Minneapolis: Fortress Press, 2007.

———. "'What She Has Done Will Be Told...': Reflections on Writing Feminist History." Pp. 3–18 in *Distant Voices Drawing Near: Essays in Honor of Antoinette Clark Wire*. Ed. Holly E. Hearon. Collegeville, MN: Liturgical Press/Michael Glazier, 2004.

Scott, James C. *Weapons of the Weak: Everyday Forms of Peasant Resistance*. New Haven: Yale University Press, 1985.

———. *Domination and the Arts of Resistance: Hidden Transcripts*. New Haven: Yale University Press, 1990.

Severy, Beth. *Augustus and the Family at the Birth of the Roman Empire*. New York: Routledge, 2003.

Shaw, Brent D. "The Age of Roman Girls at Marriage: Some Reconsiderations." *Journal of Roman Studies* 77 (1987) 30–46.

———. "Raising and Killing Children: Two Roman Myths." *Mnemosyne* 54 (2001) 31–77.

Shils, Edward. "Centre and Periphery." Pp. 117–30 in *The Logic of Personal Knowledge: Essays Presented to Michael Polanyi on His Seventieth Birthday, 11ᵗʰ March 1961*. Glencoe, Illinois: The Free Press, 1961.

Smith, Dennis E. *From Symposium to Eucharist: The Banquet in the Early Christian World*. Minneapolis: Fortress Press, 2003.

———. "The Greco-Roman Banquet as a Social Institution." 23–34 in *Meals in the Early Christian World: Social Formation, Experimentation, and Conflict at the Table*. Ed. Dennis E. Smith and Hal Taussig. Hampshire, UK: Palgrave, 2012.

Smith, Dennis E. and Hal Taussig, eds. *Meals in the Early Christian World: Social Formation, Experimentation, and Conflict at the Table*. Hampshire, UK: Palgrave, 2012.

Smith, R. R. R. "Simulcra Gentium: The Ethne from the Sebasteion at Aphrodisias." *Journal of Roman Studies* 78 (1988) 50–77.

Smith, William, William Wayte, and G. E. Marindin. *A Dictionary of Greek and Roman Antiquities*. London: John Murray, 1890.

Sokolowski, Franciszek. "Τὰ Ἔνπυρα: On the Mysteries in the Lydian and Phrygian Cults." *Zeitschrift für Papyrologie und Epigraphik* 34 (1979) 65–67.

Sölle, Dorothee. *The Silent Cry: Mysticism and Resistance*. Minneapolis: Fortress Press, 2001.

Spaeth, Barbette S. "Imperial Cult in Roman Corinth: A Response to Karl Galinsky's 'The Cult of the Roman Emperor: Uniter or Divider?.'" Pp. 61–82 in *Rome and Religion: A Cross-Disciplinary Dialogue on the Imperial Cult*. Ed. Jeffrey Brodd and Jonathan Reed. Atlanta, GA: Society of Biblical Literature, 2011.

Sperber, Dan. *Rethinking Symbolism*. Cambridge, UK: Cambridge University Press, 1975.

Standhartinger, Angela. "Women in Early Christian Meal Gatherings: Discourse and Reality." Pp. 87–108 in *Meals in the Early Christian World: Social Formation, Experimentation, and Conflict at the Table*. Ed. Dennis E. Smith and Hal Taussig. Hampshire, UK: Palgrave, 2012.

Starr, Raymond J. "Augustus as 'Pater patriae' and Patronage Decrees." *Zeitschrift
    für Papyrologie und Epigraphik* 172 (2010) 296–98.
Stevenson, Tom. "Roman Coins and Refusals of the Title '*Pater Patriae*.'" *The
    Numismatic Chronicle* 167 (2007) 119–41.
Streett, R. A. *Subversive meals: An Analysis of the Lord's Supper under Roman
    Domination during the First Century.* Eugene, OR: Pickwick Publications,
    2013.
Taussig, Hal. *In the Beginning Was the Meal: Social Experimentation and Early
    Christian Identity.* Minneapolis: Fortress Press, 2009.
Taylor, Joan E. and Philip R. Davies. "The So-Called Therapeutae of 'De Vita
    Contemplativa': Identity and Character." *Harvard Theological Review* 91, no.
    1 (1998) 3–24.
Tolmie, D. F. "Tendencies in the Research on Philemon since 1980." Pp. 1–27
    in *Philemon in Perspective: Interpreting a Pauline Letter.* Ed. D. F. Tolmie.
    Beihefte zur Zeitschrift für die Neutestamentliche Wissenschaft. Berlin: Walter
    de Gruyter, 2010.
Trümper, Monika. "Material and Social Environment of Greco-Roman Households
    in the East: the Case of Hellenistic Delos." Pp. 19–43 in *Early Christian
    Families in Context: An Interdisciplinary Dialogue.* Ed. David L. Balch and
    Carolyn Osiek. Grand Rapids, MI: William B. Eerdmans, 2003.
Tuori, Kaius. "Augustus, Legislative Power, and the Power of Appearances."
    Fundamina 20, no. 4 (2014) 938–45.
Turcan, Robert. *The Cults of the Roman Empire.* The Ancient World. Oxford, UK:
    Blackwell, 1996.
Tyrrell, William B. *Amazons: A Study in Athenian Mythmaking.* Baltimore: Johns
    Hopkins University Press, 1984.
Vander Stichele, Caroline, and Todd Penner. "Mastering the Tools or Retooling
    the Masters? The Legacy of Historical-Critical Discourse." Pp. 1–29 in *Her
    Master's Tools? Feminist and Postcolonial Engagements of Historical-Critical
    Discourse.* Ed. Caroline Vander Stichele and Todd Penner. Atlanta, GA: Society
    of Biblical Literature, 2005.
Vermaseren, Maarten J. *Corpus Cultus Cybelae Attidisque.* 7 vols. Études prélimi-
    naires aux religions orientales dans l'Empire romain 50. Leiden: E. J. Brill.
Veyne, Paul. *The Roman Empire: From Pagan Rome to Byzantium / A History
    of Private Life.* Ed. George Duby and Philippe Ariès. 1. Cambridge, MA:
    Harvard University Press, 1987.
Vuolanto, Ville. "Children and Work: Family Strategies and Socialisation in the
    Roman and Late Antique Egypt." Pp. 97–111 in *Agents and Objects: Children
    in Pre-Modern Europe.* Ed. K. Mustakallio and J. Hanska. Rome: Institutum
    Romanum Finlandiae, 2015.
Wallace-Hadrill, Andrew. "The Emperor and His Virtues." *Historia* 30 (1981)
    298–323.
———. "The Golden Age and Sin in Augustan Ideology." *Past and Present* 95
    (1982) 19–36.
———. "The Social Structure of the Roman House." *Papers of the British School at
    Rome* 56 (1988c) 43–97.
———. *Augustan Rome.* London: Bristol Classical Press, 1993.
———. "*Mutatio morum*: The Idea of a Cultural Revolution." Pp. 3–22 in *The
    Roman Cultural Revolution.* Ed. Thomas Habinek and Alessandro Schiesaro.
    Cambridge: Cambridge University Press, 1997.

————. "*Domus* and *Insulae*: Families and Housefuls." Pp. 3–18 in *Early Christian Families in Context: An Interdisciplinary Dialogue*. Ed. David L. Balch and Carolyn Osiek. Grand Rapids, MI: William B. Eerdmans, 2003.

Walters, Jonathan. "Invading the Roman Body: Manliness and Impenetrability in Roman Thought." Pp. 29–43 in *Roman Sexualities*. Ed. Judith P. Hallett. Princeton: Princeton University Press, 1998.

Weima, Jeffrey A. D. "Paul's Persuasive Prose: A Epistolary Analysis of the Letter to Philemon." Pp. 29–60 in *Philemon in Perspective: Interpreting a Pauline Letter*. Ed. D. F. Tolmie. Beihefte zur Zeitschrift für die Neutestamentliche Wissenschaft. Berlin: Walter de Gruyter, 2010.

Wendt, Heidi. *At the Temple Gates: The Religion of Freelance Experts in the Early Roman Empire*. New York: Oxford University Press, 2016.

Wessels, G. F. "The Letter to Philemon in the Context of Slavery in Early Christianity." Pp. 143–68 in *Philemon in Perspective: Interpreting a Pauline Letter*. Ed. D. F. Tolmie. Beihefte zur Zeitschrift für die Neutestamentliche Wissenschaft. Berlin: Walter de Gruyter, 2010.

White, L. M. "Paul and Pater Familias." Pp. 457–87 in *Paul in the Greco-Roman World: A Handbook*. Ed. J. P. Sampley. Harrisburg, PA: Trinity Press International/Continuum, 2003.

Whitmarsh, Tim. *Greek Literature and the Roman Empire: The Politics of Imitation*. Oxford: Oxford University Press, 2001.

Wilkerson, Margaret B. "'Ain't You Marster?': Interrogating Slavery and Gender in Philemon." Pp. 101–20 in *Onesimus, Our Brother: Reading Religion, Race, and Culture in Philemon*. Ed. Matthew V. Johnson, James A. Noel and Demetrius K. Williams. Paul in Critical Contexts. Minneapolis: Fortress Press, 2012.

Williams, Demetrius K. "'No Longer as a Slave': Reading the Interpretation History of Paul's Epistle to Philemon." Pp. 11–46 in *Onesimus, Our Brother: Reading Religion, Race, and Culture in Philemon*. Ed. Matthew V. Johnson, James A. Noel and Demetrius K. Williams. Paul in Critical Contexts. Minneapolis: Fortress Press, 2012.

Williams, Gordon. "Poetry in the Moral Climate of Augustan Rome." *Journal of Roman Studies* 52 (1962) 28–46.

Wilson, S. G. "Voluntary Associations: An Overview." Pp. 1–15 in *Voluntary Associations in the Graeco-Roman World*. Ed. John S. Kloppenborg and S. G. Wilson. London: Routledge, 1996.

Winter, Bruce W. *Roman Wives, Roman Widows: The Appearance of New Women and the Pauline Communities*. Grand Rapids, MI: William B. Eerdmans, 2003.

Winter, Sara. "Paul's Letter to Philemon." *New Testament Studies* 33 (1987) 1–15.

Wire, Antoinette C. *The Corinthian Women Prophets: A Reconstruction through Paul's Rhetoric*. Minneapolis: Fortress Press, 1995.

Wiseman, T. P. "Cybele, Virgil, and Augustus." Pp. 117–20 in *Poetry and Politics in the Age of Augustus*. Ed. Tony Woodman and David West. Cambridge: Cambridge University Press, 1984.

Wulff, David. M. "An Enduring Flame: Studies on Latino Popular Religiosity by Anthony M. Stevens-Arroyo and Ana María Díaz-Stevens; Old Masks, New Faces: Religion and Latino Identities by Anthony M. Stevens-Arroyo and Gilbert R. Cadena; Enigmatic Powers: Syncretism with African and Indigenous Peoples' Religions among Latinos by Anthony M. Stevens-Arroyo and Andres I. Pérez y Mena; Discovering Latino Religion: A Comprehensive Social Science Bibliography by Anthony M. Stevens-Arroyo and Segundo Pantoja." *Journal for the Scientific Study of Religion* 36 (1997) 480–81.

Yavetz, Z. "The Personality of Augustus: Reflections on Syme's *Roman Revolution*."
   Pp. 21–41 in *Between Republic and Empire*. Ed. Kurt A. Raaflaub and Mark
   Toher. Berkeley, CA: University of California Press, 1990.
York, Katrina E. "Feminine Resistance to Moral Legislation in the Early Empire."
   Studies in Mediterranean Antiquity and Classics 1 (2006) 1–14.
Young, Norman H. "Paidogogus: The Social Setting of a Pauline Metaphor."
   Novum Testamentum 29 (1987) 150–76.
———. "The Figure of the Paidagogos in Art and Literature." *Biblical Archaeologist*
   53 (1990) 80–86.
Zanker, Paul. *The Power of Images in the Age of Augustus*. Ann Arbor: University of
   Michigan Press, 1988.

Ancient Authors Index

Modern Authors Index

Subject Index

About the Author

Susan M. (Elli) Elliott (Ph.D., Loyola University Chicago) is a writer, lecturer, and environmental activist based in Red Lodge, Montana. In the course of a career in community organizing and ministry, she also taught for seminaries, a university, community college, and a leadership school. She is the author of *Cutting Too Close for Comfort: Paul's Letter to the Galatians in its Anatolian Cultic Context* (2003/2008). Her scholarly articles and reviews have appeared in journals including: *Journal of Biblical Literature, Semeia, Forum, Biblical Research, Listening, Catholic Biblical Quarterly,* and *Bryn Mawr Classical Review*, as well as in books of collected articles and Bible dictionaries. She recently campaigned for a legislative seat in Montana and is currently organizing a grassroots think tank in the Big Sky region.

CPSIA information can be obtained
at www.ICGtesting.com
Printed in the USA
FFOW02n0124110318
45562446-46337FF